Naval Pensioners
OF THE
UNITED STATES,
1800–1851

Naval Pensioners
OF THE
UNITED STATES,
1800–1851

Lloyd de Witt Bockstruck

Copyright © 2002
Lloyd de Witt Bockstruck
All Rights Reserved. No part of this publication
may be reproduced, in any form or by any means,
including electronic reproduction or reproduction
via the Internet, except by permission of the publisher.

Published by Genealogical Publishing Co., Inc.
1001 N. Calvert St., Baltimore, MD 21202
Library of Congress Catalogue Card Number 2002108349
International Standard Book Number 0-8063-1705-1
Made in the United States of America

Introduction

Prior to 1799 the individual states in the nation funded naval pensions. Disability pensions for seamen, marines, and officers in the navy were funded in the same manner and rate as in the regular army. Initially federal naval pensions were limited to invalids. Naval pensions, however, were administered separate and apart from the general pension system of the United States. Under the acts of 2 March 1799 and 23 April 1800, the naval pension fund was to be created from the government's share of money accruing from the sale of prizes taken at sea by vessels of the navy. The fund provided half-pay pensions for life or disability for seamen, marines, and officers. The Secretaries of Navy, Treasury, and War oversaw the pension fund, and they were required to present an annual report to Congress.

During the War of 1812 when it was necessary not only to recruit additional but also to retain talented personnel, the pension law was modified by the act of 20 January 1813 to provide half-pay pensions for a five year period to the widows of officers. If there was no widow, half-pay pensions were to be granted to the minor children under sixteen years of age of seamen and officers who died in the line of duty or who died by reasons of wounds received in the line of duty. A subsequent act of 4 March 1814 granted pensions for five years to widows or, if no widow, to the children under sixteen years of age of officers, seamen, and marines who had died since 18 June 1812 or who would later die by reason of wounds received in the line of duty. Revenue cutter officers and seamen who were wounded or disabled in the discharge of duty while operating with the Navy also became eligible for pensions.

By the act of 2 April 1816 Congress authorized pensions to those injured at Dartmoor Prison in England in April 1815 and to the widows and children of such who were killed there or who died in consequence of wounds received there.

By the act of 3 March 1817 pensions for five years were extended to widows and children under sixteen years of age of those who died from disease contracted or casualties or injuries received in the line of duty since 18 June 1812. The act of 22 January 1824 repealed this provision, but the rights which had accrued under it were reserved.

The Secretary of the Navy, by the act of 16 April 1818, was authorized to allow full monthly pensions and to extend pensions to widows and children under sixteen years of age under the act of 4 March 1814 for another five years. It also doubled the amount of the pensions.

The act of 3 March 1819 granted another term of five years' pensions to the widows and children of officers, seamen, and marines who were killed in battle, who died of wounds received in battle, or who died in the naval service during the late war. The act of 22 January 1824 granted another term of five years to widows and children. It repealed the act of 3 March 1817 but reserved the rights which had accrued under it.

Widows and orphans received an additional extension for another five year term under the act of 23 May 1828. Widows alone were granted a similar extension under the act of 28 June 1832. The act of 14 July 1832 repealed the act of 3 March 1819 which required proof of continuance of disability. Until 1832 invalids were examined biennially by surgeons to ascertain the continuance of their disability; consequently, invalid pensions were for life.

By the act of 10 July 1832 the Secretary of the Navy became the sole manager of the Naval Pension Fund. The 1834 law extended five years' pensions to widows and granted five years' pensions to widows of officers, seamen, and marines who had died in naval service since 1 January 1824 or would die thereafter by reason of disease contracted, casualties by drowning or otherwise, or of injuries received in the line of duty. Pensions were to begin with the date of the passage of the act, i.e. 30 June 1834, even though the husband might die many years thereafter.

The act of 3 March 1837 provided for pensions to widows and, if no widow, to the children under twenty-one years old of officers, seamen, and marines who had died or would die thereafter in naval service. They were to be half-pay of the navy at the rate that pay was on 1 January 1835 and were to commence from the time of death. Pensions to invalids, granted or to be granted, were to be paid from the time when they became disabled.

Under the laws of 1834 and 1837, income from the pension fund proved insufficient. By 1842 the pension fund was exhausted, and Congress began to make annual appropriations.

By the act of 26 June 1812 a privateer pension fund was also established. Within a quarter of a century, however, it too was depleted. It provided pensions to those who were wounded or were disabled on board private armed vessels of the United States involved in engagements with the enemy. If the privateer died by reason of wounds, his widow and orphans were eligible for pensions. The Secretary of the Navy also supervised the privateer pension program. The pensioners under this act were accommodated under other programs. In response to a resolution of the House of Representatives, J. K. Paulding, Secretary of the Navy, furnished a report containing the names of all of the privateer pensions ever granted on 21 April 1840. The implication was the report would contain the names of all privateer pensioners theretofore. Unfortunately, there were omissions; nevertheless, the coverage of privateer pensioners in this work does seem to be more nearly complete than for naval pensioners.

There were inequities between the pensions allowed officers and soldiers in the army and officers, seamen, and marines in the navy. Those in the army were dissatisfied with the disparity in part because those in the navy were able to draw pensions while they continued in the service.

There were, for example, forty-four officers in the navy in 1840 drawing invalid naval pensions. They also resented the fact that naval pensioners drew their pensions from the time of disability and that the widows and children of officers, seamen, and marines drew pensions for life.

The number of pensions grew from 22 in 1802 to 1,228 in 1851. The pensions in this work represent, with a few exceptions, those whose applications were approved. The government routinely returned the paperwork to claimants whose applications were rejected. Many of the annual reports to Congress containing the names of the naval pensioners survive, and this work is a consolidation of those reports and other Congressional records. The years for which reports have been located are listed below. Many of the reports include summaries giving the number of pensioners in various categories. Because many of the reports include duplicate entries, the figures are not necessarily authoritative. They do, however, reveal the growing number of pensioners.

Since all of the naval and privateer pensioners were due to disability or death, it would be expected that the names of these individuals would be included in the Old Wars pensions index. That is, however, not the case. While it might seem reasonable to attribute some of the omissions to the destruction of pension files in the fire in Washington in August 1814, there was in fact no such loss among the naval records in contrast to those of the army.

It should be pointed out that the service or disability for a naval disability pension could have antedated the year 1800. Accordingly, Revolutionary War naval veterans such as Seth Harding, Abraham Whipple, and Samuel Tucker appear among the records. Pensioners identified as Black or Colored include Edward Burke, John Butler, Henry Carter, George Evans, Jeremiah Gardner, George Thomas, and David Wilson.

While it is sometimes stated with authority that pensions were limited to veterans, their widows, or their orphans, the records reveal otherwise. Certainly the statutes themselves vary, but even knowing the regulations does not always coincide with practice. William Slam, the grandson of William Cumming, received a pension as did Cor. Vanchef, the grand heir of W. Bowne. Mothers of veterans, such as Penelope Denny and Mary Cheever, also qualified as pensioners. Sometimes, but not always, provisions for such exceptions were by private act.

The text is arranged alphabetically by the name of the veteran and/or the pensioner followed by the state of residence and rating [*i.e.* rank]. The amount of the pension, either per month or per annum, follows along with the years in which there are entries for the pensioner in the reports to Congress. Because of the dollar adjustments in the various pension acts the figure reported may not always be the highest amount paid to the pensioner. Additional data such as the nature of the disability, date of death, name of vessel on which the veteran served, and biographical details follow.

Variations in the spellings of both forenames and surnames and aliases are also given. It is evident that the one setting the type in the Congressional publications sometimes misread the manuscript record or retrieved a letter misfiled in his font box. The ability to compare the reports allows for the reduction of such errors but not necessarily for their total elimination. The selection of a spelling for an entry was sometimes based upon the first time an individual appeared in a report. Not knowing what spelling the pensioner used, or even if he or she was literate, does make it imperative that all entries for a particular surname be studied in order to insure that no relevant entry is overlooked. Entries have been consolidated if the evidence was conclusive that all of the records pertained to a single veteran. Other single entries may actually pertain to a single individual even though they appear separately.

An asterisk indicates a veteran or a dependent who appears in the Old Wars pension index. For the entries which did not identify the veterans upon which a dependent qualified for a pension, the veteran's name appears in brackets at the end of the entry based upon entries in the Old Wars pension index.

From 1802 to 1825 the reports indicated the state of residence of the pensioners. While Pennsylvania followed by Massachusetts accounted for more than half of the nation's pensioners in 1802, by 1825 New York had replaced Pennsylvania as the state with the most naval and marine pensioners. The port of New York, in part of because of the opening of the Erie Canal, had supplanted Philadelphia as the largest in the nation. Reports containing the names of pensioners for the years 1806, 1812-1815, 1817, 1831-1834, and 1849 were not found in the *American State Papers: Naval Affairs* or in the U. S. Serial Set. Information on many of the individuals included in this work, as well as other naval pensioners, will appear in the *Digested Summary and Alphabetical List of Private Claims Which Have Been Presented to the House of Representatives from the First to the 31st Congress, Exhibiting the Action of Congress on Each Claim* (Baltimore: Genealogical Publishing Company, 1970) and in *List of Private Claims Brought before the Senate of the United States.*

The federal government also set aside special funds to satisfy the claims of men lost at sea. By an act of Congress approved 3 March 1817 the heirs of the men lost on the U.S. brig *Epervier* were due the pay of the deceased on 14 July 1815 and the equivalent of six months' pay. The *Epervier* was lost at sea in 1815. It had 18 guns and weighed 477 tons. Eligible heirs included wives, orphans, parents, or siblings. There were forty-two such claimants. Similar benefits were due the heirs of those lost on U.S. Schooner *Grampus* which foundered off Charleston, South Carolina in 1843. The *Grampus* was built in 1821, had 21 guns, and weighed 184 tons. There were twenty-two claimants. Because these are little-known records and since these related records are akin to pension applications, abstracts of the files are also included in this work. It is important to bear in mind that some of the heirs of these men were also naval pensioners and would, therefore, have a regular naval pension file as well.

There are well over 3,000 entries in this compilation.

In Record Group 15, box 1, entry 32 in the National Archives is an incomplete list of pensioned Navy veterans from 1800 to 1879 who were not assigned certificate numbers. It is a card file and covers the surnames from Abbott to Grogan. Data from these cards have been incorporated into this index. *The Journals of Navy Pension Funds Accounts, 1798-1830*, NC-23, Entry 133, is a two-volume manuscript in the National Archives which contains a few references to individual naval pensioners.

    I would like to thank Johanna Johnson, Manageress of the Governments Documents of the Dallas Public Library, Dallas, Texas, and Jean L. Hort, Director of the Navy Department Library, Washington, D. C., and Dr. George K. Schweitzer, Professor Emeritus, of the University of Tennessee, Knoxville, Tennessee for their assistance in locating and interpreting relevant documents and records pertinent to this project. Patricia Law Hatcher, FASG, provided excellent technological assistance, and I am most appreciative of her efforts.

                                                                         Lloyd de Witt Bockstruck, FNGS
                                                                         Dallas, Texas

Naval Pensioners of the United States of America, 1800-1851

Year	Invalids	Widows	Orphans	Privateers	Total
1802	22				22
1803	37				37
1804	37				37
1805	49				49
1807	65				65
1808	78				78
1809	85				85
1810	90				90
1811	93				93
1816	219	33			252
1818	302	52	4		358
1819	330	58	3		391
1820	339	96	2	224	
1821	375	105			480
1822	371	120			491
1823	345	83			428
1824	393	131			524
1825	391	125	6		532
1826	444	240			686
1827	393	134			527
1828	400	134			534
1829	477	117			594
1830	474	73			517
1835	306	136		36	478
1836	308	158			468
1837	356	238	84	36	714
1838	440	302	105	36	883
1839	456	330	115		901
1840	479	344	91		914
1841	491	363	105		959
1842	503	348	95		946
1842b	503	348	95		946
1843	518				
1844	491			24	
1845	522	204		27	
1846	548	234		28	
1847	585			28	
1848	603	320	7	28	958
1850	681	389	27	29	1,060
1851	709	481	38		1,228

Naval Pensioners of the United States, 1800-1851

Abbot, Samuel. N.H. Seaman. He was pensioned at the rate of $60 per annum. He served on the frigate *Congress.* 1816. 1818. 1819. 1820. 1821. 1822. 1823. 1826. 1827. 1828. 1829. 1830 from Mass. 1835. 1836. 1837. 1839. 1840. 1841. 1842b. 1843. 1844. 1845. 1846. 1847. 1848. 1850. 1851. He also appeared as Samuel Abbett. He was disabled by a fracture of his left leg and was pensioned 22 Mar. 1815.

Abott, Stephen. Mass. Seaman. His was pensioned from 1 Feb. 1813 at the rate of $4 per month as a privateer. 1813. 1814. 1815. 1816. 1817. 1818. 1819. 1820. 1821. 1822. 1823. 1824. 1825. 1826. 1827. 1828. 1829. 1830. 1831. 1832. 1833. 1834. 1835. 1836. 1837. 1838. He was disabled by a gun shot wound of both arms. He served aboard the *Grawler.*

Achmuty, Henry J.* —. Lieutenant. His widow, Louisa Achmuty, was pensioned at the rate of $25 on 8 Oct. 1835. 1836. 1837. 1839. 1840. 1841. 1842. 1842b. 1846. 1847. 1848. 1850. She also appeared as Louisa Auchmuty.

Ackins, Andrew J. —. Seaman. His widow, Hannah Ackins, was pensioned at the rate of $6 per month from 11 Feb. 1848. 1850. 1851. He also appeared as Andrew J. Aikins and Andrew J. Arkins.

Adams, —. N.H. —. Sally Adams was pensioned on his service as a privateer at the rate of $36 per annum. 1815. 1816. 1817. 1818. 1819. 1820 increase to $72. 1821. 1822. 1823. 1824. 1825. 1826. 1827. 1828. 1829.

Adams, —. —. —. Sarah Adams was pensioned on his service as a privateer at the rate of $36 per annum. 1816. 1817. 1818. 1819. 1820 increase to $72. 1821. 1822. 1823. 1824. 1825. 1826. 1827. 1828. 1829. 1830. 1831. 1832. 1833. 1834.

Adams, —. —. Sailmaker. His son, Thomas W. Adams, was pensioned at the rate of $10 per month from 10 Sep. 1829. 1839. 1840. 1841. 1842. 1842b. 1847.

Adams, —. —. Master Commandant. His widow, Adelaide H. Adams, was pensioned 30 June 1834 at the rate of $30 per month. 1835. 1836. 1837. 1839. 1840. 1842. 1847.

Adams, Alexander. Penn. Ordinary Seaman. He was pensioned 26 Oct. 1812 at the rate of $36 per annum. 1816. 1818. 1819. 1820. 1821. 1822. 1823. 1824. 1825. 1826. 1827. 1828. 1829. 1830. 1835. 1836. 1837. 1839. 1840. 1841. 1842b. 1843. 1844. 1845. 1846. 1847. 1848. 1850. 1851. He served aboard the *Essex.* He was disabled with frostbitten feet resulting in the amputation of his toes.

Naval Pensioners of the United States, 1800-1851

Adams, George.* —. Quarter Gunner. He was pensioned at the rate of $8 per month from 19 July 1814. 1838. 1839. 1840. 1841. 1842b. 1843. 1844. 1845. 1846. 1847. 1848. 1850. He served aboard the *St. Louis* and was disabled by a fracture of his left leg.

Adams, James. Mass. Seaman. He served aboard the *Constitution* and *Java*. He was killed 29 Dec. 1812. His widow, Hannah Adams, was pensioned 7 Feb. 1818. 1820. 1821. 1822. 1825. 1827.

Adams, John.* —. Seaman. He was pensioned at the rate of $6 per month from 17 Feb. 1836. 1836. 1837. 1838. 1839. 1840. 1841. 1842. 1842b. 1843. 1844. 1845. 1846. 1847. 1848. 1850. He served aboard the *Delaware* and was disabled with a right inguinal hernia.

Adams, John. —. —. He was paid in 1842. [second of the name]

Adams, Joseph. Mass. Seaman. He was killed 29 Dec. 1812 serving aboard the *Constitution* and *Java*. His widow, Hannah Adams, was pensioned. 1824. 1825. 1828. 1830.

Adams, Nathaniel. —. Purser's Steward. His application was rejected prior to 17 Jan. 1848. He alleged employment in the revenue service, but there was no law under which the department was authorized to grant a pension under his circumstances.

Adams, William. —. Seaman. He was pensioned 25 July 1838 at $36 per annum. 1839. 1840. 1841. 1842b. 1843. 1844. 1845. 1846. 1847. 1848. 1850. 1851. He was disabled with a hernia on his left side.

Adams, William.* —. Passed Midshipman. His widow, Elizabeth Adams, was pensioned 8 Nov. 1847 at the rate of $12.50 per month. 1848. 1850. 1851.

Adee, Alvey A.* —. Surgeon. His widow, Amelia K. Adee, was pensioned from 22 Feb. 1844 at the rate of $30 per month and again on 22 Feb. 1849 at the rate of $30 per month. 1844. 1845. 1846. 1847. 1848. 1850. 1851.

Agar, Edward.* —. Purser's Clerk. His widow, Mary E. Agar, was pensioned 23 Mar. 1850 at the rate of $12.50 per month. 1851.

Agers, Samuel. —. Captain. He was pensioned from 1 Jan.1814 at the rate of $50 per month. 1838. 1839.

Aggers, Frederick.* —. Quarter Gunner. He was pensioned 19 Sep. 1845 at the rate of $3.75 per month. 1847. 1848. 1850. 1851. He also appeared as Frederick Aggens. He served aboard the U.S. brig *Bainbridge* and was disabled by a rupture.

Agnew, John.* —. Seaman. His pension began 1 Apr. 1832 at the rate of $5 per month. 1835. 1836. 1837. 1838. 1839. 1840. 1841. 1847.

Akerman, —. N.H. Marine Officer. Mary Akerman was pensioned on his service as a privateer at the rate of $60 per annum. 1815. 1816. 1817. 1818. 1819. 1820 increase to $120. 1821. 1822. 1823. 1824. 1825. 1826. 1827. 1828. 1829. She also appeared as Mary Ackerman.

Albrecht, Jacob. N.Y. Seaman. He was pensioned 4 Aug. 1814 at the rate of $72 per annum. 1816. 1818. 1819. 1820. 1821. 1822. 1823. 1824. 1825. 1826. 1827. 1828. 1829. 1830. 1835. 1836. 1837. 1839. 1840. He served aboard the *President*. He was disabled by the loss of his left arm.

Albree, George.* Mass. Cabin Boy. He was pensioned at the rate of $36 per annum starting in 1813. 1813. 1814. 1815. 1816. 1817. 1818. 1819. 1820. 1821. 1822. 1823. 1824. 1825.

Naval Pensioners of the United States, 1800-1851

1826. 1827. 1828. 1829. 1830. 1831. 1832. 1833. 1834. 1835. 1836. 1837 for half the year. He was pensioned from 1 July 1837 as a privateer pensioner at the rate of $3 per month. 1837. 1838. 1844. 1845. 1846. 1847. 1850. He served aboard the private armed brig *Holkar* and suffered from a fracture of his left leg.

Albro, George.* N.Y. Quarter Gunner. He was pensioned 3 Mar. 1819 at the rate of $72 per annum. 1818. 1821. 1822. 1823. 1824. 1825. 1826. 1827. 1828. 1829. 1830. He also appeared as George Albron. He served aboard the *Hornet*. He was disabled by a disease of the knee causing stiffness of the joint.

Alcutt, —. N.Y. Steward. His widow, Mary Alcutt, was pensioned at the rate of $9 per month. 1823.

Alden, Charles H.* —. Chaplain. His widow, Alice B. Alden, was pensioned 24 Sep. 1846 at the rate of $20 per month. 1848. 1850. 1851. He also appeared as Charles H. Adden and she as Alice B. Adden.

Alderson, Jeremiah. Penn. Quarter Gunner. He was pensioned at the rate of $60 per annum. 1818. He served aboard the *Guerriere* and was disabled by deep and extensive burns of both hands.

Alexander, Francis.* —. Lieutenant. His widow, Eliza Jane Alexander, was pensioned 11 May 1849 at the rate of $25 per month. 1850. 1851.

Alexander, George. Penn. Quarter Gunner. He was pensioned from 19 July 1814 at the rate of $96 per annum. 1819. 1820. 1821. 1822. 1823. 1824. 1825. 1826. 1827. 1828. 1829. 1830. 1835. 1836. 1837. 1839. 1840. 1841. 1842b. 1843. 1844. 1845. 1846. 1848. 1850. 1851. He served aboard the *President*. He had his left arm amputated.

Alexander, John. Penn. Seaman. He served aboard the privateer *Perry* and was accidentally disabled by a musket wound. He was pensioned at the rate of $72 per annum in 1814. 1815. 1816. 1817. 1818. 1819 in the amount of $50.80.

Alexander, John.* —. Ordinary Seaman. He was pensioned 8 Oct. 1846 at the rate of $5 per month. 1846. 1847. 1848. 1850. 1851. He served aboard the *Susannah*. He was disabled by a left inguinal hernia and paralysis of his left arm.

Allcorn James. Md. Sailing Master. He was pensioned 30 Apr. 1822 at the rate of $240 per annum. 1823. 1824. 1825. 1826. 1827. 1828. 1829. 1830. 1835. 1836. 1837. 1838. 1839. 1840. 1841. 1842. 1842b. 1843. 1844. 1845. 1846. 1847. 1848. He was disabled at Carolina Station. He also appeared as James Allcom and James Alcorn. He suffered from paralysis in his limbs due to exposure.

Allen, Alexander. Mass. Lieutenant. He was pensioned as a privateer at the rate of $144 per annum. 1814. 1815. 1816. 1817. 1818 in the amount of $143.20. He served aboard the *Prince of Neufchatel*.

Allen, Bernard. N.Y. Seaman. He was pensioned 9 Oct. 1816 at the rate of $60 per annum. 1819. 1822. 1823. 1824. 1825. 1826. 1827. 1828. 1829. 1830. He served aboard the brig *Jones* and the *Superior*. He lost the use of one finger and the use of two others on his left hand and had a severe fracture of his leg.

Allen, Charles.* —. Captain of Forecastle. He was pensioned 6 Feb. 1849 at the rate of $1.87 ½ per month. 1850. 1851. He served aboard the *Congress* and was disabled by an injury to

Naval Pensioners of the United States, 1800-1851

his left hand.

Allen, James.* —. Seaman. He was pensioned 2 June 1843 at the rate of $4 per month. 1843. 1844. 1845. 1846. 1847. 1848. 1850. 1851. He served aboard the *Pennsylvania* and was disabled by a fracture of his left arm and shoulder.

Allen, John. N. Y. Seaman. He served aboard the *United States* and was drowned 28 Oct. 1813 at New London. His widow, Mary Allen, was pensioned 8 Nov. 1821 at the rate of $6 per month. 1822. 1824. 1825. 1827. 1828. 1829. 1830. She was also called Mary Gordman.

Allen, John.* —. Armorer. His application was rejected between Mar. 1840 and 19 Jan. 1842. He failed to show by certificate from any commissioned officer or surgeon that he was injured in the service, and his injury was said to have been received prior to 1812. His application was inadmissible under the rules of evidence adopted by the Secretary of the Navy.

Allen, John D. Mass. Seaman. His widow, Lydia Allen, was pensioned at the rate of $72 per annum. 1816. 1820. 1821. 1822.

Allen, William. —. Seaman. He was pensioned 1 Jan. 1839 at the rate of $5 per month. 1843. 1844. 1845. 1846. 1847. 1848. 1850. 1851.

Allen, William C.* Penn. Quartermaster. He was pensioned 17 Mar. 1820 at the rate of $144 per annum in 1821. 1822. 1823. 1824. 1825. 1826. 1827. 1828. 1829. 1830. He served on the brig *Eagle*. He was disabled by a gun shot wound of his right leg above the ankle resulting in the ulceration of same.

Allen, William H.* —. Seaman. His pension began 23 May 1834 at the rate of $3 per month. 1835. 1836. 1837. He was disabled by a rupture of his right side.

Allen, William H. —. Lieutenant Commandant. He served aboard the schooner *Alligator* and was in pursuit of several piratical vessels near Point Hycacos on the north side of Cuba. Lt. Allen was in a launch with about thirty men when they were attacked by a schooner of the pirates. He was mortally wounded. He left no wife or children. He left a widowed mother and sister. 31 Dec. 1822.

Allen, Zephaniah.* Mass. Marine. He was pensioned 1 Nov. 1819 at the rate of $36 per annum. $48 per annum in 1821. 1822. 1823. 1824. 1825. 1826. 1827. 1828. 1829. 1830. 1835. 1836. 1837. 1838. 1839. 1840. 1841. 1842. 1842b. 1843. 1844. 1845. 1846. 1847. 1848. 1850. 1851. He served on the schooner *Herald*. He was disabled by a frozen left foot with the loss of three toes.

Allinson, Thomas. Md. Master's Mate. His widow, Mary Allinson, was pensioned at the rate of $120 per annum. 1816. 1818. 1820. 1821. 1822. 1823. 1824. 1825. She also appeared as Mary Allison and Mary Alliston. He was killed 19 June 1813.

Allison, John.* Mass. Seaman. He was pensioned at the rate of $72 per annum. 1824. 1827. 1828. 1829. He served on the *Columbus*.

Allister, Isaac.* Mass. Seaman. He was pensioned 1 July 1819 at the rate of $36 per annum. 1822. 1823. 1824. 1825. 1826. 1827. 1828. 1829. 1830. He also appeared as Isaac Alleston and Isaac Allester. He served on the schooner *Argus*.

Allister, John.* Mass. Seaman. He was pensioned at the rate of $72 per annum. 1824. 1825.

Naval Pensioners of the United States, 1800-1851

1826. He also appeared as John Allison.

Anderson, —. —. Captain Marines. His children, James W. Anderson, Benjamin F. Anderson, William Anderson, Laura V. Anderson, and Virginia N. Anderson, were pensioned at the rate of $20 per month from 13 Jan. 1830. 1837. 1839. 1840. 1841. 1842. 1842b. 1847. [The veteran was probably William Anderson according to the Old Wars pension index.]

Anderson, —. —. Lieutenant. His children, Joseph P. Anderson and Sarah Ann Anderson, were pensioned at the rate of $20 per month. 1837. 1847.

Anderson, —. —. Marine. His widow, Catharine Anderson, was pensioned at the rate of $3.50 per month. 1837. 1839. 1840. 1841. 1842. 1842b.

Anderson, —. Mass. Seaman. Sophia Anderson was pensioned on his privateer service at the rate of $36 per annum. 1815. 1816. 1817. 1818. 1819. 1820. 1821. 1822. 1823. 1824. 1825. 1826. 1827. 1828. 1829. 1830. 1831. 1832. 1833. 1834. 1835 for $6.

Anderson, Abraham.* —. Seaman. His widow, Ann Anderson, was pensioned. 1842. She was pensioned again 23 Oct. 1843 at the rate of $6 per month. 1851.

Anderson, Gabriel.* —. Seaman. He was pensioned 19 Aug. 1835 at the rate of $1.50 per month. 1842b. 1843. 1844. 1845. 1846. 1847. 1848. 1850. 1851. He served aboard the *Constitution* when he was injured.

Anderson, James.* —. Passed Midshipman. His widow, Emma Anderson, was pensioned 29 Dec.1840 at the rate of $12.50 per month. 1841. 1842b. 1845. 1848. 1850. 1851.

Anderson, John.* —. Captain of the Hold. He was pensioned 21 Oct. 1841 at $1.87 ½ per month. 1842b. 1843. 1844. 1845. 1846. 1847. 1848. 1850. 1851. He served aboard the *Macedonian* and was disabled by the loss of the third finger of his right hand.

Anderson, John.* —. Quartermaster. He was pensioned 24 Sep. 1847 at the rate of $4 per month. 1848. 1851. He served aboard the *Savannah* and was disabled by a gun shot wound of his left thigh.

Anderson, John. —. Seaman. His daughter, Ann E. Anderson, was pensioned 5 Nov. 1847 at the rate of $6 per month. 1851. He served aboard the *Pennsylvania* and was disabled by a dislocation of his left wrist.

Anderson, Lewis.* —. Seaman. He was pensioned 8 May 1847 at the rate of $3 per month. 1847. 1848. 1850. 1851. He served aboard the *Grant* and was disabled by a hernia on his right side.

Anderson, Peter.* —. Seaman. His pension began 1 Jan. 1831 at $3 per month. 1835. 1836. 1837. 1838. 1842. 1847. He served aboard the frigate *Essex* and was disabled by a gun shot wound of his right arm and leg. His left leg had to be amputated.

Anderson, Samuel T.* —. Chaplain. He was pensioned 1 July 1844 at the rate of $20 per month. 1847. 1848. 1850. 1851. He was disabled by impaired hearing.

Anderson, William. D.C. Seaman. He was pensioned at the rate of $72 per annum. 1816. He was in Mass. in 1818. 1819. 1820. 1821. 1822. He was disabled by a rupture.

Andrews, —. —. —. His widow, Cornelia Andrews, was pensioned. Her administrator received her pension. 1842.

Andrews, —. —. Gunner. His widow, Pamela Andrews, was pensioned 30 June 1834 at the rate of $10 per month. 1835. 1836.

Naval Pensioners of the United States, 1800-1851

Andrews, John. Penn. Ordinary Seaman. He received $60 per annum in 1802. 1803. 1804. 1805. 1807. 1808. 1809. 1810. 1811. He served aboard the *Constellation* and was disabled by a gun shot wound of his right leg and left thigh 6 Apr. 1799.

Andrews, Nicholas.* —. Seaman. He was pensioned 8 Aug. 1850 at the rate of $4.50 per month. 1850. 1851. He served aboard the *Cumberland* and was disabled by disease of the eyes.

Andrews, Robert.* Va. Quarter Gunner. He was pensioned 31 Aug. 1829 at $4.50 per month. 1829. 1830. 1835. 1836. 1837. 1839. 1840. 1841. 1842b. 1843. 1844. 1845. 1846. 1847. 1848. 1850. 1851. He served aboard the *Guerriere*. He also appeared as Robert Andrus. He was disabled by a fracture of his left forearm and right leg.

Andrews, Zebulon.* —. Quartermaster. His widow was Nancy L. Andrews. Her application was rejected prior to 30 Dec. 1845 since her husband drowned while on liberty in 1844 and was not on duty at the time of his death.

Angus, Samuel. N.Y. Captain. He was pensioned 2 June 1824 at the rate of $600 per annum. He was disabled by gun shot wounds in land action. 1824. 1825. 1827. 1828. 1829. 1830. 1835. 1836. 1837. 1838. 1839. 1840. 1842. 1847. He was a midshipman when he was first disabled. His widow, Ann W. Angus, was pensioned 4 Mar. 1849 at the rate of $50 per month. 1850. 1851.

Annis, John.* Mass. Seaman. He served aboard the schooner *Wasp* and died 20 Apr. 1815. His widow, Sarah Annis, was pensioned 27 Mar. 1817 at the rate of $72 per annum. 1818. 1819. 1820. 1821. 1822. 1823. 1824. 1825. 1827. 1828. 1829. 1830. 1836. 1837. 1839. 1840. 1841. 1842. 1842b. 1845. 1846. She was pensioned again at the rate of $6 per month 1 Sep. 1847. 1848. 1850. 1851. She also appeared as Sally Amies.

Anthony, James F.* —. Ship's Cook. His widow, Anna Anthony, was pensioned 10 Mar. 1849 at the rate of $9 per month. 1851.

Appleton, Daniel.* Mass. Seaman. He served aboard the sloop *Frolic*. He was from Ipswich, Mass. and sailed from Boston 18 Feb. 1814 under Capt. Bainbridge. He was taken prisoner, taken to Halifax, and then to England. He died in Dartmoor Prison 4 Jan. 1815. His widow, Abigail Appleton, was pensioned 19 Aug. 1830. 1837. 1839. 1840. 1841. 1842. 1842b. She was pensioned again 1 Sep. 1842 at the rate of $6 per annum and on 1 Sep. 1847 at the same rate. 1847. 1851.

Apsley, Joseph.* —. Ordinary Seaman. He served aboard the *United States* and was disabled by a fracture of his right thigh. He was pensioned from 4 Mar. 1839.

Arbuckle, George. Mass. Seaman. He was pensioned from 7 June 1799 at the rate of $40.04 per annum. 1802. 1803. 1804. 1805. 1807. 1808. 1809. 1810. 1811. 1816. 1818. 1819. 1820. 1821. 1822. 1824. 1825. 1826. 1827. 1828. 1829. 1830. He served on the *Constitution*. He was also reported as having served on the *Constellation*. He was disabled by a fracture of his right arm.

Arbuckle, William. Mass. Quarter Gunner. He was pensioned at the rate of $96 per annum. 1816. 1818. 1819. 1820. 1821. 1822. He also appeared as William Arbunkle. He served aboard Gunboat No. 82 and was disabled by injury of his left hip and thigh in a fall.

Archbold, J. Penn. Ordinary Seaman. He served aboard the *United States* and was killed 25 Oct. 1812. His widow, Hannah Archbold, was pensioned at the rate of $60 per annum 1820.

Naval Pensioners of the United States, 1800-1851

1821. 1822. 1824. 1825. 1827. 1829. J. A. B. Archbold was her guardian.
Archbold, —. Penn. Ordinary Seaman. His pension was paid to Mary Archbold at the rate of $60 per annum. 1824. 1825. 1827.
Archer, —.* —. —. E. M. Archer applied in Dec. 1824 at the rate of $240 per annum. [He was Richard Archer and she was Eliza M. Archer in the Old Wars pension index.]
Archer, John.* N.Y. Seaman. He was pensioned 1 July 1829 at the rate of $72 per annum. He served aboard the sloop of war *Peacock.* 1829. 1830. 1836. He was disabled with a left arm and leg diminished and enfeebled. He also appeared as John Arche.
Archer, William.* —. Seaman. His widow, Mary P. Archer, was pensioned from 12 Oct. 1839 at the rate of $6 per month. 1841. 1842. 1842b. She was pensioned again 1 Sep. 1847 at the rate of $6 per month. 1848. 1850. 1851.
Archibald, John. —. Ordinary Seaman. He served aboard the *United States* and was pensioned 28 June 1819.
Ardery, Alexander.* Md. Ordinary Seaman. He was pensioned 6 May 1821 at the rate of $72 per annum. 1824. 1825. 1826. 1827. 1828. 1829. 1830. He was disabled in Barney's flotilla. He had a rupture.
Ardis, —.* —. Carpenter's Mate. His children, Elizabeth Ardis, Ann Ardis, and Emma Ardis, were pensioned from 8 Sep. 1831 at the rate of $9.50 per month. 1839. 1840. 1841. 1842. 1842b. [The veteran was John Ardis according to the Old Wars pension index.]
Arlett, John C.* —. Marine. His widow, Mary E. Arlett, was pensioned from 5 Mar. 1842 at the rate of $3.50 per month. 1842b. 1843. 1844. 1845. 1846.
Armistead, Francis L.* —. Lieutenant of Marines. His widow, Catherine L. Armistead, was pensioned from 14 Apr. 1841 at the rate of $15 per month. 1841. 1842. 1842b. 1845. She was pensioned again 1 Sep. 1849 at the rate of $15 per month. 1850. 1851.
Armitage, —. —. Seaman. His widow, Elizabeth Armitage, was pensioned from 7 Mar. 1810 at the rate of $6 per month. 1839. 1840. 1841. 1842. 1842b. [He was Samuel Armitage according to the Old Wars pension index.]
Armstrong, —. —. Carpenter. His widow, Betsey Armstrong, was pensioned from 6 Sep. 1836 at the rate of $3.50 per month. 1837. 1839. 1840.
Armstrong, —.* —. Carpenter. His children, Ann E. Armstrong, Thomas P. Armstrong, George W. Armstrong, and Virginia Armstrong, were pensioned from 27 Nov. 1839 at the rate of $10 per month. 1841. 1842. 1842b. [He was Thomas Armstrong in the Old Wars pension index.]
Armstrong, —.* —. Sergeant Marine Corps. His children, John Armstrong, Franklin Armstrong, and Venerando Armstrong were pensioned at the rate of $7.50 per month from 23 Jan. 1835. 1837. 1839. 1840. 1841. 1842. 1842b. 1847. [He was William Armstrong in the Old Wars pension index.]
Armstrong, L. —. Quarter Gunner. His pension began 22 Nov. 1831 at the rate of $6 per month. 1835. 1836. 1837. [He was Lawrence Armstrong in the Old Wars pension index.]
Arundel, Robert. Penn. Sailing Master. He served aboard the schooner *Pert* on the lakes. He drowned 10 Nov. 1812. His widow, Margaret Arundel, was pensioned 15 Jan. 1814 at the rate of $20 per month. 1816. 1820. 1821. 1822. 1824. 1825. 1827. 1829. 1830. 1835.

Naval Pensioners of the United States, 1800-1851

1836. 1837. He also appeared as Robert Arundell.
Ashley, Joseph. —. Ordinary Seaman. He was pensioned 13 Dec. 1835 at the rate of $30 per annum. 1839. 1840. 1841. 1842b. 1843. 1844. 1845. 1846. 1847. 1848. 1850. 1851.
Ashton, Gurdon C.* —. Lieutenant. His widow, Louisa Ashton, was pensioned from 11 Oct. 1840 at the rate of $25 per month. 1841. 1842. 1842b. 1843. 1844.
Asperlin, Robert W.* —. Seaman. He was pensioned 13 Nov. 1849 at the rate of $6 per month. 1850. 1851. He was disabled with anchylosis of his right ankle and died 15 Mar. 1859. His former widow, Mary Asperlin, was Mary Leonard. [He was Robert Aspelin in the Old Wars pension index.]
Atkins, Joseph.* Mass. Seaman. He served aboard the schooner *Wasp* and died 20 Apr. 1815. His widow, Sarah Atkins, was pensioned 1 Apr. 1817 at the rate of $72 per annum. 1818. 1819. 1820. 1821. 1822. 1823. 1824. 1825. 1827. 1828. 1829. 1830. 1836. He also appeared as James Atkins. [He was Joseph Atkins in the Old Wars pension index.]
Atwood, —.* —. Purser. His widow, Martha Ann Atwood, was pensioned at the rate of $20 per month. 1837. 1839. 1840. 1841. 1842. 1842b. 1847. [He was Mathias C. Atwood in the Old Wars pension index.]
Austin, Thomas. —. Yeoman. He was pensioned 7 Dec. 1838 at the rate of $7.50 per month. 1840. 1841. 1842b. 1843. 1844. 1845. 1846. 1847. 1848. 1850. 1851. He served aboard the steamship *Fulton* and was disabled with a compound fracture of his right leg, a fracture of his left leg, and the loss of all of the toes and metatarsal bones of his left foot.
Austin, William. Mass. Commander. He was pensioned as a privateer at the rate of $180 per annum starting in 1814. 1814. 1815. 1816. 1817. 1818. 1819. 1820. 1821. 1822. 1823. 1824. 1825. 1826. 1827. 1828. 1829. 1830. 1831. 1832. 1833. 1834. 1835. 1836. 1837 for a half year. 1838. 1844. 1845. 1846. 1847. 1850. He served aboard the *Brutus* and was disabled by a gun shot wound of his right arm.
Avery, —. N.Y. Prize Master. Caroline Avery was pensioned on his service as a privateer at the rate of $120 per annum. 1818. 1819. 1820. 1821. 1822 for $60.
Awart, Charles.* —. Armorer. He was pensioned 6 Feb. 1849 at the rate of $4.50 per month. 1850. 1851. He served aboard the sloop *Dale* and was disabled by an oblique scrotal hernia.

Baab, Philip.* —. Marine. His widow, Christine Baab, was pensioned 6 Dec. 1843 at the rate of $3.50 per month. 1845. 1846. 1847. 1848. 1850.
Babbit, —. —. Landsman. His widow, Julianna S. Babbit, was pensioned from 9 Sep. 1840 at the rate of $30 per month. 1841. 1842. 1842b.
Babbit, —. —. —. Mary J. Babbit was pensioned on his service 29 Nov. 1835 at the rate of $16.66 2/3 per month. 1837. 1839. 1840. She was pensioned by special act of 2 July 1836.
Babbit, William D.* —. Surgeon. His widow, Maria Babbit, was pensioned 30 June 1834 at the rate of $25 per month. 1835. 1836. 1837. 1839. 1840. 1841. 1842. 1842b. 1845. 1846.

8

Naval Pensioners of the United States, 1800-1851

1851.
Babit, Fitz Henry. —. Lieutenant. He was killed by the British in their attack on the frigate *President*. His mother had her application rejected 2 Mar. 1821.
Bache, George M.* —. Lieutenant. His widow, Eliza C. Bache, was pensioned 9 Sep. 1846 at the rate of $25 per month. 1847. 1848. 1850. 1851.
Bacon, Frederick A.* —. Passed Midshipman. His widow, Sarah A. Bacon, was pensioned from 1 May 1839 at the rate of $12.50 per month. 1842. 1842b. 1843. She died 25 Apr. 1843. His son, Frederick A. Bacon, was pensioned from her death to 1 May 1844. He was pensioned again 1 July 1851 at the rate of $25 per month. 1851.
Badgely, James.* —. Carpenter's Mate. He was pensioned 26 June 1847 at the rate of $4.75 per month. 1847. 1848. 1850. 1851. He served aboard the *Ohio* and the receiving ship *North Carolina* and was disabled by injury to his back and hip.
Badger, Peter.* N.Y. Gunner's Mate. His widow, Catherine Badger, was pensioned 30 June 1825 at the amount of $114. Her husband was accidentally knocked overboard from the *Franklin* 18 June 1824. 1824. 1825. 1827. 1828. 1829. Her pension expired 19 June 1829.
Baggs, William. Penn. Marine. He was pensioned 1 Mar. 1814 at the rate of $36 per annum. 1816. 1818. 1819. 1820. 1821. 1822. 1823. 1824. 1825. 1826. 1827. 1828. 1829. 1830. 1835. 1836. 1837. 1839. 1840. 1841. 1842b. 1843. 1844. 1845. 1846. 1847. 1848. 1850. 1851. He was disabled on Lake Erie. He also appeared as William Boggs. He served aboard the *Niagara* and was wounded in his thigh.
Bailey, —. —. Landsman. His widow, Abigail Bailey, was pensioned at the rate of $4 per month. from 31 Dec. 1834. 1837. 1839. 1840. 1841. 1842. 1842b.
Bailey, —. —. —. Sarah Bailey was pensioned on his service. 1842.
Bailey, —. Mass. Sail Maker. Ellen Bailey was pensioned on his service as a privateer at the rate of $48 per annum from 9 Aug. 1813. 1813. 1814. 1815 for $25.07.
Bain, William. —. Quarter Gunner. He was pensioned 22 Oct. 1833 at the rate of $3.50 per month. 1837. 1838. 1839. 1840. 1841. 1842. 1842b. 1843. 1844. 1845. 1846. 1847. 1848. 1850. 1851. He also appeared as William Bayne.
Bainbridge, William. —. Captain. His widow, Susannah Bainbridge, was pensioned 30 June 1830 and Sep. 1847 at the rate of $50 per month. 1835. 1836. 1837. 1839. 1840. 1841. 1842. 1842b. 1845. 1846. 1848. 1850.
Baker, Henry. —. —. He perished aboard the *Grampus*. His widow was in Baltimore, Md. and sought compensation on 9 Dec. 1844.
Baker, Henry S.* —. Seaman. He was pensioned 11 Dec. 1838 at the rate of $4.50 per month. 1841. 1842. 1843. 1844. 1845. 1846. 1847. 1848. 1850. 1851. He served aboard the *Cyane* and was disabled by an injury to his wrist resulting in the loss of his hand.
Baker, John. —. Seaman. He served aboard the privateer *Saucy Jack* and was disabled by a gun shot wound of his right hip. He was pensioned 28 Oct. 1816 at the rate of $72 per annum from 1 May 1814.
Baker, John. —. Quartermaster. He was pensioned as a privateer at the rate of $24 per annum in 1828. 1828. 1829. 1830. 1831. 1832. 1833. 1834. 1835. 1836. 1837 for $12. He was

Naval Pensioners of the United States, 1800-1851

pensioned from 1 July 1837 for privateer service at the rate of $12 per month. 1846. 1847. 1850. He served aboard the *Roger* and was wounded in his middle, ring, and little fingers of his right hand causing contraction.

Baker, John W.* —. Seaman. He was pensioned 26 Sep. 1845 at the rate of $3 per month. 1847. 1848. 1850. 1851. He served aboard the *Brandywine* and was disabled by a left inguinal hernia.

Baker, Martin. N.Y. Seaman. He was pensioned as a privateer from 4 Sep. 1814 at the rate of $6 per month. 1814. 1815. 1816. 1817. 1818. 1819. 1820. 1821. 1822. 1823. 1824. 1825. 1826. 1827. 1828. 1829. 1830. 1831. 1832. 1833. 1834. 1835. 1836. 1837 for $36. 1838. He served aboard the *Grampus* and was disabled by a gun shot wound of his right leg causing the loss of same.

Baker, Thomas. Penn. Captain. He commanded the sloop of war *Delaware*. He was pensioned 10 Aug. 1801 at the rate of $37.50 per month. 1804. 1805. 1807. 1808. 1809. 1810. 1811. 1816. 1818. 1819. 1820. He died 3 Mar. 1820. His widow, Jane Baker, sought a pension 21 Feb. 1828, but it was not approved.

Baker, William. D.C. Ordinary Seaman. He was pensioned 1 July 1802 at the rate of $72 per annum. 1818. 1824. 1825. 1826. 1827. 1828. 1829. 1830. He served aboard the frigate *Congress*.

Balch, William.* Mass. Seaman. He was pensioned 1 July 1829 at the rate of $108 per annum. He was disabled at the Boston Navy Yard. 1830. He served aboard the *Warren* and was disabled by paralysis of his left side.

Baldwin, —.* —. Surgeon. His children, Lydia Baldwin, Margaretta Baldwin, and Georgia Baldwin, were pensioned at the rate of $27.50 per month from 1 Sep. 1819. 1837. 1839. 1842. [He was William Baldwin in the Old Wars pension index.]

Baldwin, Isaac.* N.Y. Captain's Clerk. He served aboard the *Java* and died 12 Apr. 1816. His widow, Elizabeth H. Baldwin, was pensioned 13 Dec. 1817 at the rate of $150 per annum. 1819. 1820. 1821. 1822. 1823. 1824. 1825. 1827. 1828. 1830. 1835. 1836. 1837. 1839. 1840. 1841. 1842. 1842b. 1845. 1846. 1848.

Baldwin, Isaac. S.C. Surgeon's Mate. He perished aboard the *Epervier* 1 Sep. 1815. His father was Isaac Baldwin of Beaufort District, South Carolina. His mother was Martha Baldwin. His parents were married 22 Jan. 1789, and he was born 25 Apr. 1791. His father was awarded $180 on 26 Sep. 1817.

Ball, —. N.H. Cooper. Nancy Ball was pensioned on his service as a privateer at the rate of $48 per annum. 1815. 1816. 1817. 1818. 1819. 1820. 1821 increase to $96. 1822. 1823. 1824. 1825. 1826. 1827. 1828. 1829. 1830. 1831. 1832. 1833. 1834.

Ball, John. Mass. Boatswain. He was pensioned 24 July 1815 at the rate of $108 per annum. 1818. 1819. 1820. 1821. 1822. 1823. 1824. 1825. 1826. 1827. 1828. 1829. 1830. 1835. 1836. 1837. 1838. 1839. 1840. 1842. 1847. He served on the *Enterprise*.

Ballagh, —. —. —. Mary Ballagh was pensioned on his service. 1842.

Ballard, Ebenezer.* —. Seaman. He was pensioned 1 Jan. 1846 at the rate of $8 per month. 1846. 1847. 1848. 1850. 1851. He served aboard the *Washington*. He was disabled by a fracture of his left leg and a scrotal hernia.

Naval Pensioners of the United States, 1800-1851

Ballard, Robert. Mass. Seaman. He served as a privateer aboard the *Macdonald* and was disabled by a fracture of his right arm and a withered left hand. He was pensioned in 1815 at the rate of $72 per annum. 1820.
Balster, John.* —. Seaman. He was pensioned as a privateer at the rate of $24 per annum. 1813. 1814. 1815. 1816. 1817. 1818. 1819. 1820. 1821. 1822. 1823. 1824. 1825. 1826. 1827. 1828. 1829. 1830. 1831. 1832. 1833. 1834. 1835. 1836. 1837 for $36. He was pensioned again from 1 July 1837 for privateer service at the rate of of $2 per month. 1836. 1837. 1838. 1844. 1845. 1846. 1847. 1850. He served aboard the *York* and was disabled by fracture of the bones in his nose and impaired vision in his right eye.
Banks, —. —. —. Grace Banks was pensioned on his service as a privateer at the rate of $36 per annum. 1812. 1813. 1814. 1815. 1816. 1817. 1818 increased to $72. 1819. 1820. 1821. 1822. 1823. 1824. 1825. 1826. 1827 for $60.
Banks, Edward. Penn. Seaman. He was pensioned 1 July 1819 at the rate of $72 per month. 1819. 1821 in N. H. 1822. 1823. 1824. 1825. 1826. 1827. 1828. 1829. 1830. He was disabled in Dartmoor Prison. He was disabled by paralysis of his lower extremities.
Banks, Joseph. —. Seaman. His widow, Elizabeth Banks, was pensioned at the rate of $6 per month. The date of the commencement of her pension was not reported. 1851. [He may have been the Joseph Potter Banks in the Old Wars pension index.]
Bantam, James.* —. Ordinary Seaman. He was pensioned 5 July 1833 at the rate of $4 per month. 1835. 1836. 1837. 1839. 1840. 1841. 1842. 1842b. 1843. 1844. 1845. 1846. 1847. 1848. 1850. 1851. He served aboard the *Java* and was disabled by a right inguinal hernia.
Baptiste, John. N.Y. Boy. He was pensioned 13 Feb. 1800 at the rate of $3 per month. 1803. 1804. 1805. 1807. 1808. 1809. 1810. 1811. 1816. 1818. 1819. 1820. 1821. 1822. 1823. 1824. 1825. 1826. 1827. 1828. 1829. 1830. He served aboard the *Constellation*.
Barber, Thomas.* —. 2nd Class Boy. His widow, Susan Barber, was pensioned from 24 Oct. 1840 at the rate of $3 per month. 1841. 1842. 1842b. 1846. She was pensioned again 1 Sep. 1847 at the rate of $3 per month. 1848. 1850. 1851.
Barber, Thomas.* —. Ordinary Seaman. He was pensioned from 4 May 1837 at the rate of $5 per month. 1837. 1838. 1839. 1840. 1842. 1846. 1847. He served aboard the *Lieutenant Lynch*. He was disabled by a fracture resulting in the amputation of his left leg.
Barker, Edward. —. Marine. He was pensioned 18 May 1836 at the rate of $3.50 per month. 1836. 1837. 1839. 1840. 1841. 1842b. 1843. 1844. 1845. 1846. 1847. 1848. 1850. 1851. He was disabled with chronic rheumatism.
Barker, James.* —. Quartermaster. He was pensioned 30 Apr. 1836 at the rate of $8 per month. 1838. 1839. 1840. 1841. 1842b. 1843. 1844. 1845. 1846. 1847. 1848. 1850. 1851. He served aboard the privateer *Grampus* and was disabled by a contusion of his head and partial paralysis of his right arm and leg.
Barker, Nathaniel. Mass. Seaman. He was pensioned 5 Apr. 1815 at the rate of $72 per annum. 1818. 1819. 1820. 1821. 1822. 1823. 1824. 1825. 1826. 1827. 1828. 1829. 1830. He served aboard the *Alligator*. He was disabled by a hernia.
Barker, William. Md. Ordinary Seaman. He was pensioned 1 July 1802 at the rate of $72 per

Naval Pensioners of the United States, 1800-1851

annum. 1804. 1805. 1807. 1808. 1809. 1810. 1811. 1816 in D.C. 1818. 1819. 1820. 1821. 1822. 1823. 1835. 1836. 1837. 1839. 1840. 1841. 1842b. 1843. 1844. 1845. 1846. 1847. 1848. 1850. 1851. His rank was also given as marine. He served aboard the *Congress.*

Barnard, —. —. —. His daughter, Hannah Barnard, was pensioned. 1837. 1842.

Barnard, —.* —. Carpenter's Mate. His widow, Sarah Barnard, was pensioned from 10 Sep. 1829 at the rate of $9.50 per month. 1839. 1841. 1842. 1842b. She also appeared as Sarah Bernard. [He was John Barnard in the Old Wars pension index.]

Barnard, Peter. N.Y. Ordinary Seaman. He was pensioned 1 Dec. 1814 at the rate of $4 per month. 1818. 1819. 1820. 1821. 1822. 1823. 1824. 1825. 1826. 1827. 1828. 1829. 1830. 1835. 1836. 1837. 1839. 1840. 1841. 1842b. 1843. 1844. 1845. 1846. 1847. 1848. 1850. 1851. He served aboard the *Enterprise.* He also appeared as Peter Bernard. He was disabled by a gun shot wound causing the fracture of his left arm.

Barndollar, William W.* —. Private Marine. His widow, Harriet D. Barndollar, was pensioned 18 Oct. 1847 at the rate of $3.50 per month. 1851.

Barnes, Breasted.* —. Captain. His widow, Elizabeth Barnes, was pensioned from 2 Nov. 1819 at the rate of $20 per month. 1839. 1840. 1841. 1842. 1842b. She was pensioned again at the rate of $10 per month 1 Sep. 1848. 1848. 1850. His rank was also given as Carpenter.

Barney, Joshua. Md. Captain. He was in the Chesapeake flotilla, was wounded at Bladensburg by a musket ball wound in his thigh, and died 1 Dec. 1818. He received $600 per annum in 1818. His widow, Harriet Barney, was pensioned 11 Sep. 1819 at the rate of $50 per month. 1820. 1821. 1822. 1823. 1824. 1825. 1827. 1828. 1829. 1830. 1835. 1836. 1837. She was pensioned again 1 Dec. 1843. 1846. 1848. 1850. She removed to Kentucky. He later became a Commodore.

Barnewall, Edward. N.Y. Lieutenant. He perished on the *Epervier* on 1 Sep. 1815. His mother, Mary Barnewall, was of Usher's Bridge, Dublin, Ireland. Peter Barnewall was a brother of the deceased and was the only sibling in America. Mary Barnewall appointed George Barnewall to receive the $240. She was paid 28 July 1817.

Barnwell, —. N.Y. Seaman. Mary Barnwell was pensioned on his service as a privateer at the rate of $36 per annum. 1815. 1816. 1817. 1818. 1819. 1820 increased to $72. 1821. 1822. 1823. 1824. 1825. 1826. 1827. 1828. 1829.

Barr, James, Jr. Mass. Captain's Clerk. He was pensioned at the rate of $48 per annum. 1812. 1813. 1814. 1815. 1816. 1817. 1818. 1819. 1820. 1821. 1822. 1823. 1824. 1825. 1826. 1827. 1828. 1829. 1830. 1831. 1832. 1833. 1834. 1835. 1836. 1837 for half a year. He was pensioned from 1 July 1837 for privateer service at the rate of $8 per month. 1838. 1844. 1845. 1846. 1847. 1850. He served aboard the *Growler* and was disabled by a fracture of his right leg.

Barr, John. —. Captain's Clerk. He was pensioned as a privateer from 4 Nov. 1812 at the rate of $4 per month. 1836. 1837.

Barrett, —. —. Quartermaster. His son, Samuel S. W. Barrett, was pensioned at the rate of $8 per month. 1837. 1842.

Naval Pensioners of the United States, 1800-1851

Barrett, John. Mass. Quarter Gunner. He was pensioned at the rate of $72 per annum. 1816. 1818. 1819. 1820. 1821. 1822. 1823. 1824. 1825. 1826. 1827. 1828. He served aboard the *President* and was disabled with a wound in his arm and legs caused by the bursting of a gun.

Barrett, Joseph. Mass. Quarter Gunner. He was pensioned 17 Apr. 1813 at the rate of $108 per annum. 1816. 1818. 1819. 1820. 1821. 1822. 1823. 1824. 1825. 1826. 1827. 1828. 1829. 1830. 1835. 1836. 1837. 1839. 1840. 1841. 1842b. 1843. 1844. 1845. 1846. 1847. 1848. 1850. He served aboard the frigate *United States*. He was disabled by an abdominal rupture.

Barrett, Theodore.* —. Lieutenant. His widow, Adelaide A. Barrett, was pensioned 11 Nov. 1847 at the rate of $25 per month. 1848. 1850. 1851.

Barrett, William. Mass. Quartermaster. His widow, Hannah S. Barrett, was pensioned at the rate of $108 per annum. 1816. 1818. 1819. 1820. 1821. 1822. 1823. 1824. 1825. 1827. 1828. 1829. He served aboard the *President* was killed 15 Jan. 1815. J. Foster was her guardian.

Barron, —. —. Captain. His son, Samuel Barron, was pensioned at the rate of $50 per month. 1837. 1842.

Barron, —.* N.Y. Pilot. His widow, Ida Barron, received $240 per annum. 1819. 1820. 1821. 1822. 1823. [He was Joseph Barron in the Old Wars pension index.]

Barron, James. —. Captain. He was pensioned from 22 June 1807 at the rate of $25 per month. 1839. 1840. 1841. 1842b. 1843. He served aboard the *United States*. He was wounded in his right leg and suffered a fracture of the bones in his left foot and a right inguinal hernia. [He was also pensioned for his Revolutionary War service.]

Barry, —. —. Sailing Master. His children, Robert T. Barry, Richard F. Barry, and Susannah E. Barry, were pensioned at the rate of $20 per month from 2 May 1830. 1837. 1839. 1842.

Barry, —. —. Marine. His widow, Polly Barry, was pensioned at the rate of $3.50 per month. 1837. 1839. 1840. 1841. 1842. 1842b. [He was Joseph Barry in the Old Wars pension index.]

Barry, Thomas.* —. Gunner & Master. He was pensioned from 2 May 1837 at the rate of $5 per month. 1837. 1838. 1839. 1840. 1841. 1842. He served aboard the *United States*. He was disabled by an injury in his left leg and the dislocation of his right hip. His widow, Mary Barry, was pensioned 28 June 1842 at the rate of $20 per month. 1842b. 1843. 1844. 1845. 1846. 1847. 1848. 1850. 1851.

Barry, William. Penn. Ordinary Seaman. He was pensioned at the rate of $60 per annum in 1802. N.Y. in 1803. 1804. 1805. 1807. 1808. 1809. 1810. 1811. He served aboard the *Ganges*. He was disabled by a fracture of his left leg and dislocation of his ankle joint.

Barsayline, Lawrence.* Va. Seaman. He was pensioned 18 Sep.1823 at the rate of $60 per annum. 1824. 1825. 1826. 1827. 1828. 1829. 1830. He served aboard the schooner *Decoy*. He was disabled by a fracture of his left arm.

Barstow, Charles.* —. Seaman. He was pensioned 20 Feb. 1849 at the rate of $6 per month. 1850. 1851. He served aboard the *United States*. He was disabled by a fracture of his right arm.

Naval Pensioners of the United States, 1800-1851

Bartholomew, —. N.Y. Lieutenant. Julia Ann Bartholomew was pensioned on his service as a privateer at the rate of $72 per annum. 1815. 1816. 1817. 1818. 1819. 1820. 1821. 1822. 1823. 1824. 1825. 1826. 1827. 1828. 1829.

Bartlett, —. —. Seaman. His widow, Elizabeth Bartlett, was pensioned at the rate of $6 per month. 1837. 1839. 1840. 1841. 1842. 1842b. [He was Abijah Bartlett in the Old Wars pension index.]

Bartlett, —. Mass. Seaman. Elizabeth Bartlett was pensioned on his service as a privateer at the rate of $36 per annum. 1812. 1813. 1814. 1815. 1816. 1817. 1818. 1819. 1820. 1821. 1822. 1823. 1824.

Bartlett, G. M. Mass. Boatswain's Mate. He served aboard the *Wasp* and was lost 20 Apr. 1813. His widow, Mary P. Bartlett, was pensioned 1 Jan. 1817. Her son, William G. Bartlett, was also pensioned. He was on the 1818 list. 1819. 1820. 1821. 1822. 1823. 1824. 1825. 1827. 1828. The pension was paid to Jan. 1830. His son was on the 1837 and 1842 lists. J. Droun was guardian in 1829.

Bartlett, Thomas.* —. Seaman. He was pensioned 24 Nov. 1834 at the rate of $6 per month. 1835. 1836. 1837. 1839. 1840. 1841. 1842b. 1843. 1844. 1845. 1846. 1847. 1848. 1850. 1851. He served aboard the *Boxer* and was disabled by the loss of his sight.

Bartlett, William G. Mass. Boatswain's Mate. He was pensioned at the rate of $9 per month. 1818.

Barton, George. N.Y. Quarter Gunner. He was pensioned at the rate of $54 per annum. 1824. 1825.

Bassett, —.* —. Surgeon. His son, George T. Bassett, was pensioned at the rate of $25 per month from 20 Aug. 1830. 1837. 1839. 1840. 1841. 1842. 1842b. [He was Henry W. Bassett in the Old Wars pension index.]

Bassett, Isaac. R.I. Ordinary Seaman. He was pensioned 15 May 1815 at the rate of $60 per annum. 1818. 1819. 1820. 1821. 1822. 1823. 1824. 1825. 1826. 1827. 1828. 1829. 1830. 1835. 1836. 1837. 1838. 1839. 1840. 1841. 1842. 1842b. 1843. 1844. 1845. 1846. 1847. 1848. 1850. 1851. He was disabled at the Newport station and served aboard the *Chesapeake*. He was disabled by the loss of his left leg.

Bateman, Enos. Penn. Seaman. He was pensioned 8 June 1813 at the rate of $60 per annum. 1816. 1818. 1819. 1820. 1821. 1822. 1823. 1824. 1825. 1826. 1827. 1828. 1829. 1830. He served aboard the *Constitution*. He was wounded in both knees and his left wrist.

Bates, Robert. Mass. Seaman. He served aboard the *Chesapeake* and was killed 1 June 1813. His widow, Sally Bates, was pensioned 12 May 1814 at the rate of $72 per annum. 1816. 1818. 1820. 1821. 1822. 1823. 1824. 1825. 1827. 1828. 1829.

Bates, William.* —. Master-at-Arms. His widow, Sarah Bates, was pensioned 28 Aug. 1847 at the rate of $9 per month. 1850. 1851.

Batts, Alfred.* —. Ordinary Seaman. He was pensioned 24 Oct. 1833 at the rate of $5 per month. 1839. 1840. 1841. 1842b. 1843. 1844. 1845. 1846. 1847. 1848. 1850. 1851. He served aboard the *Falmouth* and was disabled with paralysis of his right side.

Baum, George.* —. Marine. He was pensioned 3 Oct. 1847 at the rate of $3.50 per month. 1848. 1850. 1851. He was disabled with chronic ophthalmia.

Naval Pensioners of the United States, 1800-1851

Baxter, John. Penn. Seaman. He was pensioned 28 Feb. 1819 at the rate $72 per annum. 1820. 1821. 1822. 1823. 1824. 1825. 1826. 1827. 1828. 1829. 1830. 1835. 1836. 1837. 1839. 1840. 1841. 1842b. 1843. 1844. 1845. 1846. 1847. 1848. 1850. 1851. He served aboard the *United States*. He was injured in his right arm.

Bay, —. —. Quartermaster. His widow, Gratia Bay, was pensioned from 6 Jan. 1834 at the rate of $18 per month. 1839. 1840.

Bayne, William.* —. Quarter Gunner. He served aboard the *Hudson, Brandywine, St. Louis, Potomac,* and *Warren.* He was disabled by the rupture of his right groin and was pensioned in1837.

Beadle, John.* —. —. His mother, Emily Beadle, had her application rejected prior to 10 Jan. 1844. There was no law which gave a pension to the mother of an officer, seaman, or marine.

Beale, George.* —. Purser. His widow, Emily Beale, was pensioned 4 Apr. 1835. 1836. 1837. 1839. 1840. 1841. 1842. 1842b. 1845. 1846. She was pensioned again 1Sep. 1847 at the rate of $20 per month. 1848. 1850. 1851.

Bean, George W. —. Landsman. He was pensioned 12 Sep. 1849 at the rate of $4 per month. 1850. 1851. He was disabled with anchylosis of his ankle joint.

Beard, Andrew. D.C. Seaman. He was pensioned 11 Apr. 1815 at the rate of $72 per annum. 1818. 1819. He was in Md. in 1820. 1821. 1822. 1823. 1824. 1825. 1826. 1827. 1828. 1829. 1830. 1836. He served aboard the galley *United States*. He was disabled by the loss of his left hand.

Beattie, James. —. Seaman. He was pensioned 13 June 1849 at the rate of $4.75 per month. 1850. 1851. He was disabled with ophthalmia or lesions of both eyes.

Beatty, John.* N.Y. Marine. He was pensioned 1 June 1830 at the rate of $4 per month. 1830. 1835. 1836. 1837. 1839. 1840. 1841. 1842b. 1843. 1844. 1845. 1846. 1847. 1848. 1850. 1851. He was disabled on the *Vincennes*. He lost his left leg above the ankle. He also appeared as John Beaty.

Bebee, —. —. —. Patty Bebee was pensioned on his service as a privateer at the rate of $48. 1817. 1818. 1819. 1820 increase to $96. 1821. 1822. 1823. 1824. 1825. 1826. 1827. 1828. 1829.

Bebee, Jason. Conn. Corporal Marines. He was pensioned at the rate of $48 per annum in 1802. 1803. 1804. 1805. 1807. 1808. 1809. 1810. 1811. 1816. 1818. 1819. He served aboard the *Trumbull* and was disabled by a gun shot wound of his left arm resulting in amputation.

Beckford, —.* —. Landsman. His widow, Elizabeth Beckford, was pensioned from 30 Nov. 1839 at the rate of $4 per month. 1840. 1841. 1842. 1842b. [He was William Beckford in the Old Wars pension index.]

Beeler, William.* —. Corporal of Marines. His widow, Elizabeth Beeler, was pensioned from 1 July 1837. 1837. 1839. 1840. 1841. 1842. 1842b. 1846. She was pensioned again 1 Sep. 1847 at the rate of $4.50 per month. 1848. 1850. 1851.

Beers, Augustus P.* —. Surgeon. His widow, Catherine M. Beers, was pensioned at the rate of $25 per month. 1837. 1839. 1840. 1841. 1842. 1842b. She was pensioned again 1 Sep.

Naval Pensioners of the United States, 1800-1851

1847 at the rate of $25 per month. 1848. 1850. 1851. He also appeared as Augustin P. Beers.

Beeves, Allen. Md. Boatswain. He served aboard the *Sylph* and died from exposure 2 Oct. 1814. His widow, Ellen Beeves, was pensioned at the rate of $120 per annum. Ellen Beeves' infant daughter, Jane Beeves, was pensioned 13 Nov. 1815. 1816. 1818. 1819. 1820. 1821. 1822. 1823. 1824. 1825. 1827. 1828. 1829. She was paid to Jan. 1830. She also appeared as Jane Beevis.

Beggs, John.* —. Sailmaker. His widow, Sarah Beggs, was pensioned from 21 Sep. 1840 at the rate of $10 per month. 1841. 1842. 1842b. She was pensioned again 1 Sep. 1847 at the rate of $10 per month. 1848. 1850. 1851.

Begley, Joseph.* —. Ordinary Seaman. He served aboard the brig *Stromboli* in 1849. He was disabled with dysentry.

Begley, Nathaniel. Penn. Quarter Gunner. He was pensioned 8 Apr. 1812 at the rate of $108 per annum. 1816. 1818. 1819. 1820. 1821. 1822. 1823. 1824. 1825. 1826. 1827. 1829. 1830. He served aboard the *Hornet*. He was disabled with a fracture of his arm.

Bell, —. Mass. Cook. Phillis Bell was pensioned on his service as a privateer at the rate of $96 per annum from 1 Nov. 1812. 1817. 1818. 1819. 1820. 1821. 1822. 1823. 1834. 1825. 1826. 1827 for $80.

Bell, George.* —. Gunner. His widow, Margaret Bell, was pensioned at the rate of $10 per month. 1846. His children, Sophia Bell, Margaret E. Bell, and Gilbert Bell, were pensioned 7 Oct. 1846 at the rate of $10 per month. 1851.

Bell, Jacob.* —. Ship's Corporal. He was pensioned 24 Sep. 1847 at the rate of $7 per month. 1848. 1850. 1851. He served aboard the *Savannah* and was disabled with a double inguinal hernia.

Bell, James.* Penn. Seaman. He was pensioned 23 Aug. 1823 at the rate of $72 per annum. 1824. 1825. 1826. 1827. 1828. 1829. 1830. 1835. 1836. 1837. 1839. 1840. 1841. 1842b. 1843. 1844. 1845. 1846. 1847. 1848. 1850. 1851. He was disabled in Dartmoor Prison with a gun shot wound of his right wrist and thigh.

Bell, James.* —. Cook. His children, John Bell, Mary Jane Bell, Maria Bell, James Bell and Marcellus Bell, were pensioned on his service from 15 Aug. 1831 at the rate of $9.50 per month. 1839. 1840. 1841. 1842. 1842b.

Bellingham, Thomas.* —. Seaman. His widow, Elizabeth Bellingham, was pensioned from 9 Aug. 1837 at the rate of $6 per month. 1839. 1840. 1841. 1842. 1842b. She was pensioned again 1 Sep. 1847 at the rate of $6 per month. 1848. 1850. 1851.

Belmore, —. —. Seaman. His daughter, Lucy Belmore, was pensioned at the rate of $6 per month. 1837. 1842.

Bennett, —. Mass. Seaman. Anna Bennet was pensioned on his service as a privateer at the rate of $36 per annum. 1815. 1816. 1817. 1818. 1819. 1820. 1821. 1822. 1823. 1824. 1825. 1826. 1827. 1828. 1829. 1830. 1831. Paid to 1 Feb. 1832 for $36.

Bennett, Cornelius.* —. Sailing Master. His widow, Huldah Bennett, was pensioned from 18 Aug. 1840 at the rate of $20 per month. 1841. 1842. 1842b. She was pensioned again 1 Sep. 1847 at the rate of $20 per month. 1848. 1850. 1851.

Naval Pensioners of the United States, 1800-1851

Bennett, George.* —. Ordinary Seaman. He was pensioned 16 Sep. 1839 at the rate of $2.50 per month. 1841. 1842. 1843. 1844. 1845. 1846. 1847. 1848. 1850. 1851. He served aboard the *Columbia* and was disabled by the loss of sight in his left eye.

Bennett, John. N.H. Master's Mate. He was pensioned as a privateer at the rate of $84 per annum from 20 May 1813. 1813. 1814. 1815. 1816. 1817. 1818. 1819. 1820. 1821. 1822. 1823. 1824.

Bennett, John. Mass. Seaman. He was pensioned 14 Dec. 1814 at the rate of $72 per annum. 1816. 1818. 1819. 1820. 1822. 1824. 1825. 1826. 1827. 1828. 1829. 1830. 1835. 1836. 1837. 1839. 1840. 1841. 1842. 1842b. 1843. 1844. 1845. 1846. 1847. 1848. 1850. 1851. He served aboard the *General Pike*. He was disabled by the loss of his right leg.

Benson, George. —. —. He perished aboard the *Grampus*. His sister, Elizabeth C. Kolb, the widow of Joseph Kolb, was the mother of three children. She was from Baltimore, Md. and sought compensation on 10 Dec. 1844.

Benson, John.* —. Cook. He was pensioned 20 Jan. 1844 at the rate of $9 per month. 1844. 1845. 1846. 1847. 1848. 1850. 1851. He served aboard the *Boston* and was disabled with an aneurism of the aorta.

Bent, William.* —. Quartermaster. He was pensioned 15 May 1844 at the rate of $4 per month. 1847. 1848. 1850. 1851. He served aboard the *Penn* and was disabled with an injury to his left hand.

Bentley, —.* —. —. Ann E. Bentley was pensioned on his service. 1842. [He was Michael Bentley in the Old Wars pension index.]

Bently, Henry.* —. Ordinary Seaman. He was pensioned 29 June 1850 at the rate of $5 per month. 1850. 1851. He served aboard the *Brandywine* and was disabled with an injury of his back.

Bergamer, —.* —. Marine. His widow, Jane Bergamer, was pensioned from 12 Sep. 1839 at the rate of $3.50 per month. 1840. 1841. 1842b. [He was Joseph Bergamer in the Old Wars pension index.]

Berge, Peter. —. Captain's Steward. He was pensioned from 19 May 1834 at the rate of $6 per month. 1842b. 1843. He also appeared as Peter George.

Bergen, —.* —. —. James Bergen and William E. Bergen were pensioned on his service. 1842. [He was Peter Berger in the Old Wars pension index.]

Bernard, John. N.Y. Marine. He was pensioned 1 Jan. 1820 at the rate of $36 per annum. 1821. 1822. 1824. 1825. 1826. 1827. 1828. 1829. 1830. He had a long and faithful service.

Bernard, Peter. N.Y. Ordinary Seaman. He served aboard the *Enterprise*. He was pensioned at the rate of $48 per annum. 1816. 1829.

Berry, —.* —. Seaman. His widow, Mahala Berry, was pensioned from 18 May 1838 at the rate of $6 per month. 1839. 1840. 1842. She also appeared as Mahala Bury. His daughter, Elizabeth E. A. Berry, was pensioned from 9 Oct. 1840 at the rate of $6 per month. 1841. 1842. 1842b. [He was John Berry in the Old Wars pension index.]

Berry, —.* —. Lieutenant. His widow, Caroline M. Berry, was pensioned 1 June 1818 at the rate of $20 per month. 1835. 1836. 1837. 1839. 1840. 1841. 1842. 1842b. [He was

Naval Pensioners of the United States, 1800-1851

William Berry in the Old Wars pension index.]
Berry, Edward. —. Seaman. He was pensioned 4 July 1837 at the rate of $4.50 per month. 1839. 1840. 1841. 1842b. 1843. 1844. 1845. 1846. 1847. 1848. 1850. 1851. He served aboard the *Grampus* and was disabled with a scrotial hernia on the right side.
Berry, John.* —. Master-at-Arms. He was pensioned 18 Mar. 1835 at the rate of $4.50 per month. 1835. 1836. 1837. 1839. 1840. 1841. 1842b. 1843. 1844. 1845. 1846. 1847. 848. 1850. 1851. He served aboard the *Dolphin* and was disabled with a hernia of his left side.
Berry, Robert.* Mass. Seaman. He was pensioned from 22 June 1829 at the rate of $6 per month. He was disabled at the Navy Yard in Portsmouth, N.H. 1829. 1830. 1835. 1836. 1837. 1839. 1840. 1841. 1842. 1842b. 1843. 1844. 1845. 1846. 1847. 1848. 1850. He was disabled with an injury to his spine.
Berry, William. —. Boatswain. His widow, Sarah Berry, was pensioned 1 Mar. 1824 at the rate of $10 per month. 1835. 1836. 1837. 1840. 1841. 1842. 1842b. 1845. 1846. 1848. 1850.
Beverly, William B.* —. Lieutenant. His widow, Henrietta B. Beverly, was pensioned 30 Oct. 1846 at the rate of $25 per month. 1847. 1848. 1850. 1851.
Bevins, John.* —. Quarter Gunner. He was pensioned 24 Feb. 1837 at the rate of $7.50 per month. 1837. 1839. 1840. 1841. 1842b. 1843. 1844. 1845. 1846. 1847. 1848. 1850. 1851. He served aboard the *Constitution*.
Bickford, —. —. —. His daughter, Eleanor Bickford, was pensioned. 1837. 1842. She also appeared as Eleanor Beckford.
Bickham, Herman. Md. Master of Marines. He was pensioned as a privateer at the rate of $60 per annum. 1814. 1815. 1816. He was disabled with a gun shot wound in his back.
Biddison, Zachariah. —. Ordinary Seaman. He claimed to have been wounded in 1815. Since the wound was more than 25 years ago and that there was no proof that he was ever wounded or disabled while in service, his application was rejected prior to 13 Dec. 1842.
Bines, Robert M.* —. Corporal of Marines. He was pensioned 12 Sep. 1847 at the rate of $3.12 ½. 1848. 1850. 1851.
Biondi, Antoni. —. Leader of Band. He was pensioned 6 Apr. 1847 at the rate of $4.50 per month. 1850. 1851. He also appeared as Antonio Beondi. He served aboard the *Cumberland* and was disabled with a rupture.
Birchmore, William. —. Surgeon. His widow, Juliana Birchmore, was pensioned 30 June 1834 at the rate of $32.50 per month. 1835. 1836. 1837. 1839. 1840. 1841. 1842. 1842b. 1845. 1846. 1848. She also appeared as Juliana Berchmore and Juliana Burchmore.
Bird, James.* —. Seaman. He was pensioned 7 Nov. 1828 at the rate of $6 per month. 1840. 1841. 1842b. 1843. 1844. 1845. 1846. 1847. 1848. 1850. 1851.
Bishee, Lawrence. Va. Quarter Gunner. He was pensioned 27 Apr. 1813 at the rate of $48 per annum. 1816. 1818. 1819. 1820. 1821. 1824. 1825. 1826. 1827. 1828. 1829. 1830. He was disabled on Gunboat No. 10 at St. Mary's with a hernia.
Bishop, —. —. Seaman. His widow, Elizabeth Bishop, was pensioned at the rate of $6 per month. 1837. 1839. 1840. 1841. 1842. 1842b.
Bishop, —. N.Y. Lieutenant. Harriet Bishop was pensioned on his service as a privateer at the

Naval Pensioners of the United States, 1800-1851

rate of $144 per annum from 20 July 1813. 1818. 1819. 1820. 1821. 1822 for $57.60.
Bispham, John E.* —. Lieutenant. His widow, Alleta Bispham, was pensioned 24 Mar. 1849 at the rate of $25 per month. 1850. 1851.
Bissen, H. Peter. Md. Seaman. He was pensioned as a privateer at the rate of $72 per annum. 1812. 1813. 1814. 1815. 1816. 1817. 1818. 1819 for $36. He served aboard the *Nonsuch* and lost his right eye, was wounded in his head and face, and was injured in his thigh.
Black, David.* —. —. His widow, Winney B. Black, was pensioned 4 Oct. 1843 at the rate of $9 per month. 1851.
Blackburn, Alexander. Md. Ordinary Seaman. He was pensioned at the rate of $60 per annum in 1810. 1811 1816. He served aboard the *Syren* and was disabled with the loss of the thumb of his left hand.
Blade, —.* —. Ordinary Seaman. His son, James K. Blade, was pensioned at the rate of $6 per month from 26 Sep. 1834. 1837. 1839. 1840. 1841. 1842. He also appeared as James R. Blade. [He was James Blade in the Old Wars pension index.]
Blair, John.* N.Y. Seaman. He was pensioned 22 June 1818 at the rate of $60 per annum. 1819. 1820. 1821. 1822. 1823. 1824. 1825. 1826. 1827. 1828. 1829. 1830. He served aboard the *John Adams*. He was disabled with a fracture of his thigh bone.
Blair, Robert. —. Seaman. He was pensioned 1 Jan. 1832 at the rate of $6 per month. 1835. 1836. 1837. 1838. 1841. 1842. 1842b. 1843. 1844. 1845. 1846. 1847. 1848. 1850. 1851. He served aboard the *Guerriere* and was disabled with an hernia.
Blake, Daniel G.* —. Marine. His widow, Letitia Blake, was pensioned 14 Aug. 1836. 1836. 1837. 1839. 1840. 1841. 1842. 1842b. 1846. She was pensioned again 1 Sep. 1847 at the rate of $3.50 per month. 1848. 1850. 1851.
Blake, Charles. —. Surgeon's Mate. He served aboard the *Constitution* and was pensioned in 1834.
Blake, James.* Mass. Ordinary Seaman. He was pensioned 26 July 1822 at the rate of $60 per annum. 1823. 1824. 1825. 1826. 1827. 1828. 1829. 1830. 1841. 1842. 1842b. 1843. 1844. 1845. 1846. 1847. 1848. 1850. 1851. He served aboard the *Columbus*. He lost the thumb of his right hand.
Blake, Joseph. —. Orderly Sergeant. He was pensioned 26 July 1822 at the rate of $5 per month. 1835. 1836. 1837. 1839. 1840.
Blakely, J. Penn. Captain. He was the captain of the schooner *Wasp* and was lost 20 Apr. 1815. His widow, Jane Ann Blakely, was pensioned at the rate of $50 per month. She was pensioned at the rate of $50 per annum from 1 June 1816. 1818. 1819. 1820. 1821. 1822. 1824. 1823. 1825. 1827. 1829. The pension was paid to Jan. 1830. His daughter, Udna M. Blakely, was pensioned at the rate of $50 per month. 1837. R. Abbott was her guardian in 1829. 1837. 1842.
Blakesly, Abraham.* N.Y. Carpenter's Mate. He was pensioned at the rate of $114 per annum. 1824. 1825. 1827. 1828. He also appeared as Abraham Blaskley. He served aboard the *Constitution* and was disabled with a right inguinal hernia.
Blakslee, —.* —. Marine. His daughter, Julia Ann Blakslee, was pensioned at the rate of $3.50 per month from 21 July 1827. 1837. 1839. 1840. 1841. 1842. She was listed incorrectly in

Naval Pensioners of the United States, 1800-1851

      1842 as Julia Rlakeslie. 1842b. [He was John Blakslee in the Old War pensions index.]

Bliss, —.* —. Seaman. His sons were Thomas J. P. Bliss and Nathaniel Bliss. The pension was from 1 July 1838. 1839. 1840. 1841. 1842. 1842b. [He was Frederick Bliss in the Old Wars pension index.]

Bliss, —. —. Seaman. His daughter, Martha Bliss, was pensioned at the rate of $6 per month. 1837. 1842.

Bliss, Joel.* —. Carpenter's Mate. His widow, Marianna F. Bliss, was pensioned 23 June 1847 at the rate of $9.50 per month. 1848.

Blither, Nathaniel. Mass. Seaman. He was pensioned at the rate of $72 per annum. 1816. 1818. 1819. 1820. He served aboard the *President* and was disabled by the loss of his left arm. He also appeared as Nathaniel Blethen.

Bliven, —. —. —. Ann Bliven was pensioned on his service as a privateer at the rate of $60 per annum. 1812. 1813. 1814. 1815. 1816. 1817. 1818 increase to $120. 1819. 1820. 1821. 1822. 1823. 1824. 1825. 1826. 1827 for $80. She also appeared as Ann Bliver.

Blossom, E. N.Y. Carpenter's Mate. His widow, Betsey Blossom, was pensioned at the rate of $114 per annum. 1816. 1818. 1820. 1821. 1822. 1824. 1825. 1827. 1828.

Blunt, —. N.H. Lieutenant. Mary Blunt was pensioned on his service as a privateer at the rate of $72 per annum. 1815. 1816. 1817. 1818. 1819. 1820 increase to $144. 1821. 1822. 1823. 1824. 1825. 1826. 1827. 1828. 1829 for $127.60.

Boerum, William. —. Commander. His widow, Emily Boerum, was pensioned from 2 Nov. 1842 at the rate of $30 per month and again 2 Nov. 1847 at the rate of $30 per month. 1843. 1844. 1845. 1846. 1850. 1851.

Bogardus, Archibald.* —. Midshipman. He was pensioned 6 Apr. 1847 at the rate of $4.75 per month. 1847. 1848. 1850. 1851. He served aboard the *Constitution* was disabled by an injury to his right arm.

Boggs, David.* —. Orderly Sergeant of Marines. His widow, Margaret M. Boggs, was pensioned 17 Apr. 1845 at the rate of $8 per month. 1845. 1846. 1847. 1848. 1850. 1851.

Bolen, John. Md. Seaman. He was pensioned at the rate of $48 per annum. 1814. 1815. 1816. 1817. 1818. 1819. 1820. 1821. 1822. 1823. 1824. 1825 for $24. He served aboard the privateer *Vesta*. He was disabled by a gun shot wound of his breast resulting in injury to his right arm and shoulder.

Bolton, William C.* —. —. His widow, Mary H. Bolton, was pensioned 22 Feb. 1849 at the rate of $50 per month. 1850. 1851.

Bonner, George. N. Y. Seaman. He was pensioned at the rate of $145.63 per annum in 1802. 1803. 1804. 1805. 1807. 1808. 1809. 1810. 1811. He served aboard the frigate *Adams* and was disabled by an injury to his right foot.

Booker, Jacob.* N.Y. Ordinary Seaman. He was pensioned 4 May 1820 at the rate of $60 per annum. 1821. 1822. 1823. 1824. 1825. 1826. 1827. 1828. 1829. 1830. He served aboard the *Guerriere*. He was disabled by an injury to his right knee.

Boomer, David.* Mass. Seaman. He was pensioned from 1 July 1837 at the rate of $3 per month for privateer service. 1823. 1824. 1825. 1826. 1827. 1828. 1829. 1830. 1831. 1832. 1833. 1834. 1835. 1836. 1837. 1838. 1844. 1845. 1846. 1847. 1854. He also appeared as David

Naval Pensioners of the United States, 1800-1851

Boower and David Broomer. He served aboard the *Revenge* and was disabled by an injury to his left arm.
Booth, —. —. Master Commandant. His children, John S. Booth, Walter [also Waller] S. [also M.] Booth, William L. Booth, and Thomas A. Booth, were pensioned at the rate of $30 per month from 20 Aug. 1830. 1837. 1839. 1840. 1841. 1842. 1842b.
Borge, Peter.* —. Captain's Steward. He was pensioned 19 May 1834 at the rate of $6 per month. 1835. 1836. 1837. 1839. 1840. 1841. 1842b. 1844. 1845. 1846. 1847. 1848. 1850. 1851. He also appeared as Peter Boyd. He served aboard the schooner *Porpoise* and was disabled by an injury to his spine. He also appeared as Peter George.
Boston, Jacob.* —. Corporal of Marines. He was pensioned 13 Aug. 1849 at the rate of $4.50 per month. 1850. 1851. He served aboard the *Vixen* and was disabled with an injury to his back.
Bostrom, John.* —. Quarter Gunner. He was pensioned 30 May 1834 at the rate of $3 per month. 1835. 1836. 1837. 1839. 1840. 1841. 1842b. 1843. 1844. 1845. 1846. 1847. 1848. 1850. 1851. He served aboard the *Brandywine* and was disabled by an injury to his thigh bone and hip joint.
Bostwick, Melancthon. —. Purser. He perished aboard the *Epervier* 1 Sep. 1815. His parents were William W. and Lucy Bostwick of Saratoga County, New York. They were paid $240 on 11 Dec. 817.
Bosworth, Samuel.* R.I. Seaman. He was pensioned 3 July 1823 at the rate of $6 per month. 1824. 1825. 1827. 1828. 1829. 1830. 1835. 1836. 1837. 1839. 1840. 1841. 1842b. 1843. 1844. 1845. 1846. 1847. 1848. 1850. 1851. He served aboard the *Constitution*.
Boughan, James. Va. Lieutenant. His widow, Elizabeth K. Boughan, was pensioned 30 June 1834 at the rate of $25 per month. 1835. 1836. 1837. 1839. 1840. 1841. 1842. 1842b. 1844. 1845. She also appeared as Eliza H. Boughan.
Bowden, Thomas.* —. Quartermaster. He was pensioned 7 Dec. 1837 at the rate of $4 per month. 1838. 1839. 1840. 1841. 1842b. 1843. 1844. 1845. 1846. 1847. 1848. 1850. 1851. He served aboard the *Macedonian* and was disabled with an injury to his left leg.
Bowditch, Ebenezer. —. —. He was pensioned as a privateer at the rate of $48 per annum. 1813. 1814. 1815. 1816. 1817. 1818. 1819. 1820. 1821. 1822. 1823 for $22.27. He served aboard the *Matilda* and was disabled with a gun shot wound of his leg and thigh and a wound in his neck resulting in periodic dizziness and partial blindness.
Bowie, Daniel. —. —. He was pensioned. 1842.
Bowie, Henry.* N.Y. Sailing Master. He served aboard the *Epervier* and was lost 1 Sep. 1815. His widow, Belinda Bowie, was pensioned 4 June 1818 at the rate of $240 per annum. 1819. 1820. 1821. 1822. 1823. 1824. 1825. 1827. 1828. 1829. 1830. She was the former Belinda VanCleef. They were married at Flatbush, New York 30 Sep. 1802. She was paid $240 on 19 June 1817 and resided in New York, New York.
Bowie, James K.* —. Lieutenant. His widow, Cecile Bowie, was pensioned 25 Dec. 1842 at the rate of $25 per month. 1844. 1845. 1846. 1847. 1848. 1850. 1851.
Bowman, Godfrey.* Penn. Seaman. He was pensioned 1 Oct. 1825 at the rate of $72 per month. 1829. 1830. 1835. 1836. 1837. 1838. 1839. 1840. 1841. 1842. 1842b. 1843. 1844. 1845.

Naval Pensioners of the United States, 1800-1851

1846. 1847. 1848. 1850. 1851. He served aboard the schooner *Somers* on Lake Erie. He was disabled with an injury to his left arm.

Bowne, —. —. —. Sarah Bowne was pensioned on his service as a privateer at the rate of $36 per annum. 1815. 1816. 1817. 1818. 1819. 1820 increased to $72. 1821. 1822. 1823. 1824. 1825. 1826. 1827. 1828. 1829.

Bowne, H. N.J. —. His grand heirs [sic], Cornelius Vanchef, was on the pension list in 1829.

Boyd, —. —. —. Mary Boyd was pensioned on his service. 1842.

Boyd, David.* —. Marine. His widow, Rosanna Boyd, was pensioned 19 Nov. 1846 at the rate of $3.50 per month. 1847. 1848. 1850. 1851.

Boyd, John. Md. Seaman. He was pensioned as a privateer from 11 Jan. 1814 at the rate of $6 per month. 1814. 1815. 1816. 1817. 1818. 1819. 1820. 1821. 1822. 1823. 1824. 1825. 1826. 1827. 1828. 1829. 1830. 1831. 1832. 1833. 1834. 1835. 1836. 1837.

Boyd, John.* —. Marine. He was pensioned 26 Feb. 1851 at the rate of $3.50 per month. 1851. He served aboard the *Independence* and was disabled with paralysis.

Boyd, Thomas J.* —. Surgeon. His widow, Mary Ann Boyd, was pensioned from 26 Mar. 1839 at the rate of $30 per month. 1839. 1840. 1841. 1842. 1842b. 1843. 1845. 1846. She was pensioned again on 26 Mar. 1844 at the rate of $30 per month. 1848. 1850. 1851.

Boyer, Frederick.* —. Sergeant of Marines. He was pensioned 5 Sep. 1834 at the rate of $3.25 per month. 1835. 1836. 1838. 1841. 1842. 1842b. 1843. 1844. 1845. 1846. 1847. 1848. 1850. 1851. He served aboard the *Spark* and was disabled by a wound in his right knee.

Boyle, George.* —. Seaman. He was pensioned from 21 Nov. 1837 at the rate of $4 per month. 1840. 1841. 1842b. 1843. 1844. 1845. 1846. 1847. 1848. 1850. He was disabled with an injury in his neck.

Boyle, Junius J. —. Midshipman. He was pensioned from 22 Nov. 1823 at the rate of $4.75 per month. 1840. 1841. 1842b. 1843. He served aboard the *United States* and was disabled by an injury to his left elbow.

Bradlee, Thomas.* —. Sergeant of Marines. His widow, Eliza Bradlee, was pensioned from 12 Apr. 1838 at the rate of $6.50 per month. 1839. 1840. 1841. 1842. 1842b. She was pensioned again 1 Sep. 1847 at the rate of $6.50 per month. 1848. 1850. 1851.

Bradley, —. N.H. Captain's Clerk. Frances L. Bradley was pensioned on his service as a privateer at the rate of $48 per annum. 1816. 1817. 1818. 1819. 1820 increase to $96. 1821. 1822. 1823. 1824. 1825. 1826. 1827. 1828. 1829. 1830. 1831. 1832. 1833. 1834.

Bradley, Schuyler. Conn. Seaman. He was pensioned 4 Apr. 1814 at the rate of $72 per annum. 1816. 1818. 1819. 1820. 1821. 1822. 1823. 1824. 1825. 1826. 1827. 1828. 1829. 1830. He served aboard the schooner *Enterprise*. He was disabled by a gun shot wound in his breast.

Brady, John.* —. Seaman. He was pensioned 8 June 1846 at the rate of $6 per month. 1846. 1847. 1848. 1850. 1851. He served aboard the *Cumberland* and was disabled by the loss of his right arm.

Brannen, John. D.C. Marine. He was pensioned in 1810. He was paid $36 per annum in 1818. 1819. 1820. 1821. 1822. 1823. 1824. 1825. 1829. He also appeared as John Brannan. He was disabled on Gunboat No. 64.

Naval Pensioners of the United States, 1800-1851

Brannon, John. N.Y. Seaman. He was pensioned 28 June 1815 at the rate of $60 per annum. 1816. 1818. 1819. 1820. 1821. 1822. 1823. 1824. 1825. 1826. 1827. 1828. 1829. 1830. 1835. 1836. 1837. 1839. 1840. 1841. 1842b. 1843. 1844. 1845. 1846. 1847. 1848. 1850. 1851. He also appeared as John Brannan. He was disabled on the *Saratoga* on Lake Champlain.

Brazier, —. Mass. Seaman. Hannah Brazier was pensioned on his service as a privateer at the rate of $72 per annum from 6 Oct. 1812. 1817. 1818. 1819. 1820. 1821. 1822 for $55.

Breckell, Richard.* —. Seaman. He was pensioned 23 Feb. 1847 at the rate of $6 per month. 1847. 1848. 1850. 1851. He served aboard the *Saratoga*.

Breckenridge, Samuel M.* Va. Lieutenant. He served on the *Fulton* steam frigate and was killed 4 June 1829. His widow, Sarah Breckenridge, was pensioned 15 Sep. 1829. 1829. 1830.

Breese, Thomas.* —. Purser. His widow, Lucy Breese, was pensioned 11 Oct. 1846 at the rate of $20 per month. 1847. 1848. 1850. 1851.

Bremen, John. N.Y. Seaman. He was pensioned 18 July 1814 at the rate of $72 per annum. 1816. 1818. 1819. 1820. 1821. 1822. 1823. 1824. 1825. 1826. 1827. 1828. 1829. 1830. He was disabled on the flotilla in New York. He was disabled by the dislocation of his right shoulder.

Brett, Edmund.* N.Y. Private Marine. He was pensioned at the rate of $36 per annum 12 June 1815. 1818. 1819. 1820. 1821. 1822. 1823. 1824. 1825. 1826. 1827. 1829. 1830. 1835. 1836. 1837. 1839. 1840. 1841. 1842b. 1843. 1844. 1845. 1846. 1847. 1848. 1850. 1851. He served aboard the *John Adams*. He was disabled by an injury to his back and spine.

Brett, Thomas.* —. Surgeon's Steward. His widow, Ellen Brett, was pensioned 26 Apr. 1847 at the rate of $9 per month. 1850. 1851.

Brice, Robert. Conn. Seaman. His widow, Nancy Brice, was pensioned at the rate of $72 per annum. 1816. He was killed 20 Aug. 1812 aboard the *Constitution*.

Brice, Thomas. Conn. Seaman. His widow, Nancy Brice, was pensioned at the rate of $72 per annum. 1820. 1821. 1822. 1825. 1827. 1829.

Brigden, Edward. S.C. Seaman. He was pensioned as a privateer at the rate of $74 per annum from 3 Mar. 1814. 1820.

Briggs, John P. —. Surgeon. He was pensioned in 1837. 1842. He served aboard the *Saratoga* and was disabled by a wound in his left ankle and leg.

Briggs, Jotham.* Va. Seaman. He was pensioned 3 Feb. 1818 at the rate of $144 per annum. 1820. 1821. 1822. 1823. 1824. 1825. 1826. 1827. 1828. 1829. 1830. He was disabled on Gunboat No.162, *Orleans*. He lost his sight in his right eye and partial sight in his left eye.

Bright, Washington.* —. Gunner. His widow, Eliza Bright, was pensioned 17 Oct. 1846 at the rate of $10 per month. 1847. 1848. 1850. 1851.

Brimblecomb, D. Mass. Seaman. His widow, Hannah Brimblecome, received $72 per annum in 1818. 1821. 1822. 1824. 1825. She also appeared as Hannah Brimblecom.

Brimblecomb, —.* Mass. Seaman. His widow was Sarah Brimblecomb. She was pensioned at the rate of $72 per annum. 1818. 1819. 1820. 1822. 1823. In 1827 she was paid for her two children. 1828. 1829. T. Butman was their guardian. He was lost 20 Apr. 1815

Naval Pensioners of the United States, 1800-1851

aboard the *Wasp*. [He was David Brimblecomb in the Old Wars pension index.]
Brimblecomb, Philip.* Mass. Seaman. He was pensioned at the rate of $72 per annum. 1816. 1818. 1819. 1820. 1821. 1822. 1823. He served aboard the *Constitution*.
Brimblecomb, Thomas S. —. —. He was pensioned. 1842.
Brinnisholtz, William D. —. Seaman. His widow, Priscilla Brinnisholtz, was pensioned at the rate of $6 per month. The date of the commencement of her pension was not reported. 1851.
Brondie, Antonie. —. Leader of the band. He was pensioned 6 Apr. 1847 at the rate of $4.50 per month. 1848.
Brooke, John F.* —. Surgeon. His widow, Elizabeth Brooke, was pensioned 17 Oct. 1849 at the rate of $35 per month. 1850. 1851.
Brooks, —. Mass. Seaman. Betsey Brooks was pensioned on his service as a privateer at the rate of $240 per annum from 6 Oct. 1812. 1817. 1818. 1819. 1820. 1821. 1822 for $183.33.
Brooks, Richard.* —. Armorer. He was pensioned 3 Aug. 1850 at the rate of $4.50. 1850. 1851. He was disabled with a right inguinal hernia. He served aboard the *Independence*.
Broom, Charles R. —. Major Marines. His widow, Mary E. Broom, was pensioned from 14 Nov. 1840. 1841. 1842. 1842b. 1846.
Broom, Daniel. Md. Second Mate. He as pensioned as a privateer at the rate of $60 per annum from 16 Apr. 1813. 1820.
Broughton, Nicholas. —. —. He perished aboard the *Grampus*. He was born 18 Jan. 1826 and enlisted at the age of 16 on 26 Feb. 1841. He was the son of John and Elizabeth Broughton. His father was a sea captain. His mother lived in Marblehead, Mass. Their were eight siblings of the deceased, and four of them were minors on 6 May 1844.
Brown, —. —. —. Ann Brown was pensioned on his service as a privateer at the rate of $72 per annum. 1812. 1813. 1814. 1815. 1816. 1817. 1818 increase to $144. 1819. 1820. 1821. 1822. 1823. 1824. 1825. 1826. 1827. 1828. 1829. 1830. 1831. 1832 for $96.
Brown, —. Mass. Seaman. Mary Brown was pensioned on his service as a privateer at the rate of $60 per annum. 1813. 1814. 1815. 1816. 1817. 1818. 1819. 1820 increase to $120. 1821. 1822. 1823. 1824. 1825. 1826. 1827. 1828. 1829 for $80.
Brown, —. —. —. Isabella Brown was pensioned on his service as a privateer at the rate of $72 per annum. 1817. 1818. 1819. 1820. 1821. 1822. 1823. 1824. 1825. 1826. 1827 for $55.
Brown, —. Penn. Seaman. His son, John Brown, was pensioned at the rate of $6 per month. 1823.
Brown, —. —. Musician. His children, John Brown, William Brown, Richard Brown, and James Brown, were pensioned from 3 Feb. 1841 at the rate of $4 per month. 1842b.
Brown, —. —. Captain. His children, Ann Eliza Brown, Isaac C. Brown, Alexander Brown, and Emma Brown, were pensioned at the rate of $50 per month from 28 Nov. 1828. 1837. 1839. A fifth child, Eliza L. Brown, was on the 1842 roll.
Brown, —. —. Master's Mate. His daughter, Maria E. Brown, was pensioned at the rate of $10 per month. 1837.
Brown, —. —. Master's Mate. His son, Morris Brown, was pensioned at the rate of $10 per month. 1837. 1842.

Naval Pensioners of the United States, 1800-1851

Brown, —. Penn. Sailing Master. His widow, Margaret Brown, received $108 per annum in 1821.
Brown, Adam.* N.Y. Seaman. He was pensioned 26 Feb. 1820 at the rate of $72 per annum. 1821. 1822. 1823. 1824. 1825. 1826. 1827. 1828. 1829. 1830. He served aboard the brig *Spark*. He was disabled with an injury to his left hand.
Brown, Billy. —. Seaman. His application was rejected prior to 17 Jan. 1845. He was wounded prior to the passage of the act of 23 Apr. 1800 so he was not covered.
Brown, Charles.* —. Ordinary Seaman. He was pensioned from 28 Dec. 1836 at the rate of $5 per month. 1837. He served aboard the *United States* and was disabled with hemiplegia of his left side.
Brown, Charles. —. Private of Marine. He was pensioned 21 Aug. 1847 at the rate of $3.50 per month. 1848. 1850. 1851. He served aboard the *Adams* and was disabled with a double hernia.
Brown, Charles R. —. Major of Marines. His widow, Mary E. Brown, was pensioned 1 Sep. 1847 at the rate of $25 per month. 1847. 1848. 1850. 1851. She also appeared as Mary O. Brown.
Brown, Cotton. Mass. Cook. He was pensioned 22 Aug. 1809 at the rate of $108 per annum. 1811. 1816. 1818. 1819. 1824. 1825. 1826. 1827. 1828. 1829. 1830. He served on the frigate *Chesapeake*. He also appeared as Colton Brown and Collen Brown.
Brown, Daniel. N.Y. Quarter Gunner. He was pensioned at the rate of $9.00 per month in 1803. He served aboard the *President* and was wounded in his forehead.
Brown, David. —. Second Mate. He served aboard the privateer *Vesta* and was disabled by a gun shot wound of his breast, left arm, and right hand.
Brown, Edward. —. Seaman. He was pensioned at the rate of $6 per month. 1850. 1851. He was disabled by an injury from a fall. He served aboard the *Fulton*.
Brown, Eli.* —. Sailing Master. His children had their application rejected prior to 12 Dec. 1842. Their father did not die in the service.
Brown, Enoch. N.Y. Midshipman. He was pensioned at the rate of $8.50 per month in 1803. 1804. 1805. 1807. 1808. 1809. 1810. 1811. He served aboard the *Insurgent* and was disabled by a wound in left hand.
Brown, Henry.* —. Marine. He was pensioned 23 July 1849 at the rate of $1.75 per month. 1850. 1851. He was disabled with a hernia of his right side.
Brown, Henry.* —. Coal Heaver. He was pensioned 15 Apr. 1851 at the rate of $6 per month. 1851. He served aboard the *Scourge* and was disabled by an injury to his right eye.
Brown, James. —. —. He was pensioned. 1842.
Brown, James. —. Marine. He perished aboard the *Epervier* 1 Sep. 1815. Benjamin Brown of Vassalboro, Kennebec Co., Maine was his father. His brother was Benjamin Brown and was paid $36.
Brown, James.* —. Carpenter. His widow, Lydia Brown, was pensioned at the rate of $10 per month 13 Mar. 1837. 1837. 1839. 1840. 1841. 1842. 1842b. 1845. 1846. 1848. 1850.
Brown, James. Del. Seaman. He was pensioned 12 Sep. 1821 at the rate of $96 per annum. 1823 in Md. 1824. 1825. 1826. 1827. 1829. 1830. 1835. 1836. 1837. He was blind. He served

25

aboard the frigate *Congress.*

Brown, James.* N.Y. Boatswain's Mate. He was pensioned 6 June 1820 at the rate of $120 per annum.1821. 1822. 1823. 1824. 1825. 1826. 1827. 1828. 1829. 1830. He served aboard the *Constellation.* He was disabled with an injury to his left thigh.

Brown, John.* N.Y. Seaman. He was pensioned 1 July 1829 at the rate of $6 per month. 1829. 1830. 1835. 1836. 1837. 1839. 1840. 1841. 1842b. 1843. 1844. 1845. 1846. 1847. 1848. 1850. 1851. He served aboard the schooner *Dolphin.* He was disabled with a fracture of the bones of his ankles.

Brown, John, 4th.* —. Seaman. He was pensioned 31 Aug. 1825 at the rate of $3 per month. 1839. 1840. 1841. 1842b. 1843. 1844. 1845. 1846. 1847. 1848. 1850. 1851. He served aboard the *North Carolina* and was disabled with a fracture of his right collarbone.

Brown, John. Penn. Seaman. He served aboard the *Constitution* and was killed 19 Aug. 1812. His widow was Ann Brown. She was pensioned at the rate of $72 per annum. 1820. 1821. 1822. His minor child received $72 in 1822. 1824. 1825. 1827. 1829.

Brown, John. Va. Ordinary Seaman. He was pensioned 10 Jan. 1818 at the rate of $72 per annum. 1820. 1821. 1822. 1823. 1824. 1825. 1826. 1827. 1828. 1829. 1830. He served aboard the *Constellation.* He was disabled with a rupture.

Brown, Joseph.* —. Seaman. His application was rejected because his name was not found among the returns of those who were wounded on board the frigate *President* when she was captured by the British. His application was submitted between Mar. 1840 and 1 Jan. 1842.

Brown, Luke.* —. Seaman. He was pensioned at the rate of $3 per month 5 July 1834. 1835. 1836. 1837. 1839. 1840. 1841. 1842b. 1843. 1844. 1845. 1846. 1847. 1848. 1850. 1851. He served aboard the *Revenge* and was disabled by an injury to his left hand.

Brown, Obadiah. Va. Seaman. He was pensioned 1 Apr. 1819 at the rate of $60 per annum. 1824. 1825. 1826. 1827. 1828. 1829. 1830.

Brown, Samuel. —. Seaman. He was pensioned as a privateer in 1820. He was paid $45.87 for 1820 and $24 in 1821. He served aboard the *Growler* and was disabled by a wound of his head.

Brown, Stephen. Mass. Carpenter. He was pensioned as a privateer at the rate of $72 per annum. 1813. 1814. 1815. 1816. 1817 in the amount of $36. He served aboard the *Sabine* and was disabled by an injury to his left side and arm.

Brown, Thomas. Penn. Private Marine. He was pensioned 15 July 1813 at the rate of $24 per annum. 1816. 1818. 1819. 1820. 1821. 1824. 1825. 1826. 1827. 1828. 1829. 1830. He served aboard the *Constellation.* He was disabled by frost bitten toes resulting in the loss of same.

Brown, William.* —. Sergeant of Marines. He was pensioned 10 June 1851 at the rate of $6 per month. 1851. He was disabled with an injury to his left wrist.

Brown, William B.* —. Gunner. He was pensioned from 4 July 1837 at the rate of $4.50 per month. 1839. 1840. 1841. 1842b. 1843. He served aboard the *Potomac.*

Browne, —. —. —. His widow, Elizabeth Browne, had her application rejected between Mar. 1840 and 1 Jan. 1842. He was a privateersman. The privateer pension fund had long since

Naval Pensioners of the United States, 1800-1851

been exhausted. Even if the fund had been solvent, her application would have been rejected because her husband did not die in the service. She also filed an application on the service of her brother who died of wounds received in battle, but the law made no provision for a sister.

Browne, James.* —. Quartermaster. His widow, Elizabeth Browne, had her application rejected prior to 30 Dec. 1845. He did not die in the service by reason of a disease contracted while in the line of his duty.

Brownell, John. D.C. Quartermaster. He was pensioned at the rate of $108 per annum. 1816. 1818. 1819. 1820. 1821. 1822. He served aboard the *John Adams* and was disabled with a wound of his right arm.

Brownell, Thomas. —. Sailing Master. His application was rejected between Mar. 1840 and 1 Jan. 1842 because he did not produce any direct proof, other than his own statements, that the disease of which he complained was produced by a wound received on Lake Erie in 1813. He was allowed a pension from 31 Dec. 1829 at the rate of $10 per month which terminated on 1 Oct. 1840. 1842b. He served aboard the *Lawrence* and was disabled with an hernia.

Browning, Robert L.* —. Lieutenant. His widow, Leuright Browning, was pensioned 12 Aug. 1850 at the rate of $25 per month. 1850. 1851. She also appeared as Lewright Browning.

Bruce, John.* Va. Quarter Gunner. He was pensioned 1 May 1826 at the ready of $9 per month. 1827. 1828. 1829. 1830. 1835. 1836. 1837. 1839. 1840. 1841. 1842b. 1843. 1844. 1845. 1846. 1847. 1848. 1850. 1851. He served aboard the *Grampus*. He was disabled with a fracture of his thigh.

Brum, Philip. N.Y. Sailing Master. He served on the *Saratoga* on the lakes, was wounded, and died 1 June 1818. His widow, Susannah Brum, was pensioned 16 Apr. 1821 at the rate of $20 per month. 1822. 1823. 1824. 1825. 1827. 1828. 1829. 1830. 1835. 1836. She was pensioned again 1 June 1843. 1846. 1848. 1850. 1851. In 1848 it was stated that her pension was for life.

Brumley, John.* D.C. Seaman. He was pensioned 1 Sep. 1826 at the rate of $6 per month. 1827. 1828. 1829. 1830. 1835. 1836. 1837. 1839. 1840. 1841. 1842b. 1843. 1844. 1845. 1846. 1847. 1848. 1850. 1851. He was disabled on the receiving ship *Alert*. His disability was permanent. He was disabled with a fracture of his left thigh.

Bryan, Lloyd J.* —. Passed Midshipman. He was pensioned from 22 Jan. 1837 at the rate of $.83 ½ per month. 1840. 1841. 1842b. 1843. He was disabled with a gun shot wound of his knee.

Bryant, Lemuel. Mass. Ordinary Seaman. He was pensioned at the rate of $96 per annum from 1 Aug. 1814. He was disabled on Lake Ontario. 1818. 1819. 1820. 1821. 1822. 1823. 1824. 1825. 1826. 1827. 1828. 1829 in Maine. 1830. 1835. 1836. 1837. 1839. 1840. 1841. 1842b. 1843. 1844. 1845. 1846. 1847. 1848. 1850. 1851. He was incorrectly listed as Samuel Bryant in 1823. He served aboard the *Scourge* and was disabled by a wound in his abdominal muscles.

Bryant, Samuel.* N.Y. Seaman. He was pensioned 5 Mar. 1830 at the rate of $3 per month. 1830. 1835. 1836. 1837. 1839. 1840. 1841. 1842b. 1843. 1844. 1845. 1846. 1847. 1848.

Naval Pensioners of the United States, 1800-1851

1850. 1851. He served aboard the *Ontario* and was disabled by the loss of his right eye.

Buchanan, Thomas.* —. Marine. He was pensioned 4 June 1829 at the rate of $3 per month. 1835. 1836. 1837. 1838. 1839. 1840. 1841. 1842. 1842b. 1843. 1844. 1845. 1846. 1847. 1848. 1850. 1851. He served aboard the *Fulton* and was disabled by a compound fracture of his left thigh and injury to his knee and ankle joint.

Buck, Nicholas.* —. Sailmaker. His widow, Sophia H. Buck, was pensioned 16 June 1848 at the rate of $10 per month. 1850. 1851.

Buck, Peter.* —. Musician. His widow, Elizabeth Buck, was pensioned from 5 Dec. 1838 at the rate of $4 per month. 1839. 1840. 1841. 1842. 1842b. 1845. 1846. She was pensioned again 1 Sep. 1847 at the rate of $4 per month. 1848. 1850. 1851.

Buckley, —. —. Musician in Marines. His children, Eleanor Buckley, James S. Buckley, and Thomas Buckley, were pensioned at the rate of $4 per month. 1837. A fourth son, David Z. Buckley, was on the 1842 roll. [He was Thomas Buckley in the Old Wars pension index.]

Budd, —. —. Lieutenant. His sons, Thomas Budd and Charles H. Budd, were pensioned at the rate of $25 per month from 15 Mar. 1827. 1837. 1839. 1842.

Budd, George. —. Lieutenant. He was pensioned from 4 Aug. 1837 at the rate of $15 per month. 1837. 1838. 1842. He served aboard the *Chesapeake* and was disabled by a saber wound of his left shoulder and his right wrist.

Bulkley, Jonathan. —. Midshipman. He was pensioned 17 June 1834 at the rate of $9 per month. 1835. 1836. 1837. 1839. 1840. 1841. 1842b. 1843. 1844. 1845. 1846. 1847. 1848. 1850. 1851. He was disabled with a rupture.

Bull, Jacob.* Mass. Ordinary Seaman. He was pensioned 20 July 1821 at the rate of $60 annum. 1822. 1823. 1824. 1825. 1826. 1827. 1828. 1829. 1830. He served aboard the *Macedonian*. He was disabled by a musket ball through his abdomen.

Bullen, Martin.* —. Quartermaster. He was pensioned 21 Nov. 1846 at the rate of $9 per month. 1847. 1848. 1850. 1851. He served aboard the *Lawrence* and was disabled with a left inguinal hernia.

Bulley, James. —. Ordinary Seaman. He served aboard Gun Boat No. 57 and was injured in his chest and thigh. He was pensioned in Oct. 1812.

Bullock, John.* —. Captain of Forecastle. He was pensioned 9 Oct. 1846 at the rate of $7.50 per month. 1847. 1848. 1850. 1851. He served aboard the frigate *Constitution* and was disabled by an injury to his chest.

Bunch, Daniel. Md. —. He perished aboard the *Epervier* 1 Sep. 1814. His father was Daniel Bunch of Worcester Co., Md.

Bundick, —. N.Y. Sailing Master. Catherine Bundick was pensioned on his service as a privateer at the rate of $72. 1814. 1815. 1816. 1817 for $36.

Bunnell, David C.* —. Seaman. He was pensioned 27 Apr. 1813 at the rate of $3 per month. 1837. 1838. 1839. 1840. 1841. 1842. 1842b. 1843. 1844. 1845. 1846. 1847. 1848. 1850. 1851. He served aboard the *Macedonian*. He was disabled by a wound in his right knee.

Burchstead, Benjamin B.* —. Carpenter. His widow, Nabby Burchstead, was pensioned 30 June 1834 and 1 Sep. 1847 at the rate of $10 per month. 1836. 1837. 1839. 1840. 1841. 1842.

Naval Pensioners of the United States, 1800-1851

1842b. 1845. 1846. 1848. 1850. 1851.

Burdeen, John. Md. Seaman. He was pensioned 22 May 1814 at the rate of $72 per annum. 1816. 1818. 1819. 1820. 1821. 1824. 1825. 1826. 1827. 1828. 1829. 1830. He served aboard the *Lawrence* and was disabled with a gun shot wound in his right leg on Lake Erie. He also appeared as John Bardeen.

Burdett, —. —. —. Mary Burdett was pensioned on his service as a privateer at the rate of $60 per annum. 1812. 1813. 1814. 1815. 1816. 1817. 1818. 1819. 1820. 1821. 1822. 1823. 1824. 1825. 1826. 1827. 1828. 1829. 1830. 1831. 1832 for $90.

Burke, Edward.* Md. Seaman. He was pensioned 5 Jan. 1815 at the rate of $48 per annum. 1816. 1824. 1825. 1826. 1827. 1828. 1829. 1830. He was black. He served aboard the *Guerriere*. He also appeared as Edward Burk. He was disabled by the loss of the use of one of his legs by a gun powder explosion.

Burney, William. N.Y. Seaman. He was disabled 26 May 1814 at the rate of $72 per annum. 1816. 1818. 1819. 1820. 1821. 1822. 1823. 1824. 1825. 1826. 1827. 1828. 1829. 1830. He served aboard the *Peacock*. He was disabled by a rupture.

Burnham, John.* D.C. Master's Mate. He was pensioned 1 Aug. 1828 at the rate of $60 per annum. He was disabled in action 10 Sep. 1813 aboard the *Lawrence*. 1829. 1830. 1835. 1836. 1837. 1839. 1840. 1841. 1842b. 1843. 1844. 1845. 1846. 1847. 1848. 1850. 1851. He was wounded in his right leg.

Burnham, Joseph.* —. —. He was pensioned. 1842.

Burns, —. —. —. Elizabeth Burns applied in Oct. 1824 and was pensioned at the rate of $120 per annum.

Burns, —.* —. Seaman. His widow, Mary Burns, was pensioned 4 Mar. 1835 at the rate of $6 per month. 1835. 1836. 1837. 1839. [He was Daniel Burns in the Old Wars pension index.]

Burns, Dominick. N.Y. Private Marine. He was pensioned 11 May 1809 at the rate of $36 per annum. 1810. 1811. 1816. 1818. 1819. 1820. 1821. 1822. 1823. 1824. 1825. 1826. 1827. 1828. 1829. 1830. He also appeared as Dominick Barns, Dominick Barnes, Dominick Burnee, and Dominick Burnes. He was disabled on Gunboat No. 58. He was disabled with a gun shot wound of his leg below the knee.

Burns, John.* —. Ordinary Seaman. He was pensioned 29 Oct. 1844 at the rate of $5 per month. 1845. 1847. 1848. 1850. 1851. He served aboard the *Lawrence* and was disabled by the loss of his right arm above the elbow joint.

Burns, Thomas. Penn. Boatswain's Mate. He was pensioned at the rate of $91.20 per annum in 1802. 1803. 1804. 1805. 1807. 1808. 1809. 1810. 1811. He served aboard the *Philadelphia*. He was disabled by wounds in both hands resulting in the loss of the little finger of his right hand and the partial loss of the use of his left hand. In 1816 he was in New Jersey.

Burns, William W.* —. Sergeant Marines. His widow, Elizabeth Burns, was pensioned at the rate of $6.50 per month from 13 Oct. 1835. Her pension ended 31 Aug. 1842. 1843.

Burr, Nathan.* N.Y. Quarter Gunner. He was pensioned 27 May 1829 at the rate of $54 per annum. 1830. 1835. 1836. 1837. 1838. 1839. 1840. 1841. 1842. 1842b. 1843. 1844.

1845. 1846. 1847. 1848. 1850. 1851. He was disabled on Gunboat No. 162. He was disabled by a wound in his left leg.

Burr, Thomas.* Va. Ordinary Seaman. He was pensioned 1 July 1822 at the rate of $72 per annum. 1821. 1822. 1823 in Md. 1824. 1825. 1826. 1827. 1828. 1829. 1830. He served aboard the frigate *Constellation.* He also appeared as Thomas Bun. He was disabled with a hernia.

Burtch, William. N.Y. Master's Mate. He was pensioned at the rate of $120 per annum. 1818. He served aboard Gunboat No. 51 and was disabled with rheumatism.

Burton, George.* N.Y. Quarter Gunner. He was pensioned 1 July 1817 at the rate of $54 per annum. 1822. 1823. 1826. 1827. 1828. 1829. 1830. He served on Gunboat No. 110. He was disabled with a wound in his left leg. He also appeared as George Barton.

Burvell, —.* —. Seaman. His widow, Martha Burvell, was pensioned at the rate of $6 per month. 1837. 1839. 1840. 1841. 1842. 1842b. She also appeared as Martha Burrell. [He was Lemuel Burrell in the Old Wars pension index.]

Bush, —. —. —. Sarah Bush applied in May 1824 and was pensioned at the rate of $72 per annum.

Busvine, Edward J.* —. Surgeon's Steward. His widow, Elizabeth A. Busvine, was pensioned 22 Aug. 1843 at the rate of $9 per month. 1847. 1848. 1850. 1851.

Butler, John. —. Seaman. He was pensioned from 30 Apr. 1835 at the rate of $3.75 per month. 1848.

Butler, John. D.C. Seaman. He was pensioned 22 Nov. 1815 at the rate of $60 per annum in 1818. 1819. 1820. 1821. 1822. 1823. 1824. 1825. 1826. 1827. 1828. 1829. 1830. 1835. 1836. 1837. 1839. 1840. 1841. 1842b. 1843. 1844. 1845. 1846. 1847. 1848. 1850. 1851. He was black. He served aboard the *Guerriere.* He was disabled by burns.

Butler, John. N.Y. Seaman. He was pensioned 9 Oct. 1816 at the rate of $72 per annum. 1818. 1819. 1820. 1821. 1822. 1823. 1824. 1826. 1827. 1828. 1829. 1830. He served aboard the *Congress.* He was disabled with an inguinal hernia.

Butler, Philip.* N.Y. Quarter Gunner. He was pensioned at the rate of $72 per annum. 1818. 1819. 1820. 1821. 1822. He served aboard the *Tom Bowline.*

Butler, Robert.* —. Quarter Gunner. He was pensioned 30 Apr. 1835 at the rate of $3.75 per month. 1839. 1840. 1841. 1842b. 1843. 1844. 1845. 1846. 1847. 1850. 1851. He served aboard the *Constitution* and was disabled by the loss of sight in his right eye.

Butler, Samuel. Conn. Quarter Gunner. He was pensioned 28 Aug. 1815 at the rate of $96 per annum. 1816. 1818 in N.Y. 1819. 1820. 1821. 1822. 1824. 1825. 1826. 1827. 1828. 1829. 1830. 1836. 1837. 1838. 1839. 1840. 1841. 1842. 1842b. 1843. 1844. 1845. 1846. 1847. 1848. 1850. 1851. He served aboard the *Hornet.* He was disabled by grape shot in the face.

Butler, Silas.* —. Purser. His widow, Phebe Butler, was pensioned from 9 Apr. 1837 at the rate of $20 per month. 1839. 1840. 1841. 1842. 1842b. 1846. She was pensioned again 1 Sep. 1847 at the rate of $20 per month. 1848. 1850. 1851.

Butler, Thomas.* —. Captain of Foretop. He was pensioned 11 Aug. 1844 at the rate of $5.62 ½ per month. 1844. 1845. 1846. 1847. 1848. 1850. 1851. He served aboard the *Vincennes*

Naval Pensioners of the United States, 1800-1851

and was disabled by a compound fracture of his right leg.

Butler, William.* —. Landsman. His application was rejected prior to 17 Jan. 1848. He alleged to have been injured by the blowing up of the powder magazine on board the steamer, *Fulton*. The muster rolls of the vessel did not show that he was injured or disabled. The person, T. E. McKiernan, who signed the certificate of disability did not appear on the Navy Register as a medical officer of the navy.

Butt, Edmund. N.Y. Marine. He was pensioned at the rate of $36 per annum. 1828.

Butterfield, —. N.Y. Lieutenant. His widow, Eliza Butterfield, was pensioned on his service as a privateer at the rate of $144 per annum. 1818. 1819. 1820. 1821. 1822 for $31.20.

Byrne, Edmund. —. Commander. His widow, Ann Byrne, was pensioned 17 Oct. 1850 at the rate of $30 per month. 1851.

Byrnes, Patrick. —. Marine. He was pensioned 6 May 1843 at the rate of $2.62 ½ per month. 1845. 1847. 1848. 1850. 1851. He was disabled by an injury to his left hand.

Cahill, —.* —. —. Mary J. Cahill was pensioned on his service. 1842. [He was listed as Bartholomew Cahill in Old Wars pension index.]

Cain, John.* —. Ship's Corporal. His widow, Anna Cain, was pensioned 26 Oct. 1834 at the rate of $7 per month. 1839. 1840. 1841. 1842. 1842b. 1851. She also appeared Anna Crain.

Cain, Patrick. Penn. Private Marine. He was pensioned 25 Oct. 1815 at the rate of $72 per annum. 1820. 1822. 1823. 1824. 1825. 1826. 1827. 1828. 1829. 1830. He served aboard the *Constitution*. He was disabled by the loss of his right forearm.

Cain, William. N.Y. Seaman. He was pensioned 24 Aug. 1814 at the rate of $72 per annum. 1816. 1818. 1819. 1820. 1821. 1822. 1823. 1824. 1825. 1826. 1827. 1828. 1829. 1830. He served aboard the *Rattlesnake*. He was disabled by a blow to the head causing partial blindness. His ship was also given as the *Enterprise*.

Calder, George. Md. Midshipman. He was pensioned at the rate of $84 per annum in 1805. 1807. 1808. 1809. 1810. 1811. He served aboard the *Patapsco* and was disabled by a gun shot wound of his thigh.

Caldwell, —. —. Lieutenant. His son, William M. Caldwell, was pensioned from 5 June 1827 at the rate of $25 per month. 1839. 1840. 1841. 1842. 1842b.

Caldwell, William W. —. Lieutenant. His widow, Hannah Caldwell, was pensioned at the rate of $25 per month from 30 June 1834. 1837. 1839. 1842. He died of yellow fever contracted in the West Indies in September 1825. She was unsuccessful in seeking a back pension.

Caldwell, Charles.* —. Landsman. His widow, Hester Caldwell, was pensioned 4 Oct. 1848 at the rate of $4 per month. 1851.

Caldwell, Charles H.* —. Lieutenant. His widow, Elizabeth J. Caldwell, was pensioned 30 June 1834 and again on 1 Sep. 1847 at the rate of $25 per month. 1835. 1836. 1837. 1839. 1840. 1841. 1842. 1842b. 1845. 1846. 1848. 1850. 1851.

Caldwell, John. Mass. Seaman. He was pensioned 23 Apr. 1814 at the rate of $72 per annum. 1816. 1818. 1819. 1820. 1821. 1822. 1824. 1825. 1826. 1827. 1828. 1829. 1830. He served aboard the frigate *Chesapeake*. He was disabled by saber wounds resulting in the loss of both hands. He also appeared as John Chaldwell.

Caldwell, William M. —. —. His widow, Hannah Caldwell, was pensioned at the rate of $25 per month from 30 June 1834. He died of yellow fever in the West Indies in September 1825.

Cale, —. —. —. S. Cale was pensioned on his service as a privateer at the rate of $72 per annum. 1812. 1813. 1814. 1815. 1816. 1817. 1818. 1819. 1820. 1821. 1822. 1823. 1824. 1825. 1826. 1827. 1828. 1829. 1830. 1831. 1832.

Callamore, —. —. —. Maria J. Callamore and Hannah Callamore were pensioned on his service. 1842.

Calverly, John.* —. Captain of Forecastle. His application was rejected between Mar. 1840 and 1 Jan. 1842. He produced no proof that the injury of which he complained was occasioned while in the discharge of his duty as a seaman in the U.S. service.

Campbell, —. —. Lieutenant. His widow, Ann D. Campbell, was pensioned from 9 July 1833 at the rate of $10 per month. 1837. 1839. 1840. 1841. 1842. 1842b.

Campbell, Archibald.* Penn. Seaman. He was pensioned 24 Apr. 1815 at the rate of $72 per annum. 1818. 1819. 1820. 1821. 1822. 1823. 1824. 1825. 1826. 1827. 1828. 1829. 1830. He served aboard the *Macedonian*. He was disabled by an injury to his right thigh.

Campbell, Benjamin. N.Y. Sergeant Marines. He was pensioned 28 Aug. 1815 at the rate of $60 per annum. 1816. 1818. 1819. 1820. 1821. 1822. 1823. 1824. 1825. 1826. 1827. 1828. 1829. 1830. He served aboard the *Hornet*. He was disabled by a fracture of his right arm from a gun shot wound.

Campbell, George. Penn. Ordinary Seaman. He was pensioned at the rate of $60 per annum in 1805. 1807. 1808. He served aboard the *Philadelphia* and was disabled with palsy.

Campbell, John.* N.Y. Boatswain. He was pensioned 1 Aug. 1814 at the rate of $96 per annum. 1818. 1819. 1820. 1821. 1822. 1823. 1824. 1825. 1826. 1827. 1828. 1829. 1830. He was disabled on Lake Ontario by a gun shot wound in his left arm.

Campbell, Thomas. Penn. Seaman. He perished aboard the *Epervier* 1 Sep. 1815. His mother was Isabella Campbell, and she was administratrix of his estate. She was the widow of the late William Campbell and was paid $72.

Cannon, John H.* N.Y. Corporal Marines. He was pensioned 27 Oct. 1829 at the rate of $45 per annum. 1830. 1836. He served aboard the brig *Enterprise*. He was disabled with palsy.

Cannon, Joseph S. —. Midshipman. He entered the service 26 Feb. 1814, joined the naval squadron on Lake Champlain and was in battle there on 11 Sep. 1814. In 1817 he was detailed to the schooner *Asp*. His health became impaired. He was dismissed in Dec. 1828. He was pensioned at the rate of $10 per month from 1 Jan. 1829. He was disabled with pulmonary tuberculosis.

Cantrill, William.* Va. Marine. He was pensioned 8 Apr. 1830 at the rate of $2 per month. 1830. 1835. 1836. 1837. 1839. 1840. 1841. 1842b. 1843. 1844. 1845. 1846. 1847. 1848. 1850. 1851. He also appeared as William Cantrell. He served aboard the *Delaware*. He was disabled with a right inguinal hernia.

Cape, John. —. Seaman. His widow, Isabella Cape, was pensioned from 31 Jan. 1840 at the rate of $6 per month. 1840. 1841. 1842b. 1843. 1844. 1848. 1851. He also appeared as John

Naval Pensioners of the United States, 1800-1851

Cope.

Cape, William.* —. Seaman. He was pensioned 26 Feb. 1851 at the rate of $3 per month. 1851. [He was probably the one listed as William Cope in the Old Wars pension index.]

Carberry, John. N.Y. Cooper. He was pensioned 9 Dec. 1807 at the rate of $54 per annum. 1809. 1810. 1811. 1816. 1818. 1819. 1820. 1821. 1824. 1825. 1826. 1827. 1828. 1829. 1830. He served aboard the *Wasp*. He was disabled by the loss of the first and second joints of two fingers of his left hand.

Carey, Dennis.* Mass. Ordinary Seaman. He was pensioned 1 Jan. 1819 at the rate of $84 per annum. 1824. 1827. 1830. He was disabled at Boston. He also appeared as Dennis Cary. He served aboard the *Boston* and wounded in his left leg.

Carlisle, J. Penn. Marine. His widow, Nancy Carlisle, received $36 in 1822. 1823. Her children received the pension in 1824. 1825. 1827. 1829. He was killed 11 Sep. 1814 on Lake Champlain. Dr. Corey was guardian of the children.

Carlow, John.* —. Pilot. He was pensioned as a privateer at the rate of $36 per annum. 1828. 1829. 1830. 1831. 1832. 1833. 1834. 1835. 1836. 1837 for $18. He was pensioned from 1 July 1837 at the rate of $4 per month. 1838. 1844. 1845. 1846. 1847. 1850. He served aboard the *Young Teazer* and was disabled by a wound in his right knee.

Carlton, —. —. Seaman. His son, Benjamin L. Carlton, was pensioned at the rate of $6 per month. 1837. 1842. He also appeared as Benjamin F. Carleton.

Carman, —. —. —. Frances Carman was pensioned on his service as privateer at the rate of $36 per annum. 1813. 1814. 1815. 1816. 1817.

Carmick, —. —. Major Marines. His widow, Catharine Carmick, was pensioned at the rate of $25 per month from 6 Nov. 1816. 1837. 1839. 1840. 1841. 1842. 1842b. She also appeared as Catherine Carmuck. She was listed as Margaret Carmick in 1839, 1840, and 1841.

Carpenter. —. N.Y. Seaman. His widow, Catharine Carpenter, received $240 per annum in 1821. 1822. 1823.

Carpenter, Jacob.* —. Gunner. His widow, Ann Carpenter, was pensioned at the rate of $10 per month on 8 Mar. 1842. 1843. 1844. 1845. 1846. 1850.

Carpenter, Russell. N.Y. Seaman. He perished aboard the *Epervier* 1 Sep. 1815. His widow, Catherine, nee Eichel, Badger sought a pension. They were married 15 Dec. 1810. She married secondly Peter Badger. Their only child died in childhood. His widow was paid $72 on 17 Mar. 1821.

Carr, —. —. Lieutenant. His widow, Ellen Carr, was pensioned at the rate of $25 per month from 3 May 1837. 1837. 1839. 1840. She also appeared as Ellen Cars. His son, John G. Carr, was pensioned from 15 Apr. 1840 at the rate of $25 per month. 1841. 1842. 1842b. [He appeared as John A . Carr in the Old Wars pension index.]

Carr, —, —. Sailing Master. His son, Burroughs E. Carr, was pensioned at the rate of $20 per month. 1837. 1842.

Carr, Edward.* —. Seaman. He was pensioned 13 May 1835 at the rate of $6 per month. 1836. 1837. 1838. 1839. 1840. 1841. 1842. 1842b. 1843. 1844. 1845. 1846. 1847. 1848. 1850. 1851. He served aboard the *Pensacola* and was disabled by five fractures of important

Naval Pensioners of the United States, 1800-1851

bones and almost total loss of his right eye.

Carr, James E. N.Y. Sailing Master. He served aboard the *Wasp* and was lost 20 Apr. 1815. His widow, Sarah Carr, was pensioned at the rate of $240 per annum. John Tonclier was guardian. 1818. 1819. 1820. 1821. 1822. 1823. 1824. 1825. 1827. 1828. 1829. 1830. She also appeared as Sarah Care.

Carr, Patrick.* —. Marine. His widow, Julia Carr, was pensioned 5 Apr. 1850 at the rate of $3.50 per month. 1851. His child, Ann Carr, was pensioned 5 July 1850 at the rate of $3 per month. He was also known as John Carr. 1850. 1851.

Carrick, John. —. Landsman. He was pensioned 16 Sep. 1842 at the rate of $4 per month. 1842b. 1843. 1844. 1845. 1846. 1847. 1848. 1850. 1851. He served aboard the *St. Louis* and was disabled by a wound of his right thigh.

Carrier, Solomon. Md. Sergeant of Marines. He was pensioned at the rate of $54 per annum in 1808. 1809. 1810. 1811. He also appeared as Solomon Currier. He was disabled by inflamation resulting in the loss of sight in one eye.

Carroll, Arthur.* Mass. Ordinary Seaman. He was pensioned at the rate of $84 per annum in 1826. 1827. 1828. He was disabled by the loss of his right thumb. He died 1 Apr. 1827.

Carson, Robert.* Penn. Ordinary Seaman. He was pensioned at the rate of $60 per annum 26 June 1821. 1822. 1823. 1824. 1825. 1826. 1827. 1828. 1829. 1830. 1835. 1836. 1837. 1839. 1840. 1841. 1842b. 1843. 1844. 1845. 1846. 1847. 1848. 1850. 1851. He served aboard the *Macedonian*. He was wounded in his left arm resulting in partial loss of use of same.

Carswell, —.* —. —. His children, Eliza Ann Carswell and Samuel Carswell, were on the 1837 list. 1842. [He was Samuel Carswell in the Old Wars pension index.]

Carter, Charles G.* —. Musician Marines. His widow, Leah Carter, was pensioned 30 June 1834 and again 1 Sep. 1847 at the rate of $4 per month. 1835. 1836. 1837. 1839. 1840. 1841. 1842b. 1845. 1846. 1848. 1850. 1851.

Carter, Henry. —. —. He perished aboard the *Grampus*. He was a free boy and a servant to Dr. Conway and was about 21 years old. His sister, Jane Carter, was about 25 years old. Her younger sister was Fanny Carter about 16 years old. They were from Norfolk, Va. on 22 Dec. 1843.

Carter, Horace.* —. Landsman. He was pensioned 26 Feb. 1837 at the rate of $2 per month. 1839. 1840. 1841. 1842b. 1843. 1844. 1845. 1846. 1847. 1848. 1850. 1851. He served aboard the brig *Stephen* and was disabled by the loss of his left eye.

Carter, James. N.Y. Boatswain's Mate. He was pensioned as a privateer at the rate of $96 per annum. 1814. 1815. 1816. 1817. 1818. 1819. 1820. 1821. 1822. 1823. 1824. 1825. 1826. 1827. He served aboard the schooner *Whig* and was disabled with by a gun shot wound in his left arm.

Carter, James.* —. Seaman. He was pensioned 25 Apr. 1849 at the rate of $3 per month. 1850. 1851. He was disabled with an injury to the index finger of his right hand.

Carter, Nathaniel. Mass. Lieutenant. He died of yellow fever 6 Sep. 1823. His widow, Harriet Carter, was pensioned at the rate of $240 per annum. 1824. 1825. 1827. 1828. 1835. 1836. 1837. 1839. 1840. 1841. 1842. 1842b. 1845. 1846. She was pensioned again 1 Sep.

Naval Pensioners of the United States, 1800-1851

1847 at the rate of $25 per month. 1848. 1850. 1851.
Carter, William.* Md. Master's Mate. He was pensioned 1 Nov. 1814 at the rate of $96 per annum. 1819. 1820. 1821. 1822. 1823. 1824. 1825. 1826. 1827. 1828. 1829. 1830. 1836. He was disabled by an injury to his left eye and leg and a gun shot wound of his right knee. He served aboard the *Chesapeake*.
Cary, Dennis. Mass. Ordinary Seaman. He was pensioned at the rate of $84 per annum. 1824. 1825. 1826. 1828. 1829. He was disabled at Boston. He also appeared Dennis Carey.
Cash, George.* —. Seaman. His widow, Elizabeth Cash, was pensioned at the rate of $6 per month from 12 Jan. 1837. 1837. 1839. 1840. 1841. 1842. 1842b. She was pensioned again 1 Sep. 1847 at the rate of $6 per month. 1848. 1850. 1851.
Cassin, George. Mass. Seaman. He was pensioned at the rate of $60 per annum. 1820. 1823. 1824. 1827. 1829. He was disabled on Lake Champlain. He also appeared as George Carson. He served aboard the *Constitution* and was disabled by a gun shot wound in his left hand.
Cassin, John.* —. Lieutenant. His widow, Mary A. Cassin, was pensioned from 15 Oct. 1837 at the rate of $25 per month. 1839. 1840. 1841. 1842. 1842b. She was pensioned again 1 Sep. 1847 at the rate of $25 per month. 1850. 1851.
Cassin, Joseph. —. Purser. He died in Aug. 1821 of yellow fever. His widow, Eliza Cassin, was pensioned 1 Oct. 1823. 1824. 1825. 1827. 1828. 1835. 1836. 1837. 1839. 1840. 1841. 1842. 1842b. 1845. 1846. She was pensioned again 1 Sep. 1847 at the rate of $20 per month. 1848. 1850. 1851.
Cassin, Joseph. —. Lieutenant. His widow, Fanny Cassin, was pensioned 1 Sep. 1847 at the rate of $25 per month. 1835. 1836. 1837. 1839. 1840. 1841. 1842. 1842b. 1845. 1846. 1848. 1850. 1851.
Casson, John. Penn. Marine. He was pensioned 1 Aug. 1800 at the rate of $36 per annum. 1802. 1803. 1804. 1805. 1807. 1808. 1809. 1810. 1811. 1816. 1818. 1819. 1820. 1821. 1822. 1823. 1824. 1825. 1826. 1827. 1828. 1829. 1830. He served aboard the *Constellation*. He also appeared as John Cassin.
Casted, Anthony.* —. Seaman. His widow, Lucinda Casted, was pensioned 1 Apr. 1846 at the rate of $6 per month. 1847. 1848. 1850. 1851.
Caswell, —. N.H. Seaman. Polly Caswell was pensioned on his service as a privateer at the rate of $36 per annum. 1815. 1816. 1817. 1818. 1819. 1820 increase to $72. 1821. 1822. 1823. 1824. 1825. 1826. 1827. 1828. 1829.
Caswell, Abraham.* —. Ordinary Seaman. He was pensioned 30 Sep. 1838 at the rate of $2.50. 1841. 1842b. 1843. 1844. 1845. 1846. 1847. 1848. 1850. 1851. He served aboard the *Constellation* and was disabled by an injury to his head.
Caswell, Daniel.* —. Carpenter. His widow, Mary M. Caswell, had her application rejected prior to 12 Dec. 1842. He did not die of any disorder contracted in the line of duty. He died of apoplexy. Her case was not provided for by law.
Caswell, Richard W. —. Landsman. He was pensioned 6 July 1849 at the rate of $4 per month. 1850. 1851. He was disabled by a rupture of a blood vessel in his chest.
Catalano, Salvadore. —. Master. His widow, Martha Catalano, was pensioned 4 Jan. 1846 at the

rate of $20 per month. 1847. 1848. 1850. 1851. He also appeared as Salvadore Calalano.

Cathcart, Robert.* Mass. Seaman. He was pensioned 20 Sep. 1816 at the rate of $72 per annum. 1818. 1819. 1820. 1821. 1822. 1823. 1824. 1825. 1826. 1827. 1828. 1829. 1830. 1835. 1836. 1837. 1839. 1840. 1841. 1842b. 1843. 1844. 1845. 1846. 1847. 1848. 1850. 1851. He served aboard the *Macedonian*. He was disabled by a rupture on his left side.

Cathill, William. Md. Prize Master. He was pensioned as a privateer at the rate of $72 per annum. 1812. 1813. 1814. 1815. 1816. 1817. 1818. 1819. 1820. 1821 for $36. He served aboard the *Comet* and was disabled by a wound in his right arm resulting in the partial use of same. He also appeared as William Cathell.

Catlett, Elisha. D.C. 2nd Lieutenant. He was pensioned as a privateer at the rate of $120 per annum. 1813. 1814. 1815. 1816. 1817. 1818. 1819. 1820. 1821. 1822. 1823. 1824 for $104.33.

Cearson, George. Mass. Quartermaster. He was pensioned 16 Feb. 1815 at the rate of $60 per annum. 1821. 1822. 1826. 1828. 1830. He was disabled on Lake Champlain. He was also known as George Cassin and George Carson. He served aboard the *Saratoga* and was disabled by a wound through his right shoulder.

Cernon, —.* —. Ordinary Seaman. His widow, Elizabeth Cernon, was pensioned from 28 Nov. 1823 at the rate of $5 per month. 1839. 1840. 1841. 1842. 1842b. [He was listed as James Cernon in the Old Wars pension index.]

Chadbourne, —. N.H. Carpenter. Sarah Chadbourne was pensioned on his service as a privateer at the rate of $60 per annum. 1815. 1816. 1817. 1818. 1819. 1820 increase to $120. 1821. 1822. 1823. 1824. 1825. 1826. 1827. 1828. 1829.

Chaddock, John A. W. —. Lieutenant. His widow, Mary Chaddock, was pensioned from 25 Oct. 1833 at the rate of $25 per month. 1851.

Chamberlain, —. —. Sailing Master. His children, Charles R. Chamberlain and Margaret T. Chamberlain, were pensioned at the rate of $20 per month from 8 Feb. 1822. 1837. 1839. 1840. 1841. 1842. 1842b.

Chamberlain, John. Mass. Boatswain. He was pensioned 29 Mar. 1815 at the rate of $96 per annum. 1816. 1818. 1819. 1820. 1821. 1822. 1823. 1824. 1825. 1826. 1827. 1828. 1829. 1830. He served aboard Gunboat No. 160. He was disabled by a gun shot wound in his right elbow.

Chambers, Abraham.* —. Officers' Cook. His widow, Elizabeth Chambers, was pensioned 15 Nov. 1847 at the rate of $9 per month. 1851.

Chambers, Andrew. D.C. Marine. He was pensioned 10 Oct. 1815 at the rate of $60 per annum. 1818. 1819. 1820. 1821. 1822. 1823. 1824. 1825. 1826. 1827. 1828. 1829. 1830. He served aboard the *Constitution*. He was wounded in his left hand from a splinter. He also appeared as Andrew Chalmers. Compare with entry *infra*.

Chambers, Andrew. Penn. Marine. He was pensioned at the rate of $60 per annum. 1818. 1820. 1821. 1822. Compare with entry *supra*.

Champlin, John C.* —. Seaman. He was pensioned 21 May 1831 at the rate of $6 per month. 1835. 1836. 1837. 1839. 1840. 1841. 1842b. 1843. 1844. 1845. 1846. 1847. 1848. 1850. 1851. He also appeared as John C. Chaplin. He was disabled by a fracture of his right thigh. He served aboard the *St. Louis*.

Champlin, Stephen. —. Sailing Master. He was pensioned at the rate of $20 per month. 1836. 1837. 1838. 1839. 1840. 1841. 1842. 1842b. 1843. He was disabled by a gun shot wound in his left thigh.

Chandler, John R.* —. Surgeon. His widow, Elizabeth E. Chandler, was pensioned from 28 July 1841 at the rate of $30 per month. 1841. 1842. 1842b. 1845. She was pensioned again 28 July 1846 at the rate of $30 per month. 1848. 1850. 1851.

Chapman, —. —. Ordinary Seaman. His widow, Margaret Chapman, was pensioned from 5 July 1805 at the rate of $5 per month. 1841. 1842. 1842b.

Chapman, Nathaniel. Conn. Quarter Gunner. He was pensioned 1 July 1801 at the rate of $96 per annum. 1816. 1818. 1819. 1820. 1821. 1822. 1823. 1824. 1825. 1826. 1827. 1828. 1829. 1830. 1835. 1836. 1837. 1839. 1840. 1841. 1842b. 1843. 1844. 1845. 1846. 1847. 1848. 1850. 1851. He served on the schooner *Tigress*. He was disabled by a wound resulting in the loss of use of his left arm.

Chappell, William. —. Boatswain's Mate. He was pensioned 7 June 1843 at the rate of $9.50 per month. 1843. 1844. 1845. 1846. 1847. 1848. 1850. 1851. He served aboard the *North Carolina* and was disabled by disease of the eyes.

Chardelle, James. —. Marine. He perished aboard the *Epervier* 1 Sep. 1815. His parents were James and Mary Chardelle. They were paid $36 on 4 Mar. 1818.

Chase, —. —. —. Margaret Chase was pensioned on his service as a privateer at the rate of $72 per annum. 1815. 1816. 1817. 1818. 1819. 1820 increase to $144. 1821. 1822. 1823. 1824. 1825. 1826. 1827. 1828. 1829.

Chase, Leonard.* Mass. Ordinary Seaman. He was pensioned 1 Aug. 1828 at the rate of $5 per month. 1830. 1835. 1836. 1837. 1839. 1840. 1841. 1842b. 1843. 1844. 1845. 1846. 1847. 1848. 1850. 1851. He served aboard the *Warren*. He was disabled by a fracture of both thighs.

Chauncey, Isaac. —. Captain. His widow, Catherine Chauncey, was pensioned from 28 Jan. 1840 at the rate of $50 per month. 1841. 1842. 1842b. 1843. 1844. 1845. 1846. She was pensioned again 28 Jan. 1850 at the rate of $50 per month. 1848. 1850. 1851.

Chauncey, John S. —. Surgeon's Mate. He was pensioned from 30 Sep. 1817 at the rate of $4.75 per month. 1838. 1839. 1840. 1841. 1842. 1842b. 1843. His rank was given as Midshipman in 1839, 1841, 1842b, and 1843. He was disabled by the loss of an eye.

Cheever, — & —. Seamen. Mass. The two brothers served on the *Constitution* and *Java* and were killed 12 Apr. 1814. Their mother, Mary Cheever, was pensioned 17 Nov. 1814 at the rate of $160 per annum. 1816. 1818. 1819. 1820. 1821. 1822. 1824. 1825. 1827. 1828. 1830. 1835. 1836. 1837. 1839. 1840. 1841. 1842b. She was pensioned by special act.

Chew, John. Penn. —. He perished aboard the *Epervier* 1 Sep. 1815. He was born 23 Jan. 1797 in Philadelphia, Penn., son of Benjamin and Catherine Chew. He was baptized in 1799 in Christ Church St. Peter & St. James. His father was due his pay of $114.

Childs, Enos B. Md. Midshipman. He was pensioned 2 Apr. 1825 at the rate of $9.50 per month. 1827. 1828. 1829. 1830 in D.C. 1835. 1836. 1837. 1839. 1840. 1841. 1842b. 1843. 1844.

Naval Pensioners of the United States, 1800-1851

1845. 1846. 1847. 1848. 1850. 1851. He also appeared as Enos R. Childs. He served aboard the brig *Saranac*. He was disabled by a right inguinal hernia.

Christian, Charles. Penn. Seaman. $8.50 per month in 1803. 1804. 1805. 1807. 1808. 1809. 1810. 1811. He served aboard the *President* and was disabled by the loss of his left leg.

Christie, David. N.Y. Private Marines. He was pensioned 1 July 1821 at the rate of $48 per annum. 1821. 1822. 1824. 1825. 1826. 1827. 1828. 1829. 1830. He was disabled on Lake Erie. He was disabled by a wound from a splinter in his shoulder.

Christie, David. Penn. Marine. He was pensioned 16 Jan. 1816 at the rate of $48 per annum. 1819. 1820. 1823. 1824. 1825. 1826. 1829. 1830. He was disabled on the brig *Lawrence*. He was pensioned 1 Jan. 1841 at the rate of $4 per month. 1841. 1842b. 1843. 1844. 1845. 1846. 1847. 1848. 1850. 1851. He appeared as Daniel Christie in 1842.

Christopher, George. N.Y. Seaman. He was pensioned at the rate of $72 per annum. 1816. 1818. 1819. He also appeared as George Cristophers and George Christophers. He served aboard the frigate *United States* and was disabled by the loss of his right leg.

Christopher, William. N.H. Seaman. His widow, Mercy G. Christopher, was pensioned at the rate of $72 per annum. 1818. 1819. 1820. 1821. 1822. 1823. 1824. 1825. 1827 for her child. 1828. 1829. She also appeared as Mercy C. Cristopher. He was killed 1 Apr. 1814 aboard the *Essex*. Jos. Johnson was guardian of the child.

Christy, —. —. —. Caroline Christy was pensioned on his service. 1842.

Christy, —. —. Seaman. His widow, Maria Christy, was pensioned from 7 Sep. 1839 at the rate of $6 per month. 1840. 1841. 1842b. [He was John W. Christy in the Old Wars penison index.]

Churchill, Benjamin F.* —. Captain. He was pensioned as a privateer in 1814 at the rate of $240 per annum. 1814. 1815. 1816. 1817. 1818. 1819. 1820. 1821. 1822. 1823. 1824. 1825. 1826. 1827. 1828. 1829. 1830. 1831. 1832. 1833. 1834. 1835. 1836. 1837 for half a year. He was pensioned from 1 Jul. 1837 for privateer service at the rate of $20 per month. 1837. 1838. 1844. 1845. 1846. 1847. 1850. He served aboard the *Yankee* and was disabled by the loss of his right leg.

Clapp, —. —. —. Luretta C. Clapp was pensioned on his service. 1842.

Clar, John.* —. Professor of Mathematics. He was pensioned 31 July 1846 at the rate of $20 per month. 1846. 1847. 1848. 1850. 1851. He was disabled by neuralgic affection of his heart.

Clark, —. —. Ordinary Seaman. His widow, Ann Clark, was pensioned from 27 Sep. 1836 at the rate of $5 per month. 1837. 1839. 1840.

Clark, —.* N.H. Sailing Master. His widow, Phoebe A. P. Clark, was pensioned at the rate of $72 per annum. 1820. [He was Andrew Clark in the Old Wars pension index.]

Clark, Charles.* —. Landsman. He was pensioned 20 Aug. 1850 at the rate of $1.33 1/3 per month. 1850. 1851. He was disabled by an injury to his head.

Clark, James. Mass. Gunner. He served aboard the frigate *Adams* and was disabled by the loss of the use of his right arm and right leg. He was pensioned at the rate of $120 per annum. 1816. 1829 in Maine.

Clark, James. —. Ordinary Seaman. He served aboard the *Germantown* and *Franklin*. He was

Naval Pensioners of the United States, 1800-1851

pensioned in 1849 due to a fracture of his left arm and the loss of his little finger.

Clark, James H.* —. Purser. His widow, Margaret T. Clark, was pensioned 19 Sep. 1844 at the rate of $20 per month. 1845. 1846. 1847. 1848.

Clark, John.* —. Boatswain's Mate. He was pensioned 15 Jan. 1838 at the rate of $7.12 ½ per month. 1839. 1840. 1841. 1842. 1842b. 1843. 1844. 1845. 1846. 1847. 1848. 1850. 1851. He also appeared as John Clarke. He served aboard the *Constellation* and was disabled by an injury to his left knee.

Clark, John.* —. Seaman. He was pensioned 31 May 1825 at the rate of $3 per month. 1839. 1840. 1841. 1843. 1844. 1845. 1846. 1847. 1848. 1850. 1851. He was disabled by a gun shot wound causing the loss of sight in his right eye and partial loss of sight in his left eye.

Clark, Thomas R. —. Ordinary Seaman. He was pensioned 18 Feb. 1823 at the rate of $3.75 per month. 1838. 1839. 1840. 1841. 1842b. 1843. 1844. 1845. 1846. 1847. 1848. 1850. 1851. He was disabled by the loss of sight in his right eye.

Clark, Timothy.* —. Carpenter's Mate. His widow, Mary Clark, was pensioned 7 Oct. 1849 at the rate of $9.50 per month. 1850. 1851.

Clark, William. —.* Ordinary Seaman. He was pensioned 29 Aug. 1842 at the rate of $5 per month. 1842b. 1843. 1844. 1845. 1846. 1847. 1848. 1850. 1851. He served aboard the *Potomac* and was disabled by a fracture of his left thigh.

Clarke, Christian. N.Y. Seaman. He was pensioned 4 May 1813 at the rate of $48 per annum. 1816. 1818 to $72 per annum. 1819. 1820. 1821. 1822. 1823. 1824. 1825. 1826. 1827. 1828. 1829. 1830. He also appeared as Christian Clark. He served aboard the *United States*.

Clarke, James. Mass. Gunner. He was pensioned from 25 Apr. 1814 at the rate of $120 per annum. 1818. 1819. 1820. 1821. 1822. 1824. 1825. 1826. 1827. 1828. 1829. 1830 in the state of Maine. He served aboard the *Adams*. He also appeared as James Clark.

Clarke, James. —. Ordinary Seaman. He was pensioned 7 Sep. 1849 at the rate of $3.75 per month. 1850. 1851.

Clarke, Thomas J.* —. Carpenter's Mate. He was pensioned 27 Apr. 1839 at the rate of $2.37 ½ per month. 1840. 1841. 1842b. 1843. 1844. 1845. 1846. 1847. 1848. 1850. 1851. He also appeared as Thomas J. Clark. He served aboard the *Natchez* and was disabled by an injury to his left ankle.

Clarke, William.* —. Landsman. He was pensioned 17 Feb. 1851 at the rate of $2 per month. 1851. He served aboard the *Raritan* and was disabled by a fracture of his right leg.

Claxton, Alexander. —. Captain. He had previously been a Midshipman. He was pensioned at the rate of $7.12 ½ per month. 1837. 1839. 1840. He was disabled with impaired hearing. His widow, Rodolphine Claxton, was pensioned. She was on the roll in 1841. 1824. 1842b. 1843. 1844. 1845. She was pensioned 7 Mar. 1846 at the rate of $50 per month. 1848. 1850. 1851. She also appeared as Redelphine Claxton.

Clay, Charles. N.Y. Seaman. He was pensioned 11 Sep. 1810 at the rate of $72 per annum. 1816. 1818. 1819. 1820. 1821. 1822. 1823. 1824. 1825. 1826. 1827. 1828. 1829. 1830. He served aboard the *Constitution.* He was disabled with a fracture of his knee.

Naval Pensioners of the United States, 1800-1851

Clements, Isaac.* —. Seaman. He was pensioned 9 Sep. 1850 at the rate of $4.50 per month. 1850. 1851. He served aboard the *Vincennes* and was disabled by a fracture of his right wrist.

Clements, John. Mass. Seaman. He was pensioned 1 July 1812 at the rate of $72 per annum. 1816. 1818. 1819. 1820. 1821. 1822. 1823. 1824. 1825. 1826. 1827. 1828. 1829. 1830 in Conn. 1836. 1837. 1838. 1840. 1841. 1842. 1842b. 1843. 1844. 1845. 1846. 1847. 1848. 1850. 1851. He served aboard the *Constitution* and was disabled by the loss of his right leg.

Clementson, —.* —. His widow, Sarah Clementson, was pensioned at the rate of $10 month from 9 July 1833. 1837. 1839. 1840. 1841. 1842. 1842b. [He was listed as John Clementson in the Old Wars pension index.]

Clifton, —. —. —. His son, Alfred Wharton Clifton, was on the roll in 1837. 1842. [This could be an error for one of the orphans of Franklin Wharton.]

Clinton, —. N.H. Seaman. Charlotte Clinton was pensioned on his service as a privateer at the rate of $36 per annum. 1815. 1816. 1817. 1818. 1819. 1820 increase to $72. 1821. 1822. 1823. 1824. 1825. 1826. 1827. 1828. 1829.

Clinton, William.* —. Landsman. He was pensioned 27 Aug. 1846 at the rate of $4 per month. 1848. 1851.

Closs, Jacob. —. Seaman. He served aboard the *United States* and was disabled by a fracture of his shoulder. He was pensioned in 1814.

Cloud, Caleb W.* —. Assistant Surgeon. His widow, Eliza M. Cloud, was pensioned 30 June 1834 and again 1 Sep. 1847 at the rate of $15 per month. 1835. 1836. 1837. 1839. 1840. 1841. 1842. 1845. 1846. 1848. 1850. 1851.

Clough, John. —. Sailing Master. He was pensioned at the rate of $15 per month. 1837. 1838. 1839. 1840. 1841. 1842. 1842b. 1843. He was disabled by an injury to his left shoulder and ribs. His widow, Sarah A. Clough, was pensioned 19 Mar. 1847 at the rate of $25 per month. 1850. 1851.

Clunet, Peter.* Penn. Lieutenant Marines. He served aboard the *Constitution* and was killed 26 Nov. 1825 in the Navy Yard at Philadelphia. He was shot by a marine. His widow, Anna Maria Clunet, was pensioned 28 Dec. 1826 at the rate of $6 per month. 1829. 1830. 1831. 1835. 1836. 1837. 1839. 1840. 1841. 1842. 1842b. 1845. 1846. She was pensioned again 1 Sep. 1847 at the rate of $6.50 per month. 1848. 1850. 1851. She also appeared as Ann M. Cluret and Ann M. Clunett.

Coats, Russell. Mass. Quartermaster. He was pensioned 1 Dec. 1813 at the rate of $60 per annum. 1816. 1818. 1819. 1820. 1821. 1822. 1824. 1825. 1826. 1827. 1828. 1829. 1830. He served aboard the *Enterprise*. He also appeared as Russel Coates. He was disabled by a gun shot wound and loss of the ring finger on his left hand.

Cobert, —.N.Y. Carpenter's Mate. Sarah Cobert was pensioned on his service as a privateer at the rate of $72 per annum from 1 Jan. 1815.

Cochran, James. —. Private Marine. He was pensioned in Nov. 1848 due to a rupture.

Coche, Thomas.* — Seaman. He was pensioned 9 Sep. 1850 at the rate of $3 per month. 1850. 1851. He was disabled by an injury to his back. He also appeared as Thomas Cocke.

Naval Pensioners of the United States, 1800-1851

Cocke, —.* —. Lieutenant. His widow, Ann V. Cocke, was pensioned from 31 May 1835 at the rate of $38.59 per month. 1835. 1836. 1837. 1839. 1840. 1841. 1842. 1842b. [He was listed as Samuel B. Cocke in the Old Wars pension index.]

Cocke, William H. Va. Lieutenant. He was killed off Puerto Rico 6 Mar. 1823. His widow, Eliza W. Cocke, was pensioned 29 Apr. 1824 at $240 per annum. 1824. 1825. 1828. 1835. 1836. 1837. 1839. 1840. 1841. 1842. 1842b. 1846. She was pensioned again 1 Sep. 1847 at the rate of $25 per month. 1848. 1850. 1851. She also appeared as Eliza H. Cocke.

Codding, Caleb.* Md. Seaman. He was pensioned at the rate of $96 per annum. 1819. 1820. 1821. 1822. 1823. He was disabled by a gun shot wound of his right leg and a rupture.

Coffin, Ivory.* —. Seaman. He was pensioned 31 Aug. 1851 at the rate of $3 per month. 1851. He served aboard the *Savannah* and was disabled by a gun shot wound of his right knee.

Coffin, John. Penn. Seaman. He was pensioned 8 Apr. 1812 at the rate of $72 per annum. 1816. 1818. 1819. 1820. 1821. 1822. 1823. 1824. 1825. 1826. 1827. 1828. 1829. 1830. He served aboard the *Hornet*. He was disabled with chronic rheumatism.

Cogdell, R. C.* —. Passed Midshipman. He was pensioned from 24 Feb. 1839 at the rate of $6.25 per month. 1841. 1842b. 1843. He served aboard the schooner *Waves*. He was disabled by the loss of parts of two fingers.

Colby, Archibald M. —. Pilot. His widow, Louisa Colby, was pensioned 30 Jan. 1814 at the rate of $20 per month. 1851.

Cole, Daniel H.* —. Marine. He was pensioned 27 Dec. 1833 at the rate of $3 per month. 1835. 1836. 1837. 1838. 1839. 1840. 1841. 1842. 1842b. 1843. 1844. 1845. 1846. 1847. 1848. 1850. 1851. He served aboard the *Potomac* and was disabled by a gun shot wound of the chest.

Cole, Edward.* Mass. Seaman. He was pensioned from 7 Dec. 1812 for privateer service at the rate of $72 per annum. 1812. 1813. 1814. 1815. 1816. 1817. 1818. 1819. 1820. 1821. 1822. 1823. 1824. 1825. 1826. 1827. 1828. 1829. 1830. 1831. 1832. 1833. 1834. 1835. 1836. 1837 for half a year. 1837. 1844. 1845. 1846. 1847. 1850. He served aboard the *Highflyer*. He was disabled by a gun shot wound of his right arm resulting in the partial use of same.

Cole, George.* —. Seaman. He was pensioned from 30 Dec. 1839 at the rate of $6 per month. 1840. He was disabled by wounds and ulcers of his left shoulder.

Cole, George Thomas. Ga. Armorer's Mate. He perished aboard the *Epervier* 1 Sep. 1815. His surviving parent was his mother, Elizabeth Cole, of South Carolina. His brother was John David Cole of Chatham Co., Ga., and he was paid $72.

Cole, James.* —. Seaman. He was pensioned 1 May 1828 at the rate of $5 per month. 1835. 1836. 1837. 1838. 1839. 1840. 1841. 1842b. 1843. 1844. 1845. 1846. 1847. 1848. 1850. 1851. He was disabled by an injury to his left leg.

Cole, John.* New York. Ordinary Seaman. He was pensioned 1 July 1829 at the rate of $5 per month. 1829. 1830. 1835. 1836. 1837. 1839. 1840. 1841. 1842. 1842b. 1843. 1844. 1845. 1846. 1847. 1848. 1850. 1851. He was disabled at Sackett's Harbor. He was disabled with an hernia.

Cole, John. Md. Quartermaster. He was pensioned 23 Apr. 1815 at the rate of $108 per annum.

Naval Pensioners of the United States, 1800-1851

1816. 1818. 1819. 1820. 1821. 1822. 1823. 1824. 1825. 1826. 1827. 1828. 1829. 1830. He served aboard the brig *Niagara.* He was disabled by the loss of his left arm.

Cole, Richard.* —. Seaman. His widow, Elizabeth J. Cole, was pensioned 13 Jan. 1851 at the rate of $6 per month. 1851.

Cole, William.* —. Gunner's Mate. He was pensioned 25 July 1850 at the rate of $9.50 per month. 1851. He was disabled by an oblique fracture of his right thigh. He served aboard the *Portsmouth.*

Cole, William.* N.Y. Seaman. He was pensioned at the rate of $72 per annum. 1818. He was in D.C. 1819. 1820. 1821. 1822. He was disabled by the loss of his leg.

Coleman, —. Pa. Carpenter. Margaret Coleman was pensioned on his service as a privateer at the rate of $120 per annum from 4 Aug. 1812. 1816. 1817. 1818. 1819. 1820. 1821. 1822. 1823. 1824. 1825. 1826. 1827 for $71.

Coleman, Henry.* —. Gunner's Mate. He was pensioned 20 Sep. 1850 at the rate of $4.75 per month. 1850. 1851. He served aboard the *Germantown* and was disabled by a rupture of his right side.

Coleman, John A. —. Seaman. His widow, Nancy Coleman, was pensioned 26 July 1842 at the rate of $6 per month. 1851.

Coleman, Thomas.* —. Carpenter. His widow, Elizabeth Coleman, was pensioned 27 Aug. 1849 at the rate of $10 per month. 1851.

Coller, William. N.Y. Cook. He was pensioned at the rate of $72 per annum in 1805. 1807. 1808. 1809. 1810. 1811. He also appeared as William Cotter and William Colter.
He served aboard the frigate *President* and was injured in his testicles.

Collins, Henry. Penn. Seaman. He was pensioned 6 Oct. 1814 at the rate of $72 per annum. 1816. 1818. 1819. 1820. 1821. 1822. 1823. 1824. 1825. 1826. 1827. 1828. 1829. 1830. He was disabled on Lake Champlain. His pension was reduced to $4.50 per month effective 18 Mar. 1824. He served aboard the *Ticonderoga* and was disabled by a fracture of his right arm.

Collins, John. N.Y. Seaman. He was pensioned 9 Feb. 1813 at the rate of $72 per annum. 1816. 1818. 1819. 1820. 1821. 1822. 1823. 1824. 1825. 1826. 1827. 1828. 1829. 1830. 1835. 1836. 1837. 1841. 1842b. 1843. 1844. 1845. 1846. 1847. 1848. 1850. 1851. He served aboard the *United States.* He appeared incorrectly as John Colluic in 1829.

Collins, John. —. Seaman. He was pensioned 28 Feb. 1839 at the rate of $3 per month. 1839. 1840. 1842b. 1844. 1845. 1846. 1847. 1848. 1850. 1851. He served aboard the *Pioneer* and was disabled by the loss of sight in his left eye.

Collins, Michael.* —. Seaman. He was pensioned $22 Apr. 1834 at the rate of $4.50 per month. 1840. 1841. 1842b. 1843. 1844. 1845. 1846. 1847. 1848. 1850. 1851. He served aboard the *Columbia* and was disabled by a fracture of his right leg.

Collins, William. N.C. Carpenter's Mate. His widow, Ann D. Collins, was pensioned at the rate of $108 per annum. 1820. 1821. 1822. 1824. 1825. 1828 to her heirs. 1829. He was killed 6 Jan. 1815 on the flotilla at New Orleans.

Collings, William. —. —. —. He was pensioned. 1842.

Collison, Francis. —. Seaman. His widow, Catharine Collison, was pensioned 29 Sep. 1843 at

Naval Pensioners of the United States, 1800-1851

the rate of $6 per month. 1844. 1845. 1846. 1847. 1848. He also appeared as Francis Collinson.

Colsten, Samuel. N.Y. Seaman. He was pensioned 6 Sep. 1813 at the rate of $36 per annum. 1816. 1818. 1819. 1820. 1821. 1822. 1823. 1824. 1825. 1826. 1827. 1828. 1829. 1830. 1836. He also appeared as Samuel Colston. He served aboard the *Hornet*. His disability due to a gun shot wound in his left hand resulting in the loss of his forefinger. It was permanent.

Colter, James M. N.Y. Midshipman. He perished aboard the *Epervier* 1 Sep. 1815. His father was James Colter of Newburgh, Orange Co., N.Y., who was paid $114 on 10 June 1817.

Colton, Walter.* —. Captain. His widow, Cornelia P. Colton, was pensioned 22 Jan. 1851 at the rate of $20 per month. 1851.

Colton, William.* —. Purser's Steward. His widow, Rebecca A. Colton, was pensioned 1 Sep. 1847 at the rate of $9 per month. 1848. 1850. 1851.

Concklin, —. N.Y. Commander. Mary Concklin was pensioned on his service as a privateer at the rate of $120 per annum. 1815. 1816. 1817. 1818. 1819. 1820 increased to $240. 1821. 1822. 1823. 1824. 1825. 1826. 1827. 1828. 1829. 1830. 1831. 1832. 1833. 1834.

Conklin, John.* —. Seaman. He was pensioned 31 Dec. 1837 at the rate of $3 per month. 1840. 1841. 1842b. 1843. 1844. 1845. 1846. 1847. 1848. 1850. 1851. He served aboard the *Levant, Grampus, Java*, &c and was disabled by a gun shot wound in his left leg.

Conklin, John.* —. Ordinary Seaman. He was pensioned 8 Aug. 1840 at the rate of $5 per month. 1842b. 1843. 1844. 1845. 1846. 1848. He served aboard the *Penn* and was disabled by a gun shot wound in his left thigh.

Conklin, Zachariah. N.Y. Ordinary Seaman. He was pensioned 28 Aug. 1815 at the rate of $72 per annum. 1816. 1818. 1819. 1820. 1821. 1822. 1823. 1824. 1825. 1826. 1827. 1828. 1829. 1830. He served aboard the brig *Eagle*. He also appeared as Zachariah Concklin and Zachariah Conchlin. He was disabled by a wound in his shoulder resulting in the loss of the use of his arm.

Conland, William.* —. Marine. He was pensioned 28 Sep. 1847 at the rate of $1.75 per month. 1850. 1851. He served aboard the frigate *Savannah* and was disabled by a gun shot wound in his right arm.

Conner, Amasa.* D.C. Seaman. He was pensioned 1 June 1822 at the rate of $72 per annum. 1824. 1825. 1826. 1827. 1828. 1829. 1830. He was also known as Amasa Corwer, Amasa Cerner, and Amasa Corner. He served aboard the schooner *Shark*. He was disabled by the loss of the use of his left leg.

Conner, David. —. Lieutenant. He was pensioned at the rate of $16.66 2/3 per month. 1837. 1838. 1839. 1840. 1841. 1842. 1842b. 1843. He also appeared as David Connor. He served aboard the *Hornet* and was disabled by a gun shot wound in his thigh.

Conner, John. Seaman. D.C. He served aboard the *Constellation* and was disabled by a rupture. He was pensioned 3 Jan. 1812. 1816.

Conner, Michael. Md. Private Marine. He was pensioned 1 Apr. 1805 at the rate of $36 per annum. 1805. 1807. 1808. 1809. 1810. 1811. D.C. in 1816. 1818. 1821. 1822. 1823. 1824. 1825. 1826. 1827. 1828. 1829. 1830. He served aboard a gunboat under Lt.

Naval Pensioners of the United States, 1800-1851

Trippe. He was disabled by the loss of the use of his right arm.
Conrad, H. A. —. —. He was pensioned as a privateer at the rate of $48 per annum. 1817. 1818. 1819. 1820. 1821. 1822.
Conrad, Thomas J.* —. Landsman. His widow, Ann Conrad, was pensioned from 8 Mar. 1834 at the rate of $4 per month. 1839. 1840. 1841. 1842. 1842b. She was pensioned again 1 Sep. 1847 at the rate of $10 per month. 1848. 1850. 1851.
Conway, —.* —. Marine. His son, Charles W. Conway, was pensioned from 14 July 1833 at the rate of $3.50 per month. 1839. 1840. 1841. 1842. 1842b. [He was Charles Conway in the Old Wars pension index.]
Conway, Edwin.* Va. Assistant Surgeon. He perished aboard the *Grampus*. His widow Fanny S. Conway and their child were of Albemarle Co., Va. They removed to Owensboro, Ky. His widow, Fanny S. Conway, was pensioned 20 Mar. 1848 at the rate of $17.50 per month. 1845. 1846. 1847. 1848. 1850. 1851.
Cook, —. —. —. Clarissa Cook was pensioned on his service. 1842.
Cook, John.* Mass. Seaman. He was pensioned as a privateer in 1812 at the rate of $72 per annum. 1812. 1813. 1814. 1815. 1816. 1817. 1818. 1819. 1820. 1821. 1822. 1823. 1824. 1825. 1826. 1827. 1828. 1829. 1830. 1831. 1832. 1833. 1834. 1835. 1836. 1837 for half a year. He was pensioned from 1 July 1837 for privateer service at the rate of $6 per month. 1837. 1838. 1844. 1845. 1846. 1847. 1850. He served aboard the *Polly* and was disabled by the loss of his right leg.
Cook, John A.* —. Lieutenant. His widow, Frances T. Cook, was pensioned 1 Sep. 1847 at the rate of $25 per month. 1835. 1836. 1837. 1839. 1840. 1841. 1842. 1842b. 1845. 1846. 1848. 1850. 1851. She also appeared as Frances F. Cook and Frances F. Cooke.
Cook, William.* —. Cabin Cook. He was pensioned 30 June 1836 at the rate of $4.50 per month. 1836. 1837. 1839. 1840. 1841. 1842b. 1843. 1844. 1845. 1846. 1847. 1848. 1851. He served aboard the *Vincennes* and was disabled by a left inguinal hernia.
Cook, William.* —. Seaman. He was pensioned 13 June 1848 at the rate of $6 per month. 1850. 1851. He was disabled by a disease of the eyes.
Cooke, Andrew B.* —. Surgeon. His widow, Sarah Ann Cooke, was pensioned from 4 Dec. 1838 at the rate of $35 per month. 1839. 1840. 1841. 1842. 1842b. 1845. 1846. She was pensioned again 1 Sep.1847 at the rate of $35 per month. 1848. 1850. 1851. He also appeared as Andrew B. Cook.
Coombe, George.* Md. Seaman. He was pensioned 2 June 1825 at the rate of $8 per month. 1827. 1828. 1829. 1830. 1835. 1836. 1837. 1839. 1840. 1841. 1842b. 1843. 1844. 1845. 1846. 1847. 1848. 1850. 1851. He also appeared as George Coomes and George Combs. He served aboard the *Constitution*. He was disabled by a fracture of his left leg.
Coon, —. N.Y. Sailing Master. Eleanor Coon was pensioned on his service as a privateer at the rate of $144 per annum. 1818. 1819. 1820. 1821. 1822. 1823. 1824. 1825. 1826. 1827. 1828.
Cooper, —.* —. Boatswain. His widow, Rebecca G. Cooper, was pensioned from 4 Oct. 1840 at the rate of $9 per month. 1841. 1842. 1842b. [He was listed as William M. Cooper in the Old Wars pension index.]

Naval Pensioners of the United States, 1800-1851

Cooper, —. —. —. He died of yellow fever 12 July 1822. His widow was Eliza Cooper. She was pensioned 15 Oct. 1825.

Cooper, Benjamin. —. Captain. His widow, Elizabeth Cooper, was pensioned 1 June 1850 at the rate of $50 per month. 1850. 1851.

Cooper, Grenville C.* —. Purser. His widow, Jane A. Cooper, was pensioned 2 Mar. 1849 at the rate of $20 per month. 1846. 1847. 1848. 1850. 1851.

Cooper, Richard W. Mass. Seaman. He was pensioned at the rate of $8.50 per month in 1803. 1804. 1805. 1807. 1808. 1809. 1810. 1811. He served aboard the *Boston* and was disabled by a wound in his right hand and arm.

Cooper, William. Mass. Seaman. He served aboard the *Constitution* and was killed 29 Dec. 1812. His widow, Dorothea Cooper, was pensioned 24 June 1819 at the rate of $72 per annum. 1820. 1821. 1822, 1824. 1825. 1827. 1828. 1829. 1830. She also appeared as Dorothy Cooper.

Cope, William.* —. Seaman. He served aboard the *Savannah* and was disabled by a wound of his arm and thigh. He was pensioned in Apr. 1851.

Copp, —. —. —. Margaret Copp was pensioned on his service as a privateer at the rate of $60 per annum. 1815. 1816. 1817. 1818. 1819. 1820 increased to $144. 1821. 1822. 1823. 1824. 1825. 1826. 1827. 1828.

Corbett, —. —. —. S. Corbett was pensioned on his service as a privateer at the rate of $48 per annum. 1815. 1816. 1817. 1818. 1819. 1820 increased to $96.

Corbitt, —. —. Ordinary Seaman. His widow, Eunice Corbitt, was pensioned from 1 May 1823 at the rate of $5 per month. 1842b.

Cordevan, Edward.* —. Seaman. He was pensioned 28 Feb. 1836 at the rate of $3 per month. 1838. 1839. 1840. 1841. 1842b. 1843. 1844. 1845. 1846. 1847. 1848. 1850. 1851. He also appeared as Edward Cardevan and Edward Cardeven. He served aboard the *Concord* and was disabled by a rupture of his right side.

Corlette, Edward.* —. Ordinary Seaman. His widow, Susan Corlette, was pensioned from 5 July 1840 at the rate of $5 per month. 1840. 1841. 1842. 1842b. 1843. She was pensioned again 5 July 1845 at the rate of $5 per month. 1850. 1851.

Cornell, —. —. Carpenter. His widow, Mary W. Cornell, was pensioned at the rate of $10 per month. 1837. 1842.

Cornell, George. R.I. Carpenter's Mate. He was pensioned 1 Dec. 1826 at the rate of $9 per month. 1829. 1830. 1835. 1836. 1837. 1838. 1839. 1840. 1841. 1842. 1842b. 1843. 1844. 1845. 1846. 1848. 1851. He was disabled on the ship *Lawrence* on Lake Erie. He was disabled by a wound of the head.

Cornell, John.* —. Musician. His widow, Mary Cornell, was pensioned 8 July 1847 at the rate of $4 per month. 1847. 1848. 1850. 1851.

Cornyn, James.* Md. Seaman. He was pensioned 1 July 1820 at the rate of $72 per annum. 1818. 1819. 1820. 1821. 1822. 1824. 1825. 1826. 1827. 1828 in Va. 1829. 1830. He was disabled on the Chesapeake Bay flotilla, Barge No. 3. He also appeared as James Comyn, James Corning, and James Coruger. He was disabled by a hernia on his right side.

Naval Pensioners of the United States, 1800-1851

Correia, —. —. Gunner. His widow, Eleanor Correia, was pensioned at the rate of $10 per annum. 1837. 1840. 1841. 1842. 1842b.

Corse, James.* —. Seaman. He was pensioned 4 Feb. 1849 at the rate of $6 per month. 1850. He served aboard the *Ohio* and was disabled with a gun shot wound on his right hand.

Cotter, Joseph.* N.Y. Boatswain's Mate. He was pensioned 5 Nov. 1822 at the rate of $108 per annum. 1824. 1825. 1826. 1827. 1828. 1829. 1830. He was disabled at Sackett's Harbor by a fracture of his left ankle. He served aboard the brig *Jones*.

Cotter, William. —. Seaman. He was disabled by the loss of the first joint of the forefinger of his left hand. He was pensioned 28 Nov. 1811.

Cotton, Samuel. Mass. Marine. He was pensioned 5 Nov. 1813 at the rate of $36 per annum. 1816. 1818. 1819. 1820. 1821. 1822. 1825. 1826. 1827. 1828. 1829. 1830. He served aboard the *President*. He also appeared as Samuel Colton. He was disabled by a fracture of his arm and thigh.

Cotton, William. —. Purser's Steward. His widow, Rebecca A. Cotton, was pensioned at the rate of $9 per month from 3 Aug. 1830. Her pension ended 3 Aug. 1835. It was renewed in 1845.

Cottrell, James. S.C. Prize Master. He served aboard the privateer *Matilda* and was disabled with a gun shot wound of his left arm and thigh. He was pensioned 20 Apr. 1814 at the rate of $72 per annum. 1820.

Coulter, Mifflin.* —. Surgeon. His widow, Sarah Coulter, was pensioned from 12 Oct. 1840 at the rate of $25 per month. 1841. 1842. 1842b. She was listed as dead on the 1842b roll. The remainder of her pension was to be paid to her children. His children, Joseph H. Coulter, Alexander M. Coulter, and Mary Ann Coulter, were pensioned 1 Sep. 1842 at the rate of $25 per month. 1851.

Cousins, —.* —. Seaman. His daughters, Emeline Cousins and Delia Cousins, were pensioned at the rate of $6 per month from 21 May 1829. 1837. 1839. 1840. 1841. 1842. 1842b. [He was listed as John Cousins in the Old Wars pension index.]

Covell, Emerson G.* —. 1st Assistant Engineer. His widow, Ethalinda Covell, was pensioned 28 Dec. 1847 at the rate of $15 per month. 1851.

Covenhaven, —.* —. Marine. His son, James Covenhaven, was pensioned at the rate of $3.50 per month from 26 Feb. 1837. 1837. 1839. 1840. 1841. 1842. 1842b. [He was listed as William Covenhaven in the Old Wars pension index.]

Covenhaven, Francis.* N.Y. Ordinary Seaman. He served aboard the frigate *Chesapeake*. He was pensioned 23 June 1807 at the rate of $90 per annum. 1822. 1823. 1824. 1825. 1826. 1827. 1828. 1829. 1835. 1836. 1837. 1838. 1839. 1840. 1841. 1842. 1842b. 1843. 1844. 1845. 1846. 1847. 1848. 1850. 1851. He also appeared as Francis Covenhoven and Francis Covenhover. He was wounded in his left thigh, left ankle, and left shoulder.

Covie, Nathaniel. —. Quarter Gunner. He served aboard the frigate *Constellation*. He was disabled by the loss of his left leg and was pensioned 10 Jan. 1832.

Covill, Nathaniel.* —. Quarter Gunner. He was pensioned 1 Jan. 1832 at the rate of $9 per month. 1841. 1842b. 1843. 1844. 1845. 1846. 1847. 1848. 1850. 1851.

Covington, John R.* —. Gunner. His widow, Caroline L. Covington, was pensioned from 4 Nov.

Naval Pensioners of the United States, 1800-1851

1840 at the rate of $10 per month. 1841. 1842. 1842b. 1846. She was pensioned again 1 Sep. 1847 at the rate of $10 per month. 1848. 1850. 1851.

Cowan, —.* —. Gunner. His widow, Margaret Cowan, was pensioned at the rate of $10 per month from 14 Sep. 1831. 1837. 1839. 1840. 1841. 1842. 1842b. She also appeared as Margaret Cowen. [He was listed as William S. Cowen in the Old Wars pension index.]

Coward, Henry A. Md. Boy. He served aboard the privateer *Lottery* and was disabled by a gun shot wound in his right shoulder. He was pensioned 1 July 1817 at the rate of $48 per annum. 1820.

Cowell, John G. Mass. Sailing Master. He served aboard the *Essex* and was slain 18 Apr. 1814. His widow, Abigail Cowell, was pensioned from 18 Apr. 1814 at the rate of $20 per month. 1816. 1818. 1819. 1820. 1821. 1822. 1823. 1824. 1825. 1827. 1828. 1829. 1835. 1836. 1837. 1839. 1840. 1841. 1842. 1842b. 1845. 1846. She was pensioned again on 1 Sep. 1847 at the rate of $20 per month. 1848. 1850. 1851.

Cox, James S.* —. Passed Midshipman. His widow, Ellen Cox, was pensioned at the rate of $9.50 per month. 1837. 1839. 1840. 1841. 1842. 1842b. 1845. 1846. She was pensioned again 1 Sep. 1847 at the rate of $12.50 per month. 1848. 1850. 1851. She also appeared as Ellen Coxe.

Cox, John W.* —. Lieutenant. His widow, Emma M. Cox, was pensioned 7 Dec. 1842 at the rate of $25 per month. 1843. 1844. 1845. 1846. 1847. 1848. 1850. 1851.

Cox, William W.* —. Marine. His widow, Eleanor Cox, was pensioned from 10 Apr. 1837. 1840. 1841. 1842. 1842b. She was pensioned again 1 Sep. 1847 at the rate of $3.50 per month. 1848. 1850. 1851.

Crabb, Horatio N.* —. 1st Lieutenant Marines. He was pensioned at the rate of $7.50 per month. 1837. 1838. 1839. 1840. 1841. 1842. 1842b. 1843. He was disabled by a double inguinal hernia.

Crandall, Russell.* Penn. Ordinary Seaman. He was pensioned 1 Aug. 1827 at the rate of $30 per annum. 1829. 1830. He served aboard the *Cyane*. He was disabled by the loss of two joints of the little and ring fingers on his right hand.

Crane, —. —. —. Susan M. Crane was pensioned on his service. 1842.

Crawford, David R.* —. Passed Midshipman. His widow, Mary Crawford, was pensioned from 26 July 1841 at the rate of $12.50 per month. 1841. 1842. 1842b. 1843. 1844. 1845. She was pensioned again 26 July 1846 at the rate of $25 per month. 1848. 1850. 1851. His rank was also given as Lieutenant.

Crawford, George.* —. Boatswain. He was pensioned 18 May 1846 at the rate of $3 per month. 1850. 1851. He served aboard the *Congress* and was disabled by a gun shot wound in his thigh.

Crawford, Thomas.* N.Y. Seaman. He was pensioned 1 Apr. 1820 at the rate of $60 per annum. 1821. 1822. 1823. 1824. 1825. 1826. 1827. 1828. 1829. 1830. He served aboard the schooner *Firebrand.* He also appeared as Thomas Crauford. He was disabled by a gun shot wound in his left leg.

Crew, Caleb.* —. —. He died aboard the *Macedonian*. His children applied in June 1828 and were pensioned at the rate of $60 per annum.

Naval Pensioners of the United States, 1800-1851

Creighton, John Orde. —. Captain. His widow, Harriet Creighton, was pensioned from 13 Oct. 1838 at the rate of $50 per month. 1839. 1840. 1841. 1842. 1842b. 1846. She was pensioned again 1 Sep. 1847 at the rate of $50 per month. 1848. 1850. 1851.

Critchett, John. Mass. Seaman. He served aboard the *Chesapeake* and was killed 19 June 1813. His widow, Susannah Critchett, was pensioned 18 Apr. 1815 at the rate of $72 per annum. 1816. 1818. 1820. 1821. 1822. 1823. 1827 in Me. 1828. 1829. 1837. 1839. 1840. 1841. 1842. 1842b. She also appeared as Susannah Chritchet, Susannah Crickett, Susanna Crutchet, and Susanna Critchet. She was pensioned again 1 Sep. 1847 at the rate of $6 per month. 1848. 1850. 1851. He also appeared as John Crutchet and John Critchet.

Crosby, John. Mass. Seaman. He was pensioned as a privateer from 1813 at the rate of $72 per annum. 1813. 1814. 1815. 1816. 1817. 1818. 1819. 1820. 1821. 1822. 1823. 1824. 1825. 1826. 1827. He served aboard the *True Blooded Yankee* and was disabled by a wound in his left leg.

Cross, —. —. Lieutenant. His widow, Celia Cross, was pensioned at the rate of $20 from 30 June 1834. 1835. 1836. 1837. 1839. 1840. 1841. 1842. 1842b.

Crow, Benjamin.* —. Sailmaker. His widow, Margaret Ann Crow, was pensioned 31 Mar. 1845 at the rate of $10 per month. 1845. 1846. 1847. 1848. It was renewed 31 Mar. 1850. 1850. 1851.

Crowinshield, Jacob.* —. Commander. His widow, Harriet Crowninshield, was pensioned 15 July 1849 at the rate of $30 per month. 1850. 1851.

Cumming, William. N.Y. —. He was pensioned from 1 Sep. 1815 at the rate of $6 per month. His grandchild, William Slam, was pensioned at the rate of $72 per annum. 1829. 1836.

Cummings, James.* —. Ordinary Seaman. He was pensioned 16 May 1844 at the rate of $2.50 per month. 1847. 1848. 1850. 1851. He served aboard the *North Carolina* and was disabled by the loss of sight in his left eye.

Cummings, William. Mass. Seaman. He served aboard the *Epervier* and was lost 1 Sep. 1815. His widow, Margaret Cummings, was pensioned 10 Apr. 1818 at the rate of $72 per annum. 1819. 1820. 1821. 1822. 1824. 1825. 1827. 1828. 1829. 1830. 1836. She also appeared as Margaret Cummins. William Cummings and Margaret Williams were married 15 June 1800 by Alex Goudy in County Down, Ireland. Margaret Cummings lived in New York City. She had four children: Jane Cummings about 9 years old, William Cummings aged 7, Marian Cummings, and Jenny Cummings. One child died in June 1816 and another in Aug. 1816. William McConnell knew the family back in Ireland. In 1817 Jane Cummings was about 10 years old and William Cummings was 8 years old. His widow was paid $72.

Cummins, Thomas.* Ordinary Seaman. He was pensioned 12 July 1843 at the rate of $5 per month. 1844. 1845. 1846. 1847. 1848. 1850. 1851. He served aboard the *Fairfield* and was disabled by the loss of sight in both eyes.

Cumpston, —. Mass. Prize Master. Lucy Cumpston was pensioned on his service as a privateer at the rate of $60 per annum. 1815. 1816. 1817. 1818. 1819. 1820. 1821 with an increase to $120. 1822. 1823. 1824. 1825. 1826. 1827. 1828. 1829. 1830. 1831. 1832. 1833. 1834. 1835 for $10.

Naval Pensioners of the United States, 1800-1851

Cunningham, —.* N.Y. Gunner. He died 18 Apr. 1823 of yellow fever on the coast of Africa. His widow, Elizabeth Cunningham, was pensioned 18 Sep. 1824. 1824. 1825. 1827. 1828. His sons, John R. Cunningham, William B. Cunningham, and Edward T. [or F.] Cunningham were pensioned at the rate of $10 per month from 18 Apr. 1828. 1837. 1839. 1840. 1841. 1842. [He was listed as Wesley Cunningham in the Old Wars pension index.]

Cunningham, James.* —. Ordinary Seaman. His widow, Bridget Cunningham, was pensioned 5 Aug. 1849 at the rate of $5 per month. 1850. 1851.

Cunningham, R. B. —. Lieutenant. He was pensioned from 25 Mar. 1810 at the rate of $12.50 per month. 1840. 1841. 1842b. 1843.

Cunningham, Shubal.* N.Y. Seaman. He was pensioned 29 July 1814 at the rate of $72 per annum. 1822. 1823. 1824. 1825. 1826. 1827. 1828. 1829. 1830. He served aboard the frigate *Essex*. He was disabled by an injury to his right leg.

Curillier, John B. —. Musician in Marine Corps. His widow, Maria J. Curillier, was pensioned at the rate of $4 per month 30 June 1834. 1836. 1837. 1839. 1840. 1841. 1842. 1842b. 1845. 1846. She was pensioned again 1 Sep. 1847 at the rate of $4 per month. She also appeared as Maria J. Cuvillier and Maria J. Cavilier. 1848. 1850. 1851.

Currace, Antoine. —. Gunner. His widow, Eleanor Currace, was pensioned from 21 Dec. 1823 and again on 1 Sep. 1847 at the rate of $10 per month. 1839. 1848. 1850. 1851. He also appeared as Antonia Curraei and Antonio Curraei. She also appeared as Eleanor Carreia.

Curran, Nathaniel. Mass. Seaman. He served aboard the *Chesapeake* and was disabled by a fracture of his thigh. He was pensioned 30 Sep. 1813 at the rate of $48 per annum. 1816.

Currell, —. Mass. Master's Mate. Margaret Currell was pensioned on his service as a privateer at the rate of $36 per annum. 1812. 1813. 1814. 1815. 1816. 1817. 1818. 1819. 1820. 1821. 1822 for $47.60.

Currier, —. —. —. Lois Currier was pensioned on his service as a privateer at the rate of $60 per annum. 1815. 1816. 1817. 1818. 1819. 1820. 1821. 1822. 1823. 1824. 1825. 1826. 1827. 1828. 1829. 1830. 1831. 1832. 1833. 1834 for $109.33. [He was Edward Currier in the Old Wars pension index.]

Currier, William P. —. Seaman. His widow, Fanny Currier, was pensioned 28 July 1851 at the rate of $6 per month. 1851.

Currin, James. N.Y. Ordinary Seaman. He was pensioned at the rate of $7 per month in 1803. 1804. 1805. 1807. 1808. 1809. 1810. 1811. He served aboard the *Essex* and was disabled by the loss of the use of his left arm.

Curry, —. N.Y. Prize Master. Elizabeth Curry was pensioned on his service as a privateer at the rate of $120 per annum from 1 Feb. 1814.

Curtis, —. Mass. Commander. Mercy Curtis was pensioned on his service as a privateer at the rate of $240 per annum. 1817. 1818. 1819. 1820. 1821. 1822 for $200.

Curtis, William.* Md. Boatswain's Mate. He was pensioned at the rate of $108 per annum. 1819. 1820. 1821. He served aboard the *Washington* and was disabled by the fracture of the transverse process of two bones of his spine.

Cushley, John.* —. Sergeant of Marines. His widow, Mary Cushley, was pensioned 3 Oct. 1847

Naval Pensioners of the United States, 1800-1851

at the rate of $6.50 per month. 1847. 1848. 1850. 1851.

Daggett, Samuel.* —. Gunner. His widow, Laura P. Daggett, was pensioned 9 Apr. 1836. 1836. 1837. 1839. 1840. 1841. 1842. 1842b. 1845. 1846.

Dailey, James. —. Ordinary Seaman. He served aboard the *Java, Constellation, St. Louis,* and *Hudson.* He was disabled with paralysis of both legs.

Dailey, Thomas.* N.Y. Quartermaster. He was pensioned 18 Jan. 1817 at the rate of $96 per annum. 1818. 1819. 1820. 1821. 1822. 1823. 1824. 1825. 1826. 1827. 1828. 1829. 1830. He served aboard the *Hornet.* He was disabled with a gun shot wound in his left leg.

Dale, John B.* —. Lieutenant. His children, William H. Dale and John P. Dale, were pensioned 16 Feb. 1849 at the rate of $25 per month. 1850. 1851.

Daley, —. —. —. His daughter, Elizabeth Daley, was pensioned on his service. 1837. 1842. She also appeared as Elizabeth Dailey.

Dallas, Alexander. —. Captain. His widow, Mary B. Dallas, was pensioned 3 June 1849 at the rate of $50 per month. 1845. 1846. 1847. 1848. It was renewed in 1850. 1851.

Dallas, James.* —. Seaman. He was pensioned 10 June 1848 at the rate of $6 per month. 1850. 1851. He was disabled with paralysis of his left side.

Dalton, Edward. Mass. Seaman. He was pensioned as a privateer at the rate of $36 per annum from 1813. 1813. 1814. 1815. 1816. 1817. 1818. 1819. 1820. 1821. 1822. He served aboard the *Wasp* and was disabled by the loss of his right thumb.

Dalyrmple, Joseph.* —. Seaman. He was pensioned 24 Feb. 1814 at the rate of $4.50 per month. 1835. 1836. 1837. 1838. 1839. 1840. 1841. 1842. 1842b. 1843. 1844. 1845. 1846. 1847. 1848. 1850. 1851. He served aboard the *Hornet.*

Danford, —. N.H. Seaman. Sally Danford was pensioned on his service as a privateer at the rate of $36 per annum from 1 Jan. 1815. 1815. 1816. 1817. 1818. 1819. 1820 increase to $72. 1821. 1822. 1823. 1824. 1825. 1826. 1827. 1828 for $69.60. [He was Jacob Danford in the Old Wars pension index.]

Daniels, John.* N.Y. Quartermaster. He was pensioned 22 Mar. 1822 at the rate of $108 per annum. 1824. 1825. 1826. 1827. 1828. 1829. 1830. 1835. 1836. 1837. 1838. 1839. 1840. 1842. 1847. 1839. 1840. 1841. 1842b. 1843. 1844. 1845. 1846. 1847. 1848. 1850. 1851. He served aboard the sloop *Niagara.* He was disabled by a wound of his head resulting in lunacy. He was injured in a gunpowder explosion.

Danvers, Daniel.* —. Marine. He was pensioned 22 Oct. 1835 at the rate of $3 per month. 1835. 1836. 1837. 1839. 1840. 1841. 1842b. 1843. 1844. 1845. 1846. 1847. 1848. 1850. 1851. He also appeared as Daniel Denvers and David Denvers.

Darley, James. —. Ordinary Seaman. He was pensioned 1 Mar. 1838 at the rate of $5 per month. 1839. 1840. 1841. 1842b. 1843. 1844. 1845. 1846. 1847. 1848. 1850. 1851.

Darling, Benjamin F.* —. 1st Class Apprentice. He was pensioned 22 Oct. 1844 at the rate of $2 per month. 1846. 1847. 1848. 1850. 1851.

Darragh, —.* —. Purser. His daughter, Margaret P. Darrah, was pensioned from 9 Jan. 1831 at

Naval Pensioners of the United States, 1800-1851

the rate of $20 per month. 1839. 1840. 1841. 1842. 1842b. She also appeared as Margaret Danagh. [He was listed as Alexander P. Darragh in the Old Wars pension index.]

Darrington, William.* —. Yeoman. He was pensioned 18 Oct. 1841 at the rate of $3.75 per month. 1842b. 1843. 1844. 1845. 1846. 1847. 1848. 1850. 1851. He served aboard the *Macedonian* and was disabled by an injury to his right hand.

Dart, Thomas Lynch. S.C. Surgeon's Mate. His widow had her application rejected prior to 23 Dec. 1848. Her husband was discharged under the act of 1801 for reducing the navy. There was no law providing for her case.

Davidson, —. —. Boatswain. His widow, Catherine Davidson, was pensioned 27 June 1836 at the rate of $6 per month. 1836. 1837. 1839. 1840. 1842. [He was William Davidson in the Old Wars pension index.]

Davidson, John. Mass. Lieutenant. He was pensioned 1 Mar. 1801 at the rate of $20 per month. 1803. 1804. 1805. 1807. 1808. 1809. 1810. 1811. 1816. 1818. 1819. 1820. 1821. 1823. 1824. 1825. 1826. 1827. 1828. 1829. 1830. 1835. 1836. 1837. 1839. 1840. 1841. 1842b. 1843. 1844. 1845. 1846. 1847. 1848. 1850. 1851. He served aboard the *Herald*. He was disabled by a fracture of his shoulder.

Davis, —. —. —. Reliance Davis was pensioned on his service as a privateer at the rate of $36 per annum. 1812. 1813. 1814. 1815. 1816. 1817. 1818 increase to $72. 1819. 1820. 1821. 1822. 1823. 1824. 1825. 1826. 1827 for $39.

Davis, —. —. Master's Mate. His widow, Sarah Davis, was pensioned from 6 Jan. 1820 at the rate of $20 per month. 1839. 1840. 1841. 1842b.

Davis, —. —. —. His widow, Mary Davis, was pensioned from 1 July 1823 at the rate of $9 per month. 1839. 1840. 1841. 1842b.

Davis, —. —. —. Martha Davis was pensioned on his service as a privateer at the rate of $36 per annum. 1815. 1816. 1817. 1818. 1819. 1820 increase to $72. 1821. 1822. 1823. 1824. 1825. 1826. 1827. 1828. 1829. 1830. 1831. 1832. 1833.

Davis, —.* —. Carpenter. His daughter, Teresa Davis, was pensioned from 11 June 1829 at the rate of $10 per month. 1837. 1839. 1840. 1841. 1842. 1842b. [He was listed as Samuel Davis in the Old Wars pension index.]

Davis, —. N.Y. Seaman. He died of fever on the coast of Africa in Apr. 1822. His widow, Charlotte Davis, was pensioned at the rate of $72 per annum. 1824 1825.

Davis, —. N.Y. Quarter master. His widow, Mary Davis, was pensioned at the rate of $108 per annum. 1818. 1819. 1820.

Davis, Abraham. N.Y. Quartermaster. His widow, Mary Davis, received $108 per annum in 1816. 1818. 1821. 1822. 1824. 1825. 1827. 1828. 1829. He was killed 11 Sep. 1814 on the schooner *Saratoga*.

Davis, James. N.Y. Quarter Gunner. He was pensioned 18 Mar. 1847 at the rate of $108 per annum. 1818. 1819. 1820. 1821. 1822. 1823. 1824. 1825. 1826. 1827. 1828. 1829. 1830. He served aboard the *Ontario*. He was disabled by rheumatism.

Davis, James.* —. Sail Maker. His widow, Mary Frances Davis, was pensioned from 26 Jan. 1839 at the rate of $10 per month. 1839. 1840. 1841. 1842. 1842b. 1846. She was

Naval Pensioners of the United States, 1800-1851

pensioned again 1 Sep. 1847 at the rate of $10 per month. 1848. 1850. 1851.
Davis, Jesse D. —. Seaman. He was pensioned 2 Sep. 1842 at the rate of $6 per month. 1843. 1844. 1845. 1846. 1847. 1848. 1850. 1851. He served aboard the *Boston*. He was disabled by contusions of his right shoulder and ribs, dislocation of bones in his left wrist, a slight fracture of the radius, and an injury to his right thumb.
Davis, John.* —. Musician Marines. His children, Francis A. Davis and Elizabeth C. Davis, were pensioned at the rate of $4 per month from 4 July 1822. 1839. 1840. 1841. 1842. In 1841 Elizabeth C. Davis had become Elizabeth C. Enoch.
Davis, John. —. Fireman. He was pensioned 24 Aug. 1850 at the rate of $3 per month. 1850. 1851. He served aboard the *Saranac* and was disabled by an injury to his left foot.
Davis, Nathaniel. N.Y. Lieutenant. He was pensioned as a privateer at the rate of $72 per annum. 1818. 1819. 1820. 1821. 1822. 1823. 1824. 1825. 1826. 1827 for $36. He served aboard the *Saratoga* and was disabled by a wound in his right shoulder.
Davis, Thomas. —. Seaman. He served aboard the sloop *Peacock* and was disabled by a gun shot wound in his left thigh. He was pensioned in June 1815.
Davis, Thomas. —. Master's Mate. His daughter, Mary Elizabeth Davis, was pensioned at the rate of $10 per month from 26 Apr. 1820 to 6 Jan. 1828 when her mother Sarah Davis married her second husband, Mr. Drake.
Davis, Thomas, 1st. N.Y. Seaman. He was pensioned at the rate of $44 per annum. 1816. 1818. 1819. 1820. 1821. He served aboard the *Ontario* and was disabled by a saber wound of his left arm.
Davis, Thomas, 2nd. N.Y. Seaman. He was pensioned at the rate of $72 per annum. 1816. 1818. 1819. 1820. 1821. He served aboard the *President* and was disabled by the loss of his left arm.
Davis, Thomas.* —. Ship's Cook. He was pensioned 18 July 1850 at the rate of $7.20 per month. 1850. 1851. He served aboard the brig *Perry* and was disabled by a wound of his left foot.
Davis, Thomas. Penn. Seaman. He was pensioned 1 Mar. 1815 at the rate of $60 per annum. 1816. 1818. 1819. 1820. 1821. 1822. 1823. 1824. 1825. 1827. 1828. 1829. 1830. He served aboard the schooner *Ontario*.
Davis, Thomas W. —. Seaman. His widow, Abijah Davis, was pensioned 5 Apr. 1844 at the rate of $6 per month. 1850. 1851.
Davis, William. N.Y. Seaman. He was pensioned 18 Feb. 1813 at the rate of $72 per annum. 1816. 1818. 1819. 1820. 1821. 1822. 1823. 1824. 1825. 1826. 1827. 1828. 1829. 1830. He was disabled at the lakes by the loss of the use of his left eye and of his left arm. He served aboard Gunboat No. 14.
Davis, William. Penn. Seaman. He was pensioned at the rate of $60 per annum in 1826.
Davis, William. Va. Seaman. He was pensioned at the rate of $72 per annum in 1807. 1808. 1809. 1810. 1811.
Davis, William C.* —. Marine. His widow, Ann Davis, was pensioned 22 Apr. 1850 at the rate of $3.50 per month. 1851. [He was listed as William L. Davis in the Old Wars pension index.]

Naval Pensioners of the United States, 1800-1851

Davis, William P.* Penn. Prize Master. He served aboard the *Prince of Neufchatel* and was disabled by a gun shot wound in his stomach and an injury resulting in the amputation of his left hand. He was pensioned from 13 Oct. 1814 at the rate of $20 per annum. 1820.

Davis, Zebulon.* —. Second Gunner. His widow, Susan Davis, was pensioned at the rate of $7.50 per month from 10 Aug. 1800. 1837. 1839. 1840. 1841. 1842. 1842b. 1851. She was pensioned again 1 Sep. 1842 at the rate of $7.50 per month. His rank was also given as Quarter Gunner.

Dawson, William. —. Seaman. He was disabled by an injury to his left leg. He served aboard the *Mohawk* and was pensioned 1 Apr. 1823.

Day, Ebenezer.* —. Ordinary Seaman. He was pensioned from 1 June 1813 at the rate of $1.66 2/3 per month. 1838. 1839. 1840. He served aboard the *Chesapeake* and was disabled by a gun shot wound of his right thigh.

Day, Isaac.* —. Ord. Sergeant of Marine. His widow, Hannah Day, was pensioned 3 June 1846 at the rate of $8 per month. 1847. 1848. 1850. 1851.

Day, Isaac. —. —. He was pensioned as a privateer at the rate of $36 per annum. 1813. 1814. 1815. 1816. 1817. 1818. 1819. 1820. 1821. 1822. 1823. 1824 for $18. He served aboard the *York* and was disabled by a fracture of his left leg.

Day, James. Mass. Marine. His widow, Rebecca Day, received $36 per annum in 1821. 1822. 1823. 1824. 1825. 1827. 1828. 1829. He was killed 11 Sep. 1814 on Lake Champlain. Thomas Jones was guardian.

Daykin, Samuel.* —. Marine. He was pensioned 22 Oct. 1834 at the rate of $3 per month. 1835. 1836. 1837. 1839. 1840. 1841. 1842b. 1843. 1844. 1845. 1846. 1847. 1848. 1850. 1851. He was disabled by a wound in his left arm.

Dean, George. —. Seaman. His widow, Hannah Dean, had her application rejected prior to 17 Jan. 1848. He never applied for a pension, and there was no law under which the widow could claim a pension because her husband did not die in the service.

Deane, Samuel.* Mass. Seaman. He was pensioned 25 Jan. 1820 at the rate of $72 per annum. 1821. 1822. 1823. 1824 in N.Y. 1825. 1826. 1827. 1828. 1829. 1830. He also appeared as Samuel Dean. He served aboard the sloop *Erie*. He was disabled by a wound in his leg resulting in an ulcer of same.

Deane, William. Penn. Seaman. He was pensioned 1 Jan. 1811 at the rate of $72 per annum. 1816. 1818. 1819. 1820. 1821. 1822. 1823. 1824. 1825. 1826. 1827. 1828. 1829. 1830. He served on Gunboat No. 27.

Dearborn, —. —. Master Commandant. His widow, Abigail Dearborn, was pensioned at the rate of $30 per month. 1837. 1842.

Dearing, William. Penn. Seaman. He was pensioned 27 Mar. 1815 at the rate of $72 per annum. 1818. 1819. 1820. 1821. 1822. 1823. 1824. 1825. 1826. 1827. 1828. 1829. 1830. He was disabled on Lake Erie. He served aboard the *Lawrence* and was disabled by a mortification of his left foot and ankle.

DeBellevue, F.B. —. Captain Marine Corps. His application was rejected between Mar. 1840 and 1 Jan. 1842. He stated that he was wounded on 23 Dec. 1814 at New Orleans, but his name was not found on the returns of the wounded on that occasion.

Naval Pensioners of the United States, 1800-1851

Decatur, —. —. Captain. His widow, Susan Decatur, was pensioned at the rate of $50 per month from 22 Mar. 1820. 1837. 1839. 1840. 1841. 1842. 1842b.

Deddolph, Owen. Md. Gunner. He was pensioned 1 Feb. 1827 at the rate of $5 per month. 1829. 1830. 1835. 1836. 1837. 1838. 1839. 1840. 1841. 1842. 1842b. 1843. 1844. 1845. 1846. 1847. 1848. 1850. 1851. He was disabled on Barney's flotilla, St. Leonard's ck.

Deignan, Peter.* —. Private Marine. His widow, Elizabeth Deignan, was pensioned 18 Jan. 1848 at the rate of $3.50 per month. 1850. 1851. He also appeared as Peter Deigrian.

Delboeuf, Lewis.* —. Seaman. He was pensioned 14 Sep. 1849 at the rate of $2 per month. 1850. 1851. He served aboard the *Ohio*.

Demarest, —.* —. Sergeant Marines. His daughter, Emma Demarest, was pensioned at the rate of $8 per month from 24 Aug. 1824. 1837. 1839. 1840. 1841. 1842. 1842b. [He was listed as John Demarest in the Old Wars pension index.]

Demillie, Paul. S.C. Seaman. He was pensioned as a privateer at the rate of $60 per annum. 1813. 1814. 1815. 1816. 1817. 1818. 1819. 1820. 1821. 1822. 1823. 1824 for $30. He served aboard the *Hazard* and was wounded in both thighs.

DeMotte, Lewis. Mass. Seaman. He was pensioned as a privateer from 1813 at the rate of $72 per annum. 1813. 1814. 1815. 1816. 1817. 1818. 1819. 1820. 1821. 1822. 1823. 1824. 1825. 1826. 1827. 1828. 1829. 1830. 1831. 1832. 1833. 1834. 1835. 1836. 1837 for half a year. He was pensioned from 1 July 1837 for privateer service at the rate of $6 per month. 1837. 1838. 1844. 1845. 1846. 1847. 1850. He served aboard the *Young Teaser*. He was disabled by a fracture of his right leg and left arm and the loss of his left leg.

Denham, —.* —. Ordinary Seaman. His widow, Prudence Denham, was pensioned from 27 June 1837 at the rate of $5 per month. 1839. 1840. 1841. 1842. 1842b. [He was listed as John Denham in the Old Wars pension index.]

Denham, Thomas S.* D.C. Sergeant of Marines. His children, Thomas S. Denham and John E. Denham, had their application rejected prior to 23 Dec. 1848. They were barred by the act of 11 Aug. 1848. His widow, Mary Ann Denham, was pensioned from 7 Apr. 1841 at the rate of $8 per month. 1841. 1842. 1842b.

Denike, John.* N.Y. Seaman. He was pensioned 1 Dec. 1825 at the rate of $72 per annum. He was disabled by proving powder for the navy resulting in the loss of his right arm. 1827. 1828. 1829. 1830. 1836.

Denison, —.* —. Purser. His daughter, Eliza A. K. [or R.] Denison, was pensioned at the rate of $20 per month from 15 Mar. 1822. 1837. 1839. 1840. 1841. 1842. She also appeared as Eliza A. R. Dennison. [He was listed as Henry Denison in the Old Wars pension index.]

Denney, John. Md. Seaman. He was pensioned 4 Mar. 1815 at the rate of $72 per annum. 1818. 1819. 1820. 1821. 1822. 1823. 1824. 1825. 1826. 1827. 1828. 1829. 1830. He also appeared as John Denny. He was disabled at Bladensburg.

Dennis, —. Mass. Seaman. His widow, Sarah Dennis, was pensioned on his service as a privateer at the rate of $36 per annum from 19 Sep. 1812. 1812. 1813. 1814. 1815. 1816. 1817. 1818. 1819. 1820. 1821. 1822. 1823. 1824. 1825. 1826. 1827. 1828. 1829. 1830. 1831. 1832. 1833 for $51.60.

Dennis, James. S.C. Marine. He was pensioned 10 May 1810 at the rate of $36 per annum. 1811.

Naval Pensioners of the United States, 1800-1851

1816 and 1818 in Ga. 1819. 1820. 1821. 1822. 1823. 1824. 1825. 1826. 1827. 1828. 1829. 1830. He was disabled at Washington from small pox resulting in the loss of sight in one of his eyes.

Dennis, John. N.Y. Seaman. He was pensioned 25 Dec. 1815 at the rate of $60 per annum. 1818. 1819. 1820. 1821. 1822. 1823. 1824. 1826. 1827. 1828. 1829. 1830. He served aboard the *United States*. He was disabled with rheumatism.

Dennis, Thomas. N.Y. Seaman. He was pensioned 15 Nov. 1819 at the rate of $72 per annum. 1821. 1822. 1823. 1824. 1825. 1826. 1828. 1829. 1830. He served aboard the *Guerriere*.

Dennis, Thomas.* —. Seaman. He was pensioned 1 Aug. 1849 at the rate of $30 per month. 1850. 1851.

Dennison, John.* —. Sergeant of Marines. His daughters, Elmina Virginia Dennison and Mary Ellen Dennison, were pensioned 26 Apr. 1847 at the rate of $6.50 per month. 1847. 1850. 1851. His widow, Susan Dennison, was pensioned 9 Dec. 1844 at the rate of $6.50 per month. 1845. 1846. 1847. 1848.

Denny, James.* N.Y. Quarter Gunner. He was killed by pirates 9 Nov. 1822. His pension in the amount of $108 per annum was paid to his mother, Penelope Denny. 1824. 1825. 1827. 1828 in Ohio. 1829. He served aboard the schooner *Alligator*. Lt. Allen was killed at the same time. James Denny had for several months contributed half of his pay to his mother. She was pensioned by special act.

Denny, John. Md. Seaman. He was pensioned at the rate of $72 per annum. 1816.

Dent, —.* —. Captain. His widow, Elizabeth Ann Dent, was pensioned at the rate of $50 per month from 21 July 1823. 1837. 1839. 1840. 1841. 1842. 1842b. [He was listed as John H. Dent in the Old Wars pension index.]

Denver, Daniel. —. Seaman. He served in the Marine Corps and was disabled by the loss of sight in both eyes. He was pensioned 6 Nov. 1835 at the rate of $36 per annum.

Desendorf, Andrew. —. Seaman. He was pensioned as a privateer from 19 Apr. 1814 at the rate of $4 per month. 1814. 1815. 1816. 1817. 1818. 1819. 1820. 1821. 1822. 1823. 1836. 1837. 1838. 1850. He served aboard the *York* and was disabled by gunshot wounds in both hips. He also appeared as Andrew Dusendorf and Andrew Duendorf.

Desha, Robert M.* —. 1st Lieutenant Marine Corps. His children, Franklin Wharton Desha and Margaret Frances Desha, were pensioned from 6 Nov. 1822 at the rate of $15 per month. 1839. 1840. His rank was also given as Major. Margaret Frances Desha became Margaret F. Denton.

Dever, William.* —. Landsman. His widow, Ellen Dever, was pensioned at the rate of $4 per month from 23 Apr. 1823. 1837. 1839. 1840. 1841. 1842. 1842b. His son, John Dever, was pensioned from 1 Mar. 1839 at the rate of $4 per month. His pension ended 31 Aug. 1842. 1843.

Dewey, Thomas.* —. Gunner. His widow, Waitstill C. Dewey, was pensioned 16 Nov. 1849 at the rate of $10 per month. 1849. 1850. 1851. He also appeared as Thomas Davey.

Dexter, —. —. Master Commandant. His orphan, Ellen E. Dexter, was pensioned at the rate of $30 per month from 10 Oct. 1818. 1837. 1839. 1842.

Dickason, John A.* —. Carpenter. He was pensioned at the rate of $10 per month. 1837. 1838.

Naval Pensioners of the United States, 1800-1851

1839. 1840. 1841. 1842b. 1843. His widow, Joanna P. Dickason, was pensioned 28 Sep. 1847 at the rate of $10 per month. 1850. 1851. He served aboard the *Constitution* and was disabled by a left inguinal hernia.

Dickson, William. —. Seaman. He was pensioned 8 Apr. 1847 at the rate of $3 per month. 1847. 1848. 1850. 1851. He served aboard the brig *Bainbridge* and was disabled by an oblique right inguinal hernia.

Digance, James. Va. Quartermaster. He was pensioned at the rate of $108 per annum in 1805. 1807. 1808. 1809. 1810. 1811. He served aboard the frigate *Philadelphia* and was disabled by an injury to his right leg.

Dill, Eli.* —. Boatswain. His widow, Lamatre Dill, was pensioned 1 Sep. 1847 at the rate of $10 per month. 1835. 1836. 1837. 1839. 1840. 1841. 1842. 1842b. 1845. 1846. 1848. 1850. 1851. She also appeared as Lamotie Dill and Lamartie Dill.

Dillehunt, Albert. Md. Quartermaster. He perished aboard the *Grampus*. His mother was Mrs. Henrietta Dillehunt, aged about 64, of Baltimore, Md. on 14 June 1844.

Diragan, John. Md. Seaman. He was pensioned 22 Dec. 1815 at the rate of $60 per annum. 1819. 1820. 1821. 1822. 1823. 1824. 1825. 1826. 1827. 1828. 1829. 1830 [incorrectly listed as George Diragan]. 1835. 1836. 1837. 1839. 1840. 1841. 1842b. 1843. 1844. 1845. 1846. 1847. 1848. 1850. 1851. He also appeared as John Diragen and John Dixagen. He was disabled on the *Superior* with a gun shot wound of his right thigh.

Dix, John. N.Y. Surgeon. He died of yellow fever 15 Apr. 1825 on the coast of Africa. His widow, Ellen Dix, was pensioned at the rate of $300 per annum. 1824. 1825. 1827. 1828. 1835. 1836. 1837. 1839. 1840. 1841. 1842. 1842b. 1845. 1846. She was pensioned again 1 Sep. 1847 at the rate of $27.50 per month. 1848. 1850. 1851.

Dixon, James.* —. Seaman. He was pensioned 11 Nov. 1835 at the rate of $3 per month. 1836. 1839. 1840. 1841. 1842b. 1843. 1844. 1845. 1846. 1847. 1848. 1850. 1851. He served aboard the *Franklin* and was disabled by an injury to his right hand and left foot.

Dixon, Richard. —. Seaman. He was pensioned as a privateer at the rate of $60 per annum. 1812. 1813. 1814. 1815. 1816. 1817. 1818. 1819. 1820. He served aboard the *Highflyer* and was disabled by a gun shot wound in his right arm resulting in the loss of use of his right hand.

Dobson, —. N.Y. Commander. Euphemia Dobson was pensioned on his service as a privateer at the rate of $240 per annum. 1813. 1814. 1815. 1816. 1817. 1818. 1819. 1820. 1821. 1822. 1823. 1824. 1825. 1826. 1827. 1828. 1829. 1830. 1831. 1832. 1833 for $132.67. [He was William Dobson in the Old Wars pension index.]

Dodge, Edwin J.* —. Seaman. He was pensioned 18 May 1846 at the rate of $3 per month. 1846. 1847. 1848. 1850. 1851. He served aboard the *Guerriere* and was disabled by a fracture of the middle bones of the two smaller fingers of his right hand and partial dislocation of his wrist.

Dodge, Stillman.* —. Ordinary Seaman. He was pensioned 1 May 1831 at the rate of $3.33 1/3 per month. 1835. 1836. 1837. 1839. 1840. 1841. 1842. 1842b. 1843. 1844. 1845. 1846. 1847. 1848. 1850. 1851. He also appeared as Shillman Dodge and Hillman Dodge. He was disabled in the Charleston Navy Yard at Boston and was disabled by a fracture of his

Naval Pensioners of the United States, 1800-1851

right leg near the ankle.

Donigan, Timothy.* —. Ordinary Seaman. He was pensioned 27 Apr. 1837 at the rate of $2.50 per month. 1839. 1840. 1841. 1842b. 1843. 1844. 1845. 1846. 1847. 1848. 1850. 1851. He also appeared as Timothy Donegan. He was disabled at the Charleston Navy Yard by a fracture of his right forearm.

Donly, John.* —. Landsman. His widow, Jemima Donly, was pensioned 13 Aug. 1847 at the rate of $4.50 per month. 1850. 1851. He also appeared as John Donnelly and John Douly.

Donovan, James.* —. Seaman. He was pensioned 23 Nov. 1847 at the rate of $6 per month. 1848. 1850. 1851. He served aboard the *North Carolina* and was disabled by an injury to his right arm and hand.

Donovan, Richard.* —. Private Marine. His widow, Eliza Donovan, was pensioned 30 Dec. 1850 at the rate of $3.50 per month. 1851.

Dooire, —. Mass. Lieutenant. Sally Dooire was pensioned on his service as a privateer at the rate of $36 per annum from 1 Feb. 1815. 1815. 1816. 1817 for $19.10. She also appeared as Sally Dovire.

Dorgan, —.* —. —. Timothy Dorgan and Andrew Dorgan were pensioned on his service. 1842. [He was listed as Andrew Dorgan in the Old Wars pension index.]

Dorgan, John D. —. —. He was pensioned. 1842.

Dorn, Jacob. N.Y. Seaman. He was pensioned at the rate of $8.50 per month in 1803. 1804. 1805. 1807. 1808. 1809. 1810. 1811. He was pensioned 8 Dec. 1814 at the rate of $60 per annum. 1816. 1818. 1819. 1820. 1821. 1822. 1823. 1824. 1825. 1826. 1827. 1828. 1829. 1830. 1835. 1836. 1837. 1839. 1840. He also appeared as Jacob Dern, Jacob Dorne, and Jacob Dornes. He was disabled on the frigate *President*. He was disabled by an injury to his back and lower extremities.

Dorney, Bartholomew.* —. Steward. His widow, Peggy Dorney, was pensioned from 25 Jan. 1838 at the rate of $9 per month. 1839. 1840. 1841. 1842. 1842b. 1846. She was pensioned again at the rate of $9 per month 1 Sep. 1847. 1848. 1850.

Dorons, Albert S. —. Lieutenant. His widow, Martha L. Dorons, was pensioned 20 Mar. 1848 at the rate of $25 per month.

Dougan, Henry. Penn. Marine. He was pensioned 1 Jan. 1806 at the rate of $36 per annum. 1807. 1808. 1809. 1810. 1811. 1819. 1820. 1821. 1824. 1825. 1826. 1827. 1828. 1829. 1830. He also appeared as Henry Dugan. He served on the *Constellation*.

Dougherty, James. —. Corporal of Marines. His widow, Rebecca Dougherty, was pensioned at the rate of $5 per month from 17 May 1811. Her pension ended 31 Aug. 1842. She had her second application rejected prior to 12 Dec. 1842 since her husband did not die in the service. 1842. 1843. His rank was also given as seaman.

Douglas, Archibald.* —. Marine. His application was rejected prior to 10 Jan. 1844. He claimed that in Mar. 1840 he was admitted on the sick list on account of varicose veins and lameness of the left leg and that his lameness unfitted him for duty. The records showed that he afterwards served three years in the marine corps and was discharged on account of the expiration of his term of enlistment. There was no evidence that the disability alluded to continued to disable him. He was discharged in October 1842. He was

Naval Pensioners of the United States, 1800-1851

pensioned 21 Aug. 1846 at the rate of $3.50 per month. 1847. 1848. 1850. 1851. He served aboard the *Ohio* and was disabled by varicose veins and lameness of his left leg.

Douglas, Daniel.* —. Gunner. His widow, Elizabeth Douglas, was pensioned 17 June 1851 at the rate of $10 per month. 1851.

Douglass, Matthias. Md. Ordinary Seaman. He was pensioned 23 Apr. 1814 at the rate of $120 per annum. 1816. 1818. 1819. 1820. 1821. 1822. 1823. 1824. 1825. 1826. 1827. 1828. 1829. 1830. 1835. 1836. 1837. 1839. 1840. 1841. 1842b. 1843. 1844. 1845. 1846. 1847. 1848. 1850. 1851. He also appeared as Matthias Douglas and Mathias Duglas. He served aboard the *Chesapeake*. He was permanently disabled by a saber wound resulting in the fracture of his skull and contraction of the muscles in his right arm.

Dove, Marmaduke. —. Sailing Master. He was pensioned at the rate of $5 per month from 20 Apr. 1833. 1837. 1838. 1839. 1840. 1841. 1842. 1842b. 1843. He was attached to the Navy Yard in Washington, D.C. and was disabled by a hernia of his right side. His widow, Margaret Dove, was pensioned 3 July 1846 at the rate of $20 per month. 1847. 1848. 1850. 1851.

Downes, —. —. Sailing Master. His orphans, Shubal Downes, Deborah Downes, and Nathaniel Downes, were pensioned at the rate of $20 per month. 1837. 1842.

Downes, Albert E.* Mass. Lieutenant Commanding. He perished aboard the *Grampus*. His widow, Martha L. Downes, was 27 years old. Their children were Caroline Lithgow Downes aged about 6 years and Maria Gertrude Downes aged about 2 years. They lived in Charleston, Mass. His widow, Martha E. Downes, was pensioned 20 Mar. 1843 at the rate of $30 per month. 1844. 1845. 1846. 1847. 1848. 1851. He also appeared as Albert E. Downs.

Downes, John. —. Master Commandant. He was pensioned at the rate of $10 per month. 1837. 1838. 1839. 1840. 1841. 1842. 1842b. 1843. He served aboard the *Essex* and was disabled by a compound fracture of his left leg.

Downes, William B. N.Y. Seaman. He was pensioned 25 Apr. 1815 at the rate of $60 per annum. 1818. 1819. 1820. 1821. 1822. 1823. 1824. 1825. 1826. 1827. 1828. 1830. He served aboard the schooner *Saratoga*. He was disabled by a left inguinal hernia.

Downey, Thomas.* —. Musician. His widow, Mary A. Downey, was pensioned 29 July 1848 at the rate of $4 per month. 1850. 1851. She also appeared as Mary R. Downey.

Downing, William.* —. Seaman. He was pensioned 27 June 1850 at the rate of $3 per month. 1850. 1851. He served aboard the *Plymouth* and was disabled by a knife wound of his arm and wrist.

Doxy, Biscoe S. —. Sailing Master. His widow, Eliza Doxy, was pensioned from 20 May 1828 at the rate of $20 per month. 1835. 1836. 1837. 1839. 1840. 1841. 1842. 1842b. 1846. She was pensioned again 1 Sep. 1847. 1848. 1850. 1851. She also appeared as Eliza Doxey.

Drake, —. N.Y. Marine Officer. Mary Ann Drake was pensioned on his service as a privateer at the rate of $60 per annum. 1815. 1816. 1817. 1818. 1819. 1820 increased to $120. 1821. 1822. 1823. 1824.

Drew, John.* —. Sailing Master. He was pensioned at the rate of $20 per month. His widow, Sarah Drew, was pensioned from 19 Apr. 1823 at the same rate. 1837. 1839. 1840. 1841.

Naval Pensioners of the United States, 1800-1851

1842. 1842b. She was pensioned again 1 Sep. 1847 at the rate of $20 per month. 1848. 1850. 1851.

Drinkwater, Samuel. Me. Pilot. He was pensioned from 1 Jan. 1825 at the rate of $240 per annum. He served on the *Enterprise*. 1829. 1830. 1835. 1836. He was disabled with deafness.

Drury, John Temple. R.I. —. He perished aboard the *Epervier* 1 Sep. 1815. He was born in Bristol, R.I. on 5 Mar. 1790. His father was Dr. John Drury of Marblehead. John Temple Drury and his brother, Austin Drury, were baptized 2 May 1790 by the Rev. Mr. Badger at St. Michael's Church. His father was paid $240 on 17 June 1817.

Dubois, John L.* —. Seaman. He was pensioned 22 May 1834 at the rate of $4 per month. 1835. 1836. 1837. His widow, Arabella Dubois, was pensioned from 30 Aug. 1837 at the rate of $6 per month. 1839. 1840. 1841. 1842. 1842b. He was a petty officer on the *Potomac* and was disabled by a wound of his left wrist.

Duffy, James. —. Seaman. He was pensioned 1 Dec. 1842 at the rate of $2.50 per month. 1845. 1846. 1847. 1848. 1850. 1851. He served aboard the Gunboat No. 148 and was disabled by an injury to his left leg.

Dumell, Joseph.* Md. Quartermaster. He was pensioned from 10 May 1845 at the rate of $3 per month. 1845. 1846. 1847. 1848. 1850. 1851. He was also listed as Joseph Durnell. He served aboard the *Macedonian* and was disabled by an inguinal hernia.

Dumenel, George. —. Gunner. He was pensioned as a privateer at the rate of $72 per annum. 1813. 1814. 1815. 1816. 1817. 1818. 1819. 1820. 1821. 1822. 1823 for $30.60. He was disabled by grape shot wound of his left hip.

Dunbar, William.* —. Seaman. He was pensioned 31 May 1840 at the rate of $4.50 per month. 1841. 1842b. 1843. 1844. 1845. 1846. 1847. 1848. 1850. 1851. He served aboard the *Peacock* and was disabled by the loss of three fingers of his right hand.

Duncan, —.* —. Passed Midshipman. His widow, Virginia Duncan, was pensioned at the rate of $12.50 per month from 3 Aug. 1836. 1837. 1839. 1840. 1841. 1842. 1842b. [He was listed as James F. Duncan in the Old Wars pension index.]

Duncan, John.* Md. Carpenter's Mate. He was pensioned 1 Oct. 1827 at the rate of $72. He was disabled at the Navy Yard in Pensacola, Florida by a contusion of his spine. 1829. 1830.

Duncan, John.* —. Landsman. He was pensioned 6 Apr. 1846 at the rate of $4 per month. 1847. 1848. 1850. 1851. He served aboard the *Brandywine* and was disabled with cataracts of both eyes.

Duncan, Matthew. N.Y. Seaman. He was pensioned at the rate of $6 per annum. 1816.

Duncan, Silas. —. Captain. He was disabled at Plattsburgh on Lake Champlain on 11 Sep. 1814 when he was struck by a cannon ball. It carried away his whole right shoulder. His shoulder blade and collar bone were fractured. He was an acting lieutenant on the *Saratoga* 3 June 1834. The wound of his right shoulder resulted in the loss of the use of his right arm.

Dundas, Augustus. Penn. Gunner. He was pensioned 1 Jan. 1812 at the rate of $120 per annum. 1816. 1818. 1819. 1820. 1821. 1822. 1823. 1824. 1825. 1826. 1827. 1828. 1829. 1830.

Naval Pensioners of the United States, 1800-1851

He served aboard the *Wasp*. He was disabled with nearly total blindness.

Dunham, James.* —. Gunner. He was pensioned 4 July 1828 at the rate of $5 per month. 1840. 1841. 1842b. 1843. 1844. 1845. 1846. 1847. 1848. 1850. 1851. He served aboard the *Dolphin* and was injured in his right hip.

Dunham, James F. —. Passed Midshipman. His widow, Virginia Dunham, was pensioned 1 Sep. 1847 at the rate of $12.50 per month. 1848. 1850. 1851.

Dunham, Silas.* Va. Seaman. He was pensioned at the rate of $72 per annum. He was pensioned 2 June 1819 at the rate of $72 per annum. 1820. 1821. 1822. 1823. 1824. 1825. 1826. 1827. 1828. 1829. 1830. He was primarily listed as Silas Durham. He served aboard the brig *Shark*. He was disabled with a rupture.

Dunlevy, Peter. N.J. Marine. He was pensioned 10 Apr. 1817 at the rate of $60 per annum. 1818. 1819. 1820. 1821. 1822. 1823. 1824. 1826. 1825. 1827. 1828. 1829. 1830. He also appeared as Peter Dunlery and Peter Dunley. He was disabled at headquarters. He was disabled by paralysis on one side and loss of speech and memory.

Dunn, John.* N.Y. Private Marine. He was pensioned 31 May 1819 at the rate of $36 per annum. 1821. 1822. 1823. 1824. 1825. 1826. 1827. 1828. 1829. 1830. 1835. 1836. 1837. 1838. 1839. 1840. 1842. 1842b. 1843. 1844. 1845. 1846. 1847. 1848. 1850. 1851. He served aboard the *John Adams*. He was disabled with an scrotal hernia.

Dunn, Richard. Mass. Seaman. He was pensioned at the rate of $72 per annum. 1816. 1818. 1819. 1820. 1821. 1822. 1824. 1825. 1826. 1827. 1828. 1829. 1830 in N.H. 1835. 1836. 1837. 1839. 1840. 1841. 1842b. 1843. 1844. 1845. 1846. 1847. 1848. 1850. 1851. He served aboard the *Constitution*. He was disabled by the loss of his leg.

Dunn, William.* —. Gunner. He was pensioned 8 Oct. 1835 at the rate of $10 per month. 1835. 1836. 1837. 1839. 1840. 1841. 1842b. 1843. 1844. 1845. 1846. 1847. 1848. 1850. 1851. He served aboard the *Grampus* and was disabled by the loss of the thumb on his left hand.

Dunot, Christopher. Penn. Seaman. He was pensioned at the rate of $60 per annum from 1812. 1812. 1813. 1814. 1815. 1816. 1817. 1818. 1819. 1820. He served aboard the privateer *Bona* and was disabled by a gun shot wound in his left shoulder resulting in the loss of use of his left arm.

Durity, Nathaniel.* —. Ordinary Seaman. He was pensioned 8 Sep. 1851 at the rate of $2.50 per month. 1851. He served aboard the schooner *Flirt* and was disabled by an injury to his left thumb resulting in the loss of the last joint.

Dwight, Joseph.* —. Sergeant of Marines. His widow, Harriet M. Dwight, was pensioned 15 May 1849 at the rate of $6.50 per month. 1851.

Dyer, —. —. Captain. His daughter, Henrietta Dyer, was pensioned at the rate of $50 per month. 1837. 1842.

Dyer, —. Mass. Carpenter. Betsey Dyer was pensioned on his privateer service at the rate of $120 per annum from 1 Jan. 1815. 1817. 1818. 1819. 1820. 1821. 1822. 1823. 1824. 1825. 1826. 1827 for $100.

Dyer, Charles.* —. Passed Midshipman. His widow, Grace A. S. Dyer, was pensioned 23 Aug. 1850 at the rate of $12.50 per month. 1851.

Naval Pensioners of the United States, 1800-1851

Dyer, Wheatley. Mass. Ordinary Seaman. He was pensioned 10 Mar. 1815 at the rate of $60 per annum. 1816. 1818. 1819. 1820. 1821. 1822. 1823. 1824. 1825. 1826. 1827. 1828. 1829. 1830. He was disabled at Portsmouth, New Hampshire Navy Yard with a fracture of his right leg and injury to his left foot and ankle.

Eakin, —. —. —. He died of yellow fever 30 Oct. 1822. His widow, Susan W. Eakin, was pensioned 11 Apr. 1825.
Earle, —. N.Y. Sail Maker. Elizabeth Earle was pensioned on his service as a privateer at the rate of $48 per annum. 1815. 1816. 1817. 1818. 1819. 1820 increased to $96. 1821. 1822. 1823. 1824. 1825. 1826. 1827. 1828. 1829. 1830. 1831. 1832. 1833. 1834.
Earle, John.* D.C. Sailing Master. He was pensioned at the rate of $240 per annum. 1816. 1818. 1819. 1820. 1821. 1822. 1823. 1824. 1825. 1826. He also appeared as John Earl.
Earnest, Frederick. Md. Seaman. He was pensioned at the rate of $72 per annum. 1816. 1818. 1819. 1820. 1821. He served aboard the Chesapeake flotilla and was disabled by the amputation of his right arm as a result of a gun shot wound.
Easterbrook, Jeremiah. Mass. Ordinary Seaman. He was pensioned at the rate of $60 per annum. 1816. 1818. 1819. He served aboard the *Lawrence* and was disabled by a gun shot wound in his knee resulting in the loss of the use of his right leg.
Eastman, Jacob.* N.Y. Cooper. He was pensioned 1 Aug. 1828 at the rate of $108 per annum. He served aboard the *Constitution.* 1829. 1830. 1835. 1836. 1837. 1838. 1842. He was disabled by the loss of the second and third joints of the little finger of his left hand.
Eaton, Daniel. N.H. Seaman. He served aboard the privateer *Grant Turk* and was disabled by the loss of his right arm above the elbow as a result of a gun shot wound. He was pensioned from 3 Apr. 1813 at the rate of $72 per annum. He died in 1816. 1820.
Eaton, David.* —. Gunner. His widow, Susan Eaton, was pensioned. 1840. 1841. 1842. 1842b. 1843. 1844. 1845. 1846. She was pensioned again 22 Feb. 1850 at the rate of $10 per month. 1848. 1850. 1851. She also appeared as Susannah Eaton.
Eckburg, Henry.* N.Y. Corporal Marines. He was pensioned at the rate of $60 per annum. 1816. 1818. 1819. 1820. 1821. 1822. 1823. He served aboard the *Hornet* and was disabled by a gun shot wound in his thigh causing a fracture of same.
Eddo, James.* —. Captain of Forecastle. He was pensioned 16 Jan. 1835 at the rate of $1.75 per month. 1839. 1840. 1841. 1842b. 1843. 1844. 1845. 1846. 1847. 1848. 1850. 1851. He served aboard the *United States* and was disabled by a fracture of his left leg.
Edes, William.* Mass. Seaman. He was pensioned 1 Aug. 1822 at the rate of $72 per annum. 1822. 1823. 1824. 1825. 1826. 1827. 1828. 1830. He served aboard the *Columbus.* He was disabled by a rupture of his left groin.
Edgar, —. Md. Surgeon. He died of yellow fever 20 June 1823. His widow, Lavinia M. Edgar, was pensioned 24 Mar. 1824 at the rate of $300 per annum. 1824. 1825. 1827. 1828.
Edgar, Henry.* —. Boatswain's Mate. He was pensioned 19 Sep. 1843 at the rate of $9.50 per month. 1843. 1844. 1845. 1846. 1847. 1848. 1850. 1851. He served aboard the

Naval Pensioners of the United States, 1800-1851

Independence and was disabled by inflamation of his eyes.

Edgell, Washington.* Md. Seaman. He was pensioned at the rate of $72 per annum. 1818. 1819. 1820. 1821. He served aboard the *President* and was disabled by a gun shot wound in his left groin.

Edmonds, Gardner.* —. Ordinary Seaman. He was pensioned 4 June 1814 at the rate of $5 per month. 1835. 1836. 1837. 1838. 1839. 1840. 1841. 1842. 1842b. 1843. 1844. 1845. 1846. 1847. 1848. 1850. 1851. He also appeared as Gardner Edwards. He served aboard the *Superior* and was disabled by a wound in his right foot.

Edson, Alvin.* —. First Lieutenant Marine Corps. He was pensioned from 6 Feb. 1832 at the rate of $7.50 per month. 1838. 1839. 1840. 1841. 1842b. 1843. He served aboard the frigate *Potomac* and was disabled by an injury to his right leg.

Edwards, —. N.H. Seaman —. Elizabeth Edwards was pensioned on his service as a privateer at the rate of $60 per annum. 1815. 1816. 1817. 1818. 1819. 1820 increase to $120. 1821. 1822. 1823. 1824. 1825. 1826. 1827. 1828. 1829. 1830. 1831. 1832. 1833. 1834. She also appeared as Eliza Edwards.

Edwards, —. —. Lieutenant Marines. His widow, Ann Edwards, was pensioned from 16 Oct. 1800 at the rate of $25 per month. 1841. 1842b.

Edwards, David S. —. Surgeon's Mate. He was pensioned from 28 June 1822 at the rate of $7.50 per month. 1838. 1839. 1840. 1841. 1842b. 1843. He served aboard the *Grampus* and was disabled by a gun shot wound in his right hand.

Edwards, George. —. 1st Class Boy. He was pensioned 21 May 1837 at the rate of $4 per month. 1839. 1840. 1841. 1842b. 1843. 1844. 1845. 1846. 1847. 1848. 1850. 1851. He served aboard the *Constellation*.

Edwards, John. Mass. Lieutenant. He was pensioned as a privateer from 6 Dec. 1812 at the rate of $108 per annum. 1812. 1813. 1814. 1815. 1816. 1817. 1818. 1819. 1820. 1821. 1822. 1823. 1824. 1825. 1826. 1827. 1828. 1829. 1830. 1831. 1832. 1833. 1834. 1835. 1836. 1837 for half a year. He was pensioned from 1 July 1837 for privateer service at the rate of $9 per month. 1837. 1838. 1844. 1845. 1846. 1847. 1850. He served aboard the *Montgomery* and was disabled by a gun shot wound of his right arm and shoulder.

Edwards, Richard G. —. Lieutenant His widow, Ann R. Edwards, was pensioned from 1 Jan. 1838 at the rate of $25 per month. 1839. 1840. 1841. 1842. 1842b. 1847. She was pensioned again 1 Sep. 1847 at the rate of $25 per month. 1850. 1851.

Edwards, Standish F.* —. Seaman. He was pensioned 11 May 1837 at the rate of $9 per month. 1839. 1840. 1841. 1842. 1843. 1844. 1845. 1846. 1847. 1848. 1850. 1851. He served aboard the *North Carolina* and was disabled by inflamation of his eyes.

Edwards, T. —. —. He was pensioned as a privateer from 1830 at the rate of $72 per annum. 1830. 1831. 1832. 1833. 1834. 1835. 1836.

Edwards, Thomas.* N.Y. Quartermaster. He was pensioned 1 Jan. 1823 at the rate of $6 per month. 1818. 1819. 1820. 1821. 1823 in Mass. 1824. 1825. 1826. 1827. 1828. 1829. 1830. 1835. 1836. 1837. 1839. 1840. 1841. 1842. 1843. 1844. 1845. 1846. 1847. 1848. 1850. 1851. He served aboard the brig *Firefly* and was disabled by a rupture of his right side.

Naval Pensioners of the United States, 1800-1851

Egbert, —. N.J. Marine. Maria Egbert was pensioned on his service as a privateer at the rate of $36 per annum. 1814. 1815. 1816. 1817. 1818. 1819 increased to $72. 1820. 1821. 1822. 1823. 1824. 1825. 1826. 1827. 1828. 1829. 1830. 1831. 1832. 1833. 1834 for $12. [He was John Egbert in the Old Wars pension index.]

Eickhoff, Henry.* —. Marine. He was pensioned 22 June 1850 at the rate of $1.75 per month. 1850. 1851. He served board the brig *Dolphin* and was disabled by an injury to his right foot.

Elam, Jesse.* Mass. Marine. He was pensioned 1 Aug. 1828 at the rate of $6 per month. 1829. 1830. 1835. 1836. 1837. 1839. 1840. 1841. 1842. 1842b. 1843. 1844. 1845. 1846. 1847. 1848. 1850. 1851. He served aboard the frigate *Java* and was disabled by a left inguinal hernia.

Elbert, Samuel. Ga. Lieutenant. He died in the service on 20 Dec. 1812. His widow, Harriet Ann Elbert, was pensioned 13 Oct. 1817 at the rate of $240 per annum. 1820. 1821. 1822. 1827. 1828. 1829. 1830. 1835. 1836. 1837. 1839. 1840. 1841. 1842. 1842b. 1845. 1846. She was pensioned again 1 Sep. 1847 at the rate of $25 per month. 1850. 1851.

Elden, —. Mass. Gunner's Mate. Patience Elden was pensioned on his service as a privateer at the rate of $48 per annum. 1815. 1816. 1817. 1818. 1819. 1820. 1821. 1822. 1823. 1824. 1825. 1826. 1827. 1828. 1829. 1830. 1831. 1832. 1833. 1834. [He was Silas Elden in the Old Wars pension index.]

Elderkin, Bela.* N.Y. Quartermaster. He was pensioned at the rate of $72 per annum. 1821. 1822. 1823. 1824. 1825. He served aboard the *Macedonian* and was disabled by a hernia. He died 13 January 1824.

Elderkin, Stephen. Penn. Seaman. He was pensioned 1 July 1819 at the rate of $72 per annum. 1820. 1821. 1822. 1823. 1824. 1825. 1826. 1827. 1828. 1829. 1830. He was disabled on the Chesapeake flotilla. He was disabled by a fracture of his left thigh and leg.

Eldridge, —.* —. Gunner. His widow, Phebe Eldridge, was pensioned from 31 Dec. 1806 at the rate of $10 per month. 1839. 1841. 1842. 1842b. [He was listed as Daniel Eldridge in the Old Wars pension index.]

Eldridge, William.* —. Seaman. His widow, Abigail Eldridge, was pensioned at the rate of $6 per month from 2 June 1831. 1837. 1839. 1840. 1841. 1842. 1842b. She was pensioned again 1 Sep. 1847 at the rate of $6 per month. 1848. 1850. 1851.

Elliott, —. Mass. Quartermaster. Mary Elliott was pensioned on his service as a privateer at the rate of $96 per annum. 1818. 1819. 1820. 1821. 1822. 1823. 1824. 1825. 1826. 1827. 1828. 1829. 1830. 1831. 1832. 1833 for $9.33.

Elliott, Elisha C.* —. Seaman. He was pensioned 23 Dec. 1848 at the rate of $6 per month. 1850. 1851. He served aboard the frigate *United States* and was disabled by an injury to his right arm.

Elliott, Francis. Penn. Ordinary Seaman. He was pensioned 1 Jan. 1820 at the rate of $72 per annum. 1820. 1821. 1822. 1823. 1824. 1825. 1826. 1827. 1828. 1829. 1830 in Md. He served aboard the *President*. He was disabled by lameness in his right leg due to a fall from a ladder.

Elliott, Francis.* —. Marine. He was pensioned 20 Apr. 1838 at the rate of $3.50 per month.

Naval Pensioners of the United States, 1800-1851

1839. 1840. 1841. 1842b. 1843. 1844. 1845. 1846. 1847. 1848. 1850. 1851. He served aboard the *Constellation* and was disabled by the loss of his right leg.

Elliott, Jesse D. —. Captain. His widow, Frances C. Elliott, was pensioned 10 Dec. 1845 at the rate of $50 month. 1846. 1847. 1848. 1850. 1851.

Ellis, Edward.* —. Fireman. He was pensioned 23 June 1848 at the rate of $6 per month. 1850. 1851. He served aboard the *Iris* and was disabled by the loss of his right arm.

Ellis, John. —. Ordinary Seaman. His application was rejected prior to 12 Dec. 1842. It did not appear from his own statement that he was ever wounded or disabled in the service.

Ellison, Francis H. —. Sailing Master. He was pensioned at the rate of $15 per month. 1837. 1838. 1839. 1840. 1841. 1842. 1842b. 1843. He was disabled by a right inguinal hernia.

Elwell, Caleb. Mass. Seaman. He served aboard the *Macedonian* and was discharged in 1799. He was disabled by the partial loss of use of his leg. He was pensioned at the rate of $154.66 2/3 per annum.

Elwell, George. Mass. Ordinary Seaman. He was being pensioned at the rate of $154.66 2/3 per annum in 1802.

Elwell, Samuel. —. Seaman. He was pensioned as a privateer from 15 July 1812 at the rate of $60 per annum. 1812. 1813. 1814. 1815. 1816. 1817. 1818. 1819. 1820. 1821. 1822. 1823. 1824. 1825. 1826. 1827. 1828. 1829. 1830. 1831. 1832. 1833. 1834. 1835. 1836. 1837 for half a year. He was pensioned from 1 July 1837 for privateer service at the rate of $5 per month. 1837. 1842. 1844. 1845. 1846. 1847. 1850. He served aboard the *Madison* and was disabled by the loss of his right arm below the elbow.

Engles, Thomas.* Va. Seaman. He was pensioned 10 June 1823 at the rate of $48 per annum. 1824. 1825. 1826. 1827. 1828. 1829. 1830. He also appeared as Thomas Englis. He served aboard the brig *Spark*. He was disabled by a rupture. His rank was also given as boy.

English, —. —. —. Susannah English was pensioned on his service as a privateer at the rate of $60 per annum. 1812. 1813. 1814. 1815. 1816. 1817. 1818 for $56.20.

English, Thomas.* —. Ordinary Seaman. He was pensioned 14 May 1832 at the rate of $5 per month. 1835. 1836. 1837. 1839. 1840. 1841. 1842b. 1843. 1844. 1845. 1846. 1847. 1848. 1850. 1851. He served aboard the *Ontario* and was disabled by the loss of the use of three fingers on his left hand.

Enos, Abner.* Ky. Master's Mate. He was pensioned 4 June 1830 at the rate of $6 per month. 1830. 1835. 1836. 1837. 1839. 1840. 1841. 1842b. 1843. 1844. 1845. 1846. 1847. 1848. 1850. 1851. He served aboard the *Tigress*. He was disabled by a bayonet wound of his breast and a cut on his right hand.

Erskine, —. Mass. Gunner. Huldah Erskine was pensioned on his service as a privateer at the rate of $120 per annum from 1 Nov. 1812. 1817. 1818. 1819. 1820. 1821. 1822. 1823. 1824. 1825. 1826. 1827 for $100.

Eshum, —. Penn. Seaman. His widow, Sarah Eshum, received $72 in 1822. 1823. 1826.

Evans, —. —. —. His orphans, Elisha E. Evans and Albert F. Evans, were pensioned. 1837. 1842.

Evans, —.* —. Captain. His widow, Jane Evans, was pensioned from 30 June 1834 at the rate of

Naval Pensioners of the United States, 1800-1851

$50 per month. 1835. 1836. 1837. 1839. 1840. 1841. 1842. [He was Samuel Evans in the Old Wars pension index.]

Evans, —. Mass. Seaman. His widow, Susan Evans, was pensioned on his service as a privateer at the rate of $36 per annum from 11Sep. 1812.

Evans, Abner. —. Master's Mate. He was pensioned from 4 Jan. 1830 at the rate of $36 per annum. 1835.

Evans, Ebenezer. Mass. Seaman. He was pensioned 2 Mar. 1815 at the rate of $72 per annum. 1816. 1818. 1819. 1820. 1821. 1822. 1823. 1824. 1825. 1826. 1827. 1828. 1829. 1830. 1835. 1836. 1837. 1839. 1840. 1841. 1842b. 1843. 1844. 1845. 1846. 1847. 1848. 1850. 1851. He was disabled on the Chesapeake flotilla and lost his right arm.

Evans, George. —. Ordinary Seaman. He was pensioned 18 Dec. 1848 at the rate of $2.50 per month. He was colored. 1850. He served aboard the *Water Witch* and was disabled by the loss of his right thumb.

Evans, James.* —. Boatswain. His widow, Dorothy M. Evans, was pensioned 30 June 1834 and 1 Sep. 1847 at the rate of $10 per month. 1835. 1836. 1837. 1839. 1840. 1841. 1842. 1842b. 1845. 1846. 1848. 1850. 1851.

Evans, William. Penn. Quartermaster. He was pensioned 29 Mar. 1817 at the rate of $72 per annum. 1818. 1819. 1820. 1821. 1822. 1823. 1824. 1825. 1826. 1827. 1828. 1829. 1830. He served aboard the frigate *Java*. He was disabled with a hernia.

Evans, William. D.C. Marine. He was pensioned 1 May 1827 at the rate of $3 per month. 1830. 1835. 1836. 1837. 1839. 1840. 1841. 1842b. 1843. 1844. 1845. 1846. 1847. 1848. 1850. 1851. He served aboard the *United States*.

Evans, William.* —. Officer's Cook. He was pensioned 10 Dec. 1847 at the rate of $7.50 per month. 1848. 1850. 1851. He served aboard the *Spitfire* and was disabled by gun shot wounds in both thighs.

Everett, James.* —. Chaplain. His widow, Hannah Everett, was pensioned at the rate of $20 per month from 22 Apr. 1837. 1837. 1839. 1840. 1841. 1842. 1842b. 1846. She was pensioned again 1 Sep.1847 at the rate of $20 per month. 1848. 1850. 1851.

Ewell, Asa.* Mass. Ordinary Seaman. He was pensioned 9 Feb. 1816 at the rate of $60 per annum. 1818. 1819. 1820. 1821. 1822. 1823. 1824. 1825. 1826. 1827. 1828. 1829. 1830. He was disabled on the Chesapeake flotilla. He served aboard the *Ontario* and was disabled by paralysis in his right leg. He also appeared as Asa Elwell.

Ewing, Thomas. —. Seaman. His application was rejected prior to 30 Dec. 1845. He sought a pension for a wound alleged to have been received during the late war. There was no record of such. A disability of more than twenty-five years' standing had to be proved by record evidence.

Fallerhee, John.* N.Y. Landsman. He was pensioned 1 Aug. 1827 at the rate of $4 per month. 1829. 1830. 1835. 1836. 1837. 1839. 1840. 1841. 1842b. 1843. 1844. 1845. 1846. 1847. 1848. 1850. 1851. He served aboard the *Cyane*. He also appeared as John Fallabee and

Naval Pensioners of the United States, 1800-1851

John Fallakee. He was disabled with a scrotal hernia of his left side.

Falvey, John.* —. —. He was pensioned 29 Aug. 1842 at the rate of $3 per month. 1842b. 1843. 1844. 1845. 1846. 1847. 1848. 1850. 1851. He also appeared as John Falvay. He served aboard the *Potomac* and was disabled by a fracture of his right leg.

Farman, Jacob. Penn. Seaman. He was pensioned at the rate of $60 per annum in 1807. 1808. 1809. 1810. 1811. He served aboard the frigate *Philadelphia* and was disabled by an injury to his right foot.

Farragut, James.* —. Seaman. His application was rejected between Mar. 1840 and 1 Jan. 1842. He claimed that he lost the sight of an eye while in the performance of his duty. He produced no proof whatsoever. He was later pensioned 8 Jan. 1846 at the rate of $3.75 per month. 1846. 1847. 1848. 1850. 1851. He served aboard the *Experiment* and was disabled by the loss of his left eye.

Farrar, William. —. Quartermaster. He was pensioned 21 Apr. 1834 at the rate of $6 per month. 1835. 1836. 1837. 1839. 1840. He served aboard the frigate *Congress* and was disabled by injuries to his left leg, right arm, and head.

Farrell, Nicholas F. N.Y. Marine. He was pensioned 10 May 1830 at the rate of $3 per month. 1830. 1835. 1836. 1837. 1838. 1839. 1840. 1841. 1842. 1842b. 1843. 1844. 1845. 1846. 1847. 1848. 1850. 1851. He also appeared as Nicholas T. Farrell and Nicholas T. Furrel. He was disabled aboard the *Fulton* receiving ship and lost the use of his right arm.

Farrell, William.* N.Y. Seaman. He was pensioned 4 June 1829 at the rate of $6 per month. 1829. 1830. 1835. 1836. 1837. 1839. 1840. 1841. 1842b. 1843. 1844. 1845. 1846. 1847. 1848. 1850. 1851. He was disabled aboard the *Java* in the Mediterranean. He was disabled by a fracture of his right clavicle.

Farrow, Joel.* —. Quartermaster. He was pensioned 6 June 1839 at the rate of $4.50 per month. 1851. He served aboard the *Constitution* and was disabled with an hernia.

Fatio, L. C. F.* —. Midshipman. He was pensioned 25 Mar. 1825 at the rate of $2.37 ½ per month. 1842b. 1843. 1844. 1845. 1846. 1847. 1848. 1850. 1851. He served aboard the *Seagull* and was disabled by a wound in his left hand. He also appeared as L. C. F. Flatio.

Feers, —.* Mass. Seaman. Betsey Feers was pensioned on his service as a privateer at the rate of $36 per annum. 1815. 1816. 1817. 1818. 1819. 1820. 1821. 1822. 1823. 1824. 1825. 1826. 1827. 1828. 1829. She also appeared as Betsey Fears. [He was rt Fears in the Old Wars pension index.]

Fellows, Jonathan. Mass. Boatswain's Yeoman. He was pensioned 28 Aug. 1815 at the rate of $108 per annum. 1816. 1818. 1819. 1820 increased to $72 per annum. 1821. 1822. 1823. 1824. 1825. 1826. 1827. 1828. 1829. 1830. He served aboard the ship *Hornet*. He was disabled by a gun shot wound of his jaw.

Felson, Henry Alexander.* —. Officer's Steward. He was pensioned 15 Oct. 1850 at the rate of $9 per month. 1850. 1851. He served aboard the *Warren* and was disabled with a double hernia.

Felt, —. —. Seaman. His widow, Rachel Felt, was pensioned from 14 July 1815 at the rate of $6 per month. 1840. 1841. 1842.

Fenimore, Thomas E. Penn. Midshipman. He perished aboard the *Epervier* 1 Sep. 1815. His

Naval Pensioners of the United States, 1800-1851

father was Samuel Fenimore of Philadelphia. The deceased was a minor and had been brought up as a Quaker. His father was paid $114 on 5 May 1817.
Fennimore, —. —. —. Elizabeth M. Fennimore was pensioned on his service. 1842.
Fenno, John.* —. Seaman. He was pensioned 20 Sep. 1850 at the rate of $6 per month. 1850. 1851. He served aboard the *Flirt* and was disabled by the loss of his forefinger on the right hand.
Feran, John. Penn. Seaman. He perished aboard the *Epervier*. He was born 11 Nov. 1792 and was baptized 3 Dec. 1792 at St. Mary's Church in Philadelphia, the son of Thomas and Ann Ferrin. His mother, Ann Ferrin, was paid $72 on 5 June 1817.
Ferguson, —. —. Seaman. His widow, Elizabeth Ferguson, was pensioned at the rate of $6 per month. 1837. 1839. 1840. 1841. 1842. 1842b.
Ferguson, James.* —. Sailing Master. He was pensioned from 19 Feb. 1827 at the rate of $10 per month. 1839. 1840. 1841. 1842b. 1843. He also appeared as James Furguson. He served aboard the *Cyane* and was disabled with an injury to his knee.
Fernall, Tobias. N.H. Seaman. He served aboard the *Constitution* and was slain 24 Feb. 1815. His widow, Abigail C. Fernall, was pensioned 1 July 1816 at the rate of $6 per month. 1818. 1819. 1820. 1821. 1822. 1823. 1825. 1827. 1828. 1829. 1830. 1835. 1836. 1837. 1839. 1840. 1841. 1842b. She also appeared as Abigail C. Fernald.
Ferry, Daniel. N.Y. Quarter Gunner. He perished aboard the *Epervier* 1 Sep. 1815. He married sometime in 1796 Catherine ---- in Sligo, Ireland. Rev. P. Burke, a Roman Catholic priest, performed the marriage. They were the parents of nine children of whom Michael Ferry, Evert [?] Ferry, Mary Ferry, and Samuel Ferry were still living. Matthew Nevin knew they were married in Ireland. Catherine Ferry of New York City was paid $108 on 19 Mar. 1821.
Field, Edward. Conn. Surgeon's Mate. He was pensioned 15 Dec. 1813 at the rate of $180 per annum in 1802. 1803. 1804. 1805. 1807. 1808. 1809. 1810. 1811. 1816. 1818. 1819. 1820. 1821. 1822. 1823. 1824. 1825. 1826. 1827. 1828. 1829. 1830. 1835. 1836. 1837. 1839. 1840. He served aboard the *Congress*. He was disabled with a dislocation of the bones of his right forearm and a rupture of the principal tendons of same.
Fields, Bennet. N.Y. Armorer. He was pensioned at the rate of $108 per annum. 1816. 1818. 1819. 1820. 1821. 1822. 1823. 1824. 1825. 1826. 1827. 1828. He served aboard the *Essex* and was disabled by the loss of his left leg. He died 14 June 1827.
Fields, George.* —. Gunner's Mate. He was pensioned 28 Jan. 1841 at the rate of $4.75 per month. 1842b. 1843. 1844. 1845. 1846. 1847. 1848. 1850. 1851. He served aboard the *Brandywine* and was disabled by the loss of sight of his left eye and injury to his right hip joint.
Finn, Augustus. —. Landsman. He was pensioned 31 May 1845 at the rate of $4 per month. 1846. 1847. 1848. 1850. 1851. He also appeared as Augustus Fenn. He served aboard the *Ohio* and was disabled by a lumbar abscess and injury to his right thigh. He died 22 July 1869.
Finny, Robert.* —. Ordinary Seaman. He was pensioned 21 Oct. 1844 at the rate of $3.75 per month. 1844. 1845. 1846. 1847. 1848. 1850. 1851. He also appeared as Robert Finney.

Naval Pensioners of the United States, 1800-1851

He served aboard the *Erie* and was disabled by a fracture of his left leg.

Fish, —. N.Y. Seaman. Mary Fish was pensioned on his service as a privateer at the rate of $96 per annum from 10 Apr. 1813. 1815. 1816. 1817. 1818. 1819. 1820. 1821. 1822. 1823. 1824. 1825. 1826. 1827. 1828. 1829. 1830. 1831. 1832. 1833 for $26.40.

Fishburn, John.* —. Quartermaster. His widow, Maria Fishburn, was pensioned 8 Sep. 1846 at the rate of $8 per month. 1847. 1848. 1850. 1851. He also appeared as John Fishbourne.

Fisher, —. —. Corporal Marines. His daughter, Mary Ann Fisher, was pensioned at the rate of $4.50 per month from 18 May 1829. 1837. 1839. 1840. 1841. 1842. 1842b. She also appeared as Mary Jane Fisher.

Fisher, —. N.Y. Surgeon. Christina Fisher was pensioned on his service as a privateer at the rate of $48 per annum. 1815. 1816. 1817. 1818. 1819. 1820 increased to $96. 1821. 1822. 1823. 1824. 1825. 1 826. 1827. 1828. 1829. 1830. 1831. 1832. 1833. 1834 for $53.07.

Fisher, Alfred.* —. Seaman. He was pensioned 15 May 1835 at the rate of $5 per month. 1835. 1836. 1837. 1839. 1840. 1841. 1842b. 1843. 1844. 1845. 1846. 1847. 1848. 1850. 1851. He served aboard the *Vandalia* and was disabled with an inguinal hernia.

Fisher, Pero.* Penn. Ordinary Seaman. He was pensioned 20 Feb. 1815 at the rate of $60 per annum. 1819. 1820. 1821. 1822. 1823. 1824. 1825. 1826. 1827. 1828. 1829. 1830. He served aboard the schooner *Scorpion*. He lost his right arm.

Fitt, John. Mass. Seaman. He perished aboard the *Epervier* 1 Sep. 1815. He married Rachel Smith on 7 Aug. 1804 in Salem, Mass. Rachel Fitt was paid $72 on 9 Feb. 1818. He also appeared as John Felt.

Fitzgerald, George.* —. Seaman. He was pensioned 11 Oct. 1838 at the rate of $2 per month. 1839. 1840. 1841. 1842b. 1843. 1844. 1845. 1846. 1847. 1848. 1850. 1851. He served aboard the *Java* and was disabled by a rupture of his right groin.

Fitzgerald, William.* —. Seaman. He was pensioned 31 Dec. 1836 at the rate of $6 per month. 1839. 1840. 1841. 1842b. 1843. 1844. 1845. 1846. 1847. 1848. 1850. 1851. He served aboard the *Peacock* and was disabled with palsy as a result of a fever.

Fitzgibbon, Edmund. Penn. Ordinary Seaman. He was pensioned 1 Aug. 1812 at the rate of $48 per annum. 1816. 1818. 1819. 1820. 1821. 1822. 1823. 1824. 1825. 1826. 1827. 1828. 1829. 1830. He served on Gunboat No. 69. He also appeared as Edward Fitzgibbon. He was disabled due to a fall.

Fitzpatrick, Michael.* —. Master-at-Arms. He was pensioned 4 June 1829 at the rate of $9 per month. 1836. 1837. 1838. 1839. 1840. 1841. 1842. 1842b. 1843. 1844. 1845. 1846. 1847. 1848. 1850. 1851. He served aboard the *Fulton* and was disabled by the loss of sight in his right eye and an injury to his left eye.

Fitzpatrick, Patrick.* D.C. Pilot. He was disabled 1 Jan. 1828 at the rate of $120 per annum. 1829. 1830. He served aboard the U.S. sloop *Trippe* on Lake Erie. He was disabled with deafness.

Fitzsimmons, William. N.Y. Ordinary Seaman. He was pensioned 20 May 1801 at the rate of $84 per annum. 1802. 1803. 1804. 1805. 1807. 1808. 1809. 1810. 1811. 1816. 1818. 1819. 1820. 1821. 1824. 1825. 1826. 1827. 1828. 1829. 1830. He served aboard the *New York*. He was disabled with a compound fracture of his leg and foot resulting in the

Naval Pensioners of the United States, 1800-1851

amputation of same.

Flagg, Andrew. N.H. Gunner. His daughter, Lucy Flagg, was pensioned on his service at the rate of $120 per annum. 1824. 1825. 1827. 1828. 1829. 1839. 1840. 1841. 1842b. He was lost aboard the *Wasp* 20 Apr. 1815. Her guardian was Ch. Hardy.

Flagg, William. —. Lieutenant. He was pensioned 31 Oct. 1800 at the rate of $18.75 per month. 1839. 1840. 1841. 1842b. 1843. 1847. 1848. 1850. 1851. He served aboard the *John Adams* and was disabled by a rupture of his right side. He died 12 Feb. 1844.

Flanders, H. Mass. Quartermaster. His widow, Martha Flanders, received $108 per annum in 1820. 1821. 1822. 1823. 1824. 1825. 1827. 1828. 1829. He was lost 20 Apr. 1815 aboard the *Wasp*. H. Clark was guardian.

Flann, —.* —. Seaman. His widow, Susannah Flann, was pensioned from 1 Oct. 1839 at the rate of $6 per month. 1842. 1842b. [He was listed as Michael Flann, alias Edward Hughes, in the Old Wars pension index.]

Flannigan, Thomas. N.J. Seaman. He was pensioned 1 Jan. 1825 at the rate of $72 per annum 1828. 1829. 1830 in Penn. He served aboard the *Chesapeake*. He was disabled by a wound in his left hand.

Fleming, Andrew W. —. Seaman. He was pensioned 20 Dec. 1839 at the rate of $4.50 per month. 1840. 1841. 1842b. 1843. 1844. 1845. 1846. 1847. 1848. 1850. 1851. He served aboard the *Poinsett* and was disabled by a gun shot wound of his left thigh.

Fletcher, —. —. Captain. His widow, Sarah Fletcher, was pensioned at the rate of $50 per month. 1837. 1842.

Fletcher, Henry. S.C. Seaman. He was pensioned as a privateer at the rate of $48 from 3 Mar. 1814. 1815. 1816. 1817. 1818. 1819. 1820. 1821. 1822. 1823. 1824. 1825. 1826. 1827. 1828. 1829. 1830. 1831. 1832. 1833. 1834. 1835. 1836. 1837 for half a year. He was pensioned from 1 July 1837 of $4 per month. 1837. 1838. 1844. 1845. 1846. 1847. 1850. He served aboard the *Snap Dragon* and was disabled with a gun shot wound of his right thigh.

Fletcher, James. Penn. Marine. His widow, Ann Fletcher, was pensioned from 20 Jan. 1818 at the rate of $3.50 per month. 1839. 1840. 1841. She had her later application rejected prior to 23 Dec. 1848. Her claim was barred by the act of 11 Aug. 1848. She was on the 1851 list of pensioners with the date of her pension commencing 1 Sep. 1842. 1842. 1842b. 1851.

Flick, William.* —. Captain of Hold. He was pensioned 10 May 1845 at the rate of $3.75 per month. 1846. 1847. 1848. 1850. He also appeared as William Flock. He served aboard the *Macedonian* and was disabled with a right inguinal hernia.

Flinn, Philip.* —. Armorer's Mate. His widow, Johanna Flinn, was pensioned 15 Oct. 1846 at the rate of $7.50 per month. 1851. His daughter, Mary C. Flinn, was pensioned 15 May 1850 at the rate of $7.50 per month. 1850. 1851. He was also known as Patrick Flinn.

Flood, Jackson.* —. Seaman. He was pensioned 7 July 1837 at the rate of $6 per month. 1839. 1840. 1841. 1842b. 1843. 1844. 1845. 1846. 1847. 1848. 1850. 1851. He also appeared as Jack Flood. He served aboard the *Boston* and was disabled with an injury to his right hand.

Naval Pensioners of the United States, 1800-1851

Flood, William. —. Seaman. He served aboard the *Jamestown* and was disabled with an injury to his testicle. He was pensioned 8 July 1849.

Florence, —. —. —. Lydia Florence was pensioned on his service as a privateer at the rate of $24 per annum. 1813. 1814. 1815. 1816. 1817. 1818 increase to $144. 1819. 1820. 1821. 1822. 1823. 1824. 1825. 1826. 1827. 1828. 1829. 1830. 1831. 1832.

Floyd, —. N.H. Seaman. Elizabeth Floyd was pensioned on his service as a privateer at the rate of $48 per annum. 1815. 1816. 1817. 1818. 1819. 1820 increase to $60. 1821. 1822. 1823. 1824. 1825. 1826. 1827. 1828. 1829. 1830. 1831. 1832. 1833. 1834.

Floyd, William.* —. Seaman. He was pensioned 15 May 1848 at the rate of $6 per month. 1850. 1851.

Fogg, Martin B.* —. Marine. He was pensioned 6 June 1848 at the rate of $7 per month. 1848. 1850. 1851. He was disabled with the loss of his right arm.

Fogg, Warren. —. Marine. He was pensioned 1 June 1813 at the rate of $.87 ½ per month. 1841. 1842b. 1843. 1844. 1845. 1846. 1847. 1848. 1850. 1851. He served aboard the *Chesapeake* and was disabled with sword cuts on his hand and back.

Foley, Peter.* —. Marine. He was pensioned 27 June 1837 at the rate of $3.50 per month. 1837. 1838. 1839. 1840. 1841. 1842b. 1843. 1844. 1845. 1846. 1847. 1848. 1850. 1851. He served in Company B of the 2nd U.S. Mounted Marines and was disabled with a gun shot wound in his left arm.

Foot, James. Mass. Prize Master. He was pensioned as a privateer at the rate of $108 per annum from 7 Jan. 1813. 1813. 1814. 1815. 1816. 1817. 1818. 1819. 1820. 1821. 1822. 1823. 1824. 1825. 1826. 1827. 1828. 1829. 1830. 1831. 1832. 1833. 1834. 1835. 1836. 1837 for half a year. He was pensioned from 1 July 1837 at the rate of $9 per month. 1844. 1845. 1846. 1847. 1850. He served aboard the *Decatur* and was disabled by the loss of his right leg.

Foote, —. N.H. Seaman. Mary Foote was pensioned on his service as a privateer at the rate of $36 per annum. 1815. 1816. 1817. 1818. 1819. 1820 increase to $72. 1821. 1822. 1823 1824. 1825. 1826. 1827. 1828. 1829.

Ford, —. —. —. Theodosia Ford was pensioned on his service. 1842.

Ford, Daniel. Mass. Carpenter's Mate. He served aboard the *Wasp* and was lost 20 Apr. 1815. His widow, Mary Ford, was pensioned 1 Jan. 1817 at the rate of $9 per month. 1818. 1819. 1820. 1821. 1822. 1823. 1824. 1825. 1827. 1828. 1829. 1830. 1835. 1836. 1837. 1839. 1840. 1841. 1842. 1842b. 1845. 1846. She was pensioned again 1 Sep. 1847 at the rate of $9 per month. 1848. 1850. 1851.

Ford, John. N.Y. Seaman. He was pensioned 1 Apr. 1815 at the rate of $60 per annum. 1818. 1819. 1820. 1821. 1822. 1824. 1825. 1826. 1827. 1828. 1829. 1830. He was disabled at Black Rock by a wound in his thigh.

Formoso, Angello. Md. Cannonier. He was pensioned at the rate of $60 per annum in 1809. 1810. 1811. He was disabled by the loss of his left hand.

Forrest, —.* —. Sergeant Marines. His widow, Mary Forrest, was pensioned from 30 June 1834 at the rate of $5 per month. 1835. 1836. 1837. 1839. 1840. 1841. 1842. 1842b. [He was listed as Alexander Forrest in the Old Wars pension index.]

Naval Pensioners of the United States, 1800-1851

Forrest, Andrew.* —. Sergeant of Marines. His widow, Ann H. Forrest, was pensioned 18 Feb. 1849 at the rate of $8 per month. 1845. 1846. 1847. 1848. 1850. 1851.

Forrest, Dulaney. —. Lieutenant. His widow, Mary P. Forrest, was pensioned from 1 Oct. 1825 at the rate of $20 per month. 1835. 1836. 1837. 1839. 1840. 1841. 1842. 1842b. 1845. 1846. She was again pensioned Sep. 1847 at the rate of $25 per month. 1848. 1850. 1851. She also appeared as Mary T. Forrest.

Forsith, Robert. N.H. Marine. He was pensioned from 8 May 1799 at the rate of $5 per month. 1803. 1804. 1805. 1807. 1808. 1809. 1810. 1811. 1816. 1818. 1819. 1820. 1821. 1822. 1823. 1824. 1825. 1826. 1827. 1828. 1829. 1830. 1835. 1836. 1837. 1839. 1840. 1841. 1842b. 1843. 1844. 1845. 1846. 1847. 1848. 1850. 1851. He also appeared as Robert Forsyth and Robert Forsaith. He served aboard the schooner *Portsmouth*. He was disabled with a rupture.

Fort, James. —. Prize-master. He was pensioned as a privateer from 17 Jan. 1813 at the rate of $9 per month. 1837.

Fortin, William.* —. Steward. His widow, Eliza M. Fortin, was pensioned from 28 Jan. 1833 at the rate of $9 per month. 1839. 1840. 1841. 1842. 1842b. 1846. She was pensioned again 1 Sep. 1847 at the rate of $9 per month. 1848. 1850. 1851.

Fossett, James.* —. Ordinary Seaman. His widow, Susan Fossett, was pensioned from 2 Mar. 1842 at the rate of $5 per month. When she became Susan Wilkinson, wife of John Wilkinson, her pension ended on 3 Sep. 1843. 1843. 1845.

Foster, —. —. —. Mary Foster was pensioned on his service as a privateer at the rate of $48 per annum. 1812. 1813. 1814. 1815. 1816. 1817 increase to $96. 1818. 1819. 1820. 1821. 1822. 1823. 1824. 1825. 1826. 1827. 1828. 1829. 1830. 1831. 1832 for $64.

Foster, —. —. Gunner. His widow, Catharine Foster, was pensioned at the rate of $10 per month. 1837. 1842.

Foster, James.* —. Passed Midshipman. His widow, Delia H. Foster, was pensioned 11 Nov. 1847 at the rate of $12.50 per month. 1851. His daughter, Elenor Francis Foster, was pensioned 16 Sep. 1849 at the rate of $12.50 per month. 1850. 1851.

Fowler, —. —. Musician Marines. His daughter, Elizabeth Fowler, was pensioned at the rate of $4 per month. 1837. 1842.

Fowler, Ezekiel. —. Quartermaster. He was pensioned 29 Jan. 1847 at the rate of $8 per month. 1847. 1848. 1850. 1851. He served aboard the *Lawrence* and was disabled with a hernia.

Fowler, Patrick. Penn. Marine. He was pensioned at the rate of $30 per annum in 1802. 1803. 1804. 1805. 1807. 1808. 1809. 1810. 1811. He served aboard the frigate *United States* and was disabled by the fracture of his collar bone and partial use of his right arm.

Fox, James.* —. Ordinary Seaman. He was pensioned 6 May 1850 at the rate of $1.66 2/3 per month. 1850. 1851. He served aboard the *Ohio* and was disabled by the fracture of his arm.

Frame, Edward. Md. Private Marine. He was pensioned at the rate of $36 per annum. 1816. 1818. 1819. 1820. 1821. 1822. 1823. He was disabled with paralysis of his right side.

Francis, Edward.* —. Officer's Cook. He was pensioned 15 Oct. 1846 at the rate of $7.50 per month. 1847. 1848. 1850. 1851. He served aboard the *Bainbridge* and was disabled by a

Naval Pensioners of the United States, 1800-1851

gun shot wound and amputation of the index and middle fingers of his right hand.

Francis, Louis.* —. Ordinary Seaman. He was pensioned 14 July 1846 at the rate of $3.75 per month. 1846. 1847. 1848. 1850. 1851. He also appeared as Lewis Francis. He served aboard the *North Carolina* and was disabled with inflamation of his eyes.

Francisco, John. N.Y. Private Marines. He was pensioned 10 Nov. 1813 at the rate of $36 per annum. 1816. 1818. 1819. 1820. 1821. 1822. 1823. 1824. 1825. 1826. 1827. 1828. 1829. 1830. He served aboard the *United States*. He lost the use of his right arm.

Franklin, —. —. —. E. Franklin was pensioned on his service as a privateer at the rate of $36 per annum. 1812. 1813. 1814. 1815. 1816 for $8.

Franklin, Benjamin. —. Seaman. His application was rejected between Mar. 1840 and 1 Jan. 1842. He claimed to have been wounded in 1801 but did not produce testimony of any commissioned officer in support of his declaration. There was no official list showing that he was disabled. He was later pensioned under the act of 1 June 1842 at the rate of $6 per month. 1842b. 1843. 1844. 1845. 1846. 1847. 1848. 1850. 1851. He served aboard the *President* and was disabled by an injury to his right foot.

Franks, Henry.* D.C. Sergeant of Marines. His children, Elizabeth Ann Franks and Henry N. Franks, were pensioned from 27 Oct. 1840 at the rate of $6.50 per month. 1841. 1842. 1842b. They had their application rejected prior to 23 Dec. 1848. His widow, Emily Franks, was pensioned from 16 Nov. 1839 at the rate of $6.50 per month. 1840. 1842. The children were barred under the act of 11 Aug. 1848.

Frasier, David H. —. Surgeon's Mate. His widow, Eliza J. Ames, was pensioned at the rate of $15 per month. 1846.

Frazer, Daniel. Md. Quartermaster. He was pensioned at the rate of $108 per annum in 1805. 1807. 1808. 1809. 1810. 1811. He served aboard the *Enterprise* and was disabled with wounds of his right hand, right wrist, and the third finger of his hand. He also appeared as Daniel Frazier. His true identity was James North.

Frazier, James.* —. Seaman. He was pensioned 9 Mar. 1844 at the rate of $6 per month. 1844. 1845. 1846. 1847. 1848. 1850. 1851. He served aboard the *Decatur* and was disabled in a fall damaging his left testicle.

Frederick, —. —. —. Ruth Frederick was pensioned on his service as a privateer at the rate of $6 per month from 1 Jan. 1815.

Freelow, Thomas W.* —. Commander. His widow, Lydia P. Freelow, was pensioned 16 May 1847 at the rate of $30 per month. 1848. 1850. 1851. He also appeared as Thomas W. Freelon.

Freeman, John. —. Seaman. He served aboard the *Alert* and was disabled with rheumatism. He was pensioned 14 May 1818.

Freeman, Thomas. D.C. Seaman. He was pensioned at the rate of $72 per annum. 1819.

Freemody, Erie.* —. Ordinary Seaman. His widow, Catharine Freemody, was pensioned form 20 Jan. 1836 at the rate of $5 per month. 1836. 1837. 1839. 1840. 1841. 1842. 1842b. 1845. 1846. She was pensioned again 1 Sep. 1847 at the rate of $5 per month. 1848. 1850. 1851. He also appeared as Elie Freemody.

French, Moses.* —. Seaman. He was pensioned 14 Apr. 1834 at the rate of $6 per month. 1835.

Naval Pensioners of the United States, 1800-1851

1836. 1837. 1839. 1840. 1841. 1842b. 1843. 1844. 1845. 1846. 1847. 1848. 1850. 1851. He served aboard the *Enterprise* and lost his right hand.

Frost, —. N.H. Steward. Sarah Frost was pensioned on his service as a privateer at the rate of $36 per annum. 1815. 1816. 1817. 1818. 1819. 1820 increase to $72. 1821. 1822. 1823. 1824. 1825. 1826. 1827. 1828. 1829. 1830. 1831. 1832. 1833.

Fry, Henry. —. Purser. He was pensioned 1 Jan. 1838 at the rate of $20 per month. 1842b. 1843. 1844. 1845. 1846. 1847. 1848. 1850. 1851. He served aboard the *Madison* and was disabled by an injury due to a fall on the ice.

Fryer, John. Penn. Seaman. He was pensioned 25 Nov. 1815 at the rate of $72 per annum. 1819. 1820. 1821. 1822. 1823. 1824. 1825. 1826. 1827. 1828. 1829. 1830. 1835. 1836. 1837. He also appeared as John Freyer and John Fryee. He served aboard the *Guerriere*. He was disabled by a splinter wound of his right hip.

Full, James. Del. Sergeant Marines. He was pensioned at the rate of $60 per annum. 1827. 1828.

Fuller, Daniel. Md. Ordinary Seaman. He was pensioned 11 Oct. 1800 at the rate of $84 per annum in 1802. 1803. 1804. 1805. 1807. 1808. 1809. 1810. 1811. 1816. 1818. 1819. 1820. 1821. 1822. 1824. 1825. 1826. 1827. 1828. 1829. 1830. He also appeared as Daniel Fullen. He served aboard the *Experiment*. He was disabled by a gun shot wound of his arm and side.

Fuller, Franklin.* —. Music Boy Marines. He was pensioned 5 Jan. 1850 at the rate of $2 per month. 1850. 1851. He was disabled by the loss of his right eye and impaired vision of his left eye.

Fury, —. N.Y. Steward. He was lost in the *Epervier* on 1 Sep. 1815. His widow, Catherine Fury, received $108 per annum in 1822. 1823. 1824. 1825. 1827. 1828. Louis Wilcox was guardian.

Gabriel, Israel. N.Y. Seaman. He was pensioned as a privateer at the rate of $60 per annum from 4 July 1814. 1814. 1815. 1816. 1817. 1818. 1819. 1820. 1821. 1822. 1823 for $53. He served aboard the *James Monroe* and was disabled by the loss of his right arm.

Gadsden, Christopher. —. Master Commandant. His widow, Mary S. Gadsden, was pensioned from 28 Aug. 1812 at the rate of $30 per month. 1839. 1840. 1841. 1842. 1842b. She was pensioned again 1 Sep. 1847 at the rate of $30 per month. 1850. 1851.

Gale, Anthony.* —. Lieutenant Colonel Marines. He was pensioned 5 Jan. 1835 at the rate of $15 per month. 1835. 1836. 1837. 1839. 1840. 1841. 1842b. 1843. His pension was increased to $25 per month effective 1 July 1838. He was pensioned for long and faithful service. He was not disabled.

Gale, Henry. —. Quarter Gunner. He was pensioned 24 Sep. 1847 at the rate of $1.87 ½ per month. 1847. 1848. 1850. 1851. He served aboard the *Savannah* and was disabled by a fracture of the neck of his right femur.

Gallager, George. Md. Ordinary Seaman. He was pensioned 2 Mar. 1815 at the rate of $60 per annum. 1816. 1818. 1819. 1820. 1821. 1822. 1823. 1824. 1825. 1826. 1827. 1828. 1829.

1830. He served aboard the Chesapeake flotilla. He also appeared as George Gallagher. He lost his right leg.

Gallagher, John. —. Captain. His widow, Catherine H. Gallagher, was pensioned 1 Nov. 1847 at the rate of $50 per month. 1850. 1851.

Gallon, —.* —. Seaman. His widow, Mary Gallon, was pensioned at the rate of $6 per month from 28 Apr. 1825. 1837. 1839. 1840. 1841. 1842. 1842b. [He was listed as James Gallon in the Old Wars pension index.]

Gamage, Joshua, Jr. —. Seaman. He was pensioned as a privateer at the rate of $36 per annum. 1825. 1826. 1827. 1828. 1829. 1830. 1831. 1832. 1833. 1834. 1835. 1836. 1837 for $18. He was pensioned from 1 July 1837 rate of $3 per month. 1837. 1844. 1845. 1846. 1847. 1848. 1850. He served aboard the *Bristol,* was disabled by the loss of the little finger of his left hand and the third finger was rendered useless.

Gamble, John M.* —. Major Marines. His widow, Hannah L. Gamble, was pensioned from 11 Sep. 1836 at the rate of $25 per month. 1837. 1839. 1840. 1841. 1842. 1842b. 1845. 1846. She was pensioned again1 Sep. 1847 at the rate of $25 per month. 1850. 1851.

Gamble, Francis B. D.C. Lieutenant. He served aboard the *Decoy* and died of yellow fever on 30 [or 17 Sep.] June 1824. His widow, Frances W. C. Gamble, was pensioned 23 Nov. 1825. 1829. 1830.

Gansewoort, Hun. —. —. He perished aboard the *Grampus.* His brother was John M. Ganswoort who was of Cuylerville, Livingston Co., N.Y. on 29 July 1844.

Ganzler, George G. —. Apprentice. He perished aboard the *Grampus.* His father was George Ganzler of Boston, Mass. on 31 Oct. 1844. His father, a widower, had married the widow Holbrook who had a daughter, Sarah Holbrook, by her first husband. George Ganzler, Sr. had no children by his second wife who was also deceased. Sarah Holbrook was married but there was no consanguinity between her and the deceased even though their parents reared the two children as siblings. Her application was rejected.

Gardner, —. N.Y. Gunner. Sarah Gardner was pensioned on his service as a privateer at the rate of $120 per annum from 20 July 1813. 1818. 1819. 1820. 1821. 1822. 1823. 1824. 1825. 1826. 1827. 1828 for $66.33.

Gardner, —. —. —. Esther Gardner was pensioned on his service as a privateer at the rate of $36 per annum. 1812. 1813. 1814. 1815. 1816. 1817. 1818 increase to $72. 1819. 1820. 1821. 1822. 1823. 1824. 1825. 1826. 1827. 1828 for $15.80. She also appeared as Esther Gardiner.

Gardner, Andrew.* —. Landsman. His widow, Deborah Gardner, was pensioned 19 Aug. 1847 at the rate of $4 per month. 1851.

Gardner, Daniel.* —. Ordinary Seaman. He was pensioned 28 Mar. 1814 at the rate of $2.50 per month. 1839. 1840. 1841. 1842b. 1843. 1844. 1845. 1846. 1847. 1848. 1850. 1851. He served aboard the *Essex* and was disabled by deafness.

Gardner, Francis.* —. Gunner. His widow, Ann Gardner, was pensioned from 28 Apr. 1835 at the rate of $10 per month. 1835. 1836. 1837. 1839. 1840. 1841. 1842. 1842b. 1845. 1846. She was pensioned again on 1 Sep. 1847 at the rate of $10 per month. 1848. 1850. 1851.

Naval Pensioners of the United States, 1800-1851

Gardner, Jeremiah.* Md. Ordinary Seaman. He was pensioned at the rate of $60 per annum. 1819. 1820. 1821. 1822. 1823 in Va. 1824 in Md. 1825. 1826. 1827 in D.C. 1828. 1829. 1836. 1837. 1839. 1840. 1841. 1842b. 1843. 1844. 1845. 1846. 1847. 1848. 1850. 1851. He was black. He served aboard the frigate *United States*. He also appeared as Jerry Garner, Jerry Gardner, and Jerry Gardiner. He was disabled by paralysis of his left forearm.

Gardner, John.* —. Captain of Forecastle. His widow, Harriet A. Gardner, was pensioned 25 July 1849 at the rate of $7.50 per month. 1848. 1850. 1851. She also appeared as Harriet W. Gardner.

Gardner, John M. Md. Master Commandant. He served aboard the *Norfolk* and died of exposure 1 Sep. 1815. His widow, Sophia Gardner, was pensioned 28 Aug. 1817 at the rate of $360 per annum. 1818. 1819. 1820. 1821. 1822. 1823. 1824. 1825. 1827. 1828. 1829. 1830. 1835. 1836. 1837. 1839. 1840. 1841. 1842. 1842b. 1845. 1846. She was pensioned again 1 Sep. 1847 at the rate of $30 per month. 1848. 1850. 1851.

Gardner, John U.* —. Lieutenant. His widow, Harriet W. Gardner, was pensioned 27 Nov. 1847 at the rate of $25 per month. 1851. He was also listed as John M. Gardner.

Garrett, William. Mass. Seaman. He was pensioned as a privateer from 2 Mar. 1813 at the rate of $72 per annum. 1813. 1814. 1815. 1816. 1817. 1818. 1819. 1820. 1821. 1822. 1823. 1824. 1825. 1826. 1827. 1828 in the amount of $49.60. He served aboard the *True Blooded Yankee* and lost his left leg.

Garretson, —.* —. Purser. His daughter, Mary Garretson, was pensioned from 1 July 1835 at the rate of $20 per month. 1837. 1839. 1842. [He was listed as Isaac Garretson in the Old Wars pension index.]

Garrison, —.* —. Seaman. His son, Edward Garrison, was pensioned at the rate of $6 per month from 2 Apr. 1825. 1837. 1839. 1840. 1841. 1842. 1842b. [He was listed as John Garrison in the Old Wars pension index.]

Garrison, Cornelius. Md. Seaman. He was pensioned 1 Nov. 1820 at the rate of $72 per annum. 1823. 1824. 1825. 1826. 1827. 1828. 1829. 1830. He was disabled at Dartmoor Prison with a gun shot wound of his thigh.

Gatsly, Patrick.* —. Private of Marines. He was pensioned 12 Sep. 1851 at the rate of $5.25 per month. 1851. His correct identity was Patrick Gately. He served aboard the *Raritan* and was disabled by a left inguinal hernia.

Gayle, William. —. Gunner's Mate. He perished aboard the *Grampus*. His mother was Lucy G. Gayle of Matthews Co., Va. on 31 July 1844. His sister-in-law was Lucretia T. Gayle of Brooklyn, N.Y, a widower, with a 12 year old son. Her brother-in-law had been giving her $10 of his pay per month. She was also a cousin of the deceased. She had been left a widow with two small children. The deceased had a brother who was a master's mate in the service. His only sister was Lucy Ann Harris who believed their mother was dead. She lived in Boston, Mass. and had not heard from her mother in more than nine years.

Gebhart, William.* —. Seaman. He was pensioned 14 Oct. 1844 at the rate of $6 per month. 1845. 1846. 1847. 1848. 1850. 1851. He also appeared as William Gebhardt. He served aboard the *United States* and was disabled by an injury to his spine and a compound fracture of his right leg.

Gerald, John. N.Y. Seaman. He was pensioned at the rate of $60 per annum. 1818.

Gerald, John. D.C. Seaman. He was pensioned at the rate of $60 per annum. 1818. 1819. 1820. 1821. He served aboard the *Guerriere* and was disabled by a fracture of his right arm.

German, —.* —. Lieutenant. His son, Lewis S. German, was pensioned at the rate of $25 per month. 1837. 1842. [He was listed as Lewis German in the Old Wars pension index.]

Gerome, Anthony.* —. Seaman. He was pensioned 1 Jan. 1832 at the rate of $6 per month. 1835. 1836. 1837. 1839. 1840. 1841. 1842b. 1843. 1844. 1845. 1846. 1847. 1848. 1850. 1851. He served aboard the *Vincennes* and was disabled by the dislocation of the sternal portion of his clavicle.

Geyer, John. Mass. Seaman. He was pensioned 6 Apr. 1815 at the rate of $72 per annum. 1818. 1819. 1820. 1821. 1822. 1823. 1824. 1825. 1826. 1827. 1828. 1829. 1830. 1835. 1836. 1837. 1839. 1840. 1841. 1842b. 1843. 1844. 1845. 1846. 1847. 1848. 1850. 1851. He also appeared as John Geyger and John Geyee. He was disabled in the Dartmoor Massacre. He served aboard the merchant ship *Rambler* and lost his leg. His alias was John Hayden.

Gibbon, James F.* —. Quartermaster. He was pensioned 20 Feb. 1851 at the rate of $8 per month. 1851. He served aboard the *St. Louis*. He was disabled with a severe contusion of his breast.

Gibson, —. N.Y. Seaman. Mary Gibson was pensioned on his service at the rate of $36 per annum. 1815. 1816. 1817. 1818. 1829 for $27.90.

Gibson, John. D.C. Marine. He was disabled at Bladensburg by a wound of his breast and right leg. 1829.

Gibson, William. Penn. Quartermaster. He was pensioned at the rate of $144 per annum in 1821. 1822. 1823. He served aboard the *President* and was disabled with a double inguinal hernia.

Gilbert, Thomas P. Md. Seaman. He served on a flotilla and was killed 10 June 1814. His widow, Ruth Gilbert, was pensioned at the rate of $72 per annum. 1816. 1818. 1819. 1820. 1821. 1822. 1823. 1824. 1825. 1827. 1828. 1829. 1830.

Gilbody, Richard. Md. Ordinary Seaman. He was pensioned 14 Jan. 1806 at the rate of $48 per annum in 1807. Del. in 1808. 1809. 1810. 1811. 1816. 1818 in Del. 1819. 1820. 1821. 1822. 1823. 1824. 1825. He was pensioned again 14 Jan. 1826 at the rate of $4 per month. 1827. 1828. 1829. 1830. 1836. 1839. 1840. 1841. 1842b. 1843. 1844. 1845. 1846. 1847. 1848. 1850. 1851. He served aboard the *John Adams*. He also appeared as Richard Gilboy and Richard Gillbody. He was disabled with a fracture of his thigh.

Gillen, Peter. N.Y. Seaman. He was pensioned 20 Oct. 1814 at the rate of $60 per annum. 1818. 1819. 1820. 1821. 1822. 1823. 1824. 1825. 1826. 1827. 1828. 1829. 1830. He was disabled on Gunboat No. 41. He was disabled with a right femoral hernia.

Gillen, William. Md. Seaman. He was pensioned 1 Jan. 1822 at the rate of $72 per annum. 1822. 1823 in D.C. 1824. 1825. 1826. 1827. 1828. 1829. 1830. 1831. He was pensioned 1 Jan.1832 at the rate of $6 per month. 1835. 1836. 1837. 1839. 1840. 1841. 1842. 1843. 1844. 1845. 1846. 1847. 1848. 1850. He served aboard the frigate *Philadelphia*. He also appeared as William Gillon, William Gillone, and William Gillow.

Gilligan, Patrick. N.Y. Marine. He was pensioned 5 Jan. 1830 at the rate of $36 per annum. 1830. 1835. 1836. 1837. 1838. 1839. 1840. 1841. 1842. 1842b. He served aboard the receiving ship *Fulton* and was disabled by the loss of sight in his left eye.

Gilmore, —. —. Seaman. His daughter, Caroline E. Gilmore, was pensioned at the rate of $6 per month. 1837. 1842.

Gilpatrick, William. —. Seaman. His widow, Lydia Thompson, had her application rejected between Mar. 1840 and 1 Jan. 1842. Her first husband died in 1813. In 1818 she married secondly Cornelius Thompson. Her case was not provided for by law.

Ginnon, William. —. Seaman. He was pensioned 15 Jan. 1850 at the rate of $6 per month. 1850. 1851. He served aboard the *Taney* and was disabled by the loss of his right hand. He died 27 Sep. 1880.

Gist, Spencer C.* —. Lieutenant. His widow, Angeline F. Gist, was pensioned 23 Oct. 1847 at the rate of $25 per month. 1848. 1850. 1851.

Givins, Edward.* —. Landsman. He was pensioned 6 Feb. 1849 at the rate of $2.25 per month. 1850. 1851. He served aboard the *Ohio* and was disabled with a left inguinal hernia.

Glass, —. —. Carpenter's Mate. His widow, Mary Glass, was pensioned from 1 Oct. 1837 at the rate of $9.50 per month. 1839. 1841. 1842b.

Glass, James.* —. Sergeant of Marines. He was pensioned 24 Oct. 1836 at the rate of $3.25 per month. 1839. 1840. 1841. 1842b. 1843. 1844. 1845. 1846. 1847. 1848. 1850. 1851. He was disabled by a gun shot wound of his right hip joint.

Glazier, Lewis A. —. Landsman. He was pensioned 15 Mar. 1848 at the rate of $2 per month. 1851. He served aboard the *Saratoga* and was disabled with a hernia.

Gleeson, Maurice. Md. Marine. He was pensioned at the rate of $36 per annum in 1807. 1808. 1809. 1810. 1811.

Glentworth, Horatio.* —. Surgeon. His widow, Caroline E. Glentworth, was pensioned 16 Aug. 1847 at the rate of $30 per month. 1848. 1850. 1851.

Goar, John. D.C. Carpenter Yeoman. He served aboard the *President*, was wounded, and died 8 Apr. 1815. His widow, Pinetta Goar, and heirs were pensioned 14 Nov. 1820. 1830.

Goddard, John. —. Surgeon. His widow, Grace H. Goddard, was pensioned at the rate of $25 per month from 21 Aug. 1802. It ended 31 Aug. 1842. 1843.

Goelet, James F. N. Y. Sailing Master. He was pensioned at the rate of $240 per annum in 1805. 1807. 1808. 1809. He also appeared as James F. Gorlet. He served aboard the *New York* and was disabled by a contusion of his right leg.

Gold, Richard. Penn. Seaman. He was pensioned at the rate of $72 per annum in 1808. 1809. 1810. 1811.

Golding, John A.* —. Sergeant of Marines. He was pensioned 6 Nov. 1845 at the rate of $6.50 per month. 1846. 1847. 1848. 1850. 1851. He was disabled with a fracture of his right thigh and concussion of his spine.

Goldsmith, —. Mass. Seaman. Abigail Goldsmith was pensioned on his service as a privateer at the rate of $72 per annum. 1814. 1815. 1816. 1817. 1818. 1819. 1820. 1821. 1822. 1823. 1824. 1825. 1826. 1827. 1828. 1829. 1830. 1831. 1832 for $55.

Naval Pensioners of the United States, 1800-1851

Goldthwart, John. —. Ordinary Seaman. His widow, Elizabeth Goldthwart, was pensioned 1 Sep. 1837 at the rate of $5 per month. 1837. 1839. 1840. 1841. 1842. 1842b. 1850. 1851. He also appeared as John Goldthwaite.

Gondolfo, Joseph.* —. Ward-room Steward. He was pensioned 6 May 1850 at the rate of $4.50 per month. 1850. 1851. He served aboard the *Ohio* and was disabled with a hernia in his left groin.

Good, James.* Va. Seaman. He was pensioned 1 Jan. 1829 at the rate of $12 per month. 1829. 1830. 1835. 1836. 1837. 1839. 1840. 1841. 1842b. 1843. 1844. 1845. 1846. 1847. 1848. 1850. 1851. He was blind. He served aboard the *Erie* under D. Turner.

Goodell, Chester.* —. Ordinary Seaman. He was pensioned 12 Dec. 1834 at the rate of $3 per month. 1835. 1836. 1837. 1839. 1840. 1841. 1842b. 1843. 1844. 1845. 1846. 1847. 1848. 1850. 1851. He served aboard the *Constellation* and was disabled by an injury to his right hand.

Goodrum, James. —. Lieutenant. His widow, Dynoisia Goodrum, was pensioned from 9 May 1836 at the rate of $25 per month. 1837. 1839. 1840. 1841. 1842. 1842b. She was pensioned again 1 Sep. 1847 at the rate of $25 per month. 1848. 1850. 1851.

Goodshall, William M.* Md. Seaman. He was pensioned 15 July 1825 at the rate of $6 per month. 1827. 1828. 1829. 1830. 1839. 1840. 1841. 1842b. 1843. 1844. 1845. 1846. 1847. 1848. 1850. 1851. He served aboard the *Peacock*. He also appeared as William Goodshull. He was disabled by a right inguinal hernia and injury to his right testicle.

Goodwin, Amaziah. —. Seaman. He was pensioned 1 Jan. 1840 at the rate of $6 per month. 1842b. 1843. 1844. 1845. 1846. 1847. 1848. 1850. 1851. He served aboard the letter of marque schooner *Orders in Council* and was disabled by an injury to his thigh and ankle.

Goodwin, Isaac. Mass. Seaman. He was pensioned as a privateer in 1813 at the rate of $60 per annum from 20 May 1813. 1813. 1814. 1815. 1816. 1817. 1818. 1819. 1820. 1821. 1822. 1823. 1824. 1825. 1826. 1827. 1828. 1829. 1830. 1831. 1832. 1833. 1834. 1835. 1836. 1837 for half a year. He was pensioned from 1 July 1837 at the rate of $5 per month. 1837. 1838. 1844. 1845. 1846. 1847. 1850. He served aboard the *Governor Tompkins* and was disabled by a gun shot wound and fracture of his shoulder.

Goodwin, John.* —. Seaman. His widow, Joan Goodwin, was pensioned from 29 Aug. 1837 at the rate of $6 per month. 1840. 1841. 1842. 1842b. 1845. 1846. She was pensioned again 1 Sep. 1847 at the rate of $6 per month. 1848. 1850. 1851.

Goodwin, Joseph H.* —. Seaman. He was pensioned 13 Nov. 1843 at the rate of $6 per month. 1843. 1847. 1848. 1850. 1851. He also appeared as Joshua H. Goodwin. He served aboard the *Union* and was disabled by injury to his feet, fracture of his left forearm, and the loss of his left eye.

Gordon, Alexander G.* —. Commander. His widow, Julia A. Gordon, was pensioned 11 Oct. 1849 at the rate of $30 per month. 1850. 1851.

Gordon, Benjamin. Md. Quartermaster. He was pensioned as a privateer at the rate of $36 per annum from 12 Oct. 1812. 1813. 1814. 1815. 1816. 1817. 1818. 1819. 1820. 1821. 1822. 1823. 1824. 1825. 1826. 1827 for $18. He served aboard the *Dolphin* and was disabled by the loss of his forefinger on his right hand and fracture of his right arm.

Naval Pensioners of the United States, 1800-1851

Gordon, Charles.* —. Ordinary Seaman. He was pensioned 11 May 1835 at the rate of $5 per month. 1835. 1836. 1837. 1839. 1840. 1841. 1842b. He served aboard the schooner *Experiment* and was disabled by the loss of his right hand.

Gordon, Peter.* Penn. Quarter Gunner. He was pensioned 9 June 1826 at the rate of $108 per annum. 1829. 1830. 1836. He served aboard the *North Carolina*. His widow, Susan Gordon, had her application rejected between Mar. 1840 and 1 Jan. 1842 since her husband did not die in the service.

Gore, Thomas. N.Y. Ordinary Seaman. He was pensioned 1 Jan. 1822 at the rate of $30 per annum. 1822. 1824. 1825. 1826. 1827. 1828. 1829. 1830. He served aboard the *President*. He was disabled by a wound in his leg and foot.

Goshelle, Peter. Md. Seaman. He was pensioned 15 Nov. 1819 at the rate of $120 per annum. 1821. 1822. 1823. 1824. 1825. 1826. 1827. 1828. 1829. 1830. 1836. He served aboard the *Guerriere*.

Goslin, —.* —. Marine. His widow, Jane Goslin, was pensioned at the rate of $3.50 per month from 28 Dec. 1831. 1837. 1839. 1840. 1841. 1842. 1842b. [He was listed as John Goslin in the Old Wars pension index.]

Goss, —.* —. Carpenter's Mate. His children, Louisa Goss, John A. T. Goss, and Thomas Goss, were pensioned from 6 Feb. 1842 at the rate of $9.50 per month. 1842b. His widow, Mary Goss, was on the roll in 1841. [He was listed as John Goss in the Old Wars pension index.]

Gould, John. —. —. He was pensioned. 1842.

Graham, John.* —. Lieutenant. His widow, Sarah E. Graham, was pensioned 27 June 1846 at the rate of $25 per month. 1848. 1850. 1851.

Graham, Miles.* —. —. He was pensioned 27 Sep. 1845 at the rate of $4.50 per month. 1850. 1851.

Granso, John.* —. Captain of Maintop. He was pensioned 3 Mar. 1838 at the rate of $3 per month. 1839. 1840. 1841. 1842b. 1843. 1844. 1845. 1846. 1847. 1848. 1850. 1851. He also appeared as John Grandso. He served aboard the *United States* and was disabled by an injury to his right arm.

Grant, James.* N.Y. Seaman. He was pensioned 1 July 1829 at the rate of $8 per month. 1829. 1830. 1835. 1836. 1837. 1838. 1839. 1840. 1841. 1842. 1842b. 1843. 1844. 1845. 1846. 1847. 1848. 1850. 1851. He served aboard the *Delaware*. He was disabled by partial paralysis of his left side.

Grant, John. N.H. Seaman. He was pensioned 20 May 1813 at the rate of $72 per annum . 1818. 1819. 1820. 1821. 1822. 1823. 1824. 1825. 1826. 1827. 1828. 1829. 1830. 1835. 1836. 1837. 1838. 1839. 1840. 1841. 1842. 1842b. 1843. 1844. 1845. 1846. 1847. 1848. 1851. He served aboard the *Chesapeake*. He was disabled by the loss of his right eye and partial loss of sight of his left eye as a result of ophthalmia.

Grant, John. —. Ordinary Seaman. He was pensioned 1 July 1831 at the rate of $4 per month. 1835. 1836. 1837. 1839. 1840. 1841. 1842b. 1843. 1844. 1845. 1846. 1847. 1848. 1850. 1851.

Grant, John.* —. Captain of the Top. He was pensioned 5 Oct. 1844 at the rate of $2.50 per month. 1848. 1850. 1851. He served aboard the *Warren* and was injured on his left side.

Graves, Salthiel B. Mass. Commander. He was pensioned in 1813 at the rate of $120 per annum. 1813. 1814. 1815. 1816. 1817. 1818. 1819. 1820. 1821. 1822. 1823. 1824. 1825 in the amount of $107.67.

Gray, —.* —. Boatswain. His widow, Elizabeth C. Gray, was pensioned from 15 Feb. 1836 at the rate of $10 per month. 1836. 1837. 1839. 1840. 1841. 1842b. [He was listed as Richard Gray in the Old Wars pension index.]

Gray, Elias. N.Y. Sergeant Marines. He served aboard the privateer *Kemp* and was disabled by a gun shot wound in both hands. He was pensioned from 1 July 1815 at the rate of $96 per annum. 1820.

Gray, James. —. Volunteer Landsman. His application was rejected between Mar. 1840 and 1 Jan. 1841. None of the muster-rolls showed that he was wounded or in any way disabled on board the *Lawrence* on Lake Erie in September 1813.

Grayson, Alfred. Md. Captain of Marines. He died of yellow fever 30 June 1823. His widow, Elizabeth Grayson, was pensioned 3 May 1824 at the rate of $20 per month. 1824. 1825. 1836. 1837. 1839. 1840. 1841. 1842. 1842b. 1845. 1846. She was pensioned again 1 Sep. 1847 at the rate of $20 per month. 1848. 1850. 1851. She also appeared as Eliza Grayson.

Greaves, Jacob. —. Seaman. He was pensioned from 1 Jan. 1840 at the rate of $8 per month. 1842b. 1843. 1844. He was disabled by an injury to his left leg.

Green, —. —. —. Hannah Green was pensioned on his service as a privateer at the rate of $60 per annum. 1814. 1815. 1816. 1817. 1818. 1819. 1820. 1821. 1822. 1823. 1824. 1825. 1826. 1827. 1828. 1829. 1830. 1831. 1832. 1833. 1834 for $5.

Green, —. —. —. Sarah Green was pensioned on his service as a privateer at the rate of $72 per annum. 1812. 1813. 1814. 1815. 1816. 1817 increase to $144. 1818. 1819. 1820. 1821. 1822. 1823. 1824. 1825. 1826. 1827. 1828. 1829. 1830. 1831. 1832.

Green, Elliott.* —. Carpenter. His widow, Margaret F. Green, was pensioned 14 Nov. 1834 at the rate of $10 per month. 1835. 1836. 1837. 1839. 1840. 1841. 1842. 1842b. 1845. 1846. She was pensioned again 1 Sep. 1847 at the rate of $10 per month. 1848. 1850. 1851.

Green, James.* —. Seaman. He was pensioned 23 Sep. 1847 at the rate of $6 per month. 1847. 1848. 1850. 1851. He served aboard the *Savannah*.

Green, John R. —. Purser. His widow, Ann T. Green, was pensioned at the rate of $20 per month from 24 Aug. 1812. 1837. 1839. 1840. 1841. 1842. 1842b. She was pensioned again 1 Sep. 1847 at the rate of $20 per month. 1848. 1850. 1851.

Green, Leonard. N.Y. Quartermaster. He was pensioned 10 Mar. 1816 at the rate of $108 per annum. 1818. 1819. 1820. 1821. 1822. 1823. 1824. 1825. 1826. 1828. 1829. 1830. He served aboard the *Essex*.

Green, Peter. N.Y. Seaman. He was pensioned 3 Apr. 1817 at the rate of $60 per annum. 1819. 1820. 1822. 1823. 1824. 1825. 1826. 1827. 1829. 1830. 1835. 1836. 1837. 1842. 1843. 1844. 1845. 1846. He served aboard the brig *Chippewa*.

Green, Peter. —. Seaman. He was pensioned 3 Apr. 1827 at the rate of $5 per month. 1839.

1840. 1841. 1842. 1842b. 1844. 1845. 1846. 1847. 1848. 1850. 1851.
Green, Samuel H.* Mass. Quartermaster. He was pensioned 1 Jan. 1819 at the rate of $9 per month. 1824. 1825. 1826. 1827. 1828. 1829. 1830. 1835. 1836. 1837. 1839. 1840. 1841. 1842. 1842b. 1843. 1844. 1845. 1846. 1847. 1848. 1850. 1851. He served aboard the frigate *Constitution*.
Green, William N. —. —. He was pensioned as a privateer at the rate of $60 per annum from 1 Oct. 1814. 1815. 1816. 1817. 1818. 1819. 1820. 1821. 1822. 1823. 1824. 1825. 1826. 1827.
Greener, William.* R.I. Ordinary Seaman. His widow, Elizabeth Greener, was pensioned 6 Aug. 1849 at the rate of $5 per month. 1851.
Greenleaf, Joseph. N.Y. Seaman. He was pensioned at the rate of $72 per annum. 1818. 1819. 1820. 1821. 1822. 1823. 1824. 1825.
Gregory, John. Md. Cabin Boy. He was pensioned 1 Jan. 1818 at the rate of $48 per annum. 1819. 1820. 1822. 1823. 1824. 1825. 1826. 1827. 1828. 1829. 1830. He was disabled aboard the *Essex* under Com. Preble in 1800. He was disabled by a fracture of the thigh.
Gregory, William. Penn. Marine. He was pensioned 28 May 1830 at the rate of $24 per annum. 1830. 1835. 1836. 1837. 1839. 1840. 1841. 1842b. 1843. 1844. 1845. 1846. 1847. 1848. 1850. 1851. He was disabled at Bladensburg.
Grenell, —. —. Sailing Master. His daughter, Catharine A. Grenell, was pensioned at the rate of $20 per month. 1837. 1842.
Grenell, —. N.Y. Sailing Master. His widow, Catherine Grenell, received $240 per annum. 1819. 1820. 1821. 1822.
Grenell, S. H.. N.Y. Sailing Master. His widow, Sophia Grenell, received $240 per annum. 1820. 1821. 1822. 1823. 1824. 1825. 1828. He died 25 Mar. 1813 on Lake Ontario. She also appeared as Sophia Gunnell. As Sophia Cooper she was guardian of her daughter, Sophia Grenell in 1829.
Griffin, —.* —. Ordinary Seaman. His widow, Ellen Griffin, was pensioned from 25 Apr. 1835 at the rate of $5 per month. 1842b. [He was listed as Patrick Griffin in the Old Wars pension list.]
Griffin, Israel. —. Seaman. His application was rejected between Mar. 1840 and 1 Jan. 1842. He claimed to have been wounded near Black Rock while serving under Lt. Angus in 1812. His name was not found on the list of those who were wounded at that time.
Griffin, Larkin. N.Y. Surgeon. He served aboard the *Norfolk* and died of exposure 1 Nov. 1814. His widow, Mary Griffin, was pensioned 12 Dec. 1819 at the rate of $25 per month. 1819. 1820. 1821. 1822. 1823. 1824. 1825. 1827. 1828. 1829. 1830. 1835. 1836. 1837. 1839. 1840. 1841. 1842. 1842b. 1845. 1846. She was pensioned again 1 Sep. 1847 at the rate of $30 per month. 1848. 1850. 1851.
Griffin, Michael.* —. Quartermaster. His widow, Unity Griffin, was pensioned 13 July 1850 at the rate of $8 per month. 1848. 1851. He was also listed as James Griffin.
Griffing, Stewart. N.Y. Quarter Gunner. He perished aboard the *Epervier* 1 Sep. 1815. His brothers were John Griffing aged about 41 and William Griffing aged about 35 of New

Naval Pensioners of the United States, 1800-1851

York City. They were paid $108 on 24 July 1819.

Griffith, Alberto.* —. Lieutenant. His widow, Cornelia M. Griffith, was pensioned 20 Dec. 1842 at the rate of $25 per month. 1844. 1845. 1846. 1847. 1848. 1850. 1851.

Grimke, —. —. Lieutenant. His child, M. A. Secunda Grimke, was pensioned from 30 Nov. 1825 at the rate of $25 per month. 1839. 1840. 1841. 1842. 1842b. The child also appeared as M. A. S. Grinke.

Griswold, Timothy.* —. Ordinary Seaman. His children were pensioned from 1 July 1838 at the rate of $5 per month. 1841. 1842. 1842b. His widow, Laura Griswold, was pensioned at the rate of $5 per month from 29 Mar. 1837. 1837. 1839. 1842.

Grogan, David.* —. Marine. He was pensioned 15 Mar. 1851 at the rate of $3.50 per month. 1851. He was disabled by a hydrocele of his right side.

Grooms, George. Mass. Seaman. He was pensioned at the rate of $92 per annum in 1802.

Grover, William. —. Ordinary Seaman. His widow, Olive Grover, was pensioned at the rate of $5 per month from 2 Feb. 1836. 1837. 1839. 1840. 1841. 1842. 1842b. 1845. 1846.

Grymes, —.* —. Captain Marines. His widow, Ann B. Grymes, was pensioned from 25 July 1834 at the rate of $20 per month. 1835. 1836. 1837. 1839. 1840. 1841. 1842. She also appeared as Anna B. Grimes. His son, James M. Grymes, was pensioned at the rate of $20 per month from 25 Sep. 1841. 1842b. [He was listed as Charles Grymes in the Old Wars pension index.]

Gulliver, William.* —. Marine. His widow, Rebecca Gulliver, was pensioned from 31 Jan. 1822 at the rate of $3.50 per month. 1839. 1840. 1841. 1842b. 1847. 1851.

Gunnison, William.* —. Ordinary Seaman. He was pensioned 24 Nov. 1833 at the rate of $5 per month. 1835. 1836. 1837. 1838. 1839. 1840. 1841. 1842. 1842b. 1843. 1844. 1845. 1846. 1847. 1848. 1850. 1851.

Gwinn, John. —. Captain. His widow, Caroline S. Gwinn, was pensioned 4 Sep. 1849 at the rate of $50 per month. 1850. 1851.

Haas, Charles B. —. Ordinary Seaman. He was pensioned 31 Jan. 1842 at the rate of $5 per month. 1847. 1848. 1850. 1851. He also appeared as Charles B. Hass.

Hackleton, J. Mass. Seaman. He was killed on Lake Ontario 5 Dec. 1812. His widow, Mary Hackleton, was pensioned 15 June 1820 at the rate of $6 per month. 1821. 1822. 1824. 1825. 1827. 1828. 1829. 1830. 1839. 1840. 1841. 1842b.

Hadden, John. Md. Seaman. He was pensioned 15 Aug. 1807 at the rate of $72 per annum. 1808. 1809. 1810. 1811. 1816. 1818. 1819 in N.Y. 1820. 1821. 1823. 1824. 1825. 1826. 1827. 1828. 1829. 1830. He served aboard the *Chesapeake*. He also appeared as John Haddon.

Hadding, Thomas. Penn. Quartermaster. He was killed 28 Nov. 1812 on Lake Ontario. His widow, Mary Hadding, was pensioned at the rate of $108 per annum. 1825. 1827. 1829.

Haddock, Josiah P. Md. Seaman. He was pensioned as a privateer at the rate of $48 per annum from 13 Mar. 1813. 1813. 1814. 1815. 1816. 1817. 1818. 1819. 1820. 1821. 1822. 1823.

Naval Pensioners of the United States, 1800-1851

1824. 1825.

Hagernon, Daniel. N.Y. Ordinary Seaman. He was pensioned 27 Jan. 1815 at the rate of $60 per annum. 1818. 1819. 1820. 1821. 1822. 1823. 1824. 1825. 1827. 1828. 1829. 1830. He also appeared as Daniel Hagenon and Daniel Daggernon. He served aboard the *John Adams*.

Hagerty, William. Penn. Ordinary Seaman. He was pensioned 1 Aug. 1821 at the rate of $60 per annum. 1822. 1823. 1824. 1825. 1826. 1827. 1828. 1829. 1830. He also appeared as William Haggerty. He served aboard the *Columbus*.

Hale, Roswell. Mass. Ordinary Seaman. He was pensioned 25 Dec. 1819 at the rate of $60 per annum. 1821. 1822. 1823. 1824. 1825. 1826. 1827. 1828. 1829. 1830 in New York. 1835. 1836. 1837. 1839. 1840. 1841. 1842b. 1843. 1844. 1845. 1846. 1847. 1848. 1850. 1851. He was disabled on Lake Erie.

Hall, —. —. —. Eleanor Hall was pensioned on his service as a privateer at the rate of $8 per month from 1 Jan. 1813.

Hall, —.* —. Sailmaker. His widow, Ann R. Hall, was pensioned from 30 June 1834 at the rate of $10 per month. 1835. 1836. 1837. 1839. 1840. 1841. 1842. 1842b. [He was listed as Isaac Hall in the Old Wars pension index.]

Hall, —. —. —. Martha F. Hall applied in May 1824 and was pensioned at the rate of $72 per annum.

Hall, —.* —. Seaman. His son, George Joseph Hall, was pensioned at the rate of $6 per month from 10 Dec. 1834. 1837. 1839. 1840. 1841. 1842. 1842b. [He was listed as George Hall in the Old Wars pension index.]

Hall, —. D.C. Sailing Master. His widow, Elizabeth Hall, was pensioned at the rate of $240 per annum. 1818. 1819. 1820. 1821. 1822. 1824. 1825. 1827.

Hall, John.* N.Y. Quartermaster. He was pensioned 20 Oct. 1830 at the rate of $4.50 per month. 1830. 1835. 1836. 1837. 1838. 1839. 1840. 1841. 1842. 1842b. 1843. 1844. 1845. 1846. 1847. 1848. 1850. 1851. He served aboard the *Vincennes*.

Hall, John. —. Sailmaker. His widow, Martha Hall, was pensioned 13 Feb. 1851 at the rate of $10 per month. 1851.

Halsey, James M.* —. Purser. His widow, Eliza Halsey, was pensioned from 2 Jan. 1838 at the rate of $20 per month. 1839. 1840. 1841. 1842. 1842b. 1846. She was pensioned again 1 Sep. 1847 at the rate of $20 per month. 1848. 1850. 1851.

Halton, Samuel. —. Sailmaker's Mate. He was pensioned from 3 Jan. 1845 at the rate of $4.75 per month. 1850. 1851.

Hambleton, Samuel. —. Purser. He was pensioned 30 Aug. 1834 at the rate of $20 per month. 1835. 1836. 1837. 1838. 1839. 1840. 1841. 1842. 1842b. 1843. He also appeared as Samuel Hambledon.

Hamersley, George W. —. Lieutenant. He died of yellow fever 11 Sep. 1823 at Key West. His widow, Phebe Hamersley, was pensioned from 12 Sep. 1823 at the rate of $20 per month. 1824. 1825. 1827. 1828. 1829. 1835. 1836. 1837. 1839. 1840. 1841. 1842. 1842b. 1845. 1846. She was pensioned again 1 Sep. 1847 at the rate of $25 per month. 1848. 1850. 1851. She also appeared as Phebe Hammersley and Phebe Hammerley.

Naval Pensioners of the United States, 1800-1851

Hamilton, Alexander.* —. Boatswain's Mate. He was pensioned 31 May 1838 at the rate of $7.12 ½ per month. 1839. 1840. 1841. 1842b. 1843. 1844. 1845. 1846. 1847. 1848. 1850. 1851.

Hamilton, Clayton. N.Y. Seaman. He was pensioned as a privateer at the rate of $48 per annum from 19 Sep. 1814. 1814. 1815. 1816. 1817. 1818. 1819. 1820. 1821. 1822. 1823. 1824. 1825. 1826. He also appeared as Clayton Hambleton.

Hamilton, Empson. —. Marine. He was pensioned at the rate of $72 per annum in 1812. 1812. 1813. 1814. 1815. 1816. 1817. 1818. 1819. 1820. 1821. 1822. 1823. 1824. 1825. 1826. 1827. 1828. 1829. 1830. 1831. 1832. 1833. 1834. 1835. 1836. 1837 for $36. He was pensioned from 1 Jan. 1837 for privateer service at the rate of $6 per month. 1836. 1837. 1844. 1845. 1847. 1850.

Hamilton, John.* Mass. Seaman. He was pensioned 1 May 1827 at the rate of $6 per month. 1829. 1830. 1835. 1836. 1837. 1838. 1839. 1840. 1841. 1842b. 1843. 1844. 1845. 1846. 1847. 1848. 1851. He served aboard the *United States*.

Hamilton, John.* —. Seaman. He was pensioned 5 Oct. 1836 at the rate of $6 per month. 1841. 1842b. 1843. 1844. 1845. 1846. 1847. 1848. 1850. 1850. 1851.

Hamilton, John.* —. Landsman. He was pensioned 13 Dec. 1850 at the rate of $1.33 1/3 per month. 1851.

Hamilton, William.* Penn. Seaman. He was pensioned 1 July 1829 at the rate of $6 per month. 1829. 1830. 1835. 1836. 1837. 1839. 1840. 1841. 1842b. 1843. 1844. 1845. 1846. 1847. 1848. 1850. 1851. He served aboard the *Cyane*.

Hammond, Jeduthan.* Mass. Seaman. His widow, Hannah Hammond, was pensioned at the rate of $3.50 per month from 10 Nov. 18117. 1837. 1839. 1840. 1841. 1842. 1842b. She had her application rejected prior to 23 Dec. 1848. Her claim was more than the twenty-five years' standing.

Hammond, Stephen. N.Y. Seaman. He was pensioned 27 Sep. 1816 at the rate of $72 per annum. 1818. 1819. 1820. 1821. 1822. 1823. 1824. 1825. 1826. 1827. 1828. 1829. 1830. He served aboard the *President*.

Hammonds, James D. Mass. Seaman. He was disabled 29 Dec. 1829 at the rate of $72 per annum. He served aboard the *Constitution*. 1830. 1835. 1836. 1837. 1838. 1839. 1840. 1841. 1842. He also appeared as James Hammond.

Hampson, William. —. Marine. He was pensioned 29 Aug. 1842 at the rate of $2.62 ½ per month. 1842b. 1843. 1844. 1845. 1846. 1847. 1848. 1850. 1851.

Hampton, Henry.* —. Ordinary Seaman. He was pensioned 14 June 1840 at the rate of $1.66 2/3 per month. 1840. 1841. 1842b. 1843. 1844. 1845. 1846. 1847. 1848. 1850. 1851.

Hanbury, —.* —. Sergeant Marines. His widow, Ellen Nora Hanbury, was pensioned from 4 Jan. 1825 at the rate of $8 per month. 1836. 1837. 1839. 1840. 1841. 1842. 1842b. She also appeared as Ellen Nora Harbury. [He was listed as Matthew Hansbury in the Old Wars pension index.]

Hand, —. N.Y. Prize Master. Mary Hand was pensioned on his service as a privateer at the rate of $60 per annum from 1 Jan. 1815. 1815. 1816. 1817. 1818. 1819. 1820. 1821. 1822. 1823. 1824. 1825. 1826. 1827 for $16.

Naval Pensioners of the United States, 1800-1851

Handy, Albert G.* —. Acting Master. His widow, Jane Handy, was pensioned 15 May 1847 at the rate of $20 per month. 1850. 1851.

Handy, Levin.* —. Lieutenant. His widow, Henrietta D. Handy, was pensioned from 14 Sep. 1842 at the rate of $25 per month. 1844. 1845. 1846.

Hanna, Edward.* —. Gunner. His widow, Mary Hanna, was pensioned from 17 Jan. 1837 at the rate of $10 per month. 1839. 1840. 1841. 1842. 1842b. She was pensioned again 1 Sep. 1847 at the rate of $10 per month. 1848. 1850. 1851.

Hannah, Lawrence.* —. Ordinary Seaman. He was pensioned 15 Aug. 1850 at the rate of $5 per month. 1850. 1851.

Hanscom, Uriah. Mass. Ordinary Seaman. He was pensioned from 16 Oct. 1799 at the rate of $6 per month. 1803. 1804. 1805. 1807. 1808. 1809. 1810. 1811. 1816. 1818. 1819. 1820. 1821. 1824. 1825. 1826. 1827 from Maine. 1828. 1829. 1830. 1835. 1836. 1837. 1839. 1840. 1841. 1842b. 1843. 1844. 1845. 1846. 1847. 1848. 1850. 1851. He also appeared as Uriah Hanscombs and Uriah Hanscomb. He was disabled at Portsmouth.

Hansford, James H. Va. Seaman. He was pensioned at the rate of $48 per annum in 1826.

Hanson, Andrew. Mass. Seaman. He was pensioned at the rate of $8.50 per month in 1803. 1804. 1805. Penn. in 1807. 1808. 1809. [He appeared incorrectly as Andrew Harrison in this year.] 1810. 1811.

Hardin, Charles. Va. Seaman. He perished aboard the *Epervier* on 1 Sep. 1815. He married Ann Rose 2 May 1817. She was from Norfolk, Va. and was paid $72 on 2 May 1817. Ann Hardin was pensioned at the rate of $72 per annum. 1819. 1820. 1821. 1822. 1824. 1825. 1827. 1828.

Harding, Isaac.* —. Seaman. He was pensioned 9 Mar. 1834 at the rate of $5 per month. 1835. 1836. 1837. 1839. 1840. 1841. 1842b. 1843. 1844. 1845. 1846. 1847. 1848. 1850. 1851.

Harding, Seth. N.Y. Capt. He served in the Revolutionary War. He was pensioned at the rate of $360 per annum in 1808. 1809. 1810. 1811. 1816.

Hardingbrook, William. N.Y. Seaman. He was pensioned 18 Feb. 1814 at the rate of $72 per annum. 1816. 1818. 1819. 1820. 1821. 1822. 1823. 1824. 1825. 1826. 1827. 1828. 1829. 1830. 1835. 1836. 1837. 1839. 1840. 1841. 1842b. 1843. 1844. 1845. 1846. 1847. 1848. 1850. 1851. He also appeared as William Herringbrook. He served aboard the schooner *Nonsuch*.

Hardy, Isaac. Penn. Ordinary Seaman. He was killed 10 Sep. 1813 on Lake Erie. His widow, Diana Hardy, was pensioned 28 July 1820 at the rate of $5 per month. 1821. 1822. 1823. 1824. 1825. 1827. 1829. 1830. 1835. 1836. 1837. 1839. 1840. 1841. 1842. 1842b. 1844. 1845. 1846. She was pensioned again 1 Sep. 1847 at the rate of $6 per month. 1848. 1850. 1851.

Hardy, J. L. C. —. Midshipman. He was pensioned from 31 July 1821 at the rate of $4.75 per month. 1839. 1840. 1841. 1842b. 1843.

Hardy, John Jacob. S.C. Seaman. He was pensioned 25 June 1813 at the rate of $72 per annum. 1816. 1818. 1819. 1820. 1821. 1822. 1823. 1824. 1825. 1826. 1827. 1828. 1829. 1830. 1835. 1836. 1837. 1839. 1840. 1841. 1842b. 1843. 1844. 1845. 1846. 1847. 1848. 1850. 1851. He was disabled on the Georgia flotilla. He appeared as John Jacob Harding in

Naval Pensioners of the United States, 1800-1851

1829.
Harley, James. —. Seaman. He served aboard the frigate *United States*. He was pensioned at the rate of $60 per annum. 1829.

Harraden, Nathaniel. D.C. Master Commandant. He died 20 Jan. 1818 of a natural death. His widow, Susan Harraden, was pensioned at the rate of $360 per annum. 1819. 1820. 1821. 1822. 1823. 1824. 1825. 1827. 1828. 1835. 1836. 1837. 1839. 1840. 1841. 1842. 1842b. 1845. 1846. She erroneously appeared as Sarah Harraden. As Susan Harriden, she was pensioned 1 Sep. 1847 at the rate of $30 per month. 1848. 1850. 1851. She also appeared as Susan Haraden.

Harris, —. N.Y. Cook[?]. Eliza Harris was pensioned on his service as a privateer at the rate of $48 per annum. 1816. 1817. 1818. 1819. 1820. 1821. 1822. 1823. 1824. 1825. 1826. 1827. 1828. 1829 for $16.

Harris, Elijah L.* —. Marine. He was pensioned 25 Sep. 1833 at the rate of $3 per month. 1835. 1836. 1837. 1838. 1839. 1840. 1841. 1842b. 1843. 1844. 1845. 1846. 1847. 1848. 1850. 1851.

Harris, George.* —. Seaman. He was pensioned 11 Mar. 1846 at the rate of $6 per month. 1847. 1848. 1850. 1851.

Harris, John. Va.* Quarter Gunner. He was pensioned 1 Aug. 1827 at the rate of $4 per month. He was disabled on the West India squadron. He was permanently disabled. 1829. 1830. 1835. 1836. 1837. 1839. 1840. 1841. 1842b. 1843. 1845. 1846. 1847. 1848. 1850. 1851. He also appeared as John Harvis.

Harris, Richard.* —. Marine. His application was rejected between Mar. 1840 and 1 Jan. 1842. His claims were for long service, but the law had no provision for such a case.

Harris, Thompson L.* —. Chaplain. His widow, Marianne Harris, was pensioned at the rate of $20 per month on 1 Sep. 1847. 1848. 1850. He also appeared as Thompson S. Harris.

Harris, William Stewart. —. Commander. His children, William Sneed Harris and Sarah Ann Harris, were pensioned 15 May 1848 at the rate of $30 per month. 1850. 1851.

Harrison, —. —. —. Maria Harrison was pensioned on his service. 1842.

Harrison, —.* —. Ordinary Seaman. His son, John Henry Harrison, was pensioned at the rate of $5 per month from 15 Aug. 1831. 1837. 1839. 1840. 1841. 1842. 1842b. [He was listed as John Harrison in the Old Wars pension index.]

Harrison, —.* —. Surgeon's Mate. His son, Maurice J. B. Harrison, was pensioned from 1 July 1837 at the rate of $15 per month. 1839. [He was listed as John Harrison in the Old Wars pension index.]

Harrison, Horatio N. —. Passed Midshipman. He was pensioned from 15 July 1838 at the rate of $6.50 per month. 1839. 1840. 1841. 1842b. 1843.

Harrison, J. —. —. He was pensioned as a privateer at the rate of $36 per annum. 1814. 1815. 1816. 1817. 1818. 1819. 1820. 1821 for $18.

Harrod, Benjamin.* —. Seaman. He was pensioned from 28 Oct. 1836 at the rate of $3 per month. 1839. 1840. 1841.

Hart, Benjamin F.* —. Purser. His widow, Sarah Ann Hart, was pensioned 2 Nov. 1842 at the rate of $20 per month. 1843. 1844. 1845. 1846. 1848. 1850. 1851.

Naval Pensioners of the United States, 1800-1851

Hart, Clement S. —. Purser. His widow, Sarah A. Hart, was pensioned at the rate of $20 per month 1 Sep. 1842.

Hartnett, Maurice.* —. Carpenter. His widow, Mary Ann Hartnett, was pensioned at the rate of $10 per month from 9 Sep. 1830. 1837. 1839. 1840. 1841. 1842b. 1846. She was pensioned again 1 Sep. 1847 at the rate of $10 per month. 1848. 1850. 1851. She also appeared as Mary Ann Harnett and Mary Ann Harnell.

Hartwell, William B. —. Purser. His widow, Elizabeth H. Hartwell, was pensioned 12 July 1849 at the rate of $20 per month. 1850. 1851.

Harvey, —. N.H. Boatswain. Mehitable Harvey was pensioned on his service as a privateer at the rate of $60 per annum. 1815. 1816 for $35.50.

Harvey, —. Mass. Seaman. Sally Harvey was pensioned on his service at the rate of $6 per month. 1823. 1827. 1828.

Harvey, —. —. Seaman. His daughter, Miriam S. Harvey, was pensioned at the rate of $6 per month. 1837. 1842. She also appeared as Miriam S. Hervey.

Harvey, Anson.* Va. Ordinary Seaman. He was pensioned at the rate of $60 per annum. 1816 in New York. 1818. 1819. 1821. 1822. 1823. 1824. 1825. 1826. 1827. 1828. 1829. 1830. He served aboard the *President.* He also appeared as Anson Hervey.

Harvey, Thomas. Md. Mariner. He was pensioned at the rate of $36 per annum. 1816.

Haskell, —. Mass. Sailing Master. Agnes Haskell was pensioned on his service as a privateer at the rate of $144 per annum from 1 Jan. 1815. 1815. 1816. 1817. 1818. 1819. 1820. 1821. 1822. 1823. 1824. 1825. 1826. 1827. 1828. 1829. 1830. 1831. 1832. 1833. 1834.

Hassler, Charles A.* —. Surgeon. His widow, Anna J. Hassler, was pensioned 27 Nov. 1846 at the rate of $30 per month. 1848. 1850. 1851.

Hatch, James. Mass. Quarter Gunner. He was pensioned 1 July 1814 at the rate of $108 per annum. 1816. 1818. 1819. 1820. 1821. 1822. 1824. 1825. 1826. 1827. 1828. 1829 from Maine. 1830. 1835. 1836. 1837. 1839. 1840. 1841. 1842b. 1843. 1844. 1845. 1846. 1847. 1848. 1850. 1851. He served on the *General Pike.* He also appeared as James Hatchin.

Hatch, Robert.* S.C. Pilot. He served aboard the schooner *Alligator* and was killed 29 Jan. [or 5 Feb.] 1814. His widow, Mary Rawlain Hatch, was pensioned 20 July 1814 at the rate of $20 per month. 1816. 1818. 1819. 1820. 1824. 1825. 1827. 1828. 1830. 1835. 1836. 1837. 1839. 1840. 1841. 1842. 1842b. 1845. 1846. She also appeared as Mary Roulain Hatch. She was pensioned again 1 Sep. 1847 at the rate of $20 per month. 1848. 1850. 1851.

Hathaway, Ephraim.* —. Landsman. He was pensioned 15 June 1838 at the rate of $4 per month. 1839. 1840. 1841. 1842b. 1843. 1844. 1845. 1846. 1847. 1848. 1850. 1851.

Hatton, Samuel. —. Sailmaker Mate. He was pensioned 3 Jan. 1845 at the rate of $4.75 per month. 1845. 1846. 1847. 1848.

Havre, Francis.* Va. Master-at-Arms. He was pensioned at the rate of $48 per annum. 1826. 1827. 1828. 1829. 1830. He served aboard the schooner *Porpoise.* He also appeared as Francis Harvie and Francis Hayre.

Hawkins, John. D.C. Private Marine. He was pensioned 1 July 1824 at the rate of $36 per annum. 1824. 1825. 1826. 1827. 1828. 1829. 1830.

Naval Pensioners of the United States, 1800-1851

Hawkins, Samuel V.* —. Sailmaker. His widow, Jane Hawkins, was pensioned 27 July 1849 at the rate of $10 per month. 1846. 1847. 1848. 1850. 1851.

Haycock, —. —. —. George Haycock and Joseph Haycock were pensioned on his service. 1842.

Hayne, Francis. —. Seaman. He sought an increase to his pension 14 Apr. 1826.

Haynes, —. —. Seaman. His daughter, Ann Haynes, was pensioned at the rate of $6 per month. 1837. 1842.

Hays, Charles.* —. Seaman. He was pensioned 17 July 1843 at the rate of $4.50 per month. 1844. 1845. 1846. 1847. 1848. 1850. 1851.

Hays, Michael.* —. Marine. He was pensioned 4 Aug. 1846 at the rate of $2.62 ½ per month. 1850. 1851.

Haywood, John. N.Y. Master's Mate. He was pensioned at the rate of $120 per annum in 1822. 1823. 1824. 1825. 1826. 1827. 1828. He also appeared as John Hayward.

Hazen, Benjamin. Mass. Seaman. He served aboard the *Essex* and was killed 28 Mar. 1814. His widow, Hannah Hazen, was pensioned at the rate of $72 per annum 27 Feb. 1815. 1816. 1818. 1819. 1820. 1821. 1822. 1824. 1825. 1827. 1828. 1829. 1830. 1836. 1837. 1839. 1840. 1841. 1842. 1842b. 1845. 1846. His widow was pensioned again on 1 Sep.1847 at the rate of $6 per month. 1848. 1850. 1851.

Hazle, James. N.J. Seaman. He was pensioned at the rate of $60 per annum. 1818. 1819. 1820. 1821. 1822. 1823. 1824. 1825. 1826. 1827. 1828.

Hazlett, Robert.* —. Musician Marines. He was pensioned 13 Dec. 1836 at the rate of $2 per month. 1839. 1840. 1841. 1842b. 1843. 1844. 1845. 1846. 1847. 1848. 1850. 1851.

Heartle, Isaac T. Md. Acting Sailing Master. He was pensioned 1 Apr. 1817 at the rate of $240 per annum. 1818. 1819. 1820. 1821. 1822. 1823. 1824. 1825. 1826. 1827. 1828. 1829. 1830. 1835. 1836. 1837. 1841. He also appeared as Isaac T. Heartte, Isaac Heartlie, Isaac T. Hartle, and Isaac T. Hartlee. He served aboard the brig *Saranac*.

Hebard, Andrew.* —. Chief Engineer. His widow, Sarah Hebard, had her application rejected prior to 17 Jan. 1848 because the law did not provide for a pension to the widow of an engineer. She was pensioned 4 Aug. 1846 at the rate of $25 per month. 1848. 1850. 1851.

Hebberd, Seth. N.Y. Private Marine. He was pensioned from 10 May 1802 at the rate of $36 per annum in 1810. 1811. 1818. 1819. 1820. 1821. 1822. 1824. 1825. 1826. 1827. 1828. 1829. 1830. He served aboard the *Constitution*. He also appeared as Seth Hebbard.

Heckle, John.* —. Sailmaker. His son, Alfred Heckle, was pensioned 31 Oct. 1848 at the rate of $10 per month. 1850. 1851. His widow, Emily Heckle, was pensioned 15 Jan. 1847 at the rate of $10 per month. 1847. 1848.

Heerman, —. —. Surgeon. His orphans, Adolphus Heerman, Theodore Heerman, Valentine M. Heerman, Charles F. Heerman, and Clifford Heerman, were pensioned at the rate of $35 per month from 20 Apr. 1837. 1837. 1839. 1840. 1841. 1842. 1842b.

Hefferman, John M.* —. Marine. His widow, Mary H. Hefferman, was pensioned 20 Aug. 1848 at the rate of $3.50 per month. 1850. 1851.

Heffron, John.* N.Y. Boatswain's Mate. His widow, Maria Heffron, had her application rejected prior to 23 Dec. 1848. There was not proof that her husband died of disease contracted in the line of duty. She was pensioned 21 Mar. 1848 at the rate of $9.50 per month 1848.

1850. 1851. [She was also the widow of John Fishburn, Mary Fishburn.]

Hendrick, Benjamin. D.C. Marine. He was pensioned at the rate of $72 per annum. 1827. 1828. 1829. He was disabled aboard Gunboat No. 165.

Hendricks, Garrett. —. Seaman. He was pensioned 9 Aug. 1834 at the rate of $6 per annum. 1835. 1836. 1837. 1839. 1840. 1841. 1842. 1842b. 1843. 1844. 1845. 1846. 1847. 1848. 1850. 1851. He also appeared as Garret Henricks.

Henley, —. —. Captain. His widow, Mary Henley, was pensioned from 30 June 1834 at the rate of $50 per month. 1835. 1836. 1837. 1839. 1840. 1841. 1842. 1842b.

Henley, John D.* —. Captain. His widow, Eliza Henley, was pensioned from 23 May 1835 at the rate of $50 per month. 1836. 1837. 1839. 1840. 1841. 1842. 1842b. 1845. 1846. She was pensioned again 1 Sep. 1847 at the rate of $50 per month. 1848. 1850. 1851.

Henry, —.* —. Seaman. His widow, Hetty Henry, was pensioned at the rate of $6 per month from 25 May 1834. 1837. 1839. 1840. 1841. 1842. 1842b. [He was listed as John Henry as having served on the *Brandywine* in the Old Wars pension index.]

Henry, John. Md. Ordinary Seaman. He was pensioned 20 Mar. 1812 at the rate of $60 per annum. 1816. 1818. 1819. 1820. 1821. 1824. 1825. 1826. 1827. 1829. 1830. He served aboard the *Congress.*

Henry, John. —. Ordinary Seaman. He was pensioned 3 July 1845 at the rate of $2.50 per month. 1845. 1846. 1847. 1848. 1850. 1851.

Henson, —. —. —. George Henson and Mary Henson were pensioned on his service. 1842.

Hervey, Henry. Mass. Seaman. He was lost from the *Wasp* 20 Apr. 1815. His widow, Salley Hervey, was pensioned at the rate of $72 per annum. 1818. 1820. 1821. 1822. 1824. 1825. George W. Jones was guardian.

Hervey, Henry.* —. Seaman. He was pensioned 8 May 1834 at the rate of $4 per month. 1835. 1836. 1837. 1839. 1840. 1841. He also appeared as Henry Harvey.

Hibbert, —.* —. Gunner. His son, Stephen D. Hibbert, was pensioned at the rate of $10 per month from 9 July 1832. 1837. 1839. 1840. 1841. 1842. 1842b. [He was listed as Samuel Hibbert in the Old Wars pension index.]

Hibbs, Jesse L.* —. Sergeant of Marines. His application was rejected prior to 12 Dec. 1842. He claimed to have been wounded in 1814. That claim was more than 25 years old and there was no proof of his being wounded in any official return.

Hicks, Thomas.* —. Musician Marine Corps. His application was rejected between Mar. 1840 and 1 Jan. 1841. The claimant was a boy and was not wounded in any duty. On the contrary, he was injured in one of his eyes while engaged in play with his companions. The law did not cover his case.

Hicks, Thomas.* —. Drummer of Marines. His widow, Elizabeth E. Hicks, was pensioned 7 July 1847 at the rate of $4 per month. 1848. 1850. 1851.

Higby, John.* D.C. Marine. He was pensioned 1 July 1826 at the rate of $72 per annum. 1829. 1830. He served aboard the *North Carolina* under J. Rodgers.

Higdon, —. —. Gunner. His daughter, Elizabeth Higdon, was pensioned at the rate of $10 per month. 1837. 1842.

Higgins, James.* —. Seaman. His widow, Sarah Higgins, was pensioned from 28 Sep. 1834 at the rate of $6 per month. 1835. 1836. 1837. 1839. 1840. 1841. 1842. 1842b. 1845. 1846. She was pensioned again 1 Sep.1847 at the rate of $6 per month. 1848. 1850. 1851.

Higgins, Martin.* —. Coal Heaver. He was pensioned 14 Dec. 1842 at the rate of $2.50 per month. 1843. 1844. 1845. 1846. 1847. 1848. 1850. 1851.

Higgins, Noah.* —. Seaman. His widow, Rebecca Higgins, was pensioned from 30 Sep. 1837 at the rate of $6 per month. 1839. 1840. 1841. 1842b. She was pensioned again 1 Sep. 1847 at the rate of $6 per month. 1850. 1851. He also appeared as Noel Higgins.

Hilburn, —. Mass. Pilot. Martha Hilburn was pensioned on his service as a privateer at the rate of $48 per annum from 10 Oct. 1814. 1814. 1815. 1816. 1817. 1818. 1819. 1820. 1821. 1822. 1823. 1824. 1825. 1826. 1827. 1828. 1829. 1830. 1831. 1832. 1833. 1834 for $74.66.

Hill, George. Penn. Ordinary Seaman. He was killed 28 Mar. 1814 aboard the *Essex*. His widow was Sarah Hill. His minor children received $60 in 1822. 1823. 1824. 1827. 1829. James Proctor was guardian.

Hill, Justus.* —. Boatswain. His widow, Eliza Hill, was pensioned 2 Apr. 1845 at the rate of $10 per month. 1851.

Hill, Richard. Md. Seaman. He was pensioned at the rate of $72 per annum. 1818. 1819. 1820. 1821.

Hill, William. Penn. Quarter Gunner. He died 16 June 1815. He served aboard the *Guerrier*. His pension was paid to his daughter, Mary Ann Hill, at the rate of $108 per annum. 1824. 1825. 1827. 1829. William Towell was guardian.

Hillen, Edward.* —. Ordinary Seaman. He was pensioned 7 Aug. 1847 at the rate of $3.75 per month. 1848. 1850. 1851.

Hillman, Simeon. D.C. Ordinary Seaman. He was pensioned 3 July 1815 at the rate of $48 per annum. 1818. 1819. 1820. 1821. 1822. 1823. 1824. 1825. 1826. 1827. 1829. 1830. 1835. 1836. 1837. 1839. 1840. 1841. 1842b. 1843. 1844. 1845. 1846. 1847. 1848. 1850. 1851. He also appeared as Simeon Hilman and Simon Hillman. He served on Gunboat No. 23.

Hinds, —. Elizabeth Hinds was pensioned on his service at the rate of $36 per annum. 1815. 1816. 1817. 1818. 1819. 1820 increase to $72. 1821. 1822. 1823. 1824. 1825. 1826. 1827 for $33.

Hinds, William. N.Y. Boy. He was pensioned 18 Jan. 1819 at the rate of $72 per annum. 1820. 1821. 1822. 1823. 1824. 1825. 1826. 1827. 1828. 1829. 1830. He served aboard the sloop *Hornet*.

Hines, Thomas.* —. Seaman. He was pensioned at the rate of $3 per month from 1 Sep. 1849. 1850. 1851.

Hixon, Samuel C.* —. Master. His widow, Henrietta Hixon, was pensioned from 8 Sep. 1840 at the rate of $20 per month. 1841. 1842. 1842b. 1846. She was pensioned again 1 Sep. 1847 at the rate of $20 per month. 1848. 1850. 1851.

Hobbs, Hubbard H.* —. Lieutenant. His widow, Cornelia Hobbs, was pensioned from 3 Apr. 1836 at the rate of $25 per month. 1837. 1839. 1840. 1841. 1842. 1842b. 1845. 1846. She was pensioned again 1Sep. 1847 at the rate of $25 per month. 1848. 1850. 1851.

Naval Pensioners of the United States, 1800-1851

Hodding, —. Penn. Quartermaster. His widow, Mary Hodding, was pensioned at the rate of $120 per annum. 1820. 1821. 1822.

Hodge, —. —. —. His children, Eliza Hodge and Margaret Hodge, were pensioned. 1837. 1842. [Eliza Hodge only was on the 1842 list].

Hodgekins, John. N.H. Carpenter's Mate. He was pensioned 1 July 1814 at the rate of $84 per annum. 1816. 1818. 1819. 1820. 1821. 1822. 1823. 1824. 1825. 1826. 1827. 1828. 1829. 1830. 1835. 1836. 1837. 1839. 1840. 1841. 1842. He also appeared as John Hodgkins. He served aboard the schooner *Madison*.

Hodgkinson, —. N.Y. Prize Master. His widow, Ann Hodgkinson, was pensioned at the rate of $60 per annum from 16 Apr. 1814. 1820.

Hodgson, —. —. —. His daughter, Margaret Ann Hodgson, was pensioned. 1837. 1842.

Hoffman, Beekman V. —. Captain. His widow, Phebe W. Hoffman, was pensioned from 10 Dec. 1834 at the rate of $50 per month. 1835. 1836. 1839. 1840. 1841. 1842. 1842b. 1845. 1846. She was pensioned again 1 Sep. 1847 at the rate of $50 per month. 1848. 1850. 1851.

Hoffman, John.* —. Musician Marines. His widow, Theresa Hoffman, was pensioned from 30 June 1834 at the rate of $4 per month. 1836. 1837. 1839. 1840. 1841. 1842. 1842b. 1845. 1846. She was pensioned again 1 Sep. 1847 at the rate of $4 per month. 1848. 1850. 1851.

Hofford, Lawrence.* —. Quartermaster. His widow, Mary Hofford, was pensioned 16 Nov. 1842 at the rate of $8 per month. 1843. 1844. 1845. 1846. 1847. 1848. 1850. 1851.

Hogan, Daniel. Mass. Seaman. He was pensioned at the rate of $72 per annum. 1816. 1818. 1819. 1820. 1821. 1822.

Hogan, John.* Va. Seaman. He was pensioned 1 Mar. 1830 at the rate of $3 per month. 1830. 1835. 1836. 1837. 1839. 1840. 1841. 1842b. 1843. 1844. 1845. 1846. 1847. 1848. 1850. 1851. He served aboard the *Erie*.

Hogenon, Daniel. N.Y. Ordinary Seaman. He was pensioned at the rate of $60 per annum in 1826.

Hogerbets, John. Penn. Prisoner. He was pensioned 6 Apr. 1815 at the rate of $72 per annum. He had been a prisoner at Dartmoor, England. 1819. 1820. 1821. 1822. 1823. 1824. 1825. 1826. 1827. 1828. 1829. 1830. His disability was permanent. He also appeared as John Hodgerbets.

Holbert, —.* —. Corporal Marines. His widow, Mary E. Holbert, was pensioned from 30 June 1834 at the rate of $4 per month. 1835. 1836. 1837. 1839. 1840. 1841. 1842b. [He was listed as Thomas Holbert in the Old Wars pension index.]

Holbrook, Samuel F.* —. Carpenter. He was pensioned 30 Sep. 1820 at the rate of $5 per month. 1839. 1840. 1841. 1842b. 1843. 1844. 1845. 1846. 1847. 1848. 1850. 1851.

Holcomb, H. Ky. Seaman. He was drowned on 20 Feb. 1814 on the lakes. His widow, Charlotte A. Holcomb, was pensioned 10 Apr. 1818 at the rate of $72 per annum. 1819. 1820. 1821. 1822. 1823. 1824. 1825. 1827. 1828 when her child was being pensioned. 1829. 1830. He also appeared as P. Holcomb.

Holland, —. —. Carpenter's Mate. His widow, Margaret Holland, was pensioned from 10 Aug.

91

Naval Pensioners of the United States, 1800-1851

 1800 at the rate of $9.50 per month. 1841. 1842. 1842b.

Hollis, —. —. Marine. His widow, Phebe Hollis, was pensioned at the rate of $3.50 per month from 13 May 1811. 1837. 1840. 1841. 1842. 1842b.

Holmes, —. —. Armorer. His widow, Mary Ann. H. Holmes, was pensioned at the rate of 1 July 1837 at the rate of $9 per month. 1837. 1839. 1840. 1841. 1842. 1842b. [He was Samuel Holmes in the Old Wars pension index.]

Holmes, Andrew. —. Master-at-Arms. His widow, Ann J. Holmes, was pensioned from 22 Aug. 1836 at the rate of $9 per month. 1839. 1840. 1841. 1842. 1842b. She was pensioned again 1 Sep. 1847 at the rate of $9 per month. 1848. 1850. 1851.

Holmes, Edwin. —. Apprentice. He perished aboard the *Grampus*. His mother was Sarah Holmes of Boston, Mass. on 9 Jan. 1845. She was the widow of James L. Holmes, a merchant and dealer, who had been dead 15 years and was late of Plympton, Mass. The deceased was an only son and entered the service at the age of 15 in July 1840.

Holmes, John. N.Y. Seaman. He was pensioned at the rate of $72 per annum. 1816. 1818.

Holmes, John. S.C. Seaman. He was pensioned at the rate of $108 per annum. 1819. 1820. 1821. 1822. 1823.

Holmes, Silas. —. Passed Assistant Surgeon. His widow, Maria P. Holmes, was pensioned 21 May 1849 at the rate of $22.50 per month. 1850. 1851.

Holmes, William. Penn. Marine. He was pensioned 28 Oct. 1815 at the rate of $36 per annum. 1818. 1819. 1820. 1821. 1823. 1824. 1825. 1826. 1827. 1828. 1829. 1830. He also appeared as William Holins and William Holms. He served aboard the *Constitution*.

Holms, Henry H.* —. Ordinary Seaman. He was pensioned 16 Aug. 1845 at the rate of $2.50 per month. 1845. 1846. 1848. 1850. 1851. He was also known as Charles Holms, Henry Hohn, and Henry H. Holm.

Holt, Andrew McD. J. —. Purser. His widow, Susan Jane Holt, was pensioned 31 Oct. 1840 at the rate of $20 per month. 1851.

Holton, Francis M. —. —. He was pensioned 1 Jan. 1848 at the rate of $8 per month. 1848. 1850. 1851.

Homer, Charles.* —. Coxswain. He was pensioned 2 Feb. 1849 at the rate of $6.75 per month. 1850. 1851.

Hood, John.* Penn. Seaman. He was pensioned at the rate of $72 per annum. 1820. 1821. 1822. 1823.

Hooe, George M.* —. Lieutenant. His widow, Elizabeth M. A. G. Hooe, was pensioned on 10 Apr. 1845 and again 10 Apr.1850 at the rate of $25 per month. 1845. 1846. 1847. 1848. 1851. He also appeared as George Hove.

Hook, Conrad. D.C. Marine. He was killed 24 Aug. 1814 at headquarters. His widow was Susannah Hook. She was pensioned at the rate of $40 per annum on 12 Apr. 1815. Her daughter was pensioned. 1816. 1818. 1819. 1820. 1821. 1822. 1824. 1825. 1828. 1829. 1830.

Hooper, —. —. —. His son, Andrew Hooper, was pensioned. 1837. 1842.

Hooper, —. —. Seaman. His son, Thomas T. Hooper, was pensioned from 14 Feb. 1815 at the rate of $6 per month. 1842b.

Hooper, Thomas. —. —. He was pensioned. 1842.
Hooper, John A.* —. Private of Marines. He was pensioned 24 June 1851 at the rate of $1.75 per month. 1851.
Hoover, Henry. Ga. Armorer. He perished aboard the *Epervier* 1 Sep. 1815. He was the son of Godlip and Hannah, nee Dickens, Hoover who were married 18 July 1786 in South Carolina. They had twin sons, Henry Hoover and Conrad Hoover, born 26 June 1787. The father was deceased. The mother was baptized by immersion 21 Nov. 1803 at the Savannah Baptist Church. She was paid $108 on 15 Sep. 1817.
Hoover, Jacob.* Penn. Ordinary Seaman. He was pensioned at the rate of $96 per annum. 1820. 1821. 1822. 1823.
Hopkins, —.* —. —. Nathaniel G. Hopkins, Daniel H. Hopkins, and Susan S. Hopkins were pensioned on his service. 1842. [He was listed as Daniel Hopkins in the Old Wars pension index.]
Hopkins, Josias. —. Ordinary Seaman. He was pensioned 7 Dec. 1805 at the rate of $6 per month. 1835. 1836. 1837.
Horsley, Samuel. —. Surgeon. His widow, Mary Ann Horsley, was pensioned from 8 Sep. 1831 at the rate of $27.50 per month. 1839. 1840. 1841. 1842. 1842b. 1846. She was pensioned again 1 Sep. 1847 at the rate of $27.50 per month. 1848. 1850. 1851.
Horton, —. —. Midshipman. His widow, Emma Horton, was pensioned at the rate of $9.50 per month from 7 Aug. 1815. 1837. 1839. 1840. 1841. 1842. 1842b.
Horton, David. Penn. Quartermaster. He was pensioned 1 Dec. 1813 at the rate of $72 per annum. 1816. 1818. 1819. 1820. 1821. 1822. 1823. 1824. 1825. 1826. 1829. 1830. He served aboard the *Enterprise*.
Hosier, Peter.* Mass. Seaman. He was pensioned at the rate of $72 per annum from 18 Oct. 1820. 1822. 1823. 1824. 1825. 1826. 1827. 1828. 1829. 1830. He served aboard the *Columbus*. He also appeared as Peter Hozier.
House, Thomas. —. Quartermaster. He was pensioned 11 Oct. 1813 at the rate of $9 per month. 1827. 1828. 1829. 1835. 1836. He also appeared as Thomas Howse. He served aboard the *Chesapeake*.
Howard, —. N.Y. Sailmaker. Cornelia Howard was pensioned on his service as a privateer at the rate of $96 per annum. 1818. 1819. 1820.
Howel, William. Va. Ordinary Seaman. He was pensioned at the rate of $60 per annum. 1809. 1810. 1811. 1816. 1818. 1819. 1820. 1821. 1822. 1823. 1824. 1825. 1826. 1827. 1828. 1829. 1830. He also appeared as William Howell. He served aboard the *Constitution*.
Howell, Joseph. Va. —. He perished aboard the *Grampus*. He entered the Navy and deserted from the *Pennsylvania*. Afterwards he shipped aboard the *Grampus* under the name of Charles Howell. His father, John G. Howell, was alive. His mother, Ann Howell, was dead. His sisters, Henrietta Howell and Martha Ann Howell, were in Richmond, Va. 19 July 1844.
Howell, Joshua.* —. Ordinary Seaman. He was pensioned 30 June 1836 at the rate of $5 per month. 1837. 1838. 1839. 1840. 1841. 1842. 1842b. 1843. 1844. 1845. 1846. 1847. 1848. 1850. 1851.

Naval Pensioners of the United States, 1800-1851

Howland, Barney. N.Y. —. He perished aboard the *Epervier* 1 Sep. 1815. His heir was his brother Reuben Howland of New York, N.Y.

Hoxse, John. R.I. Seaman. He served aboard the *Constellation*. He was pensioned 15 Aug. 1800 at the rate of $92 per annum. 1802. 1803. 1804. 1805. 1807. 1808. 1809. 1810. 1811. 1816. 1818. 1819. 1820. 1821. 1822. 1823. 1824. 1825. 1826. 1827. 1828. 1829. 1835. 1836. 1837. 1839. 1840. 1841. 1842b. 1843. 1844. 1845. 1846. 1847. 1848. 1850. 1851. He also appeared as John Hoxe and John Hoxie.

Hubbard, Seth. N.Y. Marine. He was pensioned at the rate of $36 per annum. 1816. 1823.

Hudson, John.* —. Seaman. He was pensioned 20 Sep. 1849 at the rate of $3 per month. 1850. 1851.

Hudson, William L.* —. Sailing Master. He was pensioned at the rate of $15 per month. 1837. 1838. 1839. 1840. 1841. 1842. 1842b. 1843.

Huffstidler, George. Penn. Seaman. He was pensioned 22 Nov. 1815 at the rate of $72 per annum. 1818. 1819. 1820. 1821. 1822. 1823. 1824. 1825. 1826. 1827. 1828. 1829. 1830. He served aboard the *Guerriere*. He also appeared as George Huffstedler.

Hughes, Elias. —. Ordinary Seaman. He was pensioned 28 Aug. 1837 at the rate of $5 per month. 1837. 1839. 1840. 1841. 1842b. 1843. 1844. 1845. 1846. 1847. 1848. 1850. 1851.

Hull, —. —. —. E. Hull was pensioned on his service as a privateer at the rate of $48 per annum. 1813. 1814. 1815. 1816. 1817. 1818. 1819. 1820. 1821. 1822. 1823. 1824. 1825. 1826. 1827.

Hull, —. D.C. Sailing Master. Eliza Hull was pensioned on his service at the rate of $240 per annum. 1828.

Hull, Isaac.* —. Captain. His widow, Anna M. H. Hull, was pensioned 13 Feb. 1843 at the rate of $50 per month. 1843. 1844. 1845. 1846. 1847. 1848. 1850. 1851.

Hull, Philip. —. Landsman. He was pensioned 10 Apr. 1851 at the rate of $4 per month. 1851.

Hume, Ebenezer J.* —. Sergeant of Marines. His widow, Barbara E. Hume, was pensioned 14 Sep. 1842 at the rate of $6.50 per month. 1844. 1845. 1846. 1848. 1850. 1851.

Humphries, Joseph.* —. 2nd Class Fireman. He was pensioned 13 Sep. 1849 at the rate of $5 per month. 1850. 1851.

Hunt, —.* —. Ordinary Seaman. His daughter, Mary Ann Hunt, was pensioned from 20 Apr. 1837 at the rate of $5 per month. 1839. 1840. 1841. 1842. [He was listed as Cyrus Hunt in the Old Wars pension index.]

Hunt, Clement S.* —. Purser. His widow, Sarah Ann Hunt, was pensioned from 4 Apr. 1837 at the rate of $20 per month. 1839. 1840. 1841. 1842. 1842b. She was pensioned again 1 Sep. 1847 at the rate of $20 per month. 1848. 1850. 1851. She also appeared as Sarah Ann Huntt.

Hunter, —. —. Chaplain. His widow, Mary S. Hunter, was pensioned at the rate of $20 per month from 24 Feb. 1823. 1837. 1839. 1840. 1841. 1842. 1842b.

Hunter, —. —. Purser. His widow, Eliza Hunter, was pensioned at the rate of $20 per month from 2 Jan. 1838. 1840.

Hunter, Charles W.* —. Marine. His widow, Ellen Hunter, was pensioned from 16 May 1838 at the rate of $3.50 per month. 1839. 1840. 1841. 1842. 1842b. 1851. [He is listed as

Naval Pensioners of the United States, 1800-1851

William Hunter in the Old Wars pension index.]
Hunter, George. Penn. Midshipman. He perished aboard the *Epervier* 1 Sep. 1815. His mother, Martha Hunter, of Philadelphia, Penn. was paid $114 on 19 Jan. 1819.
Hunter, William. —. Marine. His widow, Elizabeth A. M. E. Hunter, was pensioned 1 Sep. 1842 at the rate of $3.50 per month. 1851.
Hunter, William M.* —. Captain. His widow, Harriet L. Hunter, was pensioned 5 Mar. 1849 at the rate of $50 per month. 1850. 1851.
Huntley, Thomas.* —. Seaman. He was pensioned 31 Aug. 1837 at the rate of $3 per month. 1839. 1840. 1841. 1842b. 1843. 1844. 1845. 1846. 1847. 1848. 1850. 1851.
Hurn, Edward. —. Boatswain. He was pensioned as a privateer at the rate of $120 per annum. 1835. 1836. 1837 for $60. He was pensioned again from 1 July 1837 at rate of $10 per month. 1837. 1838. 1844. 1845. 1846. 1847. 1850.
Hussey, John.* —. Ordinary Seaman. He was pensioned 1 Jan. 1832 at the rate of $5 per month. 1835. 1836. 1837. 1839. 1840. 1841. 1842b. 1843. 1844. 1845. 1846. 1847. 1848. 1850. 1851.
Huston, James G.* —. Yeoman. His widow, Pamelia Huston, was pensioned 21 Dec. 1849 at the rate of $12.50 per month. 1845. 1846. 1847. 1848. 1850. 1851.
Hutton, George. N.Y. Quarter Gunner. He was pensioned 17 June 1816 at the rate of $96 per annum. 1818. 1819. 1820. 1821. 1822. 1823. 1824. 1825. 1826. 1827. 1828. 1829. 1830. He served aboard the schooner *Alert*.
Hyatt, John. Mass. Seaman. He was pensioned 18 Mar. 1813 at the rate of $72 per annum. 1816. 1818. 1819. In New York in 1820. 1822. 1823. 1824. 1825. 1826. 1827. 1828. 1829. 1830. He served aboard the *Constitution*.
Hyberger, Nicholas. Penn. Seaman. He was pensioned 16 Oct. 1812 at the rate of $72 per annum. 1816. 1818. 1819. 1820. 1821. 1822. 1823. 1824. 1825. 1826. 1827. 1828. 1829. 1830. He served aboard the *Essex*.

Igerbrelson, Nicholas. Md. Seaman. He was pensioned 27 Dec. 1814 at the rate of $72 per annum. 1818. 1819. 1820. 1821. 1822. 1823. 1824. 1825. 1826. 1827. 1828. 1829. 1830. He served aboard the *Peacock*. He also appeared as Nicholas Ingerbretson, Nicholas Igerbreton, and Nicholas Ingerbrettsen.
Inderwick, James. N.Y. Surgeon. He perished aboard the *Epervier* 1 Sep. 1815. His father, Andrew Inderwick, was paid $300 on 1 July 1817.
Ingersoll, William.* Mass. Boatswain. He was pensioned 2 June 1821 at the rate of $120 per annum. 1822. 1823. 1824. 1825. 1826. 1827. 1828. 1829. 1830. 1836. He served aboard the schooner *Independence*.
Ingraham, —. —. Lieutenant. His son, Daniel G. Ingraham, was pensioned at the rate of $25 per month. 1837. 1842.
Ingraham, —.* —. Seaman. His widow, Hannah Ingraham, was pensioned at the rate of $6 per month from 10 Apr. 1837. 1837. 1839. 1840. 1841. 1842. 1842b. [He was listed as

Naval Pensioners of the United States, 1800-1851

    Daniel Ingraham in the Old Wars pension index.]
Ingraham, Edward.* —. Boatswain. He was pensioned 1 Apr. 1831 at the rate of $6 per month. 1835. 1836. 1837. 1839. 1840. 1841. 1842. 1843. 1844. 1845. 1846. 1847. 1848. 1850. 1851. He also appeared as Edward Ingram.
Irons, —. —. —. Phoebe Irons was pensioned on his service as a privateer at the rate of $36 per annum. 1813. 1814. 1815. 1816. 1817. 1818 increase to $72. 1819. 1820. 1821. 1822. 1823. 1824. 1825. 1826. 1827. 1828 for $48.
Irvin, Andrew.* Md. Seaman. He was pensioned 1 July 1828 at the rate of $74 per annum. 1829. 1830. 1835. 1836. 1837. He served aboard the schooner *Porpoise*. [He was listed as Andrew Irwin in the Old Wars pension index.]
Irvine, Joseph. N.Y. Corporal of Marines. He was pensioned at the rate of $48 per annum in 1808. 1809. 1810. 1811.
Irwin, Henry.* —. Marine. He was pensioned 20 Feb. 1837 at the rate of $1.75 per month. 1837. 1838. 1839. 1840. 1841. 1842b. 1843. 1844. 1845. 1846. 1847. 1848. 1850. 1851.
Irwin, Thomas.* —. Marine. He was pensioned 31 Jan. 1837 at the rate of $1.75 per month. 1841. 1842b. 1843. 1844. 1845. 1846. 1847. 1848. 1850. 1851.
Isley, —. Mass. Lieutenant. Margaret Isley was pensioned on his service as a privateer at the rate of $72 per annum from 1 Jan. 1815. 1815. 1816. 1817. 1818. 1819. 1820. 1821. 1822. 1823. 1824. 1825 increased to $144. 1826. 1827. 1828. 1829. 1830. 1831. 1832. 1833. 1834.

Jackman, Warren.* —. Landsman. He was pensioned 3 Aug. 1850 at the rate of $3 per month. 1850. 1851.
Jackson, —.* —. Gunner. His son, Benjamin Jackson, was pensioned from 26 Nov. 1831 at the rate of $10 per month. 1842b. [He was listed as George Jackson in the Old Wars pension index.]
Jackson, —. —. —. Maria Ann Jackson was pensioned on his service. 1842.
Jackson, Andrew McD.* Va. Purser. His widow, Susan Jane Jackson, was pensioned from 31 Oct. 1840 at the rate of $20 per month. 1841. 1842. She had her next application rejected prior to 23 Dec. 1848. She was barred by the act of 11 Aug. 1848.
Jackson, Henry.* —. Captain of Foretop. He was pensioned 20 Sep. 1836 at the rate of $3.75 per month. 1836. 1837. 1839. 1840. 1841. 1842b. 1843. 1844. 1845. 1846. 1847. 1848. 1850. 1851.
Jackson, Ichabod.* —. Seaman. He was pensioned 25 Jan. 1837 at the rate of $4.50 per month. 1839. 1840. 1841. 1842b. 1843. 1844. 1845. 1846. 1847. 1848. 1850. 1851.
Jackson, James. N.Y. Seaman. He was pensioned 14 Mar. 1816 at the rate of $60 per annum. 1818. 1819. 1820. 1821. 1822. 1823. 1824. 1825. 1826. 1827. 1828. 1829. 1830. 1836. 1837. 1838. 1839. 1840. 1841. 1842b. 1843. 1844. 1845. 1846. 1847. 1848. 1850. 1851. He served aboard the *Constitution*. His son, James Jackson of D.C., had his application

Naval Pensioners of the United States, 1800-1851

rejected prior to 23 Dec. 1848. He was barred by the act of 11 Aug. 1848. The pensioner at one time lived in D.C.

Jackson, Joseph.* —. Cook. He was pensioned $29 Oct. 1839 at the rate of $4.50 per month. 1840. 1841. 1842b. 1843. 1844. 1845. 1846. 1847. 1848. 1850. 1851. He appeared incorrectly as John Jackson in 1848.

Jackson, Thomas, 2d. N.Y. Quartermaster. He was pensioned 28 July 1818 at the rate of $108 per annum. 1821. 1823. 1824. 1825. 1826. 1827. 1828. 1829. 1830. 1835. 1836. 1837. 1838. 1839. 1840. 1841. 1842. 1842b. 1843. 1844. 1845. 1846. 1847. 1848. 1850. 1851. He served aboard the frigate *Chesapeake*.

Jackson, Thomas H.* —. Seaman. His widow, Mary Jackson, was pensioned from 2 May 1838 at the rate of $5 per month. 1839. 1840. 1841. 1842b. She had her application rejected prior to 30 Dec.1845. The disorder of which her husband died did not arise while he was in the line of his duty. She was pensioned 8 Apr. 1844 at the rate of $7.50 per month. His rank was given as yeoman in that list. 1848. 1850. 1851.

Jackson, William.* Penn. Seaman. He was pensioned 11 Nov. 1817 at the rate of $72 per annum. 1819. 1820. 1821. 1822. 1823. 1824. 1825. 1826. 1827. 1828. 1829. 1830. He served aboard the *United States*.

James, Reuben. —. Boatswain's Mate. He was pensioned from 27 Jan. 1836 at the rate of $9.50 per month. 1836. 1837.

Jameson, Robert. N.Y. Boatswain's Mate. He was pensioned at the rate of $108 per annum. 1818. 1819. 1820. 1821.

Jameson, Skiffington S. —. Midshipman. His widow, Mary Jameson, was pensioned from 11 Nov. 1823 at the rate of $9.50 per month. 1835. 1836. 1837. 1841. 1842. 1842b. 1845. 1846. She was pensioned again 1 Sep. 1847 at the rate of $9.50 per month. 1848. 1850. 1851.

Jameson, Sylvester.* Penn. Seaman. He was pensioned 1 Aug. 1828 at the rate of $6 per month. 1829. 1830. 1835. 1836. 1837. 1839. 1840. 1841. 1842b. 1843. 1844. 1845. 1846. 1847. 1848. 1850. 1851. He served aboard the *Warren*.

Jameson, William H.* —. Passed Midshipman. His widow, Cornelia L. T. Jameson, was pensioned 1 Sep. 1842 at the rate of $9.50 per month.

Jantzen, Lewis. S.C. Lt. He was pensioned as a privateer at the rate of $144 per annum from 1 Mar. 1815. 1820.

Jeffers, James. Va. Ordinary Seaman. He was pensioned 7 Dec. 1805 at the rate of $72 per annum. 1805. 1807. 1808. 1809. 1810. 1811. 1816. 1818. 1819. 1820. 1821. 1822. 1823. 1824. 1825. 1826. 1827. 1828. 1829. 1830. 1835. 1836. 1837. 1839. 1840. 1841. 1842b. 1843. 1844. 1845. 1846. 1847. 1848. 1850. 1851. He served on Gunboat No. 7 off Tripoli.

Jefferson, Walter.* —. Ordinary Seaman. He was pensioned 4 Nov. 1847 at the rate of $3.50 per month. 1848. 1850. 1851.

Jenkins, David.* —. Seaman. He was pensioned 1 Aug. 1828 at the rate of $6 per month. 1835. 1836. 1837. 1839. 1840. 1841. 1842b. 1843. 1844. 1845. 1846. 1847. 1848. 1850. 1851.

Jenkins, John.* —. Seaman. His widow, Ellen Jenkins, was pensioned from 2 June 1825 at the

Naval Pensioners of the United States, 1800-1851

rate of $6 per month. 1835. 1836. 1837. 1839. 1840. 1841. 1842. 1842b. 1845. 1846.

Jennett, Joseph.* —. Captain Mizzen Top. He was pensioned 12 June 1838 at the rate of $2.33 1/3 per month. 1840. 1841. 1842b. 1843. 1844. 1845. 1846. 1847. 1848. 1850. 1851. He also appeared as Joseph Jewett.

Johnson, —. —. —. Henrietta Johnson was pensioned on his service as a privateer at the rate of $72 per annum. 1813. 1814. 1815. 1816. 1817. 1818 increase to $144. 1819. 1820. 1821. 1822. 1823. 1824. 1825. 1826. 1827 for $136.40.

Johnson, —. N.H. Seaman. Nancy Johnson was pensioned on his service as a privateer at the rate of $36 per annum. 1815. 1816. 1817. 1818. 1819. 1820 increase to $72. 1821. 1822. 1823. 1824. 1825. 1826. 1827. 1828. 1829 for $69.20.

Johnson, —. —. —. Elizabeth Johnson was pensioned on his service. 1842.

Johnson, —. —. Ordinary Seaman. His daughter, Abigail Johnson, was pensioned at the rate of $5 per month. 1837. 1842. She also appeared as Abigail Johnston.

Johnson, —. —. Boatswain. His daughter, Susannah Johnson, was pensioned at the rate of $10 per month. 1837.

Johnson, Edward.* Penn. Seaman. He was pensioned at the rate of $72 per annum. 1821. 1823. 1824. 1825. 1826.

Johnson, Edward.* —. Seaman. He was pensioned 3 Dec. 1846 at the rate of $6 per month. 1847. 1848. 1850. 1851.

Johnson, Jacob.* —. Quarter Gunner. He was pensioned 22 Nov. 1843 at the rate of $3.75 per month. 1844. 1845. 1846. 1847. 1848. 1850. 1851.

Johnson, John.* —. Boat's Mate. He was pensioned 14 Dec. 1850 at the rate of $4.75 per month. 1851.

Johnson, John. N.Y. Seaman. He was pensioned 28 Mar. 1814 at the rate of $72 per annum. 1818. 1819. 1820. 1821. 1822. 1823. 1824. 1825. 1826. 1827. 1828. 1829. 1830. 1835. 1836. 1837. 1838. 1839. 1840. 1841. 1842. 1842b. 1843. 1844. 1845. 1846. 1848. 1850. 1851. [He appeared incorrectly as John Jackson in 1821.] He served aboard the *Essex*.

Johnson, John. Penn. Marine. He was pensioned at the rate of $36 per annum. 1807. 1808. 1809. 1810. 1811.

Johnson, John. —. Seaman. He was pensioned 9 May 1845 at the rate of $6 per month. 1845. 1846. 1847. 1848. 1850. 1851.

Johnson, John.* —. Seaman. He was pensioned 21 Mar. 1845 at the rate of $6 per month. 1845. 1846. 1847. 1848. 1850. 1851.

Johnson, John. —. Quarter Gunner. He was pensioned 13 Sep. 1849 at the rate of $5.62 ½ per month. 1850. 1851.

Johnson, John.* —. Gunner. His widow, Catharine Johnson, was pensioned from 11 Aug. 1818 at the rate of $10 per month. 1839. 1840. 1841. 1842. 1842b. 1846. She was pensioned again 1 Sep.1847 at the rate of $10 per month. 1847. 1848. 1850. 1851.

Johnson, Michael. —. Seaman. He was pensioned 31 Jan. 1812 at the rate of $3 per month. 1839. 1840. 1841. 1842. 1843. 1844. 1845. 1846. 1847. 1848. 1850. 1851.

Johnson, Obadiah. Va. Seaman. He was pensioned from 1 Apr. 1819 at the rate of $60 per annum. 1823. 1824. 1825. 1826. 1827. 1828. 1829. 1830. 1835. 1836. 1837. 1839. 1840.

1841. He served aboard the *Guerriere.*

Johnson, Swain.* Va. Seaman. He was pensioned 1 July 1823 at the rate of $72 per annum. 1824. 1825. 1829. 1830. He served aboard the *Shark.*

Johnson, Thomas. —. —. He perished aboard the *Grampus.* His sister with her two children were from Elk Ridge Landing on 11 Dec. 1843.

Johnson, Thomas. Pa. Carpenter's Mate. He served aboard the *Alligator* and was lost 30 June 1814. His widow, Maria T. Johnson, was pensioned 24 Mar. 1819 at the rate of $9.50 per month. 1820. 1821. 1822. 1823. 1824. 1825. 1827. 1830. 1835. 1836. 1837. 1839. 1840. 1841. 1842. 1842b. 1845. 1846. She also appeared as Mary T. Johnson.

Johnson, William. Penn. Boatswain's Mate. He was pensioned at the rate of $72 per annum. 1819.

Johnston, —.* —. Landsman. His widow, Elizabeth Johnston, was pensioned at the rate of $6 per month from 21 Feb. 1833. 1837. 1839. 1840. 1841. 1842b. [He was listed as Richard Johnston in the Old Wars pension index.]

Johnston, Stephen.* —. Lieutenant. His widow, Elizabeth A. Johnston, was pensioned 2 Apr. 1848 at the rate of $25 per month. 1848. 1850. 1851.

Jolly, —.* —. Captain of Foretop. His widow, Catharine Jolly, was pensioned from 26 Dec. 1835 at the rate of $7 per month. 1836. 1837. 1839. 1840. His children, James Jolly, Lucinda Jolly, Hannah Jolly, and Jane Jolly, were pensioned from 15 Aug. 1839 at the rate of $7 per month. 1841. 1842. 1842b. [He was listed as James Jolly in the Old Wars pension index.]

Jones, —. —. Seaman. His widow, Abigail Jones, was pensioned from 16 Aug. 1800 at the rate of $6 per month. 1837. 1839. 1840. 1841. 1842. 1842b.

Jones, —.* —. Marine. His widow, Theresa Jones, was pensioned from 26 June 1810 at the rate of $3.50 per month. 1839. 1840. 1841. 1842. 1842b. [He was listed as Richard Jones in the Old Wars pension index.]

Jones, —.* —. Master-at-Arms. His widow, Caroline Jones, was pensioned from 30 June 1834 at the rate of $9 per month. 1835. 1836. 1837. 1842. [He was listed as William Jones in the Old Wars pension index.]

Jones, —. —. Marine. His widow, Elizabeth Jones, was pensioned from 1 Sep. 1827 at the rate of $10 per month. 1835. 1836. 1837. 1839. 1840. 1841. 1842. 1842b.

Jones, —.* —. Gunner. His widow, Elizabeth Jones, was pensioned from 30 June 1834 at the rate of $10 per month. 1836. 1837. [He was listed as Stephen Jones in the Old Wars pension index.]

Jones, —. Mass. Prize Master. Frances Jones was pensioned on his service as a privateer at the rate of $72 per annum from 1 Nov. 1812. 1815. 1816. 1817. 1818. 1819. 1820. 1821. 1822. 1823. 1824. 1825. 1826. 1827. 1828. 1829. 1830. 1831. 1832 for $100.

Jones, —. N.H. Gunner. Hetty Jones was pensioned on his service as a privateer at the rate of $60 per annum. 1815. 1816. 1817. 1818. 1819. 1820. 1821. 1822. 1823. 1824.

Jones, —. N.H. Boatswain's Mate. Martha Jones was pensioned on his service as a privateer at the rate of $48 per annum. 1815. 1816. 1817. 1818. 1819. 1820 increase to $96. 1821. 1822. 1823. 1824. 1825. 1826. 1827. 1828.

Naval Pensioners of the United States, 1800-1851

Jones, —. —. Sailing Master. His children, John D. Jones, Parmelia Ann Jones, Daniel F. Jones, and Joseph B. Jones, were pensioned from 21 May 1826 at the rate of $20 per month. 1837. 1839. 1840. 1841. 1842. 1842b.

Jones, Alonzo.* —. Carpenter. His widow, Sarah V. Jones, was pensioned 17 Jan. 1848 at the rate of $10 per month. 1847. 1848. 1850. 1851.

Jones, Cave.* —. Chaplain. His widow, Mary Jones, was pensioned from 29 Jan. 1829 at the rate of $20 per month. 1836. 1837. 1839. 1840. 1841. 1842. 1842b. 1845. 1846. She was pensioned from 1 Sep. 1847 at the rate of $20 per month. 1848. 1850. 1851.

Jones, Charles.* —. Quarter Gunner. He was pensioned 7 July 1848 at the rate of $7.50 per month. 1848. 1850. 1851.

Jones, Gilbert. —. Ordinary Seaman. He was pensioned 30 June 1815 at the rate of $2.50 per month. 1838. 1839. 1840. 1841. 1842. 1842b. 1843. 1844. 1845. 1846. 1847. 1848. 1850. 1851.

Jones, Jacob. —. Captain. His widow, Ruth Jones, was pensioned 3 Aug. 1850 at the rate of $50 per month. 1850. 1851.

Jones, James.* —. Blacksmith. He was pensioned 2 June 1841 at the rate of $12 per month. 1847. 1848. 1850. 1851.

Jones, James.* —. Seaman. He was pensioned 16 Oct. 1846 at the rate of $6 per month. 1847. 1848. 1850. 1851.

Jones, James.* —. Seaman. He was pensioned 18 Sep. 1845 at the rate of $6 per month. 1846. 1848. 1850.

Jones, James.* —. Seaman. He was pensioned 20 Apr. 1844 at the rate of $6 per month. 1844. 1845. 1846. 1847. 1850.

Jones, Job.* Penn. Ordinary Seaman. He was pensioned 27 June 1822 at the rate of $60 per annum. 1823. 1824. 1825. 1826. 1827. 1828. 1829. 1830. He served aboard the *Columbus*.

Jones, John.* —. Seaman. He was pensioned 16 Sep. 1842 at the rate of $3 per month. 1842b. 1843. 1844. 1845. 1846. 1847. 1848. 1850. 1851.

Jones, John.* —. Marine. His widow, Elizabeth Jones, was pensioned from 30 June 1834 at the rate of $3 per month. 1836. 1845. 1846. She was pensioned 1 Sep. 1847 at the rate of $3 per month. 1850. 1851.

Jones, Lewis. —. Seaman. He was pensioned 27 Oct. 1835 at the rate of $6 per month. 1835. 1836. 1837. 1839. 1840. 1841. 1842b. 1843. 1844. 1845. 1846. 1847. 1848. 1850. 1851.

Jones, Lewis. —. Quartermaster. He was pensioned 27 Oct. 1835 at the rate of $8 per month. 1851.

Jones, Mark.* —. Marine. His widow, Susan Jones, was pensioned 12 Sep. 1846 at the rate of $3.50 per month. 1848. 1851. His daughter, Emeline Jones, was pensioned 16 Sep. 1849 at the rate of $3.50 per month. 1850. 1851.

Jones, Philander A. J. P. Mass. Lieutenant. His application was rejected prior to 23 Dec. 1848. There was no proof that his disability was incurred in the line of duty. He was initially pensioned 28 Dec. 1828 at the rate of $25 and was on the 1851 list.

Jones, Richard.* Mass. Cook. He served aboard the *Wasp* and was lost 20 Apr. 1815. His widow,

Naval Pensioners of the United States, 1800-1851

Abigail Jones, was pensioned 1 Jan. 1817 at the rate of $9 per month. 1818. 1819. 1821. 1822. 1823. 1824. 1825. 1827. 1828. 1829. 1830. 1835. 1836. 1837. 1839. 1840. 1841. 1842. 1842b. 1845. 1846. She was a lunatic. She was pensioned again on 1 Sep. 1847 at the rate of $9 per month. 1848. 1850. 1851.

Jones, Richard D.* —. Commander. His widow, Emily Jones, was pensioned 16 Apr. 1846 at the rate of $30 per month. 1846. 1847. 1848. 1850. 1851. He also appeared as Richard A. Jones.

Jones, Samuel.* —. Boatswain. His widow, Abigail Jones, was pensioned 16 Aug. 1850 at the rate of $3.50 per month. 1851.

Jones, Samuel. —. Boatswain's Mate. His widow, Abigail Jones, was pensioned 1 Sep. 1842 at the rate of $9 per month. 1851.

Jones, Snow. Mass. Seaman. He was pensioned at the rate of $60 per annum. 1816. 1818. 1819. 1820. 1821. 1822.

Jones, Thomas Ap Catesby.* —. Lieutenant Commanding. He was stationed on Mobile Bay and was in command of five gunboats with 182 men on 14 Dec. 1814. A British flotilla attacked with more than 1,200 men. He was severely wounded by gunshot from a ball passing through the joint of his left shoulder. It lodged between the blade and ribs. He was pensioned 15 Nov. 1831 at the rate of $20 per month. 1835. 1836. 1839. 1840. 1841. 1842. 1842b. 1843.

Jones, William. —. —. He was pensioned as a privateer at the rate of $60 per annum from 7 Dec. 1812. 1812. 1813. 1814. 1820.

Jones, William. —. Boy. He was pensioned 24 Aug. 1814 at the rate of $2.25 per month. 1837. 1838. 1839. 1840. 1841. 1842. 1842b. 1843. 1844. 1845. 1846. 1847. 1848. 1850. 1851.

Jordan, —. —. —. His daughter, Elizabeth P. Jordan, was pensioned. 1837. 1842. She also appeared as Elizabeth T. Jordan.

Jordan, Richworth.* —. Seaman. He was pensioned 15 Mar. 1836 at the rate of $2.50 per month. 1836. 1837. 1839. 1840. 1841. 1842b. 1843. 1844. 1845. 1846. 1847. 1848. 1850. 1851.

Jordan, William.* —. Carpenter. His widow, Louisa Jordan, was pensioned 5 June 1845 at the rate of $10 per month. 1847. 1848. 1850. 1851.

Joscelyn, —.* Conn. Carpenter's Mate. He died of yellow fever 17 July 1822. His widow, Elizabeth Joscelyn, was pensioned 9 Mar. 1825 at the rate of $114 per annum. 1825. 1827. 1828. She also appeared as Elizabeth Joselyn. [He was listed as Joseph Josselyn in the Old Wars pension index.]

Joseph, Frederick. Mass. Seaman. He was pensioned as a privateer in 1814 at the rate of $72 per annum from 1 July 1814. 1814. 1815. 1816. 1817. 1818. 1819. 1820. 1821. 1822. 1823. 1824. 1825. 1826. 1827. 1828. 1829. 1830.

Joseph, Peter.* —. Seaman. He was pensioned 5 Feb. 1849 at the rate of $6 per month. 1850. 1851.

Joyce, John.* —. Ordinary Seaman. He was pensioned 30 Aug. 1839 at the rate of $3.75 per month. 1840. 1841. 1842b. 1843. 1844. 1845. 1846. 1847. 1848. 1850. 1851.

Judy, Joseph. —. Carpenter's Mate. He entered the service at Boston aboard the *Chesapeake* in Apr. 1813. He was killed in an engagement with the *Shannon*. His mother, Elizabeth

Naval Pensioners of the United States, 1800-1851

Whitehead, sought a pension but was rejected 7 Mar. 1828.

Kean, Thomas.* —. Seaman. He was pensioned 13 Jan. 1847 at the rate of $3 per month. 1847. 1848. 1850. 1851.

Kearnes, William. —. Seaman. He served on the sloop *Erie* from 1823 to 1826 and was discharged. He later reenlisted. On 19 Nov. 1827 he was admitted a patient at the U.S. Naval Hospital in Portsmouth, Va. He was discharged 17 Apr. 1829. He suffered from paralysis. He was not entitled to a pension. 3 June 1834.

Kearney, John A. —. Surgeon. His widow, Mary M. Kearney, was pensioned 27 Aug. 1847 at the rate of $35 per month. 1847. 1848. 1850.

Keegan, John. Md. Quartermaster. He was pensioned 27 Mar. 1830 at the rate of $6 per month. 1830. 1839. 1840. 1841. 1842b. 1843. 1844. 1845. 1846. 1847. 1848. 1850. 1851. He served aboard the *Chesapeake*.

Keeling, Henry.* —. Gunner. He was pensioned from 30 Aug. 1834 at the rate of $5 per month. 1838. 1839. 1840. 1841. 1842b. 1843.

Keene, William C. —. Master-at-Arms. He was pensioned 10 Sep. 1843 at the rate of $9 per month. 1835. 1836. 1837. 1838. 1839. 1840. 1841. 1842. 1842b. 1843. 1844. 1845. 1846. 1847. 1848. He also appeared as William C. Keen.

Keevers, James.* —. Marine. He was pensioned 2 Mar. 1848 at the rate of $8 per month by joint resolution of 10 Aug. 1848. 1850. 1851.

Keith, Lewis G.* —. Lieutenant. His widow, Eliza M. Keith, was pensioned 1 May 1846 at the rate of $25 per month. 1846. 1847. 1848. 1850. 1851. He also appeared as Lewis G. Keeth.

Kello, Joseph N.Y. Lieutenant. He was pensioned as a privateer at the rate of $144 per annum from 17 Apr. 1814. 1814. 1815. 1816. 1817 for $72. 1820.

Kelly, —. Mass. Seaman. Hepzibah Kelly was pensioned on his privateer service at the rate of $36 per annum from 14 July 1812. 1812. 1813. 1814. 1815. 1816. 1817 with a partial increase for $53.70. 1818 at the new rate of $72. 1819. 1820. 1821. 1822. 1823. 1824. 1825. 1826. 1827 for $36.60.

Kelly, Daniel.* —. Gunner Marines. His widow, Ann M. Kelly, was pensioned from 10 June 1841 at the rate of $10 per month. 1841. 1842. 1842b. She was pensioned again 1 Sep. 1847 at the rate of $10 per month. 1850. 1851.

Kelly, Hugh. Penn. Private Marine. He was pensioned 11 May 1809 at the rate of $36 per annum. 1816. 1818. 1819. 1820. 1821. 1822. 1823. 1824. 1825. 1826. 1827. 1828. 1829. 1830. 1836. He served aboard Gunboat No. 69.

Kelly, James. R.I. Sergeant Marines. He was pensioned 18 Mar. 1830 at the rate of $36 per annum. He was disabled at Bladensburg. 1830. 1835. 1836. 1837. 1838. 1842.

Kelly, James. —. Marine. He was pensioned 24 Aug. 1814 at the rate of $4.50 per month. 1837. 1839. 1840. 1841. 1842b. 1843. 1844. 1845. 1846. 1847. 1848. 1850. 1851.

Kelly, John. Penn. Private Marine. He was pensioned at the rate of $36 per annum in 1810. 1811.

Kelly, Joseph.* —. Seaman. He was pensioned 31 Oct. 1835 at the rate of $4.50 per month.

Naval Pensioners of the United States, 1800-1851

1838. 1839. 1840. 1841. 1842b. 1843. 1844. 1845. 1846. 1847. 1848. He also appeared as Joseph Kelley.
Kelly, Thomas. N.Y. Seaman. He was pensioned 25 Apr. 1815 at the rate of $48 per annum. 1816. 1818. 1819. 1820. 1821. 1822. 1823. 1824. 1825. 1826. 1827. 1828. 1829. 1830. 1835. 1836. 1837. 1839. 1840. 1841. 1842b. 1843. 1844. 1845. 1846. 1847. 1848. 1850. 1851. He served aboard the *President*. He also appeared as Thomas Kelley.
Kelly, Thomas.* —. Marine. His widow, Mary Kelly, was pensioned 13 Sep. 1847 at the rate of $3.50 per month. 1850. 1851.
Kelsey, Joseph.* —. Quarter Gunner. His widow, Susan C. Kelsey, was pensioned 11 Nov. 1839 at the rate of $7.50 per month. 1851.
Kendrick, Benjamin. D.C. Cook. He was pensioned at the rate of $108 per annum. 1816. 1818. 1819. 1820. 1821. 1822. 1823. 1824. 1825. 1826.
Kennedy, —. —. —. Ann Kennedy was pensioned on his service as a privateer at the rate of $120 per annum. 1818. 1819. 1820. 1821. 1822 for $96.67.
Kennedy, Edmund P. —. Captain. His widow, Mary E. Kennedy, was pensioned 28 Mar. 1844 at the rate of $50 per month. 1844. 1845. 1846. 1847. 1848. 1850. 1851.
Kennedy, Michael. Va. Master's Mate. He perished aboard the *Grampus*. His sister, Mary Anne Kennedy, was from Portsmouth, Va. on 10 June 1844.
Kenney, John.* N.Y. Quarter Gunner. He was pensioned 1 July 1825 at the rate of $4.50 per month. 1827. 1828. 1829. 1830. 1835. 1836. 1837. 1839. 1840. 1841. 1842b. 1843. 1844. 1845. 1846. 1847. 1848. 1850. 1851. He served aboard the *Ontario*. He also appeared as John Kenny and John Kennedy.
Kennon, Beverly.* —. Captain. His widow, Britannia W. Kennon, was pensioned 28 Feb. 1849 at the rate of $50 per month. 1845. 1846. 1847. 1848. 1850. 1851.
Kenny, Michael.* Penn. Ordinary Seaman. He was pensioned 1 Jan. 1828 at the rate of $48 per annum. 1829. 1830. He served aboard the *United States*. He also appeared as Michael Fenny.
Kensinger, George.* Penn. Master-at-Arms. He was pensioned 22 May 1819 at the rate of $108 per annum. 1821. 1822. 1823. 1824. 1825. 1827. 1828. 1829. 1830. 1835. 1836. 1837. 1839. 1840. 1841. 1842b. 1843. 1844. 1845. 1846. 1847. 1848. 1850. 1851. He served aboard the frigate *Essex*. He also appeared as George Kinsinger and George Hensinger.
Kerney, John A. —. Surgeon. His widow, Mary M. Kerney, was pensioned 26 Aug. 1849 at the rate of $35 per month.
Kerns, William.* —. Seaman. He was pensioned 25 Aug. 1837 at the rate of $1.50 per month. 1850. 1851.
Kerns, William. —. Seaman. He was pensioned 14 Nov. 1850 at the rate of $6 per month. 1851.
Ketcham, George.* —. Seaman. He was pensioned 22 Sep. 1850 at the rate of $3 per month. 1850. 1851.
Key, Andrew. *—. Boatswain's Mate. He was pensioned 9 July 1839 at the rate of $19 per month. 1840. 1841. 1842b. 1843. 1844. 1845. 1846. 1847. 1848. 1850. 1851.
Keyas, Zenas. Mass. Marine. He was pensioned as a privateer in 1812 at the rate of $48 per annum from 6 Dec. 1812. 1812. 1813. 1814. 1815. 1816. 1817 in the amount of $28.67.

He also appeared as Zenas Keyer.

Kidder, John F.* —. Apprentice. He was pensioned 1 Mar. 1842 at the rate of $1.75 per month. 1843. 1844. 1845. 1846. 1847. 1848. 1850. 1851.

Kidwell, —.* —. Marine. His sons, William E. Kidwell and John J. Kidwell, were pensioned at the rate of $3.50 per month from 1 July 1837. 1837. 1839. 1840. 1841. 1842. 1842b.
[He was listed as Theodore Kidwell in the Old Wars pension index.]

Kiggan, John.* —. Ordinary Seaman. He was pensioned 30 Apr. 1838 at the rate of $2.50 per month. 1839. 1840. 1841. 1842b. 1843. 1844. 1845. 1846. 1847. 1848. 1850. 1851.
He also appeared as John Kiggin.

Kimball, —. —. —. Lucia Kimball was pensioned on his service at the rate of $60 per annum. 1814. 1815. 1816. 1817. 1818. 1819 increased to $120. 1820. 1821. 1822. 1823. 1824. 1825. 1826. 1827. 1828. 1829. 1830. 1831. 1832. 1833 for $100.

King, George.* —. Sergeant of Marines. His widow, Catherine C. King, was pensioned from 3 Aug. 1837 at the rate of $6.50 per month. 1839. 1840. 1841. 1842. 1842b. 1845. 1846. She was pensioned again 1 Sep. 1847 at the rate of $6.50 per month. 1848. 1850. 1851.

King, Thomas.* —. Marine. His son, William King, had his application rejected prior to 12 Dec. 1842. The law granting pensions to children was repealed in 1841 and the father died in 1842.

Kingsbury, William. N.Y. Boatswain. He was pensioned at the rate of $120 per annum. 1816. 1818. 1819. 1820. 1821. 1822. 1823. He was in D.C. in 1826. He also appeared as William Kingsberry.

Kingston, —. —. —. He was injured in 1822. Sarah Kingston applied on his service in Oct. 1825 and was pensioned at the rate of $240 per annum.

Kinnear, William. —. Marine. He was pensioned 3 Apr. 1834 at the rate of $3 per month. 1835. 1836. 1837. 1839. 1840. 1841. 1842. 1843. 1844. 1845. He also appeared as William Kennear and William Kinnead.

Kissam, Benjamin F.* —. Surgeon. His widow, Harriet J. Kissam, was pensioned from 30 June 1834 at the rate of $25 per month. 1836. 1837. 1839. 1840. 1841. 1842. 1842b. 1845. 1846. She was pensioned again 1 Sep. 1847 at the rate of $30 per month. 1848. 1850. 1851.

Kissick, John.* —. Gunner's Mate. His application was rejected prior to 30 Dec. 1845. The report of the surgeon who examined him showed his disability was not permanent. His case was not covered under the law.

Kissock, Roger. D.C. Seaman. He was pensioned at the rate of $96 per annum. 1818. 1819. 1820. 1821.

Kitchen, George.* —. Seaman. His widow, Abigail Kitchen, was pensioned from 16 Aug. 1800 at the rate of $6 per month. 1835. 1836. 1837. 1839. 1840. 1841. 1842. 1842b. 1845. 1846. She was pensioned again 1 Sep. 1847 at the rank of $6 per month. 1848. 1851.

Kitchen, John M. —. Carpenter's Mate. His widow, Mary Kitchen, was pensioned 10 Aug. 1800 at the rate of $9.50 per month. 1851.

Kitts, —.* —. Sailing Master. His widow, Eliza Kitts, was pensioned at the rate of $20 per month from 27 Sep. 1819. 1837. 1839. 1840. 1841. 1842. 1842b. [He was listed as John

Naval Pensioners of the United States, 1800-1851

Kitts in the Old Wars pension index.]
Kitts, Michael.* Penn. Marine. He was pensioned 14 Apr. 1827 at the rate of $36 per annum. 1829. 1830. He served aboard the *United States*.
Klapp, —. —. —. His daughter, Anna P. Klapp, was pensioned. 1837. 1842.
Klien, Nicholas. Penn. Sergeant of Marines. He was pensioned at the rate of $36 per annum in 1818. Md. in 1819. 1820. 1821 in D.C. 1822. 1823. 1824. 1825. 1826. 1827. 1828. 1829. 1830. 1835. 1836. 1837. 1841. 1842b. 1843. 1844. 1845. 1846. 1847. 1848. 1849. 1850. 1851. He was disabled in the Navy Yard in Boston, Mass. He also appeared as Nicholas Kleim and Nicholas Kline.
Kliess, Daniel. —. Ordinary Seaman. He was pensioned 6 May 1829 at the rate of $5 per month. 1835. 1836. 1837. 1838. 1839. 1840. 1841. 1842. 1842b. 1843. 1844. 1845. 1846. 1847.
Knight, John.* —. Landsman. His widow, Mary Knight, was pensioned 14 Nov. 1832 at the rate of $4 per month. 1851.
Kowse, Thomas. Mass. Quarter Gunner. He was pensioned 11 Oct. 1813 at the rate of $108 per annum. 1816. 1818. 1819. 1820 1821. 1822. 1823. 1824. 1825. 1826. 1839. 1840. He served aboard the *Chesapeake*. He also appeared as Thomas Kouse, Thomas Knose and Thomas House.
Kripfar, Lawrence.* D.C. Private Marine. He was pensioned 1 Jan. 1820 at the rate of $36 per annum. 1821. He was in Penn. in 1822. 1823. 1824. 1825. 1826. 1827. 1829. 1830. He served aboard the *New Orleans*. He also appeared as Lawrence Kipfar.

Lagoner, Manuel.* —. Seaman. His widow, Elizabeth Lagoner, was pensioned from 14 Mar. 1835 at the rate of $6 per month. 1835. 1836. 1837. 1839. 1840. 1841. 1842. 1842b. 1845.1846. She was pensioned again 1 Sep. 1847 at the rate of $6 per month. 1848. 1850. 1851. She also appeared as Elizabeth Lagonce and Elizabeth Lagonee.
Lagrange, John.* —. Seaman. He was pensioned 30 Nov. 1834 at the rate of $4.50 per month. 1837. 1838. 1839. 1840. 1841. 1842. 1842b. 1843. 1844. 1845. 1846. 1847. 1848. 1850. 1851.
Laighton, —. —. Gunner. His daughter, Louisa C. Laighton, was pensioned at the rate of $10 per month. 1837. 1842.
Lamb, Joseph. Ga. Ordinary Seaman. He perished aboard the *Epervier* 1 Sep. 1815. His mother was Honor Hamilton of Savannah, Georgia. Her second husband was William Hamilton. She was paid $60 on 11 June 1817.
Lambright, —. —. Boatswain. His daughter, Jane Lambright, was pensioned at the rate of $10 per month. 1837. 1842.
Lanagan, Michael.* —. Ordinary Seaman. His widow, Elizabeth Lanagan, was pensioned at the rate of $5 per month 23 Jan. 1846. 1850.
Lancey, —. Mass. Ordinary Seaman. His widow, Nancy Lancey, was pensioned at the rate of $60 per annum. 1818. 1819. 1820. 1821. 1822. 1823. 1824. 1825. 1827. 1828. She also appeared as Nancy Lancy.

Naval Pensioners of the United States, 1800-1851

Lane, —. —. —. Sally H. Lane was pensioned on his service. 1842.

Lane, Timothy.* N.Y. Cook. He was pensioned 25 Mar. 1816 at the rate of $96 per annum. 1818. 1819. 1820. 1821. 1822. 1823. 1824. 1825. 1826. 1827. 1828. 1829. 1830. 1835. 1836. 1837. 1839. 1840. 1841. 1842b. 1843. 1844. 1845. 1846. 1847. 1848. 1850. 1851. He was disabled on Gunboat No. 110 at the Charleston station.

Lang, John. —. Seaman. He was pensioned 27 July 1837 at the rate of $6 per month. 1837. 1838. 1841. 1842. 1842b. 1843. 1844. 1845. 1846. 1847. 1848. 1850. 1851.

Langley, Isaac.* —. Ordinary Seaman. He was pensioned 1 Dec. 1814 at the rate of $5 per month. 1835. 1836. 1837. 1840. 1841. 1842b. 1843. 1844. 1845. 1846. 1847. 1848. 1850. 1851.

Langley, John. —. Ordinary Seaman. He was pensioned at the rate of $5 per month. 1835. 1837. 1838. 1839. 1842.

Langrean, Peter. * —. Ordinary Seaman. His widow, Susannah Langrean, had her application rejected between Mar. 1840 and 1 Jan. 1842. Her husband had died since the 16th August last, which repealed, in part, the act of 3rd March 1837 under which last law alone she could have claimed a pension. She was pensioned 30 Aug. 1846 at the rate of $5 per month. 1850. 1851.

Lanman, John G.* —. Quarter Gunner. He was pensioned 20 June 1836 at the rate of $7.50 per month. 1839. 1840. 1841. 1842b. 1843. 1844. 1845. 1846. 1847. 1848. 1850. 1851.

Lansford, James H. Va. Seaman. He was pensioned 23 May 1814 at the rate of $48 per annum. 1818. 1819. 1820. 1821. 1822. 1823. 1824. 1825. 1827. 1829. 1828. 1830. He was disabled on Lake Champlain. He also appeared as James H. Sansford.

Lanstaff, Peter H. —. 1st Class Boy. He was pensioned 28 Feb. 1851 at the rate of $1.50 per month. 1851.

Larramee, Benjamin.* —. Boatswain. His widow, Abby Larramee, was pensioned 1 June 1849 at the rate of $10 per month. 1845. 1846. 1847. 1848. 1850. 1851. He was also known as John Brown. [He was Benjamin Laramee in Old Wars pension index.]

Laskey, —. —. —. He drowned in the service. The son of Mary Laskey applied in Jan. 1824 and was pensioned at the rate of $60 per annum.

Latham, George W.* —. Chaplain. His widow, Lucy T. Latham, was pensioned 27 Jan. 1847 at rate of $20 per month. 1847. 1848. 1850. 1851.

Lathrop, John P.* —. Chaplain. His widow, Maria M. Lathrop, was pensioned 29 Dec. 1848 at the rate of $20 per month. 1850. 1851.

Laughlin, John. —. Marine. He was pensioned at the rate of $1.75 per month. 1837. 1838. 1842. He may also have been the one listed as John Laughen on the latter list.

Laurie, —. —. Captain. His widow, Ann Eliza Laurie, was pensioned at the rate of $50 per month. 1837. 1842.

Lauson, Levin.* —. Seaman. He was pensioned 23 Sep. 1847 at the rate of $6 per month. 1847. 1848. 1850. 1851. He also appeared as Levin Lawson.

Lavis, Thomas. —. Gunner's Mate. His widow, Catherine E. Lavis, was pensioned 9 Jan. 1846 at the rate of $9 per month. 1847. 1848.

Lawrence, James. N.Y. Captain. He served aboard the *Chesapeake* and was killed 1 June 1813.

Naval Pensioners of the United States, 1800-1851

His widow, Julia M. Lawrence, was pensioned 1 June 1816 at the rate of $50 per month. 1818. 1820. 1821. 1822. 1823. 1824. 1825. 1827. 1828. 1829. 1830. 1836. 1837. 1839. 1840. 1841. 1842. 1842b. 1845. 1846. She was pensioned again 1 Sep. 1847 at the rate of $50 per month. 1848. 1850. 1851.

Lawrence, John.* —. Quarter Gunner. He was pensioned 15 Mar. 1851 at the rate of $7.50 per month. 1851.

Lazarro, John. N.Y. Seaman. He was pensioned 29 July 1814 at the rate of $72 per annum. 1816. 1818. 1819. 1820. 1821. 1822. 1823. 1824. 1825. 1826. 1827. 1828. 1829. 1830. 1835. 1836. 1837. 1838. 1842. He served aboard the *Essex*. He also appeared as John Lazanno.

Leahy, James.* N.Y. Marine. His widow, Catherine Leahy, was pensioned from 27 Dec. 1840 at the rate of $3.50 per month. 1841. 1842. 1842b. She had her next application rejected prior to 23 Dec. 1848. Her claim was barred by the act of 11 Aug. 1848. His widow was pensioned 1 Sep. 1847 at the rate of $3.50 per month. 1850. 1851. She also appeared as Catherine Leaky.

Learned, Lucas.* —. Seaman. He was pensioned 24 July 1849 at the rate of $4.50 per month. 1850. 1851.

Lecchesi, Joseph. —. Musician. His widow, Mary Lecchesi, was pensioned 28 Feb. 1850 at the rate of $4 per month. 1851.

Leckie, James.* —. Carpenter. His widow, Martha Leckie, was pensioned 12 Nov. 1843 at the rate of $10 per month. 1844. 1845. 1846. 1848. 1850. 1851.

Lecompte, Md. Seaman. Rebecca Lecompte was pensioned on his service as a privateer at the rate of $72 per annum from 4 Nov. 1812. 1817. 1818. 1819. 1820. 1821. 1822 for $61.

Lee, —.* —. Lieutenant. His widow, Elizabeth Lee, was pensioned from 30 June 1832 at the rate of $25 per month. 1835. 1836. 1837. 1839. 1840. 1842. His children, Theodore Lee and Matilda T. Lee, were pensioned from 25 Oct. 1838 at the rate of $25 per month. 1842b. [He was listed as John Lee in the Old Wars pension index.]

Lee, Richard. Conn. Quartermaster. He was pensioned 1 July 1820 at the rate of $72 per annum. 1822. 1823. 1824. 1825. 1826. 1827. 1828. 1829. 1830. 1835. 1836. 1837. 1839. 1840. 1841. 1842b. 1843. 1844. 1845. 1846. 1847. 1848. 1850. 1851. He was disabled on Lake Champlain.

Lee, Rodney. —. Barney's flotilla. His application was rejected between Mar. 1840 and 1 Jan. 1842. His name was not on the list of the wounded men who belonged to the flotilla under the command of Commodore Barney.

Lemark, Peter. N.Y. Marine. He was pensioned at the rate of $36 per annum in 1809. 1810. 1811.

Lemon, Neal C.* —. Boatswain. His widow, Martha Lemon, was pensioned 14 Aug. 1850 at the rate of $9.50 per month. 1845. 1846. 1847. 1848. 1850. 1851.

Lent, Abraham.* —. Sailmaker's Mate. His widow, Sarah Ann Lent, was pensioned from 11 Sep. 1824 at the rate of $9.50 per month. 1837. 1839. 1840. 1841. 1842. 1842b. 1845. 1846. 1848. 1850.

Lent, Peter.* —. Seaman. He was pensioned 31 May 1849 at the rate of $4.50 per month. 1850. 1851.

Naval Pensioners of the United States, 1800-1851

Leonard, Daniel. Md. Seaman. He was pensioned at the rate of $60 per annum in 1809. 1810. 1811. 1816.

Leonard, James. Penn. Seaman. He was pensioned 1 July 1829 at the rate of $108 per annum. 1829. 1830. He was disabled by disease contracted aboard the *Hornet*.

Leonard, John. —. Seaman. He was pensioned 1 July 1829 at the rate of $9 per month. 1839. 1840. 1841. 1842b. 1843. 1844. 1845. 1846. 1847. 1848. 1850. 1851.

Leppy, Henry.* Penn. Seaman. He was pensioned at the rate of $72 per annum. 1819. 1820. 1821.

Leslie, Henry P. —. Carpenter. He was pensioned from 18 Feb. 1840 at the rate of $5 per month. 1841. 1842b. 1843.

Letson, —. —. —. Alice Letson was pensioned on his service as a privateer at the rate of $36 per month. 1812. 1813. 1814. 1815. 1816. 1817. 1818. 1819. 1820. 1821. 1822. 1823. 1824. 1825. 1826. 1827 for $10.20.

Lewis, Andrew J. N.Y. —. He perished aboard the *Grampus*. His siblings were Mary J. Lewis, Elizabeth P. Lewis, Mrs. Emily C. Herring, Maria L. Lewis, Daniel B. Lewis, and Lucien L. Lewis who was not 15 years of age. They were from Brooklyn, N.Y. 15 July 1844.

Lewis, James.* —. Hospital Steward. He was pensioned 2 Dec. 1845 at the rate of $9 per month. 1846. 1847. 1848. 1850. 1851.

Lewis, James A. N.Y. Quartermaster. He was pensioned in Apr. 1814 at the rate of $108 per annum. 1816. 1818. 1819. 1820. 1821. 1822. 1823. 1825. 1826. 1827. 1828. 1829. 1830.

Lewis, John.* —. Boatswain's Mate. He was pensioned 1 Jan. 1832 at the rate of $9 per month. 1835. 1836. 1837. 1839. 1840. 1841. 1842b. 1843. 1844. 1845. 1846. 1847. 1848. 1850. 1851.

Lewis, Peter.* —. Ordinary Seaman. He was pensioned 30 July 1837 at the rate of $5 per month. 1839. 1840. 1841. 1842b. 1843. 1844. 1845. 1846. 1847. 1848. 1850. 1851.

Lewis, Richard. N.Y. Marine. He was stationed at the Navy Yard in New York and was shot 28 Aug. 1814. His widow, Mary Lewis, was pensioned 4 Oct. 1819. 1821. 1822. 1823. 1824. 1825. 1827. 1828. 1829. 1830.

Lewis, Robert.* —. Steward. He was pensioned 5 Sep. 1830 at the rate of $6.75 per month. 1839. 1840. 1841. 1842b. 1843. 1844. 1845. 1846. 1847. 1848. 1850. 1851.

Lewis, Thomas.* —. Gunner's Mate. His children, Georgia Ann Lewis and Sarah F. Lewis, were pensioned 28 Aug. 1848 at the rate of $9.50 per month. 1848. 1850. 1851.

Lewis, William. Conn. Private Marine. He served aboard the *Chesapeake*. He was pensioned 12 Dec. 1813 at the rate of $36 per annum. 1816. 1818. 1819. 1820. 1821. 1822. 1824. 1825. 1826. 1827. 1828. 1829. 1835. 1836.

Lewis, William. Va. Master Commandant. He served aboard the *Epervier* and was lost 1 Sep. 1815. He married Frances Munford Whittle 24 Apr. 1815 in Norfolk, Va. One Mary Ann Whittle, signed the license. William Fortescue Whittle was the uncle of the bride. Frances Lewis's sister was the widow of Lt. Neale who also perished on the *Epervier*. Frances Lewis was paid $360 in Aug. 1817. His widow, Frances M. Lewis, was pensioned 13 July 1818 at the rate of $30 per month. 1819. 1820. 1821. 1822. 1823. 1824. 1825. 1827. 1828. 1829. 1830. 1835. 1836. 1837. 1839. 1840. 1841. 1842. 1842b. 1845. 1846. She

Naval Pensioners of the United States, 1800-1851

was pensioned again 1 Sep. 1847 at the rate of $30 per month. 1848. 1850. 1851.
Libbis, Edward.* —. Ordinary Seaman. He was pensioned 11 June 1836 at the rate of $1.66 2/3 per month. 1839. 1840. 1841. 1842b. 1843. 1844. 1845. 1846. 1847. 1848. 1850. 1851.
Lightelle, —.* —. Marine. His sons, William E. Lightelle, Benjamin T. Lightelle, and John B. O. O'. Lightelle, were pensioned at the rate of $3.50 per month from 22 Dec. 1824. 1837. 1839. 1840. 1841. 1842. 1842b. [He was listed as John Lightelle in the Old Wars pension index.]
Lincoln, Collins. Mass. Marine. He was pensioned at the rate of $36 per annum. He was receiving his pension as early as 1 Oct. 1807. 1808. 1809. 1810. 1811.
Lincoln, Mayhen F. —. —. He was pensioned. 1842.
Lindsay, —. —. —. Elizabeth Lindsay was pensioned on his service as a privateer at the rate of $36 per annum. 1812. 1813. 1814. 1815. 1816. 1817 increase to $72. 1818. 1819. 1820. 1821. 1822. 1823. 1824. 1825. 1826 for $27.60.
Lindsey, —. —. Sailing Master. His widow, Deborah Lindsey, was pensioned at the rate of $20 per month from 19 May 1826. 1837. 1839. 1840. 1841. 1842. 1842b. She also appeared as Deborah Lindsay and Deborah Linsay.
Lindstrom, Gustavus. La. Seaman. He was pensioned as a privateer at the rate of $60 per annum from 23 Nov. 1813. 1813. 1814. 1815. 1816 for $23.83. 1820.
Lines, Orra. —. Seaman. His application was rejected between Mar. 1840 and 1 Jan. 1842. He claimed to have been wounded on Lake Champlain in 1814. His name was not on the list of those who were wounded in that action.
Linn, John.* —. Seaman. He was pensioned 1 Nov. 1831 at the rate of $6 per month. 1835. 1836. 1837.
Linn, Lewis D.* —. Purser's Steward. His widow, Elizabeth Linn, was pensioned 24 Dec. 1850 at the rate of $9 per month. 1851.
Linscott, —. —. Boatswain. His orphans, Jane P. Linscott, Mary F. Linscott, and Caroline W. Linscott, were pensioned at the rate of $10 per month from 25 May 1827. 1837. 1839. 1840. 1841. 1842. 1842b.
Linscott, James. N.Y. Seaman. He was pensioned 9 Mar. 1813 at the rate of $36 per annum. 1818. 1819. 1820. 1821. 1822. 1823. 1824. 1825. 1826. 1827. 1828. 1829. 1830. He served aboard the *Enterprise*.
Linslie, Frederick B.* —. Ship's Steward. His widow, Hannah Linslie, was pensioned 23 Sep. 1848 at the rate of $9 per month. 1851.
Lippincott, Caleb.* Penn. Ordinary Seaman. He was killed by a fall on the lakes 7 Feb. 1816. He served aboard the *Java*. His widow, Susannah Lippincott, was pensioned. 1829. 1830. She was pensioned again from 1 Jan. 1838 at the rate of $5 per month. 1839. 1840. 1841. 1842. 1842b. 1845. 1846. She was pensioned 1 Sep. 1847 at the rate of $5 per month. 1848. 1850. 1851.
Livingston, —.* —. Ordinary Seaman. His orphans, Catharine Livingston and James Livingston, were pensioned at the rate of $5 per month from 4 June 1829. 1837. 1839. 1840. 1841. 1842. 1842b. [He was listed as James Livingston in the Old Wars pension index.]
Lloyd, James. —. Marine. He was pensioned 5 Apr. 1834 at the rate of $2.62 ½ per month. 1835.

Naval Pensioners of the United States, 1800-1851

1836. 1837. 1839. 1840. 1841. 1842b. 1843. 1844. 1845. 1846. 1847. 1848. 1850. 1851.

Lloyd, John. N.H. Marine. He was pensioned 8 June 1819 at the rate of $36 per annum. 1820. 1821. 1822. 1823. 1824. 1825. 1826. 1827. 1828. 1829. 1830. 1835. 1836. 1837. 1839. 1840. 1841. 1842b. 1843. 1844. 1845. 1846. 1847. 1848. 1850. 1851. He was disabled at the navy yard at Charlestown, Mass. He also appeared as John Loyed.

Lock, —. —. —. E. Lock was pensioned on his service as a privateer at the rate of $66 per annum. 1815. 1816 for $28.60.

Lockert, James M.* —. Lieutenant. His widow, Margaret E. Lockert, was pensioned 10 Apr. 1845 at the rate of $25 per month. 1845. 1846. 1847. 1848. 1850. 1851.

Locusson, Thomas.* —. Ordinary Seaman. He was pensioned 4 Sep. 1846 at the rate of $3.75 per month. 1846. 1847. 1848. 1850. 1851.

Logue, Robert. Penn. Marine. He was stationed at Sackett's Harbor and was killed 4 Mar. 1813. His widow was Jane Logue. Her two children were pensioned 11 Nov. 1818 at the rate of $36 per annum. 1819. 1820. 1821. 1822. 1823. 1824. 1825. 1827. 1829. 1830.

Long, —. N.H. Cook. Sally Long was pensioned on his service as a privateer at the rate of $48 per annum. 1815. 1816. 1817. 1818. 1819. 1820 increase to $96. 1821. 1822. 1823. 1824. 1825. 1826 for $82.13.

Long, —. —. —. Sally Long was pensioned on his service as a privateer at the rate of $72 per annum. 1812. 1813. 1814. 1815. 1816. 1817 increase to $144. 1818. 1819. 1820. 1821. 1822. 1823. 1824. 1825. 1826. 1827. 1828. 1829. 1830. 1831. 1832 for $121.60.

Long, William. Mass. Seaman. He was pensioned at the rate of $72 per annum. 1816. 1818. 1819. 1820. 1821. 1822. 1823

Longiel, Matthew.* N.Y. Boatswain. He was lost in a boat 11 Feb. 1824 by drowning. His widow, Susannah Longiel, was pensioned 15 July 1824 at the rate of $120 per annum. 1825. 1827. 1828. 1829. Her pension expired 12 Feb.1829. She also appeared as Susannah Longill. His son, George R. Longill, was pensioned. 1837. 1842.

Longley, William S.* —. Seaman. His application was rejected prior to 10 Jan. 1844. The surgeons who examined him gave their opinion that he was not permanently disabled. They recommended that he be sent to hospital.

Lonzado, —. —. —. Agnes Lonzado was pensioned on his service as a privateer at the rate of $36 per annum. 1813. 1814. 1815. 1816. 1817. 1818 increase to $72. 1819. 1820. 1821. 1822. 1823. 1824. 1825. 1826. 1827. 1828. 1829. 1830. 1831. 1832. She also appeared as Agnes Louzado.

Look, —. Mass. Lieutenant. Eliza Look was pensioned on hi service as a privateer at the rate of $6 per month from 1 Feb. 1815.

Loomis, Erastus. —. —. He was wounded on board an armed vessel on Lake Champlain in 1814. He recovered. He alleged that he suffered from disease in consequence from the wound, but he did not prove that claim. His application was withdrawn. 23 Mar. 1826.

Lord, —.* —. Gunner. His daughter, Caroline Lord, was pensioned at the rate of $10 per month from 9 July 1829. 1837. 1839. 1840. 1841. 1842. 1842b. [He was listed as John Lord in the Old Wars pension index.]

Lord, Nathaniel.* —. Quartermaster. He was pensioned 26 Feb. 1843 at the rate of $4.50 per

Naval Pensioners of the United States, 1800-1851

month. 1843. 1844. 1845. 1846. 1847. 1848. 1850. 1851.
Lord, William.* —. Seaman. He was pensioned 9 May 1847 at the rate of $6 per month. 1847. 1848. 1850. 1851.
Loring, Noadiah M. —. Purser. His widow, Prudence C. Loring, was pensioned 3 Dec. 1808 at the rate of $20 per month. 1851.
Loscomb, John.* —. Ordinary Seaman. He was pensioned from 15 Jan. 1858 at the rate of $2.50 per month. 1838.
Loud, —. —. —. His son, Rufus W. Loud, was pensioned at the rate of $9 per month. 1837. 1842.
Loude, —. —. —. Louisa Loude was pensioned on his service. 1842.
Lovely, Henry. —. Captain. He was pensioned for privateer service from 2 Dec. 1829 at the rate of $20 per month. 1830. 1831. 1832. 1833. 1834. 1835. 1836. 1837 for $120. He was pensioned again 1 July 1837. 1838. He also appeared as Henry Lively and Henry Levely.
Lovely, John.* —. Seaman. He was pensioned 23 Apr. 1835 at the rate of $6 per month. 1838. 1840. 1841. 1842b. 1843. 1844. 1845. 1846. 1847. 1848. He also appeared as John Levely.
Lovesage, William. Penn. Seaman. He was pensioned at the rate of $72 per annum. 1819. 1820. 1821. 1822. 1823. 1824. 1825. He also appeared as William Loversage.
Lovett, —. Mass. Pay Master. Priscilla Lovett was pensioned on his service as a privateer at the rate of $60 per annum from 1 Jan. 1815. 1815. 1816. 1817. 1818. 1819. 1820. 1821. 1822. 1823. 1824. 1825. 1826. 1827. 1828. 1829. 1830.
Low, James. —. Seaman. He was pensioned 1 Jan. 1846 at the rate of $6 per month. 1846. 1847. 1848. 1850. 1851.
Low, John. —. Seaman. His widow, Betsey Low, was pensioned at the rate of $6 per month from 1 Sep. 1815. 1837. 1839. 1840. 1841. 1842. 1842b. 1845. 1846. She was pensioned again on 1 Sep. 1847 at the rate of $6 per month. 1848. 1851.
Low, John. —.Seaman. His widow, Betsey Low, was pensioned 1 Jan. 1851 at the rate of $9.50 per month. 1851.
Low, John. —. Seaman. His widow, Betsey Low, was pensioned 14 July 1815 at the rate of $3.50 per month. 1850. 1851.
Low, John. Mass. Gunner's Mate. He perished aboard the *Epervier* 1 Sep. 1815. He married Elizabeth Potter on 30 Oct. 1808 at St. Peters Church in Salem, Mass. His widow, Elizabeth Low, was paid $108 on 24 June 1817.
Low, Thomas.* —. Yeoman. His widow, Lydia Low, was pensioned from 1 Aug. 1834 at the rate of $9 per month. 1835. 1836. 1837. 1839. 1840. 1841. 1842. 1842b. 1845. 1846. She was pensioned again 1Sep. 1847 at the rate of $7.50 per month. 1848. 1850. 1851.
Lowder, George.* Md. Seaman. He was pensioned at the rate of $144 per annum. 1818. 1819. 1820. 1821. 1822. He also appeared as George Lawder.
Lowe, —.* —. Lieutenant. His orphan, Adeline K. Lowe, was pensioned at the rate of $25 per month from 2 May 1826. 1837. 1840. 1841. 1842. 1842b. She also appeared as Adeline K. Love. [He was listed as William Lowe in the Old Wars pension index.]
Lowndes, —. —. —. Jane B. Lowndes was pensioned on his service. 1842.

Naval Pensioners of the United States, 1800-1851

Lowry, . —.* —. —. His son, James Lowry, was pensioned. 1842. [He was listed as James Lowry in the Old Wars pension index.]

Lowther, R. Mass. Seaman. He served aboard the *Wasp* and was lost 20 Apr. 1815. His widow, Hannah Lowther, was pensioned at the rate of $72 per annum. 1818. 1819. 1820. 1821. 1822. 1823. 1824. 1825. 1827. 1828. 1829. She also appeared as Hannah Louther.

Lucchesi, Joseph.* —. Musician. His widow, Mary Lucchesi, was pensioned at the rate of $4 per month 23 Feb. 1850. 1850.

Ludlow, —.* —. Purser. William B. Ludlow, Augustus C. Ludlow, Mary W. Ludlow, and Robert C. Ludlow were pensioned on his service from 1 Jan. 1837 at the rate of $20 per annum. 1837. 1839. 1840. 1841. 1842. [He was listed as Robert C. Ludlow in the Old Wars pension index.]

Ludlow, William.* —. Quarter Gunner. He was pensioned 24 Sep. 1847 at the rate of $7.50 per month. 1847. 1848. 1850. 1851.

Lugler, Joseph.* —. Ord. Sergeant Marines. His widow, Sarah Jane Lugler, was pensioned 23 Oct. 1849 at the rate of $8 per month. 1850. 1851. He also appeared as Joseph Luegler.

Lumbard. —. —. —. His sons, Joshua Lumbard and John Lumbard, were pensioned. 1837. 1842.

Luscomb, John. —. Ordinary Seaman. He was pensioned 15 Jan. 1838 at the rate of $2.50 per month. 1840. 1841. 1842b. 1843. 1844. 1845. 1846. 1847. 1848. 1850. 1851.

Lutts, John.* —. Marine. His widow, Mehitable Lutts, was pensioned 19 Apr. 1848 at the rate of $3.50 per month. 1848. 1850. 1851.

Lyle, David H. N.Y. Captain's Clerk. He perished aboard the *Epervier* 1 Sep. 1815. He was the son of Henry and Getty, nee VanNess, Lyle. He was born 4 Mar. 1796. The Rev. Jeremiah Romeyn baptized him 5 Apr. 1796. His father, Henry Lyle, of Red Hook, Dutchess Co., N.Y. was paid $150 on 14 July 1817.

Lynch, John.* —. Quartermaster. He was pensioned 7 Dec. 1838 at the rate of $18 per month. 1842b. 1843. 1844. 1845. 1846. 1847. 1848. 1850. 1851.

Lyndall, —. —. Gunner. His daughter, Mary Lyndall, was pensioned at the rate of $5 per month. 1837.

Lyndell, —. —. —. Mary Lyndell was pensioned on his service. 1842.

Lyne, William B.* —. Lieutenant. His daughter, Wilhelmina B. Lyne, was pensioned 14 Feb. 1850 at the rate of $25 per month. 1850. 1851. His widow, Elizabeth B. Lyne, was pensioned at the rate of $25 per month from 1 May 1841. 1841. 1842. 1842b. 1843. 1844. 1845. 1848.

Lynn, —. N.H. Master of the Hold. Ann Eliza Lynn was pensioned on his service as a privateer at the rate of $48 per annum. 1815. 1816. 1817. 1818. 1819. 1820 increase to $96. 1821. 1822. 1823. 1824. 1825. 1826. 1827. 1828. 1829. 1830. 1831. 1832. 1833. 1834.

McArthur, William P.* —. Midshipman. He was pensioned from 15 Jan. 1838 at the rate of $4.75 per month. 1838. 1840. 1841. 1842b. 1843. His widow, Mary S. McArthur, was pensioned 23 Dec. 1850 at the rate of $30 per month. 1851 at which time his rank was given as Lieutenant Commanding.

McCall, William C.* —. Surgeon. His widow, Mary McCall, was pensioned from 15 Sep. 1831 at the rate of $25 per month. 1839. 1840. 1841. 1842. 1842b. 1845. 1846. She was pensioned again 1 Sep. 1847 at the rate of $25 per month. 1848. 1850. 1851.

McCann, —.* —. Purser's Steward. His widow, Elizabeth McCann, was pensioned from 26 Apr. 1840 at the rate of $9 per month. 1840. 1841. 1842. 1842b. [He was listed as William B. McCann in the Old Wars pension index.]

McCann, —. —. Sergeant Marines. His orphans, Mary Ann McCann and William B. McCann, were pensioned at the rate of $6.50 per month. 1837. 1842.

McCann, James.* —. Seaman. He was pensioned 31 Dec. 1847 at the rate of $6 per month. 1850. 1851.

McCann, William.* —. Ordinary Seaman. He was pensioned 9 July 1844 at the rate of $5 per month. 1844. 1845. 1846. 1847. 1848. 1850. 1851.

McCargo, John.* —. Quartermaster. He was pensioned 9 Feb. 1847 at the rate of $4 per month. 1848. 1850. 1851.

McCarthy, —. —. Ordinary Seaman. His daughter, Mary McCarthy, was pensioned at the rate of $5 per month. 1837. 1842. She also appeared as Mary McCarty.

McCarty, —.* —. Ordinary Seaman. His widow, Honora McCarty, was pensioned from 25 May 1839 at the rate of $5 per month. 1839. 1840. 1841. 1842. 1842b. She also appeared as Hannah McCarty. [He was listed as Dennis McCarty in the Old Wars pension index.]

McCarty, John. N.Y. Purser's Steward. He was pensioned 1 May 1815 at the rate of $60 per annum. 1816. 1818. 1819. 1820. 1821. 1822. 1823. 1824. 1825. 1826. 1827. 1828. 1829. 1830. He served aboard Gunboat No. 106.

McCawley, —.* —. Lieutenant. His son, James B. McCawley, was pensioned at the rate of $25 per month from 20 Feb. 1827. 1837. 1839. 1840. 1841. 1842. 1842b. He also appeared as James B. McCauley. [He was listed as George McCauley in the Old Wars pension index.]

McCawley, James.* —. Captain of Marines. His widow, Mary E. McCawley, was pensioned from 22 Feb. 1839 at the rate of $20 per month. 1839. 1840. 1841. 1842. 1842b. 1843. 1845. 1846. 1848. She was pensioned again 5 Mar. 1849 at the rate of $20 per month. 1850. 1851. He also appeared as James McCauley.

McCeaver, Peter.* N.Y. Sailmaker. He was pensioned at the rate of $90 per annum. 1818. 1819. 1820. 1821. 1822.

McCloud, —.* —. Boatswain. His orphans, John McCloud and Mary A. McCloud, were pensioned at the rate of $10 per month from 1 July 1837. 1837. 1839. 1840. 1841. 1842. 1842b. [He was listed as John McCloud in the Old Wars pension index.]

McClure, —.* —. Quarter Gunner. His widow, Mary D. McClure, was pensioned from 5 June 1834 at the rate of $7.50 per month. 1839. 1840. 1841. 1842. 1842b. [He was listed as Theophilus McClure in the Old Wars pension index.]

McCollum, Andrew.* Mass. Marine. He was pensioned 1 Apr. 1817 at the rate of $96 per annum. 1818. 1821. 1822. 1826. 1830. He was disabled at headquarters.

McConnomy, Michael.* Penn. Ordinary Seaman. He was pensioned 17 Dec. 1819 at the rate of $72 per annum. 1821. 1822. 1823. 1824. 1825. 1826. 1827. 1828. 1829. 1830. He served

Naval Pensioners of the United States, 1800-1851

aboard the brig *Argus*.

McCormick, Barney. —. Marine. His application was rejected prior to 30 Dec. 1845. He alleged to have been wounded more than twenty-five years ago. There was no record of the fact so the claim could not be allowed.

McCoy, —.* —. Seaman. His daughter, Mary Ann McCoy, was pensioned from 13 Oct. 1835 at the rate of $6 per month. 1840. 1841. 1842. 1842b. [He was listed as William McCoy in the Old Wars pension index.]

McCracken, John.* D.C. Boatswain's Mate. He was pensioned 1 Jan. 1820 at the rate of $144 per annum. 1819. 1820. 1821 in N.Y. 1822. 1823. 1824 in Mass. 1825. 1826. 1827. 1828. 1829. 1830. He served aboard the *Peacock*.

McCrae, Thomas.* —. Seaman. He was pensioned 10 Apr. 1849 at the rate of $3 per month. 1850. 1851. He also appeared as Thomas McCrea.

McCreery, George M.* Va. Lieutenant. He perished aboard the *Grampus*. His widow, Matilda McCreery, was from Richmond, Va. on 22 Dec. 1844. She was pensioned 20 Mar. 1843 at the rate of $25 per month. 1844. 1845. 1846. 1847. 1848. 1850. 1851. He also appeared as George McCreary.

McCullock, Alexander.* Mass. Sailing Master. He served aboard the schooner *Ohio*, was wounded on Lake Erie, and died 24 Aug. 1814. His widow, Ann G. McCullock, was pensioned 26 May 1815 at the rate of $20 per month. 1816. 1818. 1819. 1820. 1821. 1822. 1823. 1824. 1825. 1827. 1828. 1829. 1830. 1835. 1836. 1839. 1840. 1841. 1842. 1842b. 1845. 1846. She also appeared as Ann G. McCulloch and Ann McCullough. She was pensioned again 1 Sep. 1847 at the rate of $20 per month. 1848. 1850. 1851. He also appeared as Alexander McCullough.

McCulloh, George B.* —. Lieutenant. His widow, Susan McCulloh, was pensioned at the rate of $20 per month from 31 Dec. 1827. 1837. 1839. 1840. 1841. 1842b. She was pensioned again 1 Sep. 1842 at the rate of $25 per month. 1842. 1847. 1848. She also appeared ast Susan McCullough.

McCullum, Andrew.* Mass. Marine. He was pensioned at the rate of $96 per annum. 1818. 1819. 1820. 1823. 1824. 1825. 1827. 1828. 1829. He was disabled at headquarters. He also appeared as Andrew McCollum.

McDaniel, George. Penn. Ordinary Seaman. He was pensioned 10 Dec. 1814 at the rate of $60 per annum. 1818. 1819. 1820. 1821. 1822. 1823. 1824. 1825. 1826. 1827. 1828. 1829. 1830. He served aboard the *Congress*.

McDermott, —.* —. Quarter Gunner. His widow, Hetty McDermott, was pensioned from 30 Sep. 1837 at the rate of $7.50 per month. 1839. 1840. 1841. 1842. 1842b. [He was listed as Stephen McDermott in the Old Wars pension index.]

McDonald, Alexander.* —. Private of Marines. His widow, Asenath McDonald, was pensioned 19 Sep. 1850 at the rate of $3.50 per month. 1850. 1851.

McDonald, Hugh.* —. Sergeant of Marines. His widow, Mary McDonald, was pensioned 7 Aug. 1847 at the rate of $6.50 per month. 1848. 1850. 1851.

McDonald, James. —. Corporal of Marines. He was pensioned 31 Dec. 1814 at the rate of $2.25 per month. 1838. 1839. 1840. 1841. 1842b. 1843. 1844. 1845. 1846. 1847. 1848. 1850.

Naval Pensioners of the United States, 1800-1851

1851.

McDonald, James.* —. Seaman. He was pensioned 31 Dec. 1836 at the rate of $3 per month. 1837. 1840. 1841. 1842b. 1843. 1844. 1845. 1846. 1847. 1848. 1850. He also appeared as James McDonnell.

McDonnell, James. —. Quarter Gunner. He was pensioned at the rate of $3 per month. 1837. 1838. 1839. 1842.

McDonough, Bernard.* Penn. Private Marine. He was pensioned at the rate of $72 per annum in 1823. 1824. 1826. 1827. 1828. 1829. He was disabled by rupture.

McDonough, Henry. Mass. Seaman. He was pensioned 24 Mar. 1816 at the rate of $72 per annum. 1818. 1819. 1820. 1821. 1822. 1823. 1824. 1825. 1826. 1827. 1828. 1829. 1830. He was disabled aboard the *Guerriere*.

McDonough, John. Md. Ordinary Seaman. He was pensioned at the rate of $60 per annum in 1811. 1816.

McDowell, John A.* —. Seaman. He was pensioned 19 Mar. 1845 at the rate of $6 per month. 1845. 1846. 1847. 1848. 1850. 1851.

McEvers, —. —. Sophia McEvers was pensioned on his service as a privateer at the rate of $60 per annum. 1813. 1814. 1815. 1816. 1817. 1818. 1819 increase to $120. 1820. 1821. 1822. 1823. 1824. 1825. 1826. 1827. 1828 for $10.

McGarr, John.* —. Steward. He was pensioned 11 Nov. 1832 at the rate of $4.50 per month. 1839. 1840. 1841. 1842. 1842b. 1843. 1844. 1845. 1846. 1847. 1848. 1850. 1851. He was incorrectly listed as John M. Garr for the first two years.

McGee, John.* —. Marine. His widow, Rebecca McGee, was pensioned from 26 Jan. 1830 at the rate of $3.50 per month. 1836. 1837. 1839. 1840. 1841. 1842. 1842b. 1845. 1846. 1848. 1850. 1851.

McGee, Roger. N.Y. Marine. He was pensioned at the rate of $36 per annum. 1816. 1818. 1819. 1820. 1821. 1822. 1823. 1824. 1825. 1826. 1827. 1828. 1829. He served aboard the *Constitution*.

McGill, Mathias. Penn. Seaman. He was pensioned 24 Apr. 1815 at the rate of $96 per annum. 1821. 1822. 1823. 1824. 1825. 1826. 1827. 1828. 1829. 1830. 1835. 1836. 1837. 1838. 1839. 1840. 1841. 1842b. 1843. 1843. 1844. 1845. 1846. 1847. 1848. 1850. 1851. He also appeared as Mathias Magill. He served aboard the *President*.

McGinnes, Thomas.* —. Seaman. He was pensioned 10 Apr. 1851 at the rate of $3 per month. 1850. 1851. He also appeared as Thomas McGinnis.

McGowan, —. —. Lieutenant. His widow, Celeste McGowan, was pensioned at the rate of $25 per month from 19 Feb. 1826. 1837. 1839. 1840. 1841. 1842. 1842b.

McIsaacs, Samuel. N.Y. Boy. He was pensioned 30 July 1814 at the rate of $36 per annum. 1818. 1819. 1820. 1821. 1822. 1823. 1824. 1825. 1826. 1827. 1828. 1829. 1830. 1835. 1836. 1837. 1839. 1840. 1841. 1842b. 1843. 1844. 1845. 1846. 1847. 1848. 1850. 1851. He served aboard the *Essex*.

McKeever, Daniel.* —. Seaman. He was pensioned 10 Dec. 1844 at the rate of $3 per month. 1845. 1846. 1847. 1848. 1850. 1851.

McKeever, William.* —. Ordinary Seaman. He was pensioned 14 Oct. 1835 at the rate of $2.50

Naval Pensioners of the United States, 1800-1851

per month. 1841. 1842b. 1843. 1844. 1845. 1846. 1847. 1848. 1850. 1851.

McKennon, —. —. —. Elizabeth McKennon was pensioned on his service as a privateer at the rate of $36 per annum. 1813. 1814. 1815. 1816. 1817. 1818 increase to $72. 1819. 1820. 1821. 1822. 1823. 1824. 1825. 1826. 1827.

McKenzie, Alexander.* —. Commander. His widow, Catherine A. S. McKenzie, was pensioned at the rate of $30 per month 13 Sep. 1848. 1850. 1851. He also appeared as Alexander McKinzie.

McKenzie, John.* —. Seaman. He was pensioned 4 Oct. 1844 at the rate of $4 per month. 1845. 1846. 1847. 1848. 1850. 1851.

McKenzie, Matthew.* N.Y. Seaman. He was pensioned 10 Dec. 1819 at the rate of $72 per annum in 1821. 1822. 1823. 1824. 1825. 1826. 1827. 1828. 1829. 1830. He also appeared as Matthew McKensie. He served aboard the *Hornet*.

McKernan, James. N.Y. Seaman. He was pensioned 22 Nov. 1815 at the rate of $72 per annum. 1818. 1819. 1820. 1821. 1822. 1823. 1824. 1825. 1826. 1827. 1828. 1829. 1830. He served aboard the *Guerriere*. He also appeared as John McKernau.

McKerson, James. —. Seaman. He was pensioned. 1838.

McKim, James.* Mass. Sergeant Marines. He was a casualty during the war at Charlestown near Boston in 1814. His widow, Elizabeth McKim, received $60 per annum. 1819. 1821. 1822. 1823. 1824. 1825. 1827. 1828. 1829.

McKinney, Loring.* —. Boatswain's Mate. He was pensioned 15 Jan. 1849 at the rate of $9.50 per month. 1850.

McKnight, —. —. Captain Marines. His widow, Mary McKnight, was pensioned at the rate of $20 per month. 1837. 1842.

McLane, Charles.* —. Gunner. His widow, Catalina McLane, was pensioned 13 Nov. 1849 at the rate of $10 per month. 1850. 1851.

McLaughlin, —.* —. 1st Class Boy. His widow, Catharine McLaughlin, was pensioned at the rate of $4 per month from 15 Feb. 1837. 1837. 1839. 1840. 1841. 1842. 1842b. [He was listed as William McLaughlin in the Old Wars pension index.]

McLaughlin, Edward.* —. Private Marine Corps. His application was rejected between Mar. 1840 and 1 Jan. 1842. The surgeons who examined his wounds could not at the time decide whether his disability would be permanent.

McLaughlin, John.* —. Quarter Gunner. He was pensioned 3 Oct. 1842 at the rate of $7 per month. 1842b. 1843. 1844. 1845. 1846. 1847. 1848. 1850. 1851.

McLaughlin, John T.* —. Passed Midshipman. He was pensioned at the rate of $9.37 ½ per month from 8 Feb. 1837. 1837. 1838. 1839. 1840. 1841. 1842b. 1843. He was later promoted to Lieutenant. His widow, Salvadora McLaughlin, was pensioned 6 July 1847 at the rate of $25 per month. 1847. 1848. 1850. 1851. He was erroneously listed as G. T. McLaughlin in 1841.

McLaughlin, Patrick. N.Y. Ordinary Seaman. He was pensioned 1 Nov. 1815 at the rate of $60 per annum. 1822. 1823. 1824. 1825. 1826. 1827. 1828. 1829. 1830. 1835. 1836. 1837. 1839. 1840. 1841. 1842b. 1843. 1844. 1845. 1846. 1847. 1848. 1850. 1851. He served aboard Gunboat No. 42.

Naval Pensioners of the United States, 1800-1851

McLee, Roger. N.Y. Marine. He was pensioned 27 Apr. 1812 at the rate of $72 per annum. 1830. He served aboard the *Constitution*.

McLeod, Colin. N.Y. Boatswain. He was pensioned from Dec. 1815 at the rate of $120 per annum. 1820. 1821. 1822. 1824. 1825. 1826. 1827. 1828. 1829. 1830. He also appeared as Colin McCloud. He served aboard the brig *Argus*.

McMahan, Jeremiah. N.Y. Ordinary Seaman. He was pensioned 28 June 1815 at the rate of $60 per annum. 1819. 1820. 1821. 1822. 1823. 1824. 1825. 1826. 1827. 1828. 1829. 1830. He served aboard the brig *Firefly*. He also appeared as Jeremiah McMahon.

McMahan, Peter. Mass. Ordinary Seaman. He was pensioned 2 Nov. 1807 at the rate of $54 per annum in 1809. 1810. 1811. 1816. 1825. 1826. 1827. 1828. 1829. 1830. 1835. 1836. 1837. 1839. 1840. 1841. 1842b. 1843. 1844. 1845. 1846. 1847. 1848. 1850. 1851. He also appeared as Peter McMahon. He served aboard the frigate *Constitution*.

McMahen, John.* —. Ordinary Seaman. He was pensioned 9 July 1836 at the rate of $5 per month. 1837. 1838. 1839. 1840. 1841. 1842b. 1843. 1844. 1845. 1846. 1847. 1848. 1850. 1851. He also appeared as John McMahon.

McMane, James.* N.Y. Ordinary Seaman. He was pensioned 6 Mar. 1820 at the rate of $60 per annum. 1821. 1822. 1823. 1824. 1825. 1826. 1827. 1828. 1829. 1830. He served aboard the *Guerriere*.

McMasters, Joseph. Md. Private Marine. He was pensioned 1 Jan. 1824 at the rate of $36 per annum. 1824. 1825. 1826. 1827 [He was incorrectly listed as John McMasters in this year]. 1828 [still listed as John McMasters]. 1829. 1830.

McMenemy, James.* —. Marine. His widow, Mary Ann McMenemy, was pensioned 12 July 1849 at the rate of $3.50 per month. 1851.

McMullen, John. Penn. Gunner's Mate. He was pensioned 1 Apr. 1820 at the rate of $108 per annum. 1821. 1822. 1823. 1824. 1826. 1827. 1828. 1829. 1830.

McMullen, John.* —. Ordinary Seaman. He was pensioned 8 Dec. 1845 at the rate of $5 per month. 1846. 1847. 1848. 1850. 1851. He also appeared as John McMuller and John McMullin.

McMullen, William. Md. Marine. He was pensioned 25 Apr. 1812 at the rate of $36 per annum. 1816 and in D.C. in 1818. 1819. 1820. 1821. 1822. 1823. 1824. 1825. 1826. 1827 in D.C. 1828. 1829.1830. He served aboard the *Constellation*.

McMurray, —. N.J. Surgeon. Catherine C. McMurray was pensioned on his service as a privateer at the rate of $48 per annum. 1815. 1816. 1817. 1818. 1819 increase to $96. 1820. 1821. 1822. 1823. 1824. 1825. 1826. 1827. 1828. 1829. 1830. 1831. 1832. 1833. 1834 for $16.

McMurray, Matthew.* Va. Seaman. He was pensioned 1 Sep. 1827 at the rate of $6 per month. 1829. 1830. 1836. 1837. 1839. 1840. 1841. 1842b. 1843. 1844. 1845. 1846. 1847. 1848. 1850. 1851. He served aboard the *North Carolina*.

McMurtrie, William.* —. Purser. His widow, Elizabeth McMurtrie, was pensioned from 23 Mar. 1836 at the rate of $20 per month. 1837. 1839. 1840. 1841. 1842. 1842b. 1845. 1846. She was pensioned again on 1 Sep. 1847 at the rate of $20 per month. 1848. 1850. 1851.

McNeale, John H.* —. Seaman. He was pensioned 1 June 1831 at the rate of $3 per month. 1835. 1836. 1837. 1839. 1840. 1841. 1842b. 1843. 1844. 1845. 1846. 1847. 1848. 1850.

Naval Pensioners of the United States, 1800-1851

1851.

McNelly, —.* —. Boatswain. His widow, Martha McNelly, was pensioned from 14 July 1839. 1839. 1840. 1841. 1842. 1842b. [He was listed as John McNelly in the Old Wars pension index.]

McNelly, Joseph.* —. Gunner. His widow, Mary McNelly, was pensioned from 29 Nov. 1824 at the rate of $10 per month. 1835. 1836. 1837. 1839. 1840. 1841. 1842. 1842b. 1845. 1846. She was pensioned again 1 Sep.1847 at the rate of $10 per month. 1848. 1850. 1851. He also appeared as Joshua McNelly.

McPherson, Joseph S.* —. Master Commandant. His widow, Mary E. McPherson, was pensioned from 28 Apr. 1824 at the rate of $30 per month. 1835. 1836. 1837. 1839. 1840. 1841. 1842. 1842b. 1845. 1846. She was pensioned again 1 Sep. 1847 at the rate of $30 per month. 1848. 1850. 1851.

McPherson, William. —. Seaman. He was pensioned from 1 Jan. 1843 at the rate of $8 per month. 1844. 1845. His application was rejected prior to 10 Jan. 1844. He was wounded in 1798-99. The law granting invalid pensions to officers and seaman was not passed until 23 Apr. 1800. The Attorney General gave his opinion that no one wounded or disabled before the law was passed was entitled to its benefits.

Maccabee, —.* —. Seaman. His widow, Lydia Maccabee, was pensioned from 6 Aug. 1834 at the rate of $6 per month. 1836. 1837. 1839. 1840. 1842. She also appeared as Lydia Macabee and Lydia Marabee. [He was listed as John Macabee in the Old Wars pension index.]

Macdonough, —.* —. Captain. His orphans, Edward T. Macdonough, Charles S. Macdonough, Augustus R. Macdonough, Thomas Macdonough, and Charlotte R. Macdonough, were pensioned at the rate of $50 per month from 1 Jan. 1837. 1837. 1839. 1840. 1841. 1842. 1842b. [He was listed as Thomas Macdonough in the Old Wars pension index.]

Mack, Jeremiah.* —. Gunner. His daughter, Margaret Mack, was pensioned 1 Sep. 1846 at the rate of $10 per month. 1850. 1851. His widow, Catherine Mack, was pensioned 17 Dec. 1842 at the rate of $10 per month. 1842. 1843. 1845. 1846. 1847. 1848.

Macomber, Samuel P.* —. —. He served aborad the *Quaker* and was lost on 6 Mar. 1820. His son, George Macomber, was pensioned. 1829.

Madding, —. Penn. Quartermaster. His widow, Mary Madding, was pensioned at the rate of $108 per annum. 1824.

Madison, John R.* Ga. Lieutenant. He served aboard the *Lynx* and was lost at sea at an unknown date in 1821. His widow was Maria C. Madison. The heirs were pensioned 1 Aug. 1828. 1830. His son, John H. McIntosh Madison, was pensioned at the rate of $25 per month from 1 July 1838. 1839. 1840. 1841. 1842.

Magill, James.* Pa. Carpenter. His widow , Louisa Magill, had her claim rejected prior to 23 Dec. 1848. Her husband died in the naval asylum in Philadelphia. There was no law providing for her case. She was pensioned 14 Apr. 1848 at the rate of $10 per month.

Naval Pensioners of the United States, 1800-1851

Magin, Daniel.* —. 1st Class Boy. He was pensioned 21 July 1851 at the rate of $1.33 1/3 per month. 1851.

Maher, John. N.Y. Seaman. He was pensioned from 9 Mar. 1813 at the rate of $72 per annum. 1816. 1818. 1819. 1820. 1821. 1822. 1824. 1825. 1826. 1827. 1828. 1829. 1830. He also appeared as John Mahen. He served on the frigate *United States*.

Mahon, John.* —. Marine. His widow, Maria Mahon, was pensioned 7 Jan. 1847 at the rate of $3.50 per month. 1847. 1848. 1850. 1851.

Mahoney, Bartholomew.* —. Seaman. His application was rejected prior to 17 Jan. 1845. Dr. Sharp, Navy surgeon, certified that he was not entitled to a pension.

Malanson, —. —. Quartermaster. His daughter, Sarah Malanson, was pensioned at the rate of $8 per month. 1837. 1842.

Males, Emero. N.Y. Ordinary Seaman. He was pensioned 1 Jan. 1816 at the rate of $60 per annum. 1816. 1818. 1819. 1820. 1821. 1822. 1823. 1824. 1825. 1826. 1827. 1828. 1829. He served aboard the *Essex*.

Malon, —. N.J. Seaman. Sarah Malon was pensioned on his service as a privateer at the rate of $36 per annum from 1 Jan. 1815. She also appeared as Sarah Meloon and Sarah Malson.

Malono, Michael.* —. Private of Marines. His widow, Mary Ann Malono, was pensioned 1 Oct. 1847 at the rate of $3.50 per month. 1850. 1851. He also appeared as Michael Malone.

Malprine, John.* —. Landsman. He was pensioned 1 Feb. 1839 at the rate of $3 per month. 1840. 1841. 1842b. 1843. 1844. 1845. 1846. 1847. 1848. 1850. 1851. He also appeared as John Malprino.

Manchester, Giles.* N.J. Ordinary Seaman. He was pensioned 1 May 1827 at the rate of $5 per month. 1829. 1830. 1835. 1836. 1837. 1839. 1840. 1841. 1842b. 1843. 1844. 1845. 1846. 1847. 1848. 1850. 1851. He served aboard the frigate *United States*.

Manly, James. Mass. Quarter Gunner. He served aboard the *Wasp* and was lost 20 Apr. 1815. His widow, Elizabeth Manly, was pensioned at the rate of $108 per annum. 1818. 1819. 1820. 1821. 1822. 1823. 1824. 1825. 1828. 1829. She also appeared as Elizabeth Manley.

Maralions, —. —. —. His daughter, Susan Maralions, was pensioned. 1837. 1842. She also appeared as Susan Maralious.

Marbury, Alexander H.* —. Lieutenant. His widow, Mary B. Marbury, was pensioned 6 Dec. 1843 at the rate of $25 per month. 1845. 1847. 1848. 1850. 1851.

March, —. Mass. Seaman. Nancy March was pensioned on his service as a privateer at the rate of $72 per annum from 1 Oct. 1812. 1817. 1818. 1819. 1820. 1821. 1822. 1823. 1824. 1825 in N.Y. 1826. 1827 for $5.40.

March, John. —. —. He served aboard the *Adams* under Capt. Morris in 1814. In September he fell from the berth deck into the lower hold of the vessel and badly fractured his right shoulder blade and collar bone. He later rejoined his ship mates aboard the frigate *Congress* and was discharged in Mar. 1815. His right arm was almost useless. His application was rejected 31 Mar. 1836.

Marden, —. —. Ordinary Seaman. His daughter, Maria Marden, was pensioned at the rate of

Naval Pensioners of the United States, 1800-1851

$50 per month. 1837. 1842.

Maria, Antonio. Md. Seaman. He was pensioned 7 June 1815 at the rate of $72 per annum. 1816. 1818. 1819. 1820. 1821. 1822. 1823. 1824. 1825. 1826. 1827. 1828. 1829. 1830 in N.Y. He served aboard the schooner *Carolina*.

Marks, Andrew. —. Sergeant of Marines. He was pensioned 20 Aug. 1846 at the rate of $6.50 per month. 1850. 1851.

Marks, Enos. N.Y. Ordinary Seaman. He was pensioned 16 Feb. 1815 at the rate of $60 per annum. 1819. 1822. 1823. 1824. 1825. 1826. 1827. 1828. 1829. 1830. 1835. 1836. 1837. 1839. 1840. 1841. 1842b. 1843. 1844. 1845. 1846. 1847. 1848. 1850. 1851. He was disabled on Lake Champlain.

Marks, Jacob. —. Marine. He was pensioned 30 June 1810 at the rate of $.43 3/4 per month. 1837. 1838. 1839. 1840. 1841. 1842. 1842b. 1843. 1844. 1845. 1846. 1847. 1848. 1850. 1851.

Marks, Joseph.* N.Y. Seaman. He was pensioned 1 May 1827 at the rate of $6 per month. 1829. 1830. 1835. 1836. 1837. 1839. 1840. 1841. 1842b. 1843. 1844. 1845. 1846. 1847. 1848. 1850. 1851. He served aboard the frigate *United States*.

Marshall, —.* —. Seaman. His widow, Rachel Marshall, was pensioned from 31 Dec. 1827 at the rate of $6 per month. 1836. 1837. 1839. 1840. 1841. 1842b. [He was listed as James Marshall in the Old Wars pension index.]

Marshall, George.* —.Gunner. He was pensioned 31 Mar. 1825 at the rate of $2.50 per month. 1837. 1838. 1839. 1840. 1841. 1842b. 1843. 1844. 1845. 1846. 1847. 1848. 1850. 1851.

Marshall, Reuben. Md. Quarter Gunner. His widow, Elizabeth Marshall, was pensioned at the rate of $108 per annum. 1816. 1818. 1819. 1821. 1822. 1824. 1825. 1827.

Marshall, Thomas.* N.Y. Gunner. His widow, Mary Ann Marshall, was pensioned from 8 Aug. 1827 at the rate of $10 per month. 1827. 1828. 1839. 1840. 1842b.

Marshall, Thomas.* Md. Corporal of Marines. His widow, Elizabeth H. Marshall, was pensioned at the rate of $4.50 month from 11 Dec. 1822. 1827. 1828. 1837. 1839. 1840. 1841. 1842. 1842b. She had her application rejected prior to 23 Dec.1848. She was barred by the act of 11 Aug. 1848. She was pensioned 1 Sep. 1847 at the rate of $4.50 per month. 1850. 1851.

Marston, John, Jr. —. Midshipman. He was pensioned from 31 Dec. 1814 at the rate of $4.75 per month. 1839. 1840. 1841. 1842b. 1843.

Martin, —. —. R. Martin was pensioned on his service as a privateer from 2 Apr. 1813 to 1 July 1821.

Martin, —. —. —. Martha Martin was pensioned on his service as a privateer at the rate of $36 per annum. 1813. 1814. 1815. 1816. 1817. 1818. 1819. 1820. 1821 for $36.

Martin, —.* —. Seaman. His son, William Orleans Martin, was pensioned at the rate of $6 per month from 10 Oct. 1838. 1839. 1841. 1842. 1842b. [He was listed as Patrick Martin in the Old Wars pension index.]

Martin, —. D.C. Ordinary Seaman. His widow, Mary E. Martin, received $60 per annum. 1820. 1821. 1822. 1824. 1825. 1827. 1828.

Martin, Edward.* —. Seaman. He was pensioned 3 Mar. 1837 at the rate of $3 per month. 1838.

Naval Pensioners of the United States, 1800-1851

1839. 1841. 1842b. 1843. 1844. 1845. 1846. 1847. 1848. 1850. 1851.

Martin, Francis. Mass. Carpenter's Mate. He was pensioned as a privateer at the rate of $60 per annum from 4 Aug. 1812. 1812. 1813. 1814. 1815. 1816. 1817. 1818. 1819. 1820. 1821. 1822. 1823 for $5.

Martin, James H. Md. Sailing Master. He was pensioned at the rate of $240 per annum. 1816. 1819. 1820. 1821. 1822. He appeared as John H. Martin in 1818.

Martin, Jonathan. Mass. Quarter Gunner. He served aboard the *Wasp* and was slain 20 Apr. 1815. His widow, Ann Martin, was pensioned at the rate of $9 per month. 1818. 1819. 1821. 1822. 1823. 1824. 1825. 1827. 1828. 1829. 1830. 1835. 1836. 1837. 1839. 1840. 1841. 1842. 1842b. 1845. 1846. She was pensioned again 1 Sep. 1847 at the rate of $9 per month. 1848. 1850. 1851.

Martin, Joseph. Mass. Boatswain. He served aboard the *Wasp* and was slain 1 Sep. 1814. His widow, Elizabeth Martin, was pensioned 26 May 1815 at the rate of $120 per annum. 1816. 1818. 1819. 1820. 1821. 1822. 1823. 1825. 1827 in Maine. 1828. 1829. 1830. 1837. 1839. 1840. 1841. 1842. 1842b. 1845. 1846. She was pensioned again on 1 Sep. 1847. 1848. 1850. 1851.

Martin, Robert. Mass. Boatswain's Mate. He was pensioned as a privateer at the rate of $72 per annum from 26 Apr. 1813. 1820.

Martins, —. —. —. M. Martins was pensioned on his service as a private at the rate of $36 per annum. 1815. 1816. 1817. 1818. 1819. 1820 for $31.80.

Marwick, —. Mass. Seaman. Esther Marwick was pensioned on his service as a privateer. $17 in 1818. $5.20 in 1819.

Mason, Francis. Md. Quartermaster. He was pensioned 20 May 1814 at the rate of $108 per annum. 1816. 1818. 1819. 1820. 1821. 1822. 1823. 1824. 1825. 1826. 1827. 1828. 1829. 1830. He was disabled aboard the *Lawrence* on Lake Erie.

Mason, Joseph. —. —. He was being pensioned in 1842.

Mattee, Leonard. D.C. Seaman. He was pensioned as a privateer from 7 Dec. 1812 at the rate of $3 per month. 1812. 1813. 1814. 1815. 1816. 1817. 1818. 1819. 1820. 1821. 1822. 1823. 1824. 1825. 1826. 1827. 1828. 1829. 1830. 1836. 1837.

Matthews, Jeremiah. Penn. Quarter Gunner. He was slain 23 Nov. 1814. He served aboard the *United States*. His widow, Sarah Matthews, was pensioned 16 Mar. 1815 at the rate of $9 per month. 1816. 1818. 1819. 1820. 1821. 1822. 1823. 1824. 1825. 1827. 1829. 1830. 1835. 1836. 1837. 1839. 1840. 1841. 1842b.

Matthews, Peter. Md. Seaman. He was pensioned at the rate of $48 per annum from 25 Mar. 1812. 1813. 1814. 1815. 1816. 1817. 1818. 1819. 1820. 1821. 1822.

Mattison, Andrew. R.I. Carpenter's Mate. He was pensioned 23 May 1814 at the rate of $60 per annum. 1816. 1818. 1819. 1820. 1821. 1822. 1823. 1824. 1826. 1827. 1828. 1829. 1830. 1835. 1836. 1837. 1838. 1839. 1840. 1841. 1842. 1842b. 1843. 1844. 1845. 1846. 1847. 1848. 1850. 1851. He was disabled aboard the *Lawrence* on Lake Erie. He also appeared as Andrew Matteson.

Maury, —.* —. Lieutenant. His widow, Mary G. Maury, was pensioned from 22 June 1840 at the rate of $25 per month. 1841. 1842. [He was listed as Alexander Maury in the Old

Naval Pensioners of the United States, 1800-1851

Wars pension index.]

Maury, John M.* Va. Lieutenant. He died of yellow fever on 24 June 1823. His widow, Eliza Maury, was pensioned 8 May 1824 at the rate of $20 per month. 1824. 1825. 1827 in D.C. 1828. 1835. 1836. 1837. 1839. 1840. 1841. 1842. 1842b. 1845. 1846. She was pensioned again on 1 Sep. 1847 at the rate of $25 per month. 1848. 1850. 1851.

Maury, Matthew F.* —. Lieutenant. He was pensioned from 18 Oct. 1839 at the rate of $12.50 per month. 1840. 1841. 1842b. 1843.

Mawhiney, Adam.* —. Marine. He was pensioned 23 Oct. 1851 at the rate of $2.62 ½ per month. 1851.

Mayfield, W. —. —. He was pensioned as a privateer at the rate of $60 per annum. 1814. 1815. 1816. 1817. 1818. 1819. 1820. 1821. 1822.

Mayo, Elisha.* —. Ordinary Seaman. He was pensioned 28 May 1849 at the rate of $2.50 per month. 1850. 1851.

Mayo, Elisha. —. Ordinary Seaman. He was pensioned 10 Apr. 1851 at the rate of $5 per month. 1851.

Mayo, William.* —. Ordinary Seaman. He was pensioned 25 Feb. 1846 at the rate of $5 per month. 1847. 1848. 1850. 1851. He incorrectly appeared as William Mayer in 1850.

Mays, —. —. —. His widow, Elizabeth Mays, was pensioned from 3 Sep. 1834 at the rate of $9.50 per month. 1836. 1837. 1839. 1840. 1850. 1851. She was pensioned by special act. Compare with *infra*.

Mays, Wilson. R.I. Carpenter's Mate. He enlisted as an ordinary seaman on 16 July 1812 and was promoted to carpenter's mate. He was killed 10 Sep. 1813 on board the *Lawrence*. His mother, Elizabeth Mays, was pensioned 25 Mar. 1830. Compare with *supra*.

Meade, Samuel.* —. Seaman. He was pensioned 19 Oct. 1837 at the rate of $3 per month. 1839. 1840. 1841. 1842b. 1843. 1844. 1845. 1846. 1847. 1848. 1850. 1851. He also appeared as Samuel Mead.

Meany, Edward. Va. Ordinary Seaman. He was pensioned at the rate of $60 per annum in 1811. 1816.

Mears, Charles.* —. Landsman. He was pensioned 11 Dec. 1845 at the rate of $2 per month. 1846. 1848. 1850. 1851. He was also listed as Charles Myers and Charles Mear.

Meech, —. N.Y. Prize Master. Elizabeth Meech was pensioned on his service as a privateer at the rate of $60 per annum from 15 Mar. 1815. 1815. 1816. 1817. 1818. 1819. 1820 increase to $120. 1821. 1822. 1823. 1824. 1825 for $24.67.

Mehon, John. —. Musician in the Marines. He was pensioned 7 Jan. 1813 at the rate of $4 per month. 1851.

Meigs, John. N.Y. Seaman. He was pensioned 1 July 1819 at the rate of $120 per annum. 1816. 1818. 1819. 1820 in Ky. 1821 in Ohio. 1822. 1823. 1824. 1825. 1826. 1827. 1828. 1829. 1830. 1835. 1836. 1837. 1839. 1840. 1841. 1842b. 1843. 1844. 1845. 1846. 1847. 1848. 1850. 1851. He also appeared as John Meiggs. He served aboard the frigate *President*.

Melburn, Thomas. Mass. Seaman. He was pensioned 29 July 1814 at the rate of $72 per annum. 1819. 1820. 1821. 1822. 1823. 1824. 1825. 1826. 1827. 1828. 1829. 1830. He served aboard the *Essex*. He also appeared as Thomas Milburn.

Naval Pensioners of the United States, 1800-1851

Melvill, John. N.Y. Seaman. He was pensioned 21 Aug. 1815 at the rate of $60 per annum. 1816. 1818. 1819. 1820. 1821. 1822. 1823. 1824. 1825. 1826. 1827. 1828. 1829. 1830. He also appeared as John Melville. He served aboard the *President*.

Melvin, —. —. —. S. Melvin was pensioned on his service as a privateer at the rate of $36 per annum. 1815. 1816. 1817. 1818. 1819. 1820 increase to $72. 1821. 1822. 1823. 1824. 1825. 1826. 1827. 1828. 1829.

Melzard, —. Mass. Seaman. Sarah Melzard was pensioned on his service as a privateer at the rate of $36 per annum from 4 July 1812. 1812. 1813. 1814. 1815. 1816. 1817. 1818. 1819. 1820. 1821. 1822. 1823. 1824. 1825. 1826. 1827 for $36.60.

Merceran, Lewis.* —. Yeoman. His widow, Sarah Merceran, was pensioned 11 May 1849 at the rate of $7.50 per month. 1846. 1847. 1848. 1850. 1851. He also appeared as Lewis Mercereau and she as Sarah Mercereau.

Merchant, Richard.* —. Marine. He was pensioned 30 June 1824 at the rate of $1.75 per month. 1837. 1838. 1839. 1840. 1841. 1842. 1842b. 1843. 1844. 1845. 1846. 1847. 1848. 1850. 1851.

Mercier, —. Mass. Gunner. His widow, Martha Mercier, was pensioned from 5 July 1812. His orphans, M. Mercier and E. Mercier, were pensioned on his privateer service at the rate of $120 per annum. 1817. 1818. 1819. 1820. 1821. 1822. 1823. 1824 for $9.

Mercier, Henry J.* —. Ordinary Seaman. He was pensioned 22 May 1837 at the rate of $1.25 per month. 1839. 1840. 1841. 1842b. 1843. 1844. 1845. 1846. 1847. 1848. 1850. 1851.

Meredith, —.* —. Ordinary Seaman. His widow, Hester Meredith, was pensioned 17 Feb. 1838 at the rate of $5 per month. 1839. 1840. 1841. 1842. 1842b. [He was listed as John Meredith in the Old Wars pension index.]

Merrell, —. Mass. Master's Mate. Elizabeth Merrell was pensioned on his service as a privateer at the rate of $60 per annum. 1815. 1816. 1817. 1818. 1819. 1820 increased to $120. 1821. 1822. 1823. 1824. 1825. 1826. 1827. 1828 for $60.

Merrill, James. Mass. Ordinary Seaman. He was pensioned 23 Oct. 1819 at the rate of $60 per annum. He served on the schooner *Adams*. 1823. 1824. 1825. 1826. 1827. 1828. 1829. 1830. 1835. 1836. 1837. 1839. 1840. 1841. 1842b. 1843. 1844. 1845. 1846. 1847. 1848. 1850. 1851.

Merrill, Joseph B. —. Seaman. His widow, Tamizen Merrill, was pensioned from 28 Feb. 1813 at the rate of $6 per month. 1851.

Mervine, William. —. Midshipman. He was pensioned from 28 Nov. 1812 at the rate of $3.66 2/3 per month. 1839. 1840. 1841. 1842b. 1843.

Metz, —.* —. Landsman. His widow, Susan Metz, was pensioned at the rate of $4 per month from 12 Sep. 1823. 1837. 1839. 1840. 1842. [He was listed as George Metz in the Old Wars pension index.]

Metzer, John. —. Seaman. He was pensioned 26 Feb. 1839 at the rate of $3 per month. 1840. 1841. 1842b. 1843. 1844. 1845. 1846. 1847. 1848. 1850. 1851.

Middleton, —.* —. Quartermaster. His son, William Middleton, was pensioned at the rate of $8 per month from 1 July 1837. 1837. 1839. 1842. [He was listed as William Middleton in the Old Wars pension index.]

Naval Pensioners of the United States, 1800-1851

Middleton, William. —. Seaman. He was pensioned 1 Jan. 1837 at the rate of $8 per month. 1839. 1840. 1841. 1842b. 1843. 1844. 1845. 1846. 1847. 1848. 1850. 1851.

Midler, William. Penn. Master's Mate. He was drowned 15 Sep. 1814 at Erie, Penn. His widow, Ann Midler, was pensioned at the rate of $120 per annum. 1820. 1821. 1822. 1823. 1824. 1825. 1827. 1829. 1835. 1836. 1837. 1839. 1840. 1842. She also appeared as Ann Midlen.

Miles, —. —. —. Martha Miles was pensioned on his service as a privateer at the rate of $60 per annum. 1813. 1814. 1815. 1816. 1817. 1818 increase to $120. 1819. 1820. 1821. 1822. 1823. 1824. 1825. 1826. 1827.

Miley, Enoch M. Mass. Quarter Gunner. He was pensioned 1 Apr. 1823 at the rate of $8 per month. 1824. 1825. 1827. 1828. 1829. 1830. 1835. 1836. 1837. 1838. 1839. 1840. 1841. 1842. 1842b. 1843. 1844. 1845. 1846. 1847. 1848. 1850. 1851. He also appeared as Enoch Mileg and Enoch Meley. He served aboard the frigate *Essex*.

Milfield, William. Md. Seaman. He was pensioned as a privateer at the rate of $60 per annum from 25 Aug. 1812. 1812. 1813. 1814. 1815. 1816. 1817. 1818. 1819. 1820. 1821. 1822.

Millard, —. —. —. Mary Millard was pensioned on his service as a privateer from 4 July 1812 at the rate of $3 per month.

Miller, Frederick. —. Marine. His widow, Sarah Miller, had her application rejected prior to 10 Jan. 1844. Her husband was discharged from the service in May 1815 and died in 1836. The law did not provide a pension for a widow unless her husband died while in the service.

Miller, George. Va. Seaman. He perished aboard the *Epervier* 1 Sep. 1815. He was the son of George and Catherine Miller. His father was paid $72 on 28 May 1817 and was from Norfolk, Va.

Miller, James. —. Seaman. He was pensioned as a privateer at the rate of $72 per annum from 8 Mar. 1815. 1816. 1817. 1818. 1819. 1820. 1821. 1822. 1823. 1824. 1825. 1826. 1827. 1828. 1829. 1830. 1831. 1832. 1833. 1834. 1836 for $36. 1837. 1845. 1846. 1847. 1850.

Miller, John. Va. Seaman. He was pensioned at the rate of $108 per annum. 1827. 1828. 1829 in Md. 1830.

Miller, John. D.C. Seaman. He was pensioned 10 June 1825 at the rate of $108 per annum. 1829. 1830. He served aboard the *North Carolina*.

Miller, Samuel. —. Captain Marines. He was pensioned at the rate of $10 per month. 1837. 1838. 1839. 1840. 1841. 1842. 1842b. 1843.

Miller, Thomas.* N.Y. Seaman. He was pensioned 3 Sep. 1817 at the rate of $60 per annum. 1819. 1822. 1823. 1824. 1825. 1826. 1827. 1828. 1829. 1830 in Penn. He was disabled at Sackett's Harbor.

Miller, Thomas. —. Seaman. He was pensioned 23 Oct. 1829 at the rate of $4 per month. 1835. 1836. 1837. 1839. 1840. 1841. 1842b. 1843. 1844. 1845. 1846. 1847. 1848. 1850. 1851.

Miller, William.* —. Master. His widow, Sarah Miller, was pensioned 19 May 1847 at the rate of $20 per month. 1847. 1848. 1850. 1851.

Millet, Joseph.* —. Boatswain's Mate. He was pensioned 20 July 1843 at the rate of $4.75 per month. 1843. 1844. 1845. 1846. 1847. 1848. 1850. 1851. He also appeared as Joseph

Naval Pensioners of the United States, 1800-1851

Millett.
Mills, John.* —. —. 1st Class Fireman. His widow, Elizabeth Mills, was pensioned 31 May 1849 at the rate of $6 per month. 1850. 1851.
Mitchell, James. —. —. He was paid a pension 27 June 1805.
Mitchell, —.* —. Landsman. His widow, Catharine Mitchell, was pensioned from 30 Nov. 1832 at the rate of $4 per month. 1836. 1837. 1839. 1840. 1841. 1842. 1842b. [He was listed as James Mitchell in the Old Wars pension index.]
Mitchell, James.* —. Seaman. He was pensioned 12 June 1844 at the rate of $3 per month. 1845. 1846. 1847. 1848. 1850. 1851.
Mitchell, John.* Mass. Seaman. He was pensioned from 25 July 1818 at the rate of $120 per annum. 1820. 1821. 1822. 1823. 1824. 1825. 1826. 1827. 1828. 1829. 1830. He served aboard the *Essex*. He also appeared as John Mitchel.
Mitchell, John.* —. Seaman. He applied in 1847. 1847. 1850. 1851.
Mitchell, John.* N.Y. Seaman. He was pensioned from 12 Nov. 1821 at the rate of $72 per annum. 1824. 1825. 1829. 1830. He served aboard the *Constitution*.
Mitchell, John.* —. Quartermaster. He was pensioned 11 June 1832 at the rate of $5 per month. 1835. 1836. 1837. 1839. 1840. 1841. 1842b. 1843. 1844. 1845. 1846. 1848.
Mix, Elisha. N.Y. Commander. He was pensioned as a privateer at the rate of $144 per annum from 11 Nov. 1818. 1818. 1819. 1820. 1821. 1822. 1823. 1824. 1825. 1826. 1827. 1828. 1829. 1830. 1831.
Mix, Marvine P.* —. Commander. His widow, Ann Mix, was pensioned from 8 Feb. 1839 at the rate of $30 per month. 1839. 1840. 1841. 1842. 1842b. 1845. 1846. 1848. She was pensioned again 8 Feb.1849 at the rate of $30 per month. 1851.
Mix, Thomas M.* —. Lieutenant. His widow, Virginia R. Mix, was pensioned 24 Aug. 1849 at the rate of $25 per month. 1850. 1851.
Moffett, Archibald.* —. Ordinary Seaman. He was pensioned 1 June 1832 at the rate of $5 per month. 1835. 1836. 1837. 1839. 1840. 1841. 1842b. 1843. 1844. 1845. 1846. 1847. 1848. 1850. 1851. He also appeared as Archibald Moffatt.
Moldon, Samuel.* —. Captain of Forecastle. He was pensioned 10 Nov. 1848 at the rate of $7.50 per month. 1850. 1851.
Monteath, Walter N.* —. Lieutenant. He died in Feb. 1824 in the service. His widow, Caroline Monteath, was pensioned from 16 Oct. 1819 at the rate of $25 per month. 1837. 1839. 1840. 1841. 1842. 1842b. She was pensioned 1 Sep. 1847 at the rate of $25 per month. 1848. 1850. 1851.
Montgomery, —. N.Y. Seaman. Mary Montgomery was pensioned on his service as a privateer at the rate of $96 per annum from 1 Oct. 1812. 1817. 1818. 1819. 1820. 1821. 1822. 1823. 1824. 1825. 1826. 1827. 1828. 1829. 1830. 1831. 1832 for $80.
Montgomery, Alexander. —. Surgeon. His widow, Phebe Montgomery, was pensioned from 3 Jan. 1828 at the rate of $25 per month. 1835. 1836. 1837. 1839. 1840. 1841. 1842b. 1845. 1846. She was pensioned again 1 Sep. 1847 at the rate of $25 per month. 1848. 1850. 1851.
Montgomery, Nathaniel L.* —. Lieutenant. His widow, Joana Drinker, was pensioned at the rate of

Naval Pensioners of the United States, 1800-1851

$25 per month. 1848. [He was listed as Lawrence Montgomery in the Old Wars pension index.]

Moody, James P. —. —. He was pensioned. 1842.

Moody, Peter. Mass. Seaman. He perished aboard the *Epervier* 1 Sep. 1815. His widow was Isabella Moody of New York, N.Y. She was paid $72 on 23 July 1817. His mother also tried to claim his benefits and claimed her son had never married. Peter Moody was the son of Peter and Mary, nee Goddard, Audricourd who were married 11 Jan. 1786. They had twin sons, Peter Audricour and Richard Green Audricour, and they were baptized 25 July 1786. His father died about 30 years ago. His widowed mother married secondly William Moody on17 May 1789 at Trinity Church in Boston, Mass, and her second husband had been dead many years. His mother's sister, Bethiah D. Brown, also gave testimony.

Moody, William. —. Seaman. He was pensioned 6 Mar. 1849 at the rate of $3 per month. 1850. 1851.

Mooney, William. Penn. Private Marine. He was pensioned 20 May 1812 at the rate of $36 per annum. 1816. 1818. 1819. 1820. 1821. 1822. 1823. 1824. 1825. 1826. 1827. 1828. 1829. 1830. He served aboard the *Constitution.*

Moore, Charles. N.Y. Seaman. He was pensioned 5 Aug. 1822 at the rate of $72 per annum. 1823. 1824. 1825. 1826. 1827. 1828. 1829. 1830. 1835. 1836. 1837. 1840. He served aboard the *Constellation.*

Moore, Hamlet.* Md. Ordinary Seaman. He was pensioned 6 Oct. 1821 at the rate of $60 per annum. 1822. 1823. 1824. 1825. 1826. 1827. 1828. 1829. 1830. 1835. 1836. 1837. He served aboard the frigate *Macedonian.*

Moore, John. Penn. Seaman. He was pensioned 4 Dec. 1807 at the rate of $72 per annum. 1808. 1809. 1810. 1811. 1816. 1818. 1819. 1820. 1821. 1822. 1823. 1824. 1825. 1826. 1827. 1828. 1829. 1830. 1835. 1836. 1837. He also appeared as John More. He served aboard the *Constitution.*

Moore, John.* —. Seaman. He was pensioned 4 Dec. 1817 at the rate of $6 per month. 1839. 1840. 1841. 1842b. 1843. 1844. 1845. 1846. 1847. 1848. 1850. 1851.

Moore, John. —. Seaman. He was pensioned 9 Jan. 1838 at the rate of $4.50 per month. 1839. 1840. 1841. 1842b. 1843. 1844. 1845. 1846. 1847. 1848. 1850. 1851.

Moore, John.* —. Ordinary Seaman. He was pensioned 10 Oct. 1846 at the rate of $5 per month. 1847. 1848. 1850. 1851.

Moran, —.* —. Quarter Gunner. His son, Alexander Moran, was pensioned at the rate of $7.50 per month from 10 Sep. 1829. 1829. 1840. 1841. 1842. 1842b. [He was listed as James Moran in the Old Wars pension index.]

Moran, —.* —. Landsman. His son, John Moran, was pensioned at the rate of $4 per month from 26 Apr. 1838. 1842b. [He was listed as Michael Moran in the Old Wars pension index.]

Moran, William. N.Y. Seaman. He was pensioned 5 Dec. 1815 at the rate of $72 per annum. 1818. 1819. 1820. 1821. 1822. 1823. 1824. 1825. 1826. 1827. 1828. 1829. 1830. 1835. 1836. 1837. 1839. 1840. 1841. 1842b. 1843. 1844. 1845. 1846. 1847. 1848. 1850. 1851. He served aboard the *Guerriere.* He also appeared as William Morun.

Naval Pensioners of the United States, 1800-1851

Morgan, Alfred.* —. Coal Heaver. He was pensioned 28 Apr. 1851 at the rate of $3 per month. 1851.

Morgan, Ebenezer. —. Carpenter's Mate. His widow, Abigail Morgan, was pensioned at the rate of $9.50 from 12 Mar. 1813. No date was given. 1837. 1839. 1840. 1841. 1842. 1842b. 1851.

Morgan, James.* —. Quartermaster. He was pensioned 9 May 1847 at the rate of $9 per month. 1847. 1848. 1850. 1851.

Morley, Roderick. —. Sergeant of Marines. His application was rejected prior to 12 Dec. 1842. He claimed to have been wounded in 1800.

Morrice, Davis F.* —. Ship's Steward. His widow, Mary Ann Morrice, was pensioned 2 Aug. 1841 at the rate of $9 per month. 1842b. 1845. 1848. 1850. 1851.

Morris, —.* —. Lieutenant. His widow, Mary P. Morris, was pensioned from 5 Nov. 1837 at the rate of $25 per month. 1839. 1840. 1841. 1842. His children, Lewis R. Morris and Thomas E. Morris, were pensioned at the rate of $25 per month from 12 Aug. 1841. 1842b. [He was listed as Richard Morris in the Old Wars pension index.]

Morris, Charles W.* —. Lieutenant. He was pensioned at the rate of $12.50 per month. 1837. 1838. 1839. 1840. 1841. 1842. 1842b. 1843. His widow, Caroline D. Morris, was pensioned 11 Nov. 1846 at the rate of $25 per month. 1847. 1848. 1850. 1851.

Morris, John. N.Y. Quarter Gunner. He was pensioned at the rate of $96 per annum. 1818. 1819. 1820. 1821.

Morris, Miles. Penn. Corporal Marines. He was pensioned 1 Nov. 1815 at the rate of $60 per annum. 1816. 1818. 1819. 1820. 1821. 1822. 1823. 1824. 1825. 1826. 1827. 1828. 1829. 1830. He served aboard the *Chesapeake*.

Morris, William.* Penn. Ordinary Seaman. He was pensioned 4 May 1820 at the rate of $60 per annum. 1821. 1822. 1823. 1824. 1825. 1826. 1827. 1828. 1829. 1830. He served aboard the schooner *Franklin*.

Morrison, Jesse.* —. Carpenter. His widow, Mary A. Morrison, was pensioned 16 Apr. 1846 at the rate of $10 per month. 1846. 1847. 1848. 1850. 1851.

Morrison, Philip. Penn. Marine. He was pensioned at the rate of $54 per annum. 1802. 1803. 1804. 1805. 1807. 1808. 1809. 1810. 1811.

Morse, —. —. —. Sarah Morse was pensioned on his service. 1842.

Morse, Jacob. —. Purser's Steward. His application was rejected prior to 17 Jan. 1845. He claimed to have been wounded in the war more than twenty-five years ago. The returns did not show that he was wounded.

Morse, John. Mass. Seaman. He was pensioned at the rate of $72 per annum. 1823.

Moses, James. N.Y. Purser's Steward. He was pensioned 23 Apr. 1816 at the rate of $108 per annum. 1818. 1819. 1820. 1821. 1822. 1823. 1824. 1825. 1826. 1827. 1828. 1829. 1830. 1835. 1836. 1837. 1839. 1840. 1841. 1842b. 1843. 1844. 1845. 1846. 1847. 1848. 1850. 1851. He was disabled aboard the schooner *Lawrence* on Lake Erie.

Moss, John.* Mass. Seaman. He was pensioned at the rate of $120 per annum. 1819. 1820. 1821. 1822.

Mott, —. N.Y. Seaman. Harriet Mott was pensioned on his service as a privateer at the rate of $72

Naval Pensioners of the United States, 1800-1851

per annum. 1819. 1820. 1821. 1822. 1823. 1824. 1825. 1826. 1827. 1828. 1829 for $12.
Mott, —. —. Lieutenant. His daughter, Mary Louisa Mott, was pensioned at the rate of $20 per month from 4 July 1823. 1837. 1839. 1840. 1842.
Moulton, William. Mass. Seaman. He served aboard the *Wasp* was slain 20 Apr. 1815. His widow, Jane Moulton, was pensioned at the rate of $9 per month. 1818. 1819. 1820. 1821. 1822. 1823. 1824. 1825. 1827. 1828. 1829. 1830. 1835. 1836. 1837. 1839. 1840. 1841. 1842. 1842b. 1845. 1846. She was pensioned again at the rate of $6 per month on 1 Sep. 1847. 1848. 1850. She also appeared as Jane Maulton.
Mount, James. Va. Private Marine. He was pensioned 4 Sep. 1830 at the rate of $36 per annum. 1830. 1835. 1836. 1837. He served aboard the *Guerriere*.
Mount, James.* —. Sergeant of Marines. He was pensioned 7 June 1837 at the rate of $4.87 ½ per month. 1838. 1839. 1840. 1841. 1842. 1842b. 1843. 1844. 1845. 1846. 1847. 1848. 1850. 1851.
Mozart, —. —. —. Margaret Mozart was pensioned on his service. 1842.
Mozart, —. —. Master-at-Arms. His widow, Martha E. Mozart, was pensioned 20 Feb. 1838 at the rate of $5 per month. 1839. 1840. 1841. 1842. She also appeared as Martha Mosart. There was a listing for a daughter, Martha E. Mozart, at the rate of $9 per month form 16 Aug. 1839. 1841. 1842b.
Mull, Jacob. —. Sailing Master. He was pensioned 28 May 1849 at the rate of $20 per month. 1850. 1851. His widow, Mary Mull, was pensioned 29 Jan. 1851 at the rate of $20 per month. 1851.
Mullen, —. —. Quartermaster. His son, John Mullen, was pensioned at the rate of $6 per month. 1837. 1842.
Mullen, Francis. Penn. Marine. He was pensioned at the rate of $72 per annum in 1821. 1823.
Mullen, John.* Mass. Quarter Gunner. He served aboard the *Wasp* and was slain 20 Apr. 1815. His widow was Judetha Mullen who was pensioned at the rate of $108 per annum. The two orphan children, [Elizabeth P. Mullen and John Mullen], were pensioned. 1818. 1819. 1821. 1822. 1823. 1824. 1825. 1827. 1829. 1830. She also appeared as Judith Mullen.
Mulliniffe, James. Md. Ordinary Seaman. He was pensioned 3 Apr. 1815 at the rate of $60 per annum. 1816. 1818. 1819 in Va. 1820. 1821. 1822. 1823. 1824. 1825. 1826. 1827. 1828. 1829. 1830. He also appeared as James Mulleniffe and James Mulliniff. He was disabled on the Chesapeake flotilla.
Mulloy, —. Mass. Seaman. Sally Mulloy was pensioned on his service as a privateer at the rate of $36 per annum. 1815. 1816. 1817. 1818. 1819. 1820. 1821. 1822. 1823. 1824. 1825. 1826. 1827. 1828. 1829. 1830. 1831. 1832. 1833. 1834.
Muncey, Daniel. Penn. Seaman. He was pensioned at the rate of $96 per annum in 1824. 1825. 1826. 1827. 1828.
Muncey, Edward. Md. Sergeant Marines. He was pensioned at the rate of $54 per annum. 1828.
Munday, William. Md. Seaman. He was pensioned at the rate of $72 per annum in 1816. 1818. 1819. 1820. 1821.
Munroe, —.* —. Boatswain. His daughter, Margaret R. Munroe, was pensioned at the rate of $10 per month from 27 Mar. 1832. 1837. 1839. 1840. 1841. 1842. 1842b. [He was listed

as Richard Munroe in the Old Wars pension index.]
Munroe, H. Penn. Seaman. He served aboard the *Chesapeake* and was killed 1 June 1813. His widow, Eleanor Munroe, was pensioned at the rate of $72 per annum. 1820. 1821. 1822. 1823. 1824. 1825. 1827. 1829. She also appeared as Eleanor Monroe. His daughter was Mary Ann Munroe. Martin McCormick was her guardian.
Munroe, John.* —. Seaman. He was pensioned 22 July 1835 at the rate of $4.50 per month. 1837. 1838. 1839. 1840. 1841. 1842b. 1843. 1844. 1845. 1846. 1847. 1848. 1850. 1851.
Murdock, —. —. —. Eleanor R. Murdock was pensioned on his service. 1842.
Murdock, Edward. —. Ordinary Seaman. He was pensioned. 1838.
Murdock, Thomas.* —. Seaman. He was pensioned 30 June 1836 at the rate of $6 per month. 1837. 1839. 1840. 1841. 1842. 1842b. 1843. 1844. 1845. 1846. 1847. 1848. 1850. 1851. He also appeared as Thomas Murdoch.
Murphy, —.* —. Corporal Marines. His widow, Hester Murphy, was pensioned at the rate of $4.50 per month from 26 Dec. 1831. 1837. 1839. 1840. 1841. 1842. 1842b. [He was listed as William Murphy in the Old Wars pension index.]
Murphy, —. Md. Commander. Eleanor Murphy was pensioned on his service as a privateer at the rate of $120 per annum. 1814. 1815. 1816. 1817. 1818. 1819 increased to $240. 1820. 1821. 1822. 1823. 1824 for $162.
Murphy, David.* —. Marine. His widow, Mary Ann Murphy, was pensioned 14 Oct. 1847 at the rate of $3.50 per month. 1848. 1850. 1851.
Murphy, John. —. Landsman. He perished aboard the *Grampus*. His parents and his brother died within the last year. His sister, Mary Murphy, was a minor in Boston, Mass. on 11 July 1844.
Murphy, Patrick. —. Ordinary Seaman. He was pensioned 19 Oct. 1836 at the rate of $5 per month. 1839. 1840. 1841. 1842b. 1843. 1844. 1845. 1846. 1847. 1848. 1850. 1851.
Murphy, Patrick. —. Ordinary Seaman. He was pensioned 1 Jan. 1846 at the rate of $5 per month. 1850. 1851.
Murray, —.* —. —. Hannah Murray and Charles B. Murray were pensioned on his service. [He was listed as James Murray in the Old Wars pension index.]
Murray, Colton.* —. Boatswain's Mate. He was pensioned 1 Aug. 1831 at the rate of $9 per month. 1835. 1836. 1837. 1839. 1840. 1841. 1842b. 1843. 1844. 1845. 1846. 1847. 1848. 1850. 1851. He also appeared as Cotton Murray.
Murray, Edward. Md. Sergeant Marines. He was pensioned 1 Jan. 1801 at the rate of $54 per annum. 1802. 1803. 1804. 1805. 1807. 1808. 1809. 1810. 1811. 1816. 1818. 1819. 1820. 1821. 1822. 1824. 1825. 1826. 1827. 1829. 1830. He served aboard the *Baltimore*.
Murray, Francis. —. Seaman. His application was rejected prior to 10 Jan. 1844. He claimed to have been wounded as long ago as 1799. The Attorney General had ruled that anyone wounded or disabled before the passage of the law on 23 Apr. 1800 was ineligible.
Murray, John.* —. 1st Class Boy. He was pensioned 16 Aug. 1845 at the rate of $.87 ½ per month. 1845. 1846. 1847. 1848. 1850. 1851.
Mushaway, John. N.H. Boatswain. He was pensioned 4 July 1800 at the rate of $10 per month. 1803. 1804. 1805. 1807. 1808. 1809. 1810. 1811. 1816. 1818. 1819. 1820. 1821. 1822. 1823. 1824. 1825. 1826. 1827. 1828. 1829. 1830. He served aboard the *Congress*. He

Naval Pensioners of the United States, 1800-1851

also appeared as John Mashaway.
Mussey, —. —. —. He drowned. Mary Mussey applied in Apr. 1827 and was pensioned at the rate of $60 per annum.
Myer, —. N.Y. Sailing Master. Mary Myer was pensioned on his service as a privateer at the rate of $72 per annum. 1815. 1816. 1817. 1818. 1819. 1820 increase to $144. 1821. 1822. 1823. 1824. 1825. 1826. 1827. 1828. 1829.
Myers, —.* —. Marine. His widow, Elizabeth Myers, was pensioned from 10 Oct. 1839 at the rate of $3.50 per month. 1840. 1841. 1842. 1842b. [He was listed as George Myers in the Old Wars pension index.]
Myers, Augustine.* —. Seaman. He was pensioned 14 Oct. 1844 at the rate of $3 per month. 1845. 1846. 1847. 1848. 1850. 1851. He also appeared as Augustus Myers.
Myers, Edward.* —. Seaman. He was pensioned 27 May 1837 at the rate of $3 per month. 1839. 1840. 1841. 1842. 1843. 1844. 1845. 1846. 1847. 1848. 1850.
Myers, John.* N.Y. Seaman. He was pensioned 1 Nov. 1828 at the rate of $6 per month. 1829. 1830. 1835. 1836. 1837. 1839. 1840. 1841. 1842b. 1843. 1844. 1845. 1846. 1847. 1848. 1850. 1851. He served aboard the *Vincennes* under William B. Finch.
Myers, John.* —. Captain of the Hold. He was pensioned 3 May 1849 at the rate of $7.50 per month. 1850. 1851.
Myers, Joseph.* —. Private of Marines. His widow, Mary Myers, was pensioned 28 July 1847 at the rate of $3.50 per month. 1850. 1851.
Myrick, John.* —. Gunner. He was pensioned 7 Aug. 1837 at the rate of $5 per month. 1841. 1842b. 1843. 1844. 1845. 1846. 1847. 1848. 1850. 1851.

Nabb, William. Md. Seaman. He was wounded on the Chesapeake flotilla and died 1 July 1814. Sarah Hopkins was paid $72 per annum as guardian of his son, Nelson Nabb, in 1818. 1819. 1821. 1822. 1824. 1825. 1827. 1828. 1829.
Nagle, James. —. Seaman. He was pensioned 30 June 1835 at the rate of $5 per month. 1835. 1836. 1837. 1839. 1840. 1841. 1842b. 1843. 1844. 1845. 1846. 1847. 1848. 1850. 1851.
Nagle, Joseph.* —. Boatswain. His widow, Elizabeth Nagle, was pensioned from 19 Nov. 1834 at the rate of $9.50 per month. 1835. 1836. 1837. 1839. 1840. 1841. 1842. 1842b. 1846. She was pensioned again on 1 Sep. 1847 at the rate of $9.50 per month. 1848. 1850. 1851.
Nants, John. —. Lieutenant. He was pensioned from 1 Jan. 1824 for privateer service at the rate of $12 per month. 1825. 1826. 1827. 1828. 1829. 1830. 1831. 1832. 1833. 1834. 1835. 1836. 1837 for $72. 1845. 1846. 1847. 1850. He also appeared incorrectly as John Mantz.
Nants, John.* —. Sailing Master. His widow, Ann Nants, was pensioned at the rate of $20 per month from 27 Dec. 1824. 1837. 1838. 1839. 1840. 1841. 1842. 1842b. 1846. She was pensioned again 1 Sep. 1847 at the rate of $20 per month. Her husband died of a natural death. 1848. 1850. 1851. She also appeared as Ann Nantz.

Naval Pensioners of the United States, 1800-1851

Napier, William. Penn. Corporal of Marines. He was pensioned 1 July 1825 at the rate of $4 per month. 1829. 1830. 1835. 1836. 1837. 1839. 1840. 1841. 1842. 1842b. 1843. 1844. 1845. 1846. 1847. 1848. 1850. 1851. He served aboard the *President.*

Nash, Thomas.* —. Ordinary Seaman. He was pensioned 23 Dec. 1834 at the rate of $5 per month. 1835. 1836. 1837. 1838. 1842.

Nason, —. —. —. Sally Nason was pensioned on his service. 1842.

Navarro, David.* N.Y. Sailmaker. He died of yellow fever 1 Oct. 1823. His widow, Margaret Navarro, was pensioned from 2 Oct. 1823 at the rate of $10 per month. 1824. 1825. 1827. 1828. 1835. 1836. 1837. 1839. 1840. 1841. 1842. 1842b. 1845. 1846. She was pensioned again 1 Sep. 1847 at the rate of $10 per month. 1848. 1850. 1851. She also appeared as Margaret Navarre.

Neagle, —.* —. Sergeant Marines. His sons, William Neagle and Godfrey B. Neagle, were pensioned at the rate of $6.50 per month from 5 Aug. 1838. 1839. 1840. 1842. [He was listed as Michael Neagle in the Old Wars pension index.]

Neal, Benjamin J [or I]. Va. Lieutenant. He was lost in the *Epervier* 1 Sep. 1815. He married Mary L. Whittle 13 Dec. 1814 in Norfolk, Va. She was paid $140 in Aug. 1817. His widow, Mary Neal, was pensioned 13 July 1813 at the rate of $20 per month. 1819. 1821. 1822. 1823. 1824. 1825. 1827. 1828. 1837. 1839. 1840. 1841. 1842. 1842b. 1845. 1846. She was pensioned again on 1 Sep.1847 at the rate of $25 per month. 1848. 1850. 1851. She also appeared as Mary Neale.

Needham, Josiah.* —. Quarter Gunner. He was pensioned 4 May 1842 at the rate of $4.80 per month. 1842b. 1843. 1844. 1845. 1846. 1847. 1848. 1850. 1851.

Neilson, John.* —. Quarter Gunner. He was pensioned 1 Jan. 1832 at the rate of $9 per month. 1835. 1836. 1837. 1839. 1840. 1841. 1842. 1843. 1844. 1845. 1846. 1847. 1848. 1850. 1851.

Nelson, —.* —. Seaman. His widow, Ann Nelson, was pensioned from 11 Nov. 1837 at the rate of $6 per month. 1839. 1840. 1841. 1842. 1842b. [He was listed as William Nelson in the Old Wars pension index.]

Nelson, —. —. Gunner. His daughter, Elizabeth A. Nelson, was pensioned. 1837. 1842.

Nelson, Henry. Mass. Seaman. He was pensioned at the rate of $72 per annum in 1807. 1808. 1809. 1810. 1811. 1816. 1823.

Nelson, John.* —. Seaman. He was pensioned 8 July 1845 at the rate of $4.80 per month. 1845. 1847. 1848. 1850. 1851.

Nelson, Thomas. Md. Cook. He was pensioned at the rate of $120 per annum. 1823. 1824. 1825.

Nesbet, William. N.Y. Seaman. He was pensioned 18 Apr. 1815 at the rate of $48 per annum. 1816. 1818. 1819. 1820. 1821. 1822. 1823. 1824. 1825. 1826. 1827. 1828. 1829. 1830. 1836. He also appeared as William Nesbit. He served aboard the *President.*

Netts, John.* —. Captain's Steward. His widow, Eliza Netts, was pensioned from 6 Dec. 1838 at the rate of $9 per month. 1840. 1841. 1842b. She was pensioned again 1 Sep. 1847 at the rate of $9 per month. 1848. 1851. He also appeared as John Netto.

Newberry, David.* —. Ordinary Seaman. He was pensioned 15 Apr. 1826 at the rate of $2 per month. 1837. 1838. 1839. 1840. 1841. 1842. 1842b. 1843. 1844. 1845. 1846. 1847.

Naval Pensioners of the United States, 1800-1851

1848. 1850. 1851. He also appeared as David Newbury and David Newburg.

Newcomb, Henry S. —. Lieutenant. His widow, Rhoda Newcomb, was pensioned from 1 Nov. 1825 at the rate of $25 per month. 1835. 1836. 1837. 1839. 1840. 1841. 1842. 1842b. 1845. 1846. She was pensioned again on 1 Sep. 1847 at the rate of $25 per month. 1848. 1850. 1851.

Newhall, Asa. Mass. Seaman. He was pensioned at the rate of $48 per annum. 1816.

Newman, Timothy. —. Master Commandant. His widow, Abigail Fuller, had her application rejected prior to 12 Dec. 1842. The children of Timothy Newman had already received the pension to which their mother would have been entitled if she had not married a second time.

Newman, William D.* —. Commander. His widow, Miriam S. Newman, was pensioned 9 Oct. 1844 at the rate of $30 per month. 1845. 1846. 1847. 1848. 1850. 1851.

Newton, Benjamin.* Penn. Seaman. He was pensioned at the rate of $72 per annum. 1818. 1819. 1820. 1821. 1822. 1823. 1824. 1825. 1826. 1827. 1828. 1829. 1830. He served aboard *Washington*.

Newton, William. —. Ordinary Seaman. He was pensioned 11 Sep. 1814 at the rate of $1.25 per month . 1839. 1840. 1841. 1842b. 1843. 1844. 1845. 1846. 1847. 1848. 1850. 1851.

Nichols, —. —. Seaman. His widow, Teresa Nichols, was pensioned from 30 June 1838 at the rate of $6 per month. 1840. 1841. 1842. 1842b. She also appeared as Teresa Nicholas.

Nichols, —.* —. Sailing Master. His widow, Sarah H. Nichols, was pensioned at the rate of $20 per month. 1837. 1839. 1840. 1841. 1842. 1842b. She also appeared as Sarah H. Nicholls. [He was listed as Thomas Nichols in the Old Wars pension index.]

Nichols, Francis B. —. Midshipman. He was pensioned from 1 June 1818 at the rate of $4.75 per month. 1837. 1838. 1839. 1840. 1841. 1842. 1842b. 1843. 1844. 1845. 1846. 1847. 1848. 1850. 1851.

Nicholls, William. Mass. Ordinary Seaman. He was pensioned 29 July 1814 at the rate of $60 per annum. 1818. 1819. 1820. 1821. 1822. 1824. 1825. 1826. 1827. 1828. 1829. 1830. He served aboard the *Essex*. He also appeared as William Nichols.

Nicholson, —. —. —. Ann E. Nicholson was pensioned on his service. 1842.

Nicholson, —. —. Captain. His daughters, Maria Nicholson and Elizabeth R. Nicholson, were pensioned at the rate of $50 per month. 1837. 1842.

Nicholson, —.* —. Lieutenant. His sons, James W. A. Nicholson and Frederick A. G. Nicholson, were pensioned at the rate of $25 per month from 24 June 1829. 1837. 1839. 1840. 1841. 1842. [He was listed as Nathaniel D. Nicholson in the Old Wars pension index.]

Nicholson, Isaac. Md. Cook. He was pensioned 28 Sep. 1814 at the rate of $108 per annum. 1819. 1820. 1821. 1822. 1823. 1824. 1825. 1826. 1827. 1828. 1829. 1830. He was disabled on the Chesapeake flotilla.

Nicholson, John. D.C. Carpenter. He was wounded in the Potomac River and died 8 Sep. 1814. His widow, Charity Nicholson, was pensioned 23 Nov. 1815 at the rate of $120 per annum. 1816. 1818. 1819. 1821. 1822. 1823. 1824. 1825. 1827. 1828. 1829. 1839. 1840. 1841. 1842b.

Naval Pensioners of the United States, 1800-1851

Nicholson, John.* —. Ordinary Seaman. He was pensioned 30 Aug. 1842 at the rate of $5 per month. 1842b. 1843. 1844. 1845. 1846. 1847. 1848. 1850. 1851.

Nicholson, Joseph J. —. Captain. His widow, Laura C. Nicholson, was pensioned from 12 Dec. ' 1838 at the rate of $50 per month. 1839. 1840. 1841. 1842. 1842b. 1846. She was pensioned again 1 Sep. 1847 at the rate of $50 per month. 1848. 1850. 1851.

Nickerson, J. C. Mass. Seaman. He served abroad the *Guerriere* and was slain 17 June 1815. His widow, Elizabeth S. Nickerson, was pensioned 1 July 1816 at the rate of $72 per annum. 1818. 1819. 1820. 1821. 1822. 1823. 1824. 1825. 1827. 1828. 1829. 1830. She also appeared as Eliza S. Nickerson.

Nickerson, James. N.Y. Seaman. He was pensioned 15 July 1815 at the rate of $72 per annum. 1821. 1822. 1823. 1824. 1825. 1826. 1827. 1828. 1830. 1835. 1836. 1837. 1839. 1840. 1841. 1842. 1842b. 1843. 1844. 1845. 1846. 1847. 1848. 1850. 1851. He served aboard the *President*. He also appeared as James Pickerson.

Nightingale, Brister. —. —. He was pensioned as a privateer at the rate of $48 per annum from 15 June 1815. 1815. 1816. 1817. 1818. 1819. 1820. 1821. 1822.

Niles, N. —. —. He was pensioned as a privateer at the rate of $36 per annum. 1814. 1815. 1816. 1817. 1818. 1819. 1820. 1821. 1822. 1823. 1824. 1825. 1826. 1827. 1828. 1829. 1830. 1831. 1832. 1833. 1834. 1835. 1836. 1837 for $18.

Noble, Philemon. —. Seaman. His children, Mary Noble and Philemon Noble, were pensioned at the rate of $3 per month from 28 July 1800. Mary Noble was paid to 25 June 1820; Philemon Noble was paid to 23 Aug. 1821.

Nogle, John. Mass. Ordinary Seaman. He was pensioned at the rate of $48 per annum. 1818. 1819. 1820. 1821. 1822. 1824. 1825. 1826. 1827. 1828. 1829. He also appeared as John Vogle. He was disabled on the frigate *Constitution*.

Norcrose, Benjamin. Penn. Seaman. He was pensioned 11 July 1815 at the rate of $60 per annum. 1818. 1819. 1820. 1821. 1822. 1823. 1824. 1825. 1826. 1827. 1828. 1829. 1830. He served aboard the *Constitution*. He also appeared as Benjamin Norcross. His rank was also given as Sergeant of Marines.

Norris, —.* —. Master Commandant. His children, Maria C. Norris and Shubrick Norris, were pensioned at the rate of $30 per month from 1 Jan. 1838. 1839. 1840. 1841. 1842. 1842b. He was listed as Otho Norris in the Old Wars pension index.]

Norris, James.* —. Assistant Surgeon. He was pensioned 1 July 1848 at the rate of $20 per month. 1850. 1851.

North, —. Pa. Seaman. Mary North was pensioned on his service as a privateer at the rate of $36 per annum He received $14.70 in 1812 and $12.50 in1813.

Noyer, John F.* Penn. Marine. He was pensioned 17 Nov. 1821 at the rate of $5 per month. 1824. 1825. 1827. 1828. 1829. 1830. 1835. 1836. 1837. 1839. 1840. 1841. 1842b. 1843. 1844. 1845. 1846. 1847. 1848. 1850. 1851. His disability was permanent.

Noyes, Ebenezer.* —. Ship's Carpenter. His widow, Sarah L. Noyes, was pensioned from 9 Oct. 1835 at the rate of $7 per month. 1837. 1839. 1840. 1841. 1842. 1842b. She was pensioned again 1 Sep. 1847 at the rate of $7 per month. 1848. 1850. 1851. He also appeared as Ebenezer Noys.

Naval Pensioners of the United States, 1800-1851

Nugent, John. Penn. Seaman. He was pensioned 1 Apr. 1815 at the rate of $72 per annum. 1816. 1818. 1819. 1820. 1821. 1822. 1823. 1824. 1825. 1826. 1827. 1828. 1829. 1830. 1835. 1836. 1837. 1838. 1839. 1840. 1841. 1842. 1842b. 1843. 1844. 1845. 1846. 1848. 1850. 1851. He served aboard the *Argus*.

Nugent, John.* —. Marine. His widow, Jane Nugent, was pensioned 12 Aug. 1845 at the rate of $3.50 per month. 1845. 1846. 1847. 1848. 1850. 1851.

Oatman, John.* —. Landsman. He was pensioned 3 Apr. 1844 at the rate of $4 per month. 1844. 1845. 1846. 1847. 1848. 1851.

Obear, William.* —. Master-at-Arms. He was pensioned 6 Aug. 1847 at the rate of $6.75 per month. 1850. 1851.

O'Conner, Nicholas. Penn. Sailing Master. He was pensioned at the rate of $240 per annum. 1818. 1819. 1820. 1821. 1822. He also appeared as Nicholas O'Connor.

Odiorne, Samuel, Jr.* N.H. Seaman. He was pensioned 1 July 1829 at the rate of $6 per month. 1829. 1830. 1835. 1836. 1837. 1838. 1839. 1840. 1841. 1842. 1842b. 1843. 1844. 1845. 1846. 1847. 1848. 1850. 1851. He was disabled at the navy yard in Portsmouth. He also appeared as Samuel Ordiorne.

Oellers, —. —. Seaman. His widow, Rebecca Oellers, was pensioned from 21 Mar. 1839 at the rate of $6 per month. 1839. 1840. 1841. 1842. 1842b.

O'Hare, Richard.* —. Carpenter's Mate. His widow, Elizabeth O'Hare, was pensioned from 28 Aug. 1838 at the rate of $9.50 per month. 1839. 1840. 1841. 1842. 1842b. She was pensioned again 1 Sep. 1847 at the rate of $9.50 per month. 1848. 1850. 1851.

Olcutt, R. K. D.C. Steward. He served aboard the schooner *Hamilton* and was lost 8 Aug. 1813. His widow, Mary Olcutt, received $108 per annum in 1821. 1822. 1824 in N.Y. 1825. 1827. 1828. 1829.

Oliver, John.* —. Gunner. His widow, Eliza A. Oliver, was pensioned at the rate of $10 per month from 30 Mar. 1834. 1836. 1837. 1839. 1840. 1841. 1842. 1842b. 1846. She was pensioned again 1 Sep. 1847 at the rate of $10 per month. 1848. 1850. 1851.

Oliver, Thomas. N.Y. Seaman. He was pensioned 29 July 1814 at the rate of $72 per annum. 1816. 1818. 1819. 1820. 1821. 1822. 1823. 1824. 1825. 1826. 1827. 1828. 1829. 1830. He served aboard the *Essex*. He also appeared as Thomas Olliver.

O'Mally, Patrick.* —. Ordinary Seaman. He was pensioned 20 Oct. 1842 at the rate of $2.50 per month. 1843. 1844. 1845. 1846. 1847. 1848. 1850. 1851.

Omans, Isaac.* Mass. Seaman. He was pensioned 26 June 1821 at the rate of $72 per annum. 1821. 1823. 1824. 1825. 1826. 1827. 1828. 1829. 1835. 1836. 1837. 1839. 1840. 1841. 1842b. 1843. 1844. 1845. 1846. 1847. 1848. 1850. 1851. He also appeared as Isaac Omant and Issac Owmans. He served aboard the sloop *Argus*.

O'Neal, Cornelius.* N.Y. Seaman. He was pensioned 15 July 1825 at the rate of $72 per annum. 1827. 1828. 1829. 1830. He served aboard the *Peacock*.

O'Neal, Robert H.* —. Boatswain. His widow, Jennett O'Neal, was pensioned 4 Aug. 1847 at the rate of $10 per month. 1847. 1848. 1850. 1851.

Orr, James.* —. Sergeant of Marines. He was pensioned 7 Feb. 1848 at the rate of $8 per month

Naval Pensioners of the United States, 1800-1851

by a joint resolution of 10 Aug. 1848. 1850. 1851.

Osborne, Elisha. Md. Marine. He was pensioned at the rate of $48 per annum. 1816. 1818. 1819. 1820. 1821.

Osbourn, —.* —. Seaman. His widow, Elizabeth Osbourn, was pensioned from 16 Aug. 1834 at the rate of $6 per month. 1835. 1836. 1837. 1839. 1840. 1841. 1842b. She was listed as Margaret Osbourn in 1837, 1839, 1840, 1841, and 1842. [He was listed as Archibald Osbourn in the Old Wars pension index.]

Osgood, —.Mass. —. Sarah Osgood was pensioned on his service as a privateer at the rate of $72 per annum from 31 July 1812. 1817. 1818. 1819. 1820. 1821. 1822. 1823. 1824. 1825. 1826. 1827. 1828 for $42.

Osgood, Joseph. N.Y. Sailing Master. He served aboard the schooner *Scourge* and died 8 Aug. 1813 in an upset on the lake. His widow, Susannah L. Osgood, was pensioned at the rate of $240 per annum. 1816. 1818. 1821. 1822. 1823. 1824. 1825. 1827. 1828. 1829.

O'Sullivan, John.* —. Purser's Steward. His son, Thomas O'Sullivan, was pensioned at the rate of $9 per month from 30 Oct. 1831. His pension ended 31 Aug. 1842. 1843.

Otternell, John. N.Y. Carpenter's Mate. He was pensioned at the rate of $72 per annum. 1818. 1819. 1820. 1821. 1822. 1823. 1824. 1825. 1826. 1827. 1828. 1829. He was disabled on Lake Champlain. He also appeared as John Otterwell and John Ottenvell.

Overman, John.* —. Carpenter. His children, Sarah Ann Overman, Charles Carroll Overman, Isabella Overman, and John Oliver Overman, were pensioned 17 Aug. 1849 at the rate of $10 per month. 1850. 1851. His widow, Elizabeth Overman, was pensioned 19 Mar. 1845 at the rate of $10 per month. 1845. 1846. 1847. 1848.

Overstocks, —. N.Y. Commander. Lucinda Overstocks was pensioned on his service as a privateer at the rate of $120 per annum from 1 Feb. 1813. 1813. 1814. 1815. 1816. 1817. 1818. 1819 increased to $240. 1820. 1821. 1822. 1823.

Owens, Asael.* —. Seaman. He was pensioned from 22 Jan. 1838 at the rate of $3 per month. 1838. 1840. 1841. 1842b. 1843. 1844. 1845.

Owings, Thomas. N.C. Quartermaster. He was pensioned 2 May 1814 at the rate of $96 per annum. 1816. 1818. 1819. 1820. 1821. 1822. 1823. 1824. 1825. 1826. 1827. 1828. 1829. 1830. He served aboard the brig *Enterprise*.

Packett, —. —. Lieutenant. His children, Mary Ann Packett and John B. Packett, were pensioned at the rate of $25 per month from 29 Mar. 1837. 1837. 1839. 1842.

Page, —. —. Sailing Master. His widow, Eliza Page, was pensioned from 16 Sep. 1826 at the rate of $20 per month. 1835. 1836. 1837. 1839. 1840. 1841. 1842. 1842b.

Page, Moses. Mass. Seaman. He was pensioned as a privateer at the rate of $72 per annum from 20 Nov. 1816. 1816. 1817. 1818. 1819. 1820. 1821. 1822 in the amount of $36.

Page, James.* —. Surgeon. His widow, Maria Page, was pensioned from 15 Mar. 1832 at the rate of $25 per month. 1835. 1836. 1837. 1839. 1840. 1841. 1842. 1842b. 1845. 1846. She was pensioned again on 1 Sep. 1847 at the rate of $25 per month. 1848. 1850. 1851.

Naval Pensioners of the United States, 1800-1851

Paine, Thomas. —. Sailing Master. He was pensioned 7 Feb. 1834 at the rate of $20 per month. 1835. 1836. 1837. 1838. 1839. 1840. 1841. 1842. 1842b. 1843. He also appeared as Thomas Payne.

Palmer, —.* —. Passed Assistant Surgeon. His widow, Jane R. Palmer, was pensioned from 6 Nov. 1836 at the rate of $17.50 per month under the act of 3 Mar. 1837. 1837. 1839. 1840. 1841. 1842. His son, G. J. O'Neill Palmer, was pensioned at the rate of $17.50 from 5 Jan. 1840. 1842b. [He was listed as George Palmer in the Old Wars pension index.]

Palmer, Morris.* —. Drummer M.C. His widow, Cornelia Palmer, was pensioned 28 Feb. 1845 at the rate of $4 per month. 1845. 1846. 1847. 1848. 1850.

Palmer, Morris.* —. Orderly Sergeant Marines. His widow, Ann Palmer, was pensioned from 13 Oct. 1841 at the rate of $8 per month. 1842. 1842b. 1843. 1844. 1845. She was pensioned again 13 Oct. 1846 at the rate of $8 per month. 1848. 1850. 1851.

Parker, Benjamin H.* N.Y. Seaman. He was pensioned 30 Sep. 1821 at the rate of $54 per annum. 1822. 1823. 1824. 1825. 1826. 1827. 1828. 1829. 1830. He served aboard the schooner *Columbus*.

Parker, George. Mass. Captain. He served aboard the *Syren* and died 11 Mar. 1814 from exposure in the service. His widow, Elizabeth Parker, was pensioned at the rate of $360 per annum 1818. 1819. 1821. 1822. 1823. 1824. 1825. 1827. 1829. She was also listed as Eliza Parker. His rank was also given as Master Commandant.

Parker, James L.* —. Lieutenant. His widow, Mary Parker, was pensioned 12 July 1847 at the rate of $25 per month. 1848. 1850. 1851.

Parker, Lewis.* —. Gunner. His son, Lewis Parker, had his application rejected prior to 30 Dec. 1845 because there was no law providing for the child of a deceased officer or seaman. His widow, Susan Ann Parker, was pensioned 31 Aug. 1845 at the rate of $10 per month. 1850. 1851. He also appeared as Louis Parker.

Parker, Nehemiah.* —. Carpenter. His widow, Frances W. Parker, was pensioned from 26 Aug. 1830 at the rate of $10 per month. 1837. 1839. 1840. 1841. 1842. 1842b. 1846.

Parker, Richard.* —. Seaman. He was pensioned 31 July 1842 at the rate of $6 per month. 1843. 1844. 1845. 1846. 1847. 1848. 1850. 1851.

Parker, William. N.Y. Seaman. He was pensioned 4 Aug. 1813 at the rate of $72 per annum. 1816. 1818. 1819. 1820. 1821. 1822. 1823. 1824. 1825. 1826. 1827. 1828. 1829. 1830. 1835. 1836. 1837. 1838. 1839. He served aboard the schooner *Governor Tompkins*.

Parker, William. —. —. He was pensioned. 1842.

Parkham, Alexander B. —. Commander. His widow, Lydia H. Parkham, was pensioned at the rate of $30 per month 23 July 1848. 1850.

Parrott, —.* —. Ordinary Seaman. His widow, Abigail Parrott, was pensioned from 3 Mar. 1832 at the rate of $5 per month. 1839. 1840. 1841. 1842. 1842b. [He was listed as Nathaniel Parrott in the Old Wars pension index.]

Parsells, George.* N.Y. Sailmaker. He died in a fall from aloft 20 Aug. 1819. His widow, Margaret Parsells, received $120 per annum in 1821. 1822. 1823. 1824. 1825. 1827. 1828. 1829. 1835. 1836. 1837. 1839. 1840. 1841. 1842. 1842b. 1845. 1846. She was

Naval Pensioners of the United States, 1800-1851

pensioned again on 1 Sep. 1847 at the rate of $10 per month. 1848. 1850. 1851. He also appeared as George Parsell. She also appeared as Margaret Purcelles and Margaret Parcels.

Parsons, Samuel B. N.Y. Armorer. He was pensioned as a privateer at the rate $72 per annum from 12 Apr. 1813. 1813. 1814. 1815. 1816. 1817. 1818. 1819. 1820 for $41.40.

Parsons, Thomas B. —. Seaman. He was pensioned 30 May 1835 at the rate of $9 per month. 1835. 1836. 1837. 1838. 1839. 1840. 1841. 1842. 1842b. 1843. 1844. 1845. 1846. 1847. 1848. 1850. 1851. He served on the ship *Charles* from Newburyport, Mass. in 1807 as a mate. He was discharged at New Orleans due to the embargo and enlisted in the service of the U.S. in 1808 as a seaman on Gunboat No. 11 under Commandant John Rush. He next served on Gunboat No. 20 under Lt. John D. Henley. He then served on Gunboat No. 22 under Sailing Master Brown and midshipman Thomas Ap Catesby Jones who was the acting lieutenant. The vessel filled with water and capsized on the Sabine River. He saved Lt. Jones, Capt. Thomas Ap Catesby Jones (who could not swim), Brown, and five seamen. Commandant David Porter then took command of the New Orleans station and Lt. Douglas took command of Gunboat No. 22. Parsons was made quartermaster. He was discharged with the disability of a rupture. During the War of 1812 he took to sea again as sailing master of the privateer *Fox*. He sought unsuccessfully to be pensioned at the rank of quartermaster.

Parsons, Usher. —. Surgeon. He was pensioned 7 Feb. 1816 at the rate of $12.50 per month. 1835. 1836. 1837. 1838. 1839. 1840. 1841. 1842. 1842b. 1843. 1844. 1845. 1846. 1847. 1848. 1851.

Pasco, John. Penn. Seaman. He was pensioned 4 Dec. 1807 at the rate of $72 per annum. 1808. 1809. 1810. 1811. 1816. 1818. 1819. 1820. 1821. 1822. 1823. 1824. 1825. 1826. 1827. 1828. 1829. 1830. He served aboard the *Constitution.*

Passenger, A. Mass. Seaman. He served aboard the *Wasp* and was lost 20 Apr. 1815. His widow, Charlotte Passenger, received $72 per annum. 1819. 1821. 1822. 1824. 1825. 1827. 1829.

Pasture, Charles. Md. Ordinary Seaman. He was pensioned 24 Mar. 1815 at the rate of $60 per annum. 1819. 1820. 1821. 1822. 1823. 1824. 1825. 1826. 1827. 1828. 1829. 1830. 1835. 1836. 1837. 1839. 1840. 1841. 1842b. 1843. 1844. 1845. 1846. 1847. 1848. 1850. 1851. He also appeared as Charles Parture and Charles Pastine. He was disabled on the Chesapeake flotilla.

Patch, —. Mass. Seaman. Hannah Patch was pensioned on his service as a privateer at the rate of $36 per annum. 1815. 1816. 1817. 1818. 1819 increased to $72. 1820. 1821. 1822. 1823. 1824. 1825. 1826. 1827. 1828. 1829. 1830. 1831. 1832. 1833. 1834 for $3

Patch, Nicholas. Mass. Seaman. He served aboard Gunboat No. 149 and died of exposure 29 Oct. 1812. His widow, Nancy Patch, was pensioned 15 Apr. 1819 at the rate of $6 per month. 1822. 1827. 1829. 1830. 1835. 1836. 1837. 1839. 1840. 1841. 1842. 1842b. 1845. 1846. She was pensioned again 1 Sep. 1847 at the rate of $6 per month. 1848. 1850. 1851.

Patfield, Joshua. —. Seaman. His widow, Mrs. Graffam, had her application rejected prior to 30

Naval Pensioners of the United States, 1800-1851

Dec. 1845. Her deceased husband served on a private armed vessel, and there was no law in existence providing for the widows of privateersmen.

Patten, John.* N.Y. Ordinary Seaman. His widow, Rachel Patten, was pensioned from 11 Aug. 1835 at the rate of $5 per month. 1839. 1840. 1841. 1842. 1842b. She had her application rejected prior to 23 Dec. 1848. She was barred by the act of 11 Aug. 1848. She was pensioned 30 June 1847 at the rate of $5 per month. 1851. She also appeared as Sarah Patton.

Patterson, —.* —. Boatswain. His widow, Mary Ann Patterson, was pensioned at the rate of $10 per month from 13 Dec. 1836. 1837. 1839. 1840. 1841. 1842. 1842b. [He was listed as John Patterson in the Old Wars pension index.]

Patterson, —. —. Seaman. His daughter, Eunice Patterson, was pensioned at the rate of $6 per month. 1837. 1842.

Patterson, Daniel T.* —. Captain. His widow, Georgeanne Patterson, was pensioned from 25 Aug. 1839 at the rate of $50 per month. 1839. 1840. 1841. 1842. 1842b. 1843. 1845. 1846. She was pensioned again 25 Aug. 1849 at the rate of $50 per month. 1848. 1850. 1851.

Patterson, John. Md. Seaman. He was pensioned 1 May 1815 at the rate of $120 per annum. 1818. 1819. 1820. 1821. 1822. 1823. 1824. 1825. 1826. 1827. 1828. 1829. 1830. He served aboard the schooner *Superior*.

Patterson, Neal. Md. Seaman. He was disabled in 1805 and pensioned at the rate of $72 per annum. 1807. 1808. 1809. 1810. 1811. 1816. 1818. 1819. He was pensioned 1 July 1820 at the rate of $8 per month. 1820. 1821. 1822. 1823. 1824. 1825. 1826. 1827. 1828. 1829. 1830. 1835. 1836. 1837. 1839. 1840. 1841. 1842b. 1843. 1844. 1845. 1846. 1847. 1848. 1850. He served aboard the *Enterprise*.

Paul, —. —. —. Mary Paul was pensioned on his service as a privateer at the rate of $36 per annum. 1814. 1815. 1816. 1817. 1818. 1819. 1820 increased to $72. 1821. 1822. 1823. 1824. 1825. 1826. 1827. 1828. 1829 for $34.40.

Payne, William. R.I. Ordinary Seaman. He was pensioned from 9 Sep. 1814 at the rate of $60 per annum. 1819. 1820. 1821. 1822. 1823. 1824. 1825. 1826. 1827. 1828. 1829. 1830. He served aboard the *Independence*.

Payton, James. N.Y. Ordinary Seaman. He was pensioned at the rate of $60 per annum in 1821. 1822. 1823. 1824. 1825. 1826. 1827. 1828. 1829. He served aboard the *United States*. He was listed as dead in 1829. He also appeared as James Peyton.

Peabody, —. —. —. Phebe Peabody was pensioned on his service. 1842.

Peaco, John W. —. Surgeon. His widow, Georgianna A. Peaco, was pensioned from 23 May 1827 at the rate of $25 per month. 1835. 1836. 1837. 1839. 1840. 1841. 1842. 1842b. 1845. 1846. She was pensioned again 1 Sep. 1847 at the rate of $25 per month. 1848. 1850. 1851.

Pearce, George.* D.C. Lieutenant. He died of yellow fever 7 Aug. 1823. His widow, Eliza L. Pearce, was pensioned 16 May 1823 at the rate of $20 per month. 1824. 1825. 1827. 1828. 1835. 1836. 1837. 1845. 1846. She was pensioned again on 1 Sep. 1847 at the rate of $25 per month. 1847. 1848. 1850. 1851.

Naval Pensioners of the United States, 1800-1851

Pearce, George.* —. Seaman. He was pensioned 8 Jan. 1847 at the rate of $6 per month. 1848. 1850. 1851.
Pearson, John.* —. Boatswain's Mate. His widow, Frances E. Pearson, was pensioned 16 Sep. 1848 at the rate of $9.50 per month. 1850. 1851.
Pease, Levi.* —. Carpenter. His widow, Almira Pease, was pensioned 12 May 1842 at the rate of $10 per month. 1842b. 1843. 1844. 1845. 1846. 1850. 1851.
Peck, Daniel.* N.Y. Seaman. He was pensioned 1 July 1829 at the rate of $6 per month. 1829. 1830. 1835. 1836. 1837. 1839. 1840. 1841. 1843. 1844. 1845. 1846. 1847. 1848. 1850. 1851. He was disabled aboard the *Java* in the Mediterranean.
Peck, Joseph. —. Seaman. He was pensioned 19 Oct. 1836 at the rate of $2.50 per month. 1837. 1839. 1840. 1841. 1842b. 1843. 1844. 1845. 1846. 1847. 1848. 1850. 1851.
Peck, Joseph. —. Ordinary Seaman. He was pensioned 3 Jan. 1851 at the rate of $5 per month. 1851.
Peed, John.* —. Sailmaker. His widow, Rachel B. Peed, was pensioned 23 Feb. 1851 at the rate of $10 per month. 1851.
Peed, Nathaniel B.* —. Sailmaker. His widow, Frances M. Peed, was pensioned 9 May 1845 at the rate of $10 per month. 1846. 1847. 1848. 1850. 1851.
Pelt, James. Va. Seaman. He was pensioned at the rate of $102 per annum in 1811.
Penn, John. N.Y. Quarter Gunner. He perished aboard the *Epervier* 1 Sep. 1815. He had served earlier on the *Essex* under Capt. David Porter where he was disabled by a wound in his right foot and ankle for which he was pensioned from 29 July 1814 at the rate of $6 per month. His executor was James Jones of New York, N.Y. 1816. 1818. 1819.
Penny, William. Mass. —. He perished on the *Grampus*. There were conflicting claims from his mother and a woman who claimed to be his widow. His mother was Elizabeth Penny of Malden, Mass. His older brother was James G. Penny of Saugus, Mass. He was aged 38 and was three years and five months older than the deceased. Their father, William Penny, was living in Malden. The deceased was of Charleston, Mass. when he married Fanny Grover of Saugus on 16 Feb. 1835. They lived together two days. He went to sea. About six months later she cohabited with Lucius Grover of Saugus, her cousin. They eloped to Rhode Island where they were married. On 14 May 1837 they had a child. They had four or more five children. Her brother and sister-in-law were Benjamin and Almira Grover of Cambridge. Eliza Davis of Saugus was a sister of Fanny Grover. Gilbert Grover was a brother of Fanny Grover, and it was he who sought to apply for the benefits due his sister as the widow of William Penny. Asa Grover was the father of Fanny Grover and told his son Gilbert Grover that it would be wrong to apply for the benefits. James G. Penny, brother of the deceased, obtained a warrant for adultery for Lucius Grover and Fanny Grover believing that they had been married. Lucius Grover fled before the arrival of the sheriff. Henry Grover took his sister Fanny Grover to Rhode Island where she married Lucius Grover. They were residents of Becket. Henry Grover was in prison at Charlestown.
Percival, John.* —. Lieutenant. He was pensioned at the rate of $12.50 per month. 1837. 1838. 1839. 1840. 1841. 1842. 1842b. 1843.
Perkins, —. Mass. Sailing Master. Hannah Perkins was pensioned as a privateer at the rate of $72

Naval Pensioners of the United States, 1800-1851

per annum. 1815. 1816. 1817. 1818. 1819 increased to $144. 1820. 1821. 1822. 1823. 1824. 1825. 1826. 1827. 1828. 1829. 1830.

Perkins, —. Mass. Seaman. Elizabeth Perkins was pensioned on his service as a privateer at the rate of $36 per annum. 1816. 1817. 1818. 1819. 1820 increased to $72. 1821. 1822. 1823. 1824. 1825. 1826. 1827. 1828. 1829. 1830. 1831. 1832. 1833. 1834. 1835 for $12.50.

Perkins, —. N.H. Seaman. Mary Perkins was pensioned on his service as a privateer at the rate of $36 per annum. 1815. 1816. 1817. 1818. 1819. 1820 increase to $72. 1821. 1822. 1823. 1824. 1825. 1826. 1827. 1828. 1829. 1830. 1831. 1832. 1833. 1834.

Perkins, James. Penn. Able Seaman. He was pensioned at the rate of $24 per annum in 1809. 1810. 1811.

Perkins, Samuel. M. N.H. Ordinary Seaman. He served aboard the *Chesapeake* and was killed 1 June 1813. His widow was Lucy Perkins. Their children, Mary Perkins, Nancy Perkins, and Caroline Perkins, were pensioned at the rate of $60 per month. 1816. 1818. 1822. 1824. 1825. 1827 in Mass. 1828. 1829. 1842.

Perreau, —. —. —. Margaret Perreau was pensioned on his service as a privateer at the rate of $36 per annum. 1814. 1815. 1816. 1817 for $14.50.

Perry, —. —. Lieutenant. His children, James DeWolf Perry, Nancy B. Perry, and Alexander Perry, were pensioned at the rate of $25 per month from 1 July 1837. 1837. 1839. 1840. 1841. 1842b.

Perry, Charles.* —. Seaman. He was pensioned 30 Nov. 1837 at the rate of $4.50 per month. 1839. 1840. 1841. 1842b. 1843. 1844. 1845. 1846. 1847. 1848. 1850. 1851.

Perry, Ebenezer. —. —. He perished aboard the *Grampus*. His mother was Sarah Perry of Bangor, Me. on 24 May 1844.

Perry, Hyman. Md. Seaman. He was pensioned at the rate of $72 per annum. 1816.

Perry, James.* Va. Ship's Corporal. He was pensioned 1 Sep. 1827 at the rate of $9 per month. 1829. 1830. 1835. 1836. 1837. 1839. 1840. 1841. 1842b. 1843. 1844. 1845. 1846. 1847. 1848. 1850. 1851. He served aboard *North Carolina*.

Perry, James H. —. 1ˢᵗ Class Boy. He was pensioned 20 Nov. 1849 at the rate of $4 per month. 1850. 1851.

Perry, Nathaniel H.* —. Purser. His widow, Lucretia M. Perry, was pensioned from 8 May 1832 at the rate of $20 per month. 1835. 1836. 1837. 1839. 1840. 1841. 1842. 1842b. 1845. 1846. She was pensioned again 1 Sep. 1847 at the rate of $20 per month. 1848. 1850. 1851.

Perry, Oliver Hazard. —. Captain. He died on board the *John Adams* at Port Trinidad in Aug. 1819. His widow, Elizabeth C. Perry, was pensioned from 23 Aug. 1820 at the rate of $50 per month. 1837. 1839. 1840. 1841. 1842. 1842b. 1845. 1846. She was pensioned again 1 Sep. 1847 at the rate of $50 per month. 1848. 1850. 1851. His mother, Sarah Perry of Rhode Island, had another son, Lt. James Alexander Perry, who also died in the service leaving his mother and sister without any support. He had fought at the age of 13 with his brother at the memorable engagement on Lake Erie. Her father also held a commission in the naval service. She sought a pension 21 Jan. 1823.

Perry, Payne. —. Seaman. He was pensioned 6 Apr. 1836 at the rate of $6 per month. 1836.

Naval Pensioners of the United States, 1800-1851

1837. 1839. 1840. 1841. 1842b. 1843. 1844. 1845. 1846. 1847. 1848. 1850. 1851.
Perry, William.* Mass. Seaman. He was pensioned 9 Apr. 1825 at the rate of $6 per month. 1827. 1828. 1829 in D.C. 1830. 1835. 1836. 1837. 1839. 1840. 1841. 1842b. 1843. 1844. 1845. 1846. 1847. 1848. 1850. 1851. He served aboard the schooner *Grampus* in the 1830 roll. [The name of the vessel was seemingly in error. It was likely the *North Carolina*.]
Peterson, John. Mass. Ordinary Seaman. He was pensioned 10 Sep. 1813 at the rate of $60 per annum. 1816. 1818. 1819. 1820. 1821. 1822. 1824. 1825. 1826. 1827. 1828. 1829. 1830. 1835. 1836. 1837. 1839. 1840. 1841. 1842b. 1843. 1844. 1845. 1846. 1847. 1848. 1850. 1851. He served aboard the *Chesapeake*.
Peterson, John. N.Y. Seaman. He was pensioned from 24 May 1816 at the rate of $72 per annum. 1820. 1821. 1822. 1823. 1824. 1825. 1826. 1827. 1828. 1829. 1830. He served aboard the schooner *Madison*.
Peterson, John.* —. Quarter Gunner. He was pensioned 6 Aug. 1847 at the rate of $3.75 per month. 1846. 1847. 1848. 1850. 1851.
Peterson, Thomas.* —. Seaman. He was pensioned 25 Mar. 1846 at the rate of $3 per month. 1847. 1848. 1850. 1851.
Pettingell, Joseph.* —. Marine. His widow, Eliza E. Pettingell, was pensioned 11 Aug. 1846 at the rate of $3.50 per month. 1847. 1848. 1850. 1851.
Phillips, —. —. Landsman. His widow, Catharine Phillips, was pensioned from 18 Feb. 1834 at the rate of $4 per month. 1842b.
Phillips, —.* —. Marine. His widow, Sarah Phillips, was pensioned from 22 Oct. 1834 at the rate of $3.50 per month. 1835. 1836. 1837. 1839. 1840. 1841. 1842. 1842b. [He was listed as George W. Phillips in the Old Wars pension index.]
Phillips, James. N.Y. Seaman. He was pensioned as a privateer at the rate of $72 per annum from Sep. 1814. 1814. 1815. 1816. 1817. 1818. 1819. 1820. 1821. 1822. 1823. 1824. 1825. 1826. 1827. 1828. 1829. 1830. 1831. 1832. 1833 for $69.20.
Phillips, John.* —. Carpenter. His widow, Charlotte Phillips, was pensioned 21 Aug. 1845 at the rate of $10 per month. 1850. 1851. She was also known as Praxedes Phillips.
Phillips, Nathaniel. —. Seaman. His application was rejected 17 Jan. 1845. He claimed to have been wounded in the late war. There was no record evidence of the fact, and the law required that a wound of more than twenty-five years' standing be proved by record evidence. He was pensioned 1 Jan. 1845 at the rate of $4 per month. 1847. 1848. 1850. 1851.
Phillips, Samuel.* —. Carpenter. He was pensioned at the rate of $7.50 per month. 1836. 1837. 1838. His widow, Sarah T. Phillips, was pensioned from 9 Oct. 1839 at the rate of 10 per month. 1840. 1841. 1842. 1842b. She was pensioned again 1 Sep. 1847 at the rate of $10 per month. 1848. 1850. 1851.
Phippen, —. —. —. Margaret Phippen was pensioned on his service. 1842.
Phyfer, Stephen.* N.Y. Ordinary Seaman. He was pensioned 4 Apr. 1825 at the rate of $84 per annum. 1827. 1828. 1829. 1830. 1835. 1836. 1837. 1839. 1840. 1841. 1842. 1842b. 1843. 1844. 1845. 1846. 1847. 1848. 1850. 1851. He was disabled at Sackett's Harbor.
Pickering, Daniel. N.H. Carpenter's Mate. He was pensioned as a privateer at the rate of $72 per

Naval Pensioners of the United States, 1800-1851

annum from 18 Oct. 1812. 1812. 1813. 1814. 1815. 1816. 1817. 1818. 1819. 1820. 1821. 1822. 1823. 1824. 1825. 1826. 1827. 1828. 1829. 1830. 1831. 1832. 1833. 1834. 1835. He was pensioned from 1 Jan. 1837 at the rate of $6 per month. 1845. 1846. 1847. 1850.

Pickering, Henry.* —. Landsman. He was pensioned 3 Mar. 1847 at the rate of $4 per month. 1847. 1848. 1850. 1851.

Pickeson, James. —. Seaman. He served aboard the *President*. He was pensioned at the rate of $72 per annum. 1829.

Pierce, —. —. Lieutenant. His widow, Eliza L. Pierce, was pensioned from 7 Aug. 1822 at the rate of $25 per month. 1837. 1839. 1840. 1841. 1842. 1842b.

Pierce, —.* —. Carpenter's Mate. His widow, Catharine Ann Pierce, was pensioned at the rate of $9.50 per month from 10 Sep. 1829. 1837. 1839. 1840. 1841. 1842. 1842b. [He was listed as Wilder W. Pierce in the Old Wars pension index.]

Pierce, George. N.Y. Seaman. He was pensioned 22 Nov. 1815 at the rate of $60 per annum. 1818. 1819. 1820. 1821. 1822. 1823. 1824. 1825. 1826. 1827. 1828. 1829. 1830. He also appeared as George Peirce. He served aboard the *Guerriere*.

Pierce, John. S.C. Gunner. He was pensioned at the rate of $108 per annum in 1821.

Piercy, William P.* —. Commander. His widow, Henrietta Piercy, was pensioned 14 July 1847 at the rate of $30 per month. 1847. 1848. 1850. 1851.

Pierson, Peter.* —. Seaman. He was pensioned 20 Mar. 1836 at the rate of $6 per month. 1836. 1837. 1839. 1840. 1841. 1842b. 1843. 1844. 1845. 1846. 1847. 1848. 1850. 1851.

Pillsbury, —. Mass. Seaman. Margery Pillsbury was pensioned on his service as a privateer at the rate of $36 per annum. 1816. 1817. 1818. 1819. 1820 increased to $72. 1821. 1822. 1823. 1824. 1825. 1826. 1827. 1828. 1828. 1829.

Piner, John.* N.Y. Ordinary Seaman. He was pensioned 6 Nov. 1828 at the rate of $5 per month. 1829. 1830. 1835. 1836. 1837. 1839. 1840. 1841. 1843. 1844. 1845. 1846. 1847. 1848. 1850. 1851. He served aboard the *Macedonian* under J. Biddle. He also appeared as John Pinee.

Pinkham, Alexander B.* —. Commander. His widow, Lydia H. Pinkham, was pensioned 23 July 1843 at the rate of $30 per month. 1843. 1844. 1848. 1851.

Pinkham, Reuben.* —. Lieutenant. His widow, Lydia G. Pinkham, was pensioned from 27 Oct. 1839 at the rate of $25 per month. 1840. 1841. 1842. 1842b. 1845. 1846. She was pensioned again 1 Sep. 1847 at the rate of $25 per month. 1847. 1850. 1851.

Pinkney, Henry.* —. Commander. His daughter, Emily Maria Pinkney, was pensioned 16 May 1848 at the rate of $30 per month. 1848. 1850. 1851.

Pippen, Joseph. Mass. Coxswain. He served aboard the *Wasp* and was lost 20 Apr. 1815. His widow, Nabby Pippen, was pensioned 1 Jan. 1817 at the rate of $60 per annum. 1818. 1819. 1821. 1822. 1823. 1824. 1825. 1827. 1828. 1829. 1830. She was pensioned again from 11 Apr. 1835 at the rate of $5 per month. 1839. 1840. 1841. 1842b. He also appeared as Joseph Phippen and she as Nabby Phippen.

Pitman, —. N.Y. Seaman. Susan Pitman was pensioned on his service as a privateer at the rate of $36 per annum. 1815. 1817. 1818 for $18.50.

Pitman, William. Md. Boy. He was pensioned at the rate of $36 per annum in 1804. 1805. 1807.

Naval Pensioners of the United States, 1800-1851

1808. 1809. 1810. 1811. 1816 in D.C. 1818. 1819. 1820. 1821. He also appeared as William Pittman.

Pitt, James. Va. Seaman. He was being pensioned at the rate of $108.80 per annum in 1802. 1803. 1804. 1805. 1807. 1808. 1809. 1810. He also appeared as James Pitts and James Pelt.

Pitt, John.* Penn. Seaman. He was pensioned 1 Aug. 1821 at the rate of $72 per annum. 1822. 1823. 1824. 1825. 1826. 1827. 1828. 1829. 1830. He served aboard the *Columbus*.

Place, John.* N.Y. Ordinary Seaman. He served aboard the *Hornet* and was killed 23 Feb. 1813. His widow, Sarah Place, received $60 per annum in 1822. 1823. His orphans, Sarah Place, Cornelia Place, and Gilbert J. Place, received $60 per annum. 1824. 1825. 1827. 1828. 1829. Israel Vandyke was their guardian.

Place, John. —. Seaman. His mother, Nancy Tompkins, was pensioned at the rate of $8.33 ½ per month from 6 Dec. 1847 by special act of 22 Feb. 1849. 1850.

Place, John. N.Y. Armorer. He was pensioned at the rate of $96 per annum. 1818. 1819. 1820. 1821. 1822. 1823. 1824. 1825. 1826. 1827. 1828.

Platt, Charles F. —. —. He was pensioned. 1842. [second of the name on the list]

Platt, Charles T.* —. Lieutenant. He was pensioned at the rate of $25 per month from 4 June 1829. 1837. 1838. 1839. 1840. 1841. 1842. 1842b. 1843.

Platt, Peter. Pa. Seaman. He was pensioned as a privateer at the rate of $72 per annum from 25 Dec. 1814. 1814. 1815. 1816. 1817. 1818. 1819. 1820. 1821. 1822. 1823. 1824. 1825. 1826.

Plinter, —. —. —. Harriet Plinter was pensioned on his service. 1842.

Poland, Jacob. Mass. Boatswain. He was pensioned as a privateer at the rate of $60 per annum from 27 Apr. 1813. 1814. 1815. 1816. 1817. 1818. 1819. 1820. 1821. 1822 in the amount of $30.

Poland, William. Mass. Seaman. He was pensioned as a privateer at the rate of $48 per annum from 25 Nov. 1812. 1820.

Pons, Antonie.* —. Seaman. His widow, Marie Pons, was pensioned 30 June 1847 at the rate of $6 per month. 1851.

Porter, —. Mass. Commander. Lois Porter was pensioned on his service as a privateer at the rate of $120 per annum from 1 Feb. 1815. 1815. 1816. 1817. 1818. 1819 increased to $240. 1820. 1821. 1822. 1823. 1824. 1825. 1826. 1827. 1828. 1839. 1830 for $20.

Porter, David.* —. Captain. He was pensioned from 24 Jan. 1825 at the rate of $40 per month. 1839. 1840. 1841. 1842. 1842b. His widow, Evelina Porter, had her application rejected prior to 17 Jan. 1848. He did not die in the service. He had already left the navy.

Porter, John.* —. Master Commandant. His widow, Eliza C. Porter, was pensioned from 2 Sep. 1831 at the rate of $30 per month. 1835. 1836. 1837. 1839. 1840. 1841. 1842. 1842b. 1845. 1846. She was pensioned again 1 Sep. 1847 at the rate of $30 per month. 1848. 1850. 1851.

Potter, Joseph. Penn. Seaman. He perished aboard the *Epervier* 1 Sep. 1815. He married Elizabeth Kemp on18 Mar. 1809 in Philadelphia, Penn. James Bateman of the Methodist Episcopal Church performed the marriage at the house of Isaac Cropper. They had a daughter, Hannah Potter, born in July 1814. His widow was paid $72 on 22 May 1818.

Naval Pensioners of the United States, 1800-1851

Potter, Luke.* —. Captain of Hold. He was pensioned 14 Sep. 1850 at the rate of $3.75 per month. 1850. 1851.

Pottinger, William.* —. Lieutenant. His widow, Frances Pottinger, was pensioned from 5 Feb. 1833 at the rate of $25 per month. 1835. 1836. 1837. 1839. 1840. 1841. 1842. 1842b. 1845. 1846. She was pensioned again 1 Sep. 1847 at the rate of $25 per month. 1848. 1850. 1851. She also appeared as Frances Pottenger.

Potts, James B.* —. Sailing Master. His widow, Sarah Potts, was pensioned from 8 May 1839 at the rate of $20 per month. 1839. 1840. 1841. 1842. 1842b. 1846. She was pensioned again 1 Sep. 1847 at the rate of $20 per month. 1848. 1850. 1851.

Potts, Samuel. Penn. Seaman. He perished aboard the *Epervier* 1 Sep. 1815. He was the son of Jasper and Mary, nee Dellsil [?], Potts who were married in the German Lutheran St. Michaels and Zions Church in Philadelphia, Penn. He was born 26 Sep. 1782. His mother of Frankford, Penn. was paid $72 on 20 Sep. 1817.

Poulton, Robert. Mass. Ordinary Seaman. He was pensioned 11 Dec. 1814 at the rate of $60 per annum. 1816. 1818. 1819. 1820. 1821. 1822. 1824. 1825. 1826. 1827. 1828. 1829. 1830. He served aboard the *Constitution*.

Powell, Henry.* —. Seaman. He was pensioned 10 Feb. 1840 at the rate of $3 per month. 1840. 1841. 1842b. 1843. 1844. 1845. 1846. 1847. 1848. 1850. 1851.

Powell, William J.* —. Surgeon. His widow, Angelica T. Powell, was pensioned 6 Feb. 1848 at the rate of $27.50 per month. 1848. 1850. 1851.

Power, Edward.* —. Ordinary Seaman. He was pensioned 27 May 1834 at the rate of $5 per month. 1839. 1840. 1841. 1842b. 1843. 1844. 1845. 1846. 1847. 1848. 1850. 1851.

Powers, John. Mass. Quartermaster. He was pensioned as a privateer at the rate of $48 per annum from 6 Jan. 1813. 1813. 1814. 1815. 1816. 1817 for $24.

Powers, John.* N.Y. Marine. He was pensioned 1 July 1826 at the rate of $36 per annum. 1829. 1830. He served aboard the *Franklin*.

Prather, —.* —. Marine. His widow, Henrietta M. Prather, was pensioned from 14 Sep. 1834 at the rate of $3.50 per month. 1835. 1836. 1837. 1839. 1840. 1841. 1842b. [He was James Prather in the Old Wars pension index.]

Pratt, Richard M. —. Seaman. His widow, Elizabeth Pratt, was pensioned from 8 Jan. 1819 at the rate of $6 per month. 1851.

Pray, E. —. —. He was pensioned as a privateer at the rate of $96 per annum. 1815. 1816. 1817.

Preble, —. —. Captain. His widow, Mary Preble, was pensioned from 25 Aug. 1837 at the rate of $50 per month. 1837. 1839. 1840. 1841. 1842. 1842b.

Prentiss, John E.* —. Lieutenant. His widow, Eleanor H. Prentiss, was pensioned from 5 July 1840 at the rate of $25 per month. 1841. 1842. She was pensioned again 1 Sep.1847 at the rate of $25 per month. 1848. 1850. 1851.

Prentiss, Nathaniel A.* —. Sailing Master. He was pensioned at the rate of $10 per annum. 1837. 1838. 1839. 1840. 1841. 1842. 1842b. 1843.

Preston, William. —. Boatswain. His application was rejected between Mar. 1840 and 1 Jan. 1842. He claimed to have been wounded on Lake Champlain in September 1814, but his name was not on the list of those who were.

Naval Pensioners of the United States, 1800-1851

Price, —.* —. Lieutenant. His daughter, Rachel W. Price, was pensioned at the rate of $25 per month. 1837. 1842. [He was listed as George Price in the Old Wars pension index.]
Price, John. —. Seaman. He was pensioned 11 May 1835 at the rate of $6 per month. 1835. 1836. 1837. 1839. 1840. 1841. 1843. 1844. 1845. 1846. 1847. 1848. 1850. 1851.
Price, John.* —. Seaman. He was pensioned 30 Aug. 1842 at the rate of $6 per month. 1842b. 1843. 1844. 1845. 1846. 1848.
Price, Nelson.* —. Ordinary Seaman. He was pensioned 31 May 1850 at the rate of $3.75 per month. 1850. 1851.
Price, Simeon.* —. Landsman. He was pensioned 8 May 1844 at the rate of $1.33 1/3 per month. 1850. 1851.
Price, William.* Penn. Seaman. He was pensioned 1 Jan. 1819 at the rate of $72 per annum. 1822. 1823. 1824. 1825. 1826. 1827. 1828. 1829. 1830. He served aboard the brig *Argus*.
Prichard, —. Mass. Seaman. He was pensioned on his service as a privateer at the rate of $72 per annum from 6 Dec. 1812. 1820.
Primrose, John R. —. Apprentice. He perished aboard the *Grampus*. His sister was Rachel Ann Primrose of New York, N.Y. 8 June 1844. She was 17 years old in 1843. His parents were Daniel and Amelia Primrose. His father died about 5 years ago, and his mother about 2 years ago. His half-sister was Mary Western, a widow aged 43, who lived at 11 Division St.
Proctor, —. —. Carpenter's Mate. His daughter, Bathsheba Proctor, was pensioned at the rate of $9.50 per month. 1837.
Proctor, —. —. Seaman. His daughter, Mary Proctor, was pensioned at the rate of $6 per month. 1837. 1841. 1842. 1842b.
Proctor, Benjamin.* —. Seaman. He was pensioned 1 Mar. 1832 at the rate of $4 per month. 1836.
Proctor, Charles. Mass. Steward. He perished aboard the *Epervier* 1 Sep. 1815. He married Mary Kelly on 8 Feb. 1807 in Roxbury, Mass. The Rev. Eliphalet Porter of the First Church of Roxbury performed the marriage. The groom was from Boston. William Basson was an uncle of the deceased. Charles Proctor had been a lieutenant in the army prior to entering the Navy. His widow, Mary Proctor, was paid $108 on 5 June 1817.
Proctor, Charles.* —. Steward. His daughter, Mary Proctor, was pensioned from 1 July 1837 at the rate of $9 per month. 1839. 1840. 1845. 1846. 1848. 1850. 1851.
Pugal, Stephen. N.Y. Seaman. He was pensioned as a privateer at the rate of $72 per annum from 11 Mar. 1813. 1813. 1814. 1815. 1816. 1817. 1818. 1819. 1820. 1821. 1822 for $36.
Purdy, John.* —. Ordinary Seaman. He was pensioned 13 Dec. 1850 at the rate of $.62 ½ per month. 1851.

Quantin, Peter. Penn. Ordinary Seaman. He was pensioned 17 Sep. 1813 at the rate of $60 per annum. 1820. 1821. 1822. 1823. 1824. 1825. 1826. 1827. 1828. 1829. 1830. 1835. 1836. 1837. 1839. 1840. He served aboard the *Chesapeake*. He also appeared as Peter

Naval Pensioners of the United States, 1800-1851

Quantier.
Quigley, Michael.* Mass. Ordinary Seaman. He was pensioned 11 Mar. 1825 at the rate of $60 per annum. He was disabled in the Charlestown Navy Yard. 1827. 1828. 1829. He served on the *Constitution*.
Quills, David. Mass. Quartermaster. He was pensioned 20 Feb. 1815 at the rate of $60 per annum. 1822. 1823. 1824. 1825. 1826. 1827. 1828. 1829. 1830. 1835. 1836. 1837. 1839. 1840. 1841. 1842. 1842b. 1843. 1844. 1845. 1846. 1847. 1848. 1850. 1851. He also appeared as David Quill.
Quinnell, Henry.* —. Seaman. He was pensioned 26 Sep. 1845 at the rate of $2 per month. 1845. 1846. 1847. 1848. 1850. 1851.

Rackliff, —.* —. Ordinary Seaman. His widow, Susan Rackliff, was pensioned from 6 July 1841 at the rate of $5 per month. 1842b. [He was listed as Benjamin Rackliff in the Old Wars pension index.]
Racks, John. N.Y. Boatswain's Mate. He was pensioned at the rate of $96 per annum. 1816. He also appeared as John Rack.
Radcliff, James.* —. Corporal, Marines. His widow, Damaris Radcliff, was pensioned 9 May 1846 at the rate of $4.50 per month. 1850. 1851.
Ragan, Burnett. —. Landsman. He was pensioned 6 June 1838 at the rate of $2 per month. 1839. 1840. 1841. 1842b. 1843. 1844. 1845. 1846. 1847. 1848. 1850. 1851. He also appeared as Burnett Rogan.
Rainey, Joseph. Md. Ordinary Seaman. His widow, Rebecca Rainey, was pensioned from 11 Nov. 1804 at the rate of $5 per month. 1839. 1840. 1841. 1842. 1842b. She had her application rejected prior to 23 Dec. 1848. She was barred under the act of 11 Aug. 1848. She also appeared as Rebecca Ramey.
Ramsay, Robert.* —. Steward. He was pensioned from 30 Dec. 1837 at the rate of $5 per month and again on 1 June 1848 at the rate of $8 per month. 1843. 1844. 1845. 1846. 1847. 1848. 1850. 1851.
Randall, John. Md. Private Marine. He was pensioned 2 Sep. 1805 at the rate of $36 per annum. 1805. 1807. 1808. 1809. 1810. 1811. 1816. 1818. 1819. 1820. 1821. 1822. 1823. 1824. 1825. 1826. 1827. 1828. 1829. 1830. 1835. 1836. 1837. 1839. 1840. 1841. 1842b. 1843. 1844. 1845. 1846. 1847. 1848. 1850. 1851. He also appeared as John Randal. He was disabled at New Orleans.
Randolph, Burwell S.* D.C. Midshipman. He was pensioned 20 Feb. 1820 at the rate of $72 per annum. 1821. 1822. 1823. 1824. 1825. 1826. 1827. 1828. 1829. 1830. 1836. 1837. 1838. 1839. 1840. 1841. 1842. 1842b. 1843. 1844. 1845. 1846. 1847. 1848. 1850. 1851. He served aboard the *Constellation*.
Randolph, Richard Bland. —. Midshipman. He entered the service on 1 May 1800 on the *Insurgente* and was sent to shore sick in Sept. 1800. He was sick 20 months 18 days. He sought a pension for his wounds 17 May 1824. His application was withdrawn.

Naval Pensioners of the United States, 1800-1851

Rankin, —. —. —. Mary Rankin was pensioned on his service as a privateer at the rate of $72 per annum. 1812. 1813. 1814. 1815. 1816. 1817. 1818. 1819. 1820. 1821. 1822. 1823. 1824. 1825. 1826. 1827. 1828. 1829. 1830. 1831. 1832.

Rankin, George. Penn. Ordinary Seaman. He drowned in Lake Erie on 18 Sep. 1814. His widow, Margaret Rankin, received $60 in 1822. 1823. 1824. 1825. 1827. 1828. 1829. Their son was George Rankin.

Rankin, James. *—. Seaman. He was pensioned 8 June 1839 at the rate of $4.50 per month. 1840. 1841. 1842b. 1843. 1844. 1845. 1846. 1847. 1848. 1850. 1851.

Rantin, —. Pa. Commander. Elizabeth H. Rantin was pensioned on the service as a privateer at the rate of $120 per annum. 1813. 1814. 1815. 1816. 1817. 1818 increased to $240. 1819. 1820. 1821. 1822. 1823. 1824. 1825. 1826. 1827.

Rassmassen, Andrew. N.Y. Pilot. He served aboard the schooner *Pert* and was killed on Lake Erie on 22 July 1813. His widow, Catherine Rassmassen, was pensioned 2 Aug. 1814 at the rate of $20 per month. 1816. 1818. 1821. 1823. 1824. 1825. 1827. 1828. 1829. 1830. 1836. 1837. 1840. 1841.1842. 1842b. She also appeared as Catherine Rasmussen, Catherine Rossmussoin, and Catherine Rusmussen.

Rathbon, John.* Penn. Ordinary Seaman. He was pensioned 1 July 1819 at the rate of $72 per annum. 1829. 1830. 1836. He served aboard the schooner *Shark.*

Ratler, John. N.Y. Quartermaster. He was pensioned 1 July 1822 at the rate of $72 per annum. 1824. 1825. 1826. 1827. 1828. 1829. 1830. He served aboard the schooner *Ontario.* He also appeared as John Rattler.

Rattle, Thomas. Md. Seaman. He was pensioned as a privateer at the rate of $48 per annum from 28 Nov. 1812. 1812. 1813.

Ray, Hyde.* —. Surgeon. His widow, Catharine S. M. Ray, was pensioned from 7 Sep. 1835 at the rate of $35 per month. 1836. 1837. 1839. 1840. 1841. 1842. 1842b. 1845. 1846. She was pensioned again 1 Sep. 1847 at the rate of $35 per month. 1848. 1850. 1851.

Read, Benjamin F. —. Lieutenant. His widow, Catharine C. Read, was pensioned at the rate of $25 per month from 6 Jan. 1812. 1837. 1839. 1840. 1841. 1842. 1842b. She was pensioned again 1 Sep. 1847 at the rate of $25 per month. 1848. 1850. 1851.

Read, Jasper. —. Seaman. He was pensioned 28 Mar. 1814 at the rate of $3 per month. 1840. 1841. 1842b. 1843. 1844. 1845. 1846. 1847. 1848. 1850. 1851.

Read, John. D. C. Private Marine. He was pensioned 1 Apr. 1820 at the rate of $36 per annum. 1821. 1823. 1824. 1825. 1826. 1827. 1828. 1829. 1830. He served aboard the *Tom Bowline.* He also appeared as John Reed.

Read, Richard.* —. Boatswain's Mate. He was pensioned 18 Dec. 1850 at the rate of $4.75 per month. 1851.

Reagan, John.* N.Y. Private Marine. He was pensioned 1 May 1815 at the rate of $60 per annum. 1816. 1818. 1819. 1820. 1821. 1822. 1823. 1824. 1825. 1826. 1827. 1828. 1829. 1830. He served aboard the *President.*

Reak, —. —. —. Mary Reak was pensioned on his service at the rate of $72 per annum. 1818. 1819. 1820. 1821. 1822. 1823. 1824. 1825. 1826. 1827. She also appeared as Mary Reaux.

Naval Pensioners of the United States, 1800-1851

Reany, —.* —. Purser's Steward. His daughter, Mary K. Reany, was pensioned at the rate of $9 per month from 3 Jan. 1831. 1839. 1840. 1841. 1842. 1842b. [He was listed as John K. Reany in the Old Wars pension index.]

Reaux, —. N.Y. Lt. Mary Leaux was pensioned on his service at the rate of $144 per annum. 1820.

Reddington, John.* —. Armorer. He was pensioned 30 Jan. 1843 at the rate of $4.50 per month. 1844. 1845. 1846. 1847. 1848. 1850. 1851.

Redfield, John G.* —. Quartermaster. His widow, Susan M. Redfield, was pensioned 7 Nov. 1847 at the rate of $8 per month. 1850. 1851.

Reed, James C.* —. Ordinary Seaman. He was pensioned 5 May 1837 at the rate of $2.50 per month. 1837. 1838. 1839. 1840. 1841. 1842b. 1843. 1844. 1845. 1846. 1847. 1848. 1850. 1851. He also appeared as James C. Read.

Reed, Thomas. N.Y. Seaman. He was pensioned 10 Nov. 1815 at the rate of $60 per annum. 1818. 1819. 1820. 1821. 1822. 1823. 1824. 1825. 1826. 1827. 1828. 1829. 1830. He also appeared as Thomas Read. He served aboard the *Peacock*.

Reid, James. —.* Ordinary Seaman. He was pensioned 14 Jan. 1838 at the rate of $5 per month. 1839. 1840. 1841. 1842b. 1843. 1844. 1845. 1846. 1847. 1848. 1850. 1851.

Reid, Washington. —. Lieutenant. His widow, Mary Reid, was pensioned 18 Feb. 1850 at the rate of $25. 1850. 1851.

Reilly, Philip.* —. Marine. His widow, Mary Reilly, was pensioned 5 July 1850 at the rate of $3.50 per month. 1851.

Reinburg, Lewis.* —. Marine. He was pensioned 28 Jan. 1843 at the rate of $1.75 per month. 1843. 1844. 1845. 1846. 1847. 1848. 1850. 1851. He also appeared as Lewis Reineburg.

Renshaw, James.* —. Captain. His widow, Charlotte E. Renshaw, was pensioned 29 May 1846 at the rate of $50 per month. 1848. 1850. 1851.

Revel, John.* —. Ordinary Seaman. He was pensioned 20 Aug. 1833 at the rate of $2.50 per month. 1837. 1838. 1839. 1840. 1841. 1842b. 1843. 1844. 1845. 1846. 1847. 1848. 1850. 1851.

Reynolds, —. —. N.Y. Boatswain. His daughter, Amanda H. Reynolds, was pensioned at the rate of $10 per month from 23 Apr. 1835. 1839. 1840. He died of yellow fever 21 May 1823. His widow, Phoebe Reynolds, was pensioned 15 July 1824 at the rate of $10 per month. 1824. 1825. 1827. 1828. 1830. 1835. 1836. 1837. 1839. 1840. 1841. 1842b. [He was listed as William Reynolds in the Old Wars pension list.]

Rhodes, —. —. —. Rachel Rhodes was pensioned on his service as a privateer at the rate of $72 per annum. 1819. 1820. 1821. 1822. 1823. 1824. 1825. 1826. 1827 for $36.

Rhodes, Frederick.* —. Corporal Marines. He was pensioned 27 Nov. 1833 at the rate of $2.50 per month. 1835. 1836. 1837.

Rhodes, Rosnante.* N.Y. Seaman. He was pensioned 5 Dec. 1815 at the rate of $72 per annum. 1818. 1819. 1820. 1821. 1822. 1823. 1824. 1825. 1826. 1827. 1828. 1830. 1835. 1836. 1837. 1839. 1840. 1841. 1842b. 1843. 1844. 1845. 1846. 1847. 1848. 1850. 1851. He served aboard the *Guerriere*. He also appeared as Rosmante Rhodes and Rosnanti Rhodes.

Naval Pensioners of the United States, 1800-1851

Rice, Christopher.* —. Purser. His widow, Eliza M. Rice, was pensioned 5 Mar. 1846 at the rate of $20 per month. 1846. 1847. 1848. 1850. 1851.

Rice, John.* N.Y. Seaman. He was pensioned from 29 July 1830 at the rate of $6 per month. 1835. 1836. 1837. 1839. 1840. 1841. 1842b. 1843. 1844. 1845. 1846. 1847. 1848. 1850. 1851. He served aboard the *Vincennes*.

Richardet, —. —. Sailing Master. His children, James B. Richardet and Samuel Richardet, were pensioned at the rate of $20 per month. 1837. 1842.

Richards, —. —. —. A. P. Richards was pensioned on his service as a privateer at the rate of $72 per annum. 1817. 1818. 1819. 1820. 1821. 1822. 1823. 1824. 1825. 1826. 1827 for $67.

Richards, John. La. Quarter Gunner. He was pensioned 20 Oct. 1829 at the rate of $108 per annum. 1829. 1830. 1835. 1836. 1837. 1839. 1840. 1841. 1842b. 1843. 1844. 1845. 1846. 1847. 1848. He was disabled on the M. flotilla, Lake Borgne.

Richards, John.* —. Seaman. He was pensioned 12 Apr. 1848 at the rate of $3 per month. 1848. 1850. 1851.

Richards, Stephen. Mass. Seaman. He was pensioned as a privateer at the rate of $48 per annum from 3 Apr. 1813. 1813. 1814. 1815. 1816. 1817. 1818. 1819. 1820 in the amount of $24.

Richardson, —. Mass. Gunner. Harriet Richardson was pensioned on his service as a privateer at the rate of $72 per annum. 1814. 1815. 1816. 1817. 1818. 1819. 1820. 1821. 1822. 1823. 1824. 1825. 1826. 1827. 1828. 1829. 1830. 1831. 1832. 1833. 1834 for $47.40.

Richardson, —.* —. Boatswain's Mate. His widow, Sarah Richardson, was pensioned from 9 Jan. 1837 at the rate of $9.50 per month. 1839. 1840. 1841. 1842b. [He was listed as Robert Richardson in the Old Wars pension index.]

Richardson, Benjamin I.* La. Master's Mate. He was pensioned 8 Oct. 1829 at the rate of $10 per month. 1830. 1835. 1836. 1837. 1839. 1840. 1841. 1842b. 1843. 1844. 1845. 1846. 1847. 1848. 1850. 1851. He was disabled at the Navy Yard in Pensacola.

Richardson, John. —. Quarter Gunner. He was pensioned from 20 Oct. 1829 at the rate of $9 per month. 1850. 1851.

Richardson, Robert.* —. Gunner's Mate. He was pensioned 14 Dec. 1850 at the rate of $4.75 per month. 1851.

Richardson, William. Mass. Master's Mate. He was pensioned as a privateer at the rate of $72 per annum from 28 May 1813. 1813. 1814. 1815. 1816. 1817. 1818. 1819. 1820. 1821. 1822. 1823. 1824. 1825. 1826. 1827 in the amount of $22.50.

Richmond, John. —. Marine. He was pensioned 31 July 1816 at the rate of $1.75 per month. 1839. 1840. 1841. 1842. 1843. 1844. 1845. 1846. 1847. 1848. 1850. 1851.

Riddle, Samuel. —. Seaman. He was pensioned 30 June 1836 at the rate of $3 per month. 1839. 1840. 1841. 1842b. 1843. 1844. 1845. 1846. 1847. 1848. 1850. 1851.

Riddle, Thomas. Penn. Boy. He served on Gunboat No. 21 under Capt. William Sheed. On 29 July 1813 in action with the enemy at the entrance to Delaware Bay he lost his leg. After the amputation, he was employed at the navy yard in Philadelphia. He was pensioned on 30 May 1814 at the rate of $3 per month for life. 1816. 1818. 1819. 1820. 1821. 1822. 1823. He also appeared as Thomas Riddels.

Naval Pensioners of the United States, 1800-1851

Ridgeway,* Ebenezer. —. Commander. His widow, Maria Ridgeway, had her application rejected between Mar. 1840 and 1 Jan. 1842. Her husband died 16 Aug. 1841. The law did not cover her case. She was pensioned 1 Nov. 1841 at the rate of $30 per month. 1842b. 1843. 1844. 1845. 1848. 1850. 1851.

Ridley, —. Mass. Seaman. Rachel Ridley was pensioned on his service as a privateer at the rate of $36 per annum. 1815. 1816. 1817. 1818. 1819 increased to $72. 1820. 1821. 1822. 1823. 1824. 1825. 1826. 1827. 1828. 1829. 1830. 1831. 1832. 1833. 1834. 1835 for $6.

Riggs, Andrew. Mass. Seaman. He served aboard the schooner *Madison* and was killed on Lake Ontario 27 Dec. 1814. He was pensioned at the rate of $48 per annum from 19 Oct. 1812. His widow, Nancy Riggs, was pensioned at the rate of $6 per month. 1818. 1819. 1820. 1821. 1822. 1823. 1824. 1825. 1827. 1829. 1830. 1835. 1836. 1837. 1839. 1840. 1841. 1842b. She appeared as Nancy Briggs in 1820 and 1821.

Riggs, Daniel. —. Ordinary Seaman. He was pensioned 18 May 1836 at the rate of $3.75 per month. 1836. 1837. 1838. 1841. 1842. 1842b. 1843. 1844. 1845. 1846. 1847. 1848. 1850. 1851.

Riley, Bartholomew. —. Marine. He was pensioned 1 June 1832 at the rate of $3 per month. 1835. 1836.

Riley, Jeremiah. Penn. Seaman. He was pensioned at the rate of $81.60 per annum in 1802. 1803. 1804. 1805.

Riley, John. —. Marine. He was pensioned 1 July 1831 at the rate of $3 per month. 1835. 1836. 1837. 1839. 1840. 1841. 1842b. 1843. 1844. 1845. 1846. 1847. 1848. 1850. 1851.

Riley, Philip. Penn. Seaman. He was pensioned at the rate of $72 per annum in 1821. 1822. 1823.

Riley, Thomas.* —. Gunner. He was pensioned from 23 June 1837 at the rate of $7.50 per month. 1839. 1840. 1841. 1842b. 1843. His widow, Esther Riley, was pensioned 11 Mar. 1845 at the rate of $10 per month. 1845. 1846. 1847. 1848.

Ring, —.* —. Boatswain. His widow, Eliza Ring, was pensioned from 25 Sep. 1835 at the rate of $10 per month. 1836. 1837. 1839. 1840. 1842. [He was listed as Thomas Ring in the Old Wars pension list.]

Rinker, Samuel. —. Sailing Master. His widow, Catharine Rinker, was pensioned from 10 July 1823 at the rate of $20 per month. 1836. 1837. 1839. 1840. 1841. 1842. 1842b. 1845. 1846. She was pensioned again 1 Sep. 1847 at the rate of $20 per month. 1848. 1850. 1851.

Ripley, Edin M.* —. Boatswain's Mate. He was pensioned 7 Nov. 1850 at the rate of $9.50 per month. 1851.

Risley, —. N.Y. Steward. Lavinia Risley was pensioned on his service as a privateer at the rate of $96 per annum from 20 July 1813. 1818. 1819. 1820. 1821. 1822. 1823. 1824. 1825. 1826. 1827. 1828 for $53.07.

Risley, —. N.Y. Surgeon's Mate. Rachel A. Risley was pensioned on his service as a privateer at the rate of $96 per annum 1 Mar. 1814. 1820.

Ritchie, —.* —. Lieutenant. His daughter, Mary R. Ritchie, was pensioned at the rate of $25 per month from 26 June 1831. 1837. 1839. 1840. 1841. 1842. 1842b. [He was listed as John

Naval Pensioners of the United States, 1800-1851

T. Ritchey in the Old Wars pension index.]
Ritchie, Thomas.* —. Seaman. He was pensioned 14 May 1839 at the rate of $3 per month. 1840. 1841. 1842b. 1843. 1844. 1845. 1846. 1847. 1848. 1850. 1851. He also appeared as Thomas Richie.
Roach, —. N.Y. Marine. Sarah Roach was pensioned on his service as a privateer at the rate of $144 per annum. 1817. 1818. 1819. 1820. 1821. 1822. 1823. 1824. 1825. 1826. 1827. 1828. 1829. 1830. 1831. 1832 for $108.
Roach, John.* —. Ord. Sergeant of Marines. He was pensioned 14 May 1850 at the rate of $2 per month. 1851.
Roath, Stephen B.* —. Gunner's Mate. He was pensioned in Aug. 1842 at the rate of $4.75 per month. 1842b. 1843. 1844. 1845. 1846. 1847. 1848. 1850. 1851.
Roberts, —.* —. Musician Marines. His daughters, Mary Roberts and Margaret Roberts, were pensioned on his service at the rate of $4 per month from 1 Oct. 1836. 1839. 1840. 1841. 1842. 1842b. [He was listed as Francis Roberts in the Old Wars pension index.]
Roberts, —. Mass. Carpenter. Hannah Roberts was pensioned on his service as a privateer at the rate of $60 per annum. 1815. 1816. 1817. 1818. 1819. 1820 increased to $120. 1821. 1822. 1823. 1824. 1825. 1826. 1827. 1828. 1829. 1830. 1831. 1832. 1833. 1834. 1835 for $10.
Roberts, James.* —. Quarter Gunner. He was pensioned 14 Apr. 1832 at the rate of $1.87 ½ per month. 1837. 1838. 1839. 1840. 1841. 1842b. 1843. 1844. 1845. 1846. 1848. 1850. 1851.
Roberts, John. —. Seaman. He was pensioned from 21 Apr. 1836 at the rate of $3 per month. 1836. 1837. 1838. 1839. 1840. 1841. 1842. 1842b. 1843. 1844. 1845. 1846. 1847. 1848. 1850. 1851.
Roberts, John. Penn. Gunner's Yeoman. He was pensioned 2 May 1815 at the rate of $108 per annum. 1818. 1819. 1820. 1821. 1822. 1823. 1824. 1825. 1826. 1827. 1828. 1829. 1830. He served aboard the *Guerriere*.
Roberts, Joseph. —. —. He was pensioned. 1842.
Roberts, Nelson V.* —. 1st Sergeant Marines. His widow, Elizabeth Roberts, was pensioned from 14 Feb. 1838. 1839. 1840. 1841. 1842. 1842b. 1845. 1846. He also appeared as Nelson Roberds.
Robertson, —.* —. Purser. His children, Susan D. Robertson and Elizabeth R. Robertson, were pensioned at the rate of $20 per month from 1 Jan. 1837. 1837. 1839. 1840. 1842. In 1842 his children were William J. H. Robertson, Samuel Robertson, Susan D. Robertson, and Elizabeth B. W. Robertson. In 1840 the latter was listed as Eliza W. B. Robertson. [He was listed as Samuel Robertson in the Old Wars pension index.]
Robertson, Henry P.* —. Lieutenant. His widow, Mary E. Robertson, was pensioned 4 Nov. 1850 at the rate of $25. 1851.
Robey, —. —. Musician Marine Corps. His widow, Eleanor Ann Robey, was pensioned at the rate of $4 per month. 1837. 1842.
Robins, William. Md. Seaman. He was pensioned at the rate of $72 per annum in 1807. 1808. 1809. 1810 [He appeared as William Roberts in this year]. 1811.
Robinson, —. N.C. Lieutenant. Martha Robinson was pensioned on his service as a privateer at the rate of $144 per annum. 1818. 1819. 1820. 1821. 1822. 1823. 1824. 1825. 1826. 1827. 1828.

1829. 1830. 1831. 1832 for $32.40.

Robinson, —. —. Ordinary Seaman. His widow, Sarah Robinson, was pensioned from 10 June 1838 at the rate of $5 per month. 1839. 1840. 1842.

Robinson, —.* —. Ordinary Seaman. His orphans, Sarah Robinson and Susan Robinson, were pensioned from 10 Mar. 1841 at the rate of $5 per month. 1842. 1842b. [He was listed as William Robinson in the Old Wars pension index.]

Robinson, Charles H.* —. Seaman. He was pensioned 18 May 1848 at the rate of $6 per month. 1848. 1850. 1851.

Robinson, John. N.Y. Seaman. He was pensioned 16 Apr. 1813 at the rate of $72 per annum. 1816. 1818. 1819. 1820. 1821. 1822. 1823. 1824. 1825. 1826. 1829. 1830. He also appeared as John Robenson. He served aboard the *United States*.

Robinson, John. —. Master's Mate. He was pensioned 1 Jan. 1813 at the rate of $1.25 per month. 1839. 1840. 1841. 1842b. 1843. 1844. 1845. 1846. 1847. 1848. 1850. 1851.

Robinson, John.* —. Captain of Forecastle. He was pensioned 2 Apr. 1845 at the rate of $9 per month. 1845. 1846. 1847. 1848. 1850. 1851.

Robinson, John.* —. Seaman. He was pensioned 30 June 1849 at the rate of $6 per month. 1850. 1851.

Robinson, John.* —. Seaman. He was pensioned 3 July 1848 at the rate of $4.50 per month. 1850. 1851.

Robinson, John.* —. Boatswain's Mate. His widow, Elizabeth Robinson, was pensioned 27 Aug. 1849 at the rate of $9.50 per month. 1850. 1851.

Robinson, William. N.J. Marine. He was pensioned 5 June 1807 at the rate of $6 per month. 1808. 1809. 1810. 1811. 1816. 1818. 1819. 1820. 1821. 1822. 1823. 1824. 1825. 1826. 1827. 1828. 1829. 1830. 1835. 1836. 1837. 1839. 1840. 1841. 1842b. 1843. 1844. 1845. 1846. 1847. 1848. 1850. 1851. He was disabled in the barracks.

Roderigue, Peter. Md. Boatswain's Mate. He was pensioned as a privateer from 23 Sep. 1812 at the rate of $96 per annum. 1812. 1813. 1814. 1815. 1816. 1817. 1818. 1819. 1820. 1821. 1822. 1823. 1824. 1825. 1826. 1827. 1828. 1829. 1830. 1831. 1832. 1833. 1834. 1835. 1836 for $23. 20. 1837. 1838.

Rodgers, —. —. —. Ellen Rodgers was pensioned on his service. 1842.

Rodgers, George W.* —. Captain. His widow, Anna M. Rodgers, was pensioned from 21 May 1832 at the rate of $50 per month. 1835. 1836. 1837. 1839. 1840. 1841. 1842. 1842b. 1845. 1846. She was pensioned again 1 Sep. 1847 at the rate of $50 per month. 1848. 1850. 1851.

Rodgers, William. N.Y. Quarter Gunner. He was pensioned 25 Apr. 1815 at the rate of $96 per annum. 1816. 1818. 1819. 1820. 1821. 1822. 1823. 1824. 1825. 1826. 1827. 1828. 1829. 1830. He also appeared as William Rogers. He served aboard the *President*.

Rogers, —.* —. Assistant Surgeon. His sons, Augustine Rogers and Theophilus Rogers, were pensioned on his service at the rate of $20 per month from 1 July 1838. 1839. 1840. 1842. [He was Wilmot Rogers in the Old Wars pension index.]

Rogers, Andrew. —. Marine. His application was rejected prior to 30 Dec. 1845. There was no record evidence of his disability which had been presented within the twenty-five

Naval Pensioners of the United States, 1800-1851

year limit after the injury was received.

Rogers, George H. Md. Sergeant of Marines. Md. He was pensioned at the rate of $54 per annum in 1811. 1813. 1816.

Rogers, James. N.Y. Sailing Master. He was pensioned 27 July 1815 at the rate of $20 per month. 1818. 1819. 1820. 1821. 1822. 1823. 1824. 1825. 1826. 1827. 1828. 1829. 1830. 1835. 1836. 1837. 1839. 1840. 1841. 1842b. 1843. 1844. 1845. 1846. 1847. 1848. 1850. 1851. He served aboard the *President*. He also appeared as James Rodgers. He was permanently disabled.

Rogers, John.* —. Carpenter's Yeoman. He was pensioned 18 May 1832 at the rate of $4.50 per month. 1835. 1836. 1837. 1839. 1840. 1841. 1842. 1843. 1844. 1845. 1846. 1847. 1848. 1850. 1850. 1851. His rank was also given as captain's yeoman. He also appeared as John Rodgers.

Rogers, John. —. Captain. He was pensioned at the rate of $25 per month. 1837. 1838. He also appeared as John Rodgers.

Rogers, John.* —. Captain. His widow, Minerva Rogers, was pensioned from 1 Aug. 1838 at the rate of $50 per month. 1839. 1840. 1841. 1842. 1842b. 1843. 1845. 1846. 1848. She was pensioned again 1 Aug. 1848 at the rate of $50 per month. 1851.

Rogers, Richard. Md. Sergeant of Marines. He perished aboard the *Epervier* 1 Sep. 1815. His father, William Rogers of St. Mary's Co., Md., was paid $54 in Apr. 1821.

Rogers, Telemachus. —. —. He was pensioned. 1842.

Rogson, William. —. Ordinary Seaman. He was pensioned 6 Sep. 1847 at the rate of $1.25 per month. 1847.

Rolfe, Nathaniel. Mass. Seaman. He was pensioned at the rate of 14 Dec. 1813 at the rate of $72 per annum. 1816. 1818. 1819. 1820. 1821. 1822. 1824. 1825. 1826. 1827. 1828. 1829. 1830. 1835. 1836. 1837. 1839. 1840. 1841. 1842b. 1843. 1844. 1845. 1846. 1847. 1848. 1850. 1851. He also appeared as Nathan Rolfe, Nathaniel Rolph, and Nathaniel Rolf. He served on the frigate *United States*.

Romaine, Michael.* —. Seaman. He was pensioned 20 Jan. 1845 at the rate of $3 per month. 1845. 1846. 1847. 1848. 1850. 1851.

Romeo, John.* Penn. Ordinary Seaman. He was pensioned 1 Apr. 1828 at the rate of $5 per month. 1829. 1830. 1835. 1836. 1837. 1839. 1840. 1841. 1842. 1842b. 1843. 1844. 1845. 1846. 1847. 1848. 1850. 1851. He was disabled in the Navy yard at Erie Station.

Rose, —.* —. Master Commandant. His widow, Mary W. Rose, was pensioned from 27 Aug. 1830 at the rate of $30 per month. 1835. 1836. 1837. 1839. 1840. 1841. 1842. 1842b. [He was listed as Robert M. Rose in the Old Wars pension index.]

Rose, Francis. Mass. Seaman. He was pensioned at the rate of $102 per annum in 1802. N.Y. in 1803. 1804. 1805. 1807. 1808. 1809. 1810.

Rose, John. Penn. Seaman. He served aboard the *Lawrence* and was killed 10 Sep. 1813 on Lake Erie. His widow, Martha Rose, was pensioned from 2 Aug. 1814 at the rate of $6 per month. 1824. 1825. 1827. 1828. 1829. 1836. 1837. 1839. 1840. 1841. 1842. 1842b. She was pensioned again 1 Sep. 1847 at the rate of $6 per month. 1848. 1850. 1851.

Rose, Samuel.* —. Seaman. He was pensioned from 24 May 1836 at the rate of $4.50 per month.

Naval Pensioners of the United States, 1800-1851

1839. 1840. 1841. 1842b. 1843. 1844. 1845. 1846. 1847. 1848. 1850. 1851.

Rosier, John. Penn. Marine. He was pensioned at the rate of $36 per annum in 1807. 1808. 1809. 1810. 1811.

Ross, Andrew.* —. Lieutenant of Marines. His widow, Ann J. Ross, was pensioned at the rate of $15 per month from 11 Dec. 1836. 1837. 1839. 1840. 1841. 1842. 1842b. 1845. 1846. She was pensioned again 1 Sep. 1847 at the rate of $15 per month. 1848. 1850. 1851.

Ross, Edward.* N.Y. Boy. He was pensioned 1 Jan. 1827 at the rate of $3 per month. 1829. 1830. 1835. 1836. 1837. 1839. 1840. 1841. 1842b. 1843. 1844. 1845. 1846. 1847. 1848. 1850. 1851. He served aboard the *Constitution* under D. T. Patterson.

Ross, John W.* —. Seaman. He was pensioned 3 June 1846 at the rate of $6 per month. 1846. 1847. 1848. 1850. 1851.

Ross, William.* —. Marine. His widow, Sarah Ross, was pensioned 1 Sep. 1842 at the rate of $3.50 per month. 1841. 1842. 1842b. 1851.

Rossou, William.* —. Ordinary Seaman. He was pensioned 6 Sep. 1847 at the rate of $1.25 per month. 1848. 1850. 1851. He also appeared as William Rosson.

Roth, —. N.Y. Seaman. Grace Roth was pensioned on his service as a privateer at the rate of $72 per annum from 10 May 1813. 1818. 1819. 1820. 1821. 1822. 1823. 1824. 1825. 1826. 1827. 1828. 1829. 1830. 1831. 1832. 1833 for $25.80. She also appeared as Grace Roath.

Rouin, John.* —. Seaman. He was pensioned at the rate of $6 per month. 1847. 1848. 1850. 1851. He also appeared as John Rowan.

Rounds, —. Mass. Seaman. Anna Rounds was pensioned on his service as a privateer at the rate of $36 per annum. 1815. 1816. 1817. 1818. 1819. 1820. 1821. 1822. 1823. 1824. 1825. 1826. 1827. 1828. 1829.

Roundy, Cornelius M. —. —. He was pensioned. 1842.

Rowe, —. —. —. Polly Rowe was pensioned on his service. 1842.

Rowe, James. Mass. Prize Master. He was pensioned as a privateer from 19 Oct. 1812 at the rate of $6 per annum. 1812. 1813. 1814. 1815. 1816. 1817. 1818. 1819. 1820. 1821. 1822. 1823. 1824. 1825. 1826. 1827. 1828. 1829. 1830. 1831. 1832. 1833. 1834. 1835. 1836. 1837 for half a year. He was pensioned from 1 July 1837 at the rate of $3.33 1/3 per month. 1837. 1838. 1844. 1845. 1846. 1847. 1850. He also appeared as James Row.

Rowland, Edmond. N.Y. Ordinary Seaman. He was pensioned 29 Mar. 1815 at the rate of $48 per annum. 1818. 1819. 1820. 1821. 1822. 1823. 1824. 1825. 1826. 1827. 1828. 1829. 1830. 1835. 1836. 1837. 1838. 1839. 1840. 1842. 1842b. 1843. 1844. 1845. 1846. 1847. 1848. 1850. 1851. He was disabled on Lake Champlain. He also appeared as Edward Rowland.

Rowland, George. D.C. Marine. He was pensioned at the rate of $48 per annum. 1819. 1820. 1821. 1822.

Rowley, Alonzo.* —. Ordinary Seaman. He was pensioned 15 Mar. 1836 at the rate of $5 per month. 1836. 1837. 1839. 1840. 1841. 1842b. 1843. 1844. 1845. 1846. 1847. 1848. 1850. 1851. He also appeared as Alonzo Rouley.

Ruff, Samuel W.* —. —. Dr. Ruff died in October 1841. His widow, Sarah Ruff, had her application was rejected before 1 Jan. 1842 since the law did not cover her case.

Naval Pensioners of the United States, 1800-1851

Rugg, Charles.* —. Marine. He was pensioned 3 July 1845 at the rate of $3.50 per month. 1845. 1846. 1847. 1848. 1850. 1851.

Rumney, —.* —. Sailing Master. His widow, Eliza Rumney, was pensioned from 31 Mar. 1823 at the rate of $20 per month. 1839. 1840. 1841. 1842. 1842b. [He was listed as Edward Rumney in the Old Wars pension index.]

Rundlett, Edward. —. Marine. He was pensioned 29 July 1845 at the rate of $2.62 ½ per month. 1845. 1846. 1847. 1848. 1850. 1851.

Ruppert, David. —. Marine. His widow, Joanna Ruppert, was pensioned 27 Apr. 1851 at the rate of $3.50 per month. 1851.

Russell, —.* —. Lieutenant. His widow, Elizabeth J. Russell, was pensioned from 21 July 1838 at the rate of $25 per month. 1839. 1840. 1841. 1842. 1842b. [He was listed as Edmund Russell in the Old Wars pension index.]

Russell, —. —. Ordinary Seaman. His daughter, Abigail Russell, was pensioned at the rate of $5 per month. 1837. 1842.

Russell, George. S.C. Prize Master. He was pensioned at the rate of $120 per annum from 16 Feb. 1813. 1818. He died that year.

Russell, Thomas. —. Master's Mate. His widow, Sally Russell, was pensioned at the rate of $10 per month from 17 Oct. 1813. 1837. 1839. 1840. 1841. 1842. 1842b. 1848. 1850.

Russell, William.* —. Sergeant Marines. His widow, Mary Russell, was pensioned from 7 July 1829 at the rate of $4.50 per month. 1836. 1837. 1839. 1840. 1841. 1842. 1842b. 1845. 1846. She was pensioned 1 Sep.1847 at the rate of $6.50 per month. 1848. 1850. 1851.

Ryall, —. —. —. Mary Ryall was pensioned on his service. 1842.

Ryan, John.* N.Y. Captain of Foretop. He perished aborad the *Grampus*. His widow was Mary Ryan of Brooklyn, Kings Co., N.Y. He married Mary Gillespie on 19 Nov. 1841 in St. James Roman Catholic Church in Brooklyn. There were no children. His widow, Mary Ryan, was pensioned 3 Mar. 1848 at the rate of $7.50 per month. 1847. 1848. 1850. 1851.

Sage, —. N.Y. Seaman. Lois Sage was pensioned on his service as a privateer at the rate of $36 per annum. 1815. 1816. 1817. 1818. 1819. 1820 increase to $72. 1821. 1822. 1823. 1824. 1825. 1826. 1827. 1828. 1829.

Sage, Otis.* —. Corporal of Marines. He was pensioned 16 Nov. 1835 at the rate of $4.50 per month. 1835. 1836. 1837. 1839. 1840. 1841. 1842b. 1843. 1844. 1845. 1846. 1847. 1848. 1850. 1851.

Salter, Horatio. Md. Boy. He was pensioned from 1 July 1820 at the rate of $48 per annum. 1826. 1829. 1830. He served aboard the brig *Argus*.

Sanderson, —. —. Lieutenant. His daughter, Hannah T. Sanderson, was pensioned at the rate of $25 per month from 23 Aug. 1831. 1837. 1839. 1840. 1841. 1842. 1842b. She also appeared as Hannah T. Saunderson.

Naval Pensioners of the United States, 1800-1851

Sandwich, William. Penn. Marine. He was pensioned at the rate of $36 per annum in 1807. 1808. 1809. 1810. 1811. 1816. 1818. 1819. 1820. 1821. 1822. 1823. He also appeared as William Sandwith.

Sandys, Charles. Mass. Sailmaker's Mate. He was pensioned at the rate of $8.50 per month in 1803. 1804. 1805. 1807. 1808. 1809. 1810. 1811.

Sardo, Joseph.* —. Musician. His widow, Ann Eliza Sardo, was pensioned from 20 Dec. 1835 at the rate of $4 per month. 1835. 1836. 1837. 1839. 1840. 1841. 1842. 1842b. 1845. 1846. She was pensioned again 1 Sep. 1847 at the rate of $4 per month. 1848. 1850. 1851.

Sarria, Joseph R. Mass. Officer's Steward. He perished aboard the *Grampus*. His widow, Esperanza Pons Sarria of Boston, was pensioned 20 Mar. 1843 at the rate of $9 per month. 1851. He was Jose Sarria of a province of Minorca.

Saunders, Daniel. Mass. Quarter Gunner. He was pensioned at the rate of $108 per annum. 1819. 1820 in D.C. 1821.

Saunders, Daniel. Ga. Seaman. He was pensioned at the rate of $72 per annum in 1808. 1809. 1810. 1811. 1816. 1818. 1819. 1820. 1821. 1822. 1823.

Saunders, James. Va. Lieutenant. He died 7 Dec. 1816 of a natural death. His widow, Harriet H. Saunders, was pensioned 27 Mar. 1817 at the rate of $20 per month. 1818. 1819. 1821. 1822. 1823. 1824. 1825. 1827 in Va. 1828. 1829. 1830. 1835. 1836. 1837. 1839. 1840. 1841. 1842. 1842b. 1845. 1846. He also appeared as James Sanders. She was pensioned again 1 Sep. 1847 at the rate of $25 per month. 1848. 1850. 1851. She also appeared as Harriet H. Sanders.

Saunders, Robert.* Mass. Seaman. He was pensioned at the rate of $72 per annum. 1818. 1819. 1820. 1821. 1822. 1823. 1824. 1825. 1826. 1827. 1828. 1829. He was also listed as Robert Willet and Robert Sanders. He was disabled in the Dartmoor Massacre.

Sawtell, Jason L.* —. Coal Heaver. He was pensioned 22 Sep. 1846 at the rate of $4.50 per month. 1847. 1848. 1850. 1851.

Sawyer, Horace B. —. Midshipman. He was pensioned from 3 June 1813 at the rate of $4.75 per month. 1838. 1839. 1840. 1841. 1842b. 1843.

Sawyer, James.* —. Prize Master. He was pensioned as a privateer at the rate of $120 per annum. 1834. 1835. 1836. He was pensioned from 1 Jan. 1837 at the rate of $10 per month. 1837. 1838. 1844. 1845. 1846. 1847. 1850.

Sawyer, John H. N.Y. Seaman. He perished aboard the *Epervier* 1 Sep. 1815. His mother, Essey Combs, of New York was paid $72 on 4 Mar. 1818.

Sawyer, Samuel. Mass. Seaman. He was pensioned 16 Feb. 1815 at the rate of $72 per annum. 1816. 1818. 1819. 1820. 1821. 1822. 1823. 1824. 1825. 1826. 1827. 1828. 1829. 1830. He served aboard the schooner *Ticonderoga*.

Scanton, Patrick. Mass. Ordinary Seaman. He was pensioned 1 Jan. 1810 at the rate of $72 per annum. 1816. 1818. 1819. 1820. 1821. 1822. 1823. 1824. 1825. 1826. 1827. 1828. 1829. 1830. 1835. 1836. 1837. 1839. 1840. 1841. 1842b. 1843. 1844. 1845. 1846. 1847. 1848. 1850. 1851. He also appeared as Patrick Scranton. He served aboard the *Constitution*.

Scates, John.* —. Marine. His widow, Emily L. Scates, was pensioned 10 Aug. 1846 at the rate of $3.50 per month. 1848. 1850. 1851.

Naval Pensioners of the United States, 1800-1851

Scatterly, Robert. —. Seaman. He was pensioned 1 Nov. 1832 at the rate of $4 per month. 1835. 1836. 1837. 1838. 1839. 1840. 1842.

Schannal, Peter. —. Boy. He perished abroad the *Grampus*. His mother was Joanna Schannal of Boston, Mass. on 8 May 1844. His father was Cornelius Schannal who inquired if he would have a claim. Michael Flaherty of Boston testified that he was a neighbor of the family in Seamount near Cove, County Cork, Ireland on 29 June 1824 when Peter Schannal was born. He had been in United States nine years.

Schlosser, —.* —. Seaman. His widow, Sally Schlosser, was pensioned at the rate of $6 per month from 5 Feb. 1831. 1837. 1839. 1840. 1841. 1842. 1842b. She also appeared as Sally Sclosser. [He was Lewis Schlosser in the Old Wars pension index.]

Schnell, —. —. —. Margaret V. Schnell was pensioned on his service. 1842.

Schriver, Jacob. —. Seaman. He was pensioned 15 Mar. 1836 at the rate of $6 per month. 1836. 1837. 1839. 1840.

Schrouder, John. N.Y. Seaman. He was pensioned 20 June 1814 at the rate of $72 per annum. 1816. 1818. 1819. 1820. 1821. 1822. 1823. 1824. 1825. 1826. 1827. 1828. 1829. 1830. 1835. 1836. 1837. 1839. 1840. 1841. 1842. 1842b. 1843. 1844. 1845. 1846. 1847. 1848. 1850. 1851. He was disabled aboard the *Lawrence* on Lake Erie. He also appeared as John Shrouder and John Schroader.

Scott, —.* —. Lieutenant. His widow, Clarissa B. Scott, was pensioned from 16 Feb. 1830 at the rate of $25 per month. 1835. 1836. 1837. 1839. 1842. [He was listed as Henry D. Scott in the Old Wars pension index.]

Scott, Belleger.* —. 2nd Class Boy. He was pensioned 1 Sep. 1847 at the rate of $2.25 per month. 1848. 1850. 1851. He also appeared as Billinger Scott.

Scott, Thomas.* Md. Ordinary Seaman. He was pensioned 1 Sep. 1827 at the rate of $60 per annum. 1829. 1830. He served aboard the United States *Alert*.

Scriver, John. N.Y. Seaman. He was pensioned 10 Apr. 1811 at the rate of $60 per annum. 1816. 1818. 1819. 1820. 1821. 1822. 1823. 1824. 1825. 1826. 1827. 1828. 1829. 1830. 1835. 1836. 1837. 1839. 1840. 1841. 1842b. 1843. 1844. 1845. 1846. 1847. 1848. He also appeared as John Schriver. He served aboard the *Hornet*.

Searcy, —.* D.C. Lieutenant. He died of yellow fever 1 Nov. 1822. His widow, Isabella R. Searcy, was pensioned 29 Apr. 1824 at the rate of $240 per annum. 1824. 1825. 1827. 1828. [He was listed as Robert Searcy in the Old Wars pension index.]

Seawell, James.* —. Seaman. He was pensioned 31 Aug. 1843 at the rate of $4.50 per month. 1843. 1844. 1845. 1846. 1847. 1848. 1850. 1851.

Sellers, Hamilton. Penn. Ordinary Seaman. He was pensioned at the rate of $8.50 per month in 1803. 1804. 1805. 1807. 1808. 1809. 1810. 1811. 1816. 1818. 1819. 1820. 1821. 1822. 1823. 1824. 1825. 1826. 1827. 1828.

Selmore, George.* —. Seaman. He was pensioned 2 July 1849 at the rate of $4.50 per month. 1850. 1851.

Sevier, Alexander G.* —. Captain Marines. His widow, Elizabeth A. Sevier, was pensioned from 9 May 1827 at the rate of $20 per month. 1835. 1836. 1837. 1839. 1840. 1841. 1842b. 1845. 1846. She was pensioned again 1 Sep. 1847 at the rate of $20 per month.

Naval Pensioners of the United States, 1800-1851

1848. 1850. 1851.

Seward, —. Mass. Cook. His widow, Jane Seward, was pensioned at the rate of $73 per annum. 1820.

Seymour, —. —. —. Eliza Seymour and Susan Seymour were pensioned on his service. 1842.

Seymour, William. —. Seaman. He was pensioned 17 Feb. 1836 at the rate of $5 per month. 1836. 1837. 1839. 1840. 1841. 1842.

Shackerly, Peter. —. Carpenter. He served aboard the frigate *Chesapeake* when it was attacked by the British ship of war *Leopard*. He was killed. His orphans, Harriet Shackerly, Sarah Shackerly, and Mary Shackerly, applied for a pension. Since their father's death was prior to June 1812, they were not eligible. 23 Mar. 1820.

Shaler, —. N.Y. Commander. Ann Shaler was pensioned on his service as a privateer at the rate of $120 per annum. 1815. 1816. 1817. 1818. 1819. 1820 for $240. 1821. 1822. 1823. 1824. 1825. 1826. 1827. 1828. 1829 for $40.

Shanklin, James.* —. Ordinary Seaman. He was pensioned 1 June 1813 at the rate of $2.50 per month. 1838. 1839. 1840. 1841. 1842b. 1843. 1844. 1845. 1846. 1847. 1848. 1850. 1851.

Shannamon, John. Md. Seaman. He was pensioned 28 July 1806 at the rate of $72 per annum. 1808. 1809. 1810. 1811. 1816 in D.C. 1818. 1819. 1820. 1821. 1822. 1823. 1824. 1825. 1826. 1827. 1828. 1829. 1830. He served aboard the *Constitution*.

Shapely, John. Mass. Cook. He was pensioned 11 June 1801 at the rate of $108 per annum. 1802. 1803. 1804. 1805. 1807. 1808. 1809. 1810. 1811. 1816. 1818. 1819. 1820. 1821. 1822. 1823. 1824. 1825. 1826. 1827. 1828. 1829. 1830. He served aboard the schooner *Boston*. He also appeared as John Shapeley.

Sharp, Reuben. —. Quarter Gunner. He was pensioned 13 Jan. 1845 at the rate of $5.62 ½ per month. 1845. 1846. 1847. 1848. 1850. 1851. He was also known as Robert Gray.

Shaw, —.* —. Purser. His widow, Margaret E. Shaw, was pensioned from 17 Oct. 1820 at the rate of $20 per month. 1836. 1837. 1839. 1840. 1841. 1842. [He was listed as John R. Shaw in the Old Wars pension index.]

Shaw, John.* Mass. Seaman. He was pensioned 1 May 1817 at the rate of $72 per annum. 1818. 1821. 1822. 1823. 1824. 1825. 1826. 1827. 1828. 1829. 1830. He served aboard the *United States*.

Shaw, John.* —. Captain. His widow, Mary B. Shaw, was pensioned from 17 Sep. 1823 at the rate of $50 per month. 1836. 1837. 1839. 1840. 1841. 1842. 1842b. 1845. 1846. She was pensioned again 1 Sep. 1847 at the rate of $50 per month. 1848. 1850. 1851.

Sheater, Charles.* S.C. Boatswain's Mate. He was pensioned at the rate of $72 per annum 1 Nov. 1822. 1823. 1824. 1825. 1826. 1827. 1828. 1829. 1830. He served aboard the schooner *Revenge*. He was pensioned 1 Nov. 1832 at the rate of $9.50 per month. 1835. 1836. 1837. 1839. 1840. 1841. 1842b. 1843. 1844. 1845. 1846. 1847. 1848. 1850. 1851. He also appeared as Charles Sheeter, Charles Sheeten, Charles Shoter, and Charles Shuter.

Sheffield, Robert L.* —. Carpenter. His widow, Harriet E. Sheffield, was pensioned 17 Mar. 1849 at the rate of $10 per month. 1850. 1851.

Shehan, —. Mass. Gunner. Bethia Shehan was pensioned on his service as a privateer at the rate of $120 per annum. 1817. 1818. 1819. 1820. 1821. 1822. 1823. 1824. 1825. 1826. 1827 for

Naval Pensioners of the United States, 1800-1851

$103.33.

Sheldon, Nathaniel. S.C. Seaman. He was pensioned as a privateer at the rate of $72 per annum from 11 Jan. 1814. 1820.

Shepherd, —. —. —. Patience Shepherd was pensioned on his service as a privateer at the rate of $36 per annum. 1815. 1816. 1817. 1818. 1819. 1820 increased to $72. 1821. 1822. 1823. 1824. 1825. 1826. 1827. 1828. 1829. 1830. 1831. 1832. 1833. 1834.

Shepherd, Yankee. Mass. Boy. He was pensioned as a privateer at the rate of $72 per annum from 26 Feb. 1815. 1815. 1816. 1817. 1818. 1819. 1820. 1821. 1822. 1823. 1824. 1825 for $51.

Sherburne, John H.* —. Lieutenant. His widow, Frances P. Sherburne, was pensioned at the rate of $25 per month 2 Nov. 1849. 1850. 1851. She also appeared as Frances P. Shuburne.

Sherburne, Jonathan W.* —. Lieutenant. His widow, Louisa B. Sherburne, was pensioned from 30 June 1834 at the rate of $25 per month. 1835. 1836. 1837. 1839. 1840. 1841. 1842. 1842b. 1845. 1846. 1848. 1850. 1851. She also appeared as Louisa B. Shuburne.

Sherlock, Edward. N.Y. Steward. He was pensioned at the rate of $96 per annum. 1819. 1820. 1821. 1822. 1823. He also appeared as Edward Sherblock.

Shinney, John. D.C. Private Marine. He was pensioned 1 July 1824 at the rate of $36 per annum. 1824. 1825. 1826. 1827. 1828. 1829. 1830. He was disabled from exposure.

Shockley, Nehemiah.* —. Seaman. He was pensioned 18 Sep. 1843 at the rate of $6 per month. 1843. 1844. 1845. 1846. 1847. 1848. 1850. 1851.

Shroeder, Henry.* —. Sailmaker's Mate. His widow, Rosanna Shroeder, was pensioned 8 Sep. 1846 at the rate of $7.50 per month. 1847. 1848. 1850. 1851.

Shubrick, —. N.Y. Lieutenant. He was lost on 1 Sep. 1815 in the *Epervier*. His widow, Elizabeth Shurbrick, received $240 per annum. 1819. 1821. 1822. 1824. 1825. 1827. 1828.

Shubrick, —. —. Lieutenant. His son, Edmund T. Shubrick, was pensioned at the rate of $25 per month. 1837. 1842.

Shubrick, Edward R.* —. Captain. His widow, Esther M. Shubrick, was pensioned 12 Mar. 1849 at the rate of $50 per month. 1845. 1846. 1847. 1848. 1850. 1851.

Shubrick, Irvine.* —. Commander. His widow, Julia S. Shubrick, was pensioned 5 Apr. 1849 at the rate of $30 per month. 1850. 1851.

Shubrick, John Templar. N.Y. Lieutenant. He perished aboard the *Epervier* 1 Sep. 1815. He married Elizabeth Matilda Ludlow 6 June 1814 at Brooklyn, Long Island, N.Y. Elizabeth Matilda Shubrick was paid $240 on 30 Oct. 1817.

Simmons, —. Mass. Seaman. Nancy Simmons was pensioned on his service as a privateer at the rate of $60 per annum. 1813. 1814. 1815. 1816. 1817. 1818 increase to $120. 1819. 1820. 1821. 1822. 1823. 1824. 1825. 1826. 1827. 1828 for $80. She also appeared as Nancy Simonds.

Simmons, —. —. Marine. His widow, Elizabeth Simmons, was pensioned from 30 Jan. 1811 at the rate of $3.50 per month. 1839. 1840. 1841. 1842. 1842b.

Simonds, Benjamin. Mass. Seaman. He was pensioned as a privateer from 1 Nov. 1812 at the rate of $60 per annum. 1812. 1813. 1814. 1815. 1816. 1817. 1818. 1819. 1820. 1821. 1822. 1823. 1824 in the amount of $43.

Naval Pensioners of the United States, 1800-1851

Simonds, Daniel*. Mass. Seaman. He served aboard the *Chesapeake* and was killed 1 June 1813. His widow, Nancy Simonds, was pensioned at the rate of $72 per annum for her child. 1816. 1818. 1820. 1821. 1822. 1824. 1825. 1827. 1829. Jesse Cutler was guardian. She also appeared as Nancy Simmons and Nancy Simmonds.

Simpson, —. —. —. Sally K. Simpson was pensioned on his service. 1842.

Simpson, Stephen.* —. Marine. He was pensioned 16 Nov. 1835 at the rate of $3.50 per month. 1835. 1836. 1837. 1839. 1840. 1841. 1842b. 1843. 1844. 1845. 1846. 1847. 1848. 1850. 1851.

Sinclair, —. —. Captain. His son, Arthur Sinclair, was pensioned at the rate of $50 per month. 1837. 1842.

Sinclair, —.* —. Captain. His children, George T. Sinclair, William H. Sinclair, and Gilberta F. Sinclair, were pensioned from 1 Jan. 1837 at the rate of $50 per month. 1837. 1839. 1840. 1841. 1842. 1842b. [He was listed as Arthur Sinclair in the Old Wars pension index.]

Sinclair, —. Mass. Commander. Mary Sinclair was pensioned as a privateer at the rate of $120 per annum. 1815. 1816. 1817. 1818. 1819. 1820 increased to $240. 1821. 1822. 1823. 1824. 1825. 1826. 1827. 1828. 1829. 1830. 1831. 1832. 1833. 1834.

Sisson, Alexander. N.Y. Sailing Master. He served aboard the *Madison* and was slain at Niagara on Lake Ontario 7 Dec. 1812. His widow, Sarah Sisson, was pensioned at the rate of $240 per annum. 1816. 1821. 1822. 1824. 1825. His daughter, Matilda Sisson, was pensioned in 1827. 1828. 1829. 1837. 1842. J. Ditchell was guardian.

Sitcher, —.* Drummer. His widow, Eliza Sitcher, was pensioned from 28 Feb. 1841 at the rate of $4 per annum. 1841. 1842. She also appeared as Eliza Stitcher. [He was William Sitcher in the Old Wars pension index.]

Siteber, William.* —. Musician Marines. He was pensioned 26 Nov. 1835 at the rate of $3.50 per month. 1835. 1836. 1837. 1838. 1839. 1840. 1841. 1842. 1842b. He also appeared as William Sitcher.

Sivers, —.* —. Sergeant Marines. His children, John Sivers and Nancy Sivers, were pensioned from 1 Jan. 1842 at the rate of $6.50 per month. 1842. 1842b. [He was listed as John Sivers on the Old Wars pension list.]

Sivery, John.* —. Seaman. His widow, Mary Sivery, had her application rejected between Mar. 1840 and 1 Jan. 1842. Her husband died after he was discharged from the U.S. service. Her case was not covered by the law.

Slade, George.* —. Yeoman. He was pensioned 17 Apr. 1851 at the rate of $7.50 per month. 1851.

Slater, Horatio. Penn. Boy. He was pensioned at the rate of $48 per annum. 1816. 1818. 1819. 1820. 1821 in Md. 1822. 1823. 1824. 1825. 1827. 1828. He also appeared as Horatio Salter.

Sloane, John. N.Y. Seaman. He was pensioned at the rate of $60 per annum. 1819. 1820. 1821. 1822. 1823. He also appeared as John Sloan.

Small, William. Penn. Marine. He was pensioned at the rate of $18.50 per annum in 1802. Va. in 1803. 1804. 1805. 1807. 1808. 1809. 1810. 1811.

Small, William.* —. Seaman. His widow, Ann Small, was pensioned 16 Oct. 1846 at the rate of

Naval Pensioners of the United States, 1800-1851

$6 per month. 1851.

Smart, John. N.Y. Seaman. He was wounded and died on Lake Champlain on 15 Oct. 1814. His widow, Eleanor Smart, was pensioned 19 June 1819 at the rate of $6 per month. 1821. 1822. 1823. 1824. 1825. 1827. 1828. 1829. 1830. 1835. 1836. 1837. 1839. 1840. 1841. 1842. 1842b. 1845. 1846. She was pensioned again 1 Sep. 1847 at the rate of $6 per month. 1848. 1850. 1851.

Smart, William.* N.Y. Ordinary Seaman. He was pensioned at the rate of $5 per month on 1 June 1827. 1829. 1830. 1835. 1836. 1837. 1838. 1839. 1840. 1842. 1842b. 1843. 1844. 1845. 1846. 1847. 1848. 1850. 1851. He served aboard the *United States*.

Smidt, —.* —. Marine. Catharine Smidt was pensioned on his service from 18 Mar. 1837 at the rate of $3.50 per month. 1839. 1840. 1841. 1842b. She also appeared as Catherine Smith. [He was listed as John Smidt in the Old Wars pension index.]

Smiley, —. —. Seaman. His widow, Alice Smiley, was pensioned at the rate of $6 per month from 27 Feb. 1813. 1837. 1839. 1840. 1841. 1842. 1842b.

Smith, —.* —. Lieutenant. His son, Alonzo P. Smith, was pensioned from 1 Jan. 1840 at the rate of $25 per month. 1840. 1841. 1842. 1842b. [He was listed as Frederick Smith in the Old Wars pension index.]

Smith, —. —. Master Commandant. His children, Catherine M. Smith was pensioned at the rate of $30 per month. No date was given. 1841. 1842. 1842b.

Smith, —. N.H. Seaman. Lydia Smith was pensioned on his service as a privateer at the rate of $36 per annum. 1815. 1816. 1817. 1818. 1819 for $71.40.

Smith, —. —. Lieutenant. His daughter, Lavinia Smith, was pensioned on his service at the rate of $25 per month. 1837. 1842.

Smith, —.* —. Midshipman. His widow, Jane Smith, was pensioned at the rate of $9.50 per month from 21 Mar. 1831. 1837. 1839. 1840. 1841. 1842. 1842b. [He was listed as Ferdinand Smith in the Old Wars pension index.]

Smith, —.* —. Lieutenant. His widow, Louisa Ann Smith, was pensioned at the rate of $25 per month from 30 Nov. 1836. 1837. 1839. 1840. 1841. 1842. 1842b. [He was Jno. H. Smith in the Old Wars pension index.]

Smith, —. —. —. Margaret Smith was pensioned on his service as a privateer at the rate of $72 per annum. 1817. 1818. 1819. 1820. 1821. 1821. 1822. 1823. 1824. 1825. 1826 for $36.

Smith, —. N.Y. Seaman. Maria Smith was pensioned on his service as a privateer at the rate of $72 per annum. 1819. 1820. 1821. 1822. 1823. 1824. 1825. 1826. 1827. 1828.

Smith, —. N.H. Carpenter's Mate. Margaret Smith was pensioned on his service as a privateer at the rate of $48 per annum. 1815. 1816. 1817. 1818. 1819. 1820 increase to $96. 1821. 1822. 1823. 1824. 1825. 1826. 1827. 1828. 1829.

Smith, —. Mass. Seaman. Mary Smith was pensioned on his service as a privateer at the rate of $36 per annum. 1813. 1814. 1815. 1816. 1817 increase to $72. 1818. 1819. 1820. 1821. 1822. 1823. 1824. 1825. 1826. 1827. 1828 for $.40.

Smith, —. —. Boatswain. Patty Smith applied in Dec. 1825 and was pensioned at the rate of $72 per annum from 17 June 1815. 1839. 1840. 1841. 1842. 1842b. She also appeared as Patty Wilson.

Naval Pensioners of the United States, 1800-1851

Smith, —. —. Master Commandant. Phoebe Ann Smith applied in May 1827 and was pensioned at the rate of $120 per annum. She later received $30 per month. 1836. 1837. 1842.

Smith, —.* —. Steward. His widow, Sarah Smith, was pensioned from 19 Dec. 1820 at the rate of $9 per month. 1839. 1840. 1841. 1842. 1842b. [He was listed as Elisha Smith in the Old Wars pension index.]

Smith, —. New York. Boatswain's Mate. His widow, Sarah Smith, was pensioned at the rate of $114 per annum. 1818. 1819.

Smith, Aaron.* Mass. Ordinary Seaman. He was pensioned 1 Aug. 1828 at the rate of $2.50 per month. 1830. 1835. 1836. 1837. 1839. 1840. 1841. 1842b. 1843. 1844. 1845. 1846. 1847. 1848. 1850. 1851. He served aboard the frigate *Constitution*.

Smith, Adam. —. Seaman. His application was rejected prior to 17 Jan. 1845. He claimed to have been injured in the Tripolitan War. There was no record to prove his disability of more than twenty-five years' standing.

Smith, Alexander.* —. Seaman. He was pensioned 26 July 1836 at the rate of $3 per month. 1839. 1840. 1841. 1842b. 1843. 1844. 1845. 1846. 1847. 1848.

Smith, Alfred.* —. Ordinary Seaman. He was pensioned 27 Sep. 1837 at the rate of $2.50 per month. 1838. 1839. 1840. 1841. 1842b. 1843. 1844. 1845. 1846. 1847. 1848. 1850. 1851.

Smith, Benjamin. Md. Master's Mate. He was pensioned as a privateer from 20 Oct. 1812 at the rate of $8 per month. 1812. 1813. 1814. 1815. 1816. 1817. 1818. 1819. 1820. 1821. 1822. 1823. 1824. 1825. 1826. 1827. 1828. 1829. 1830. 1831. 1832. 1836. 1837. 1838.

Smith, Charles, 3rd.* —. Seaman. He was pensioned 19 Aug. 1841 at the rate of $3 per month. 1842b. 1843. 1844. 1845. 1846. 1847. 1848. 1850. 1851.

Smith, Charles.* —. Seaman. He was pensioned 3 Apr. 1849 at the rate of $3 per month. 1850. 1851.

Smith, Daniel. N.Y. Seaman. He was pensioned 6 July 1816 at the rate of $60 per annum. 1818. 1819. 1820. 1821. 1822. 1823. 1824. 1825. 1826. 1827. 1828. 1829. 1830. He was disabled aboard the schooner *Superior* on Lake Ontario.

Smith, Edward. —. Ordinary Seaman. He was pensioned 25 Feb. 1845 at the rate of $2.50 per month. 1845. 1846. 1847. 1848. 1850. 1851.

Smith, Frederick.* —. Captain of Forecastle. He was pensioned 14 June 1842 at the rate of $7 per month. 1842b. 1843. 1844. 1845. 1846. 1847. 1848. 1850. 1851.

Smith, J. —. —. He was pensioned as a privateer at the rate of $72 per annum. 1815. 1816. 1817. 1818. 1819 for $36.

Smith, James. —.* Ordinary Seaman. He was pensioned 2 Dec. 1837 at the rate of $2.50 per month. 1839. 1840. 1841. 1842b. 1843. 1844. 1845. 1846. 1847. 1848. 1850. 1851.

Smith, Jesse.* —. Lieutenant. His widow, Mehitable Smith, was pensioned from 10 Sep. 1829 at the rate of $25 per month. 1835. 1836. 1837. 1839. 1840. 1841. 1842. 1842b. 1845. 1846. She was pensioned again 1 Sep. 1847 at the rate of $1 Sep. 1847. 1848. 1850. 1851.

Smith, John.* —. Boatswain. He was pensioned 31 Dec. 1827 at the rate of $5 per month. 1837. 1838. 1841. 1842. 1842b. 1843. 1844. 1845. 1846. 1847. 1848. 1850. 1851.

Smith, John. Mass. Quartermaster. He was pensioned from 1 Oct. 1817 at the rate of $72 per annum.

Naval Pensioners of the United States, 1800-1851

    1819. 1820. 1821. 1822. 1823. 1824. 1825. 1826. 1827. 1828. 1829. 1830. He served aboard the frigate *Guerriere*.

Smith, John.* N.Y. Ordinary Seaman. He was pensioned 1 June 1826 at the rate of $60 per annum. 1827. 1828. 1829. 1830. He served aboard the *Brandywine*.

Smith, John. N.Y. Ordinary Seaman. He was pensioned at the rate of $48 per annum in 1805. 1807. 1808. 1809. 1810. 1811.

Smith, John. N.Y. Seaman. He was pensioned 1 July 1822 at the rate of $72 per annum . 1823. 1824. 1825. 1826. 1827. 1828. 1829. 1830. He served aboard Gunboat No. 163.

Smith, John.* N.Y. Ordinary Seaman. He served aboard the *Franklin*. He was lost in a boat 20 Mar. 1822. His widow, Mary Smith, was pensioned 30 Jun. 1825. 1827. 1828. 1830.

Smith, John. Penn. Marine. He was pensioned at the rate of $48 per annum in 1821. 1822.

Smith, John. —. Seaman. He was pensioned from 31 Aug. 1834 at the rate of $3 per month. 1839. 1840. 1841. 1842b. 1843. 1844. 1845. 1846. 1847. 1848. 1850. 1851.

Smith, John.* —. Seaman. His widow, Jane Elizabeth Smith, was pensioned 25 June 1850 at the rate of $6 per month. 1851.

Smith, John, 5th.* —. Seaman. He was pensioned from 5 May 1837 at the rate of $3 per month. 1840. 1841. 1842b. 1843. 1844.

Smith, John H.* —. Lieutenant. His daughters, Catharine F. Smith and Emeline B. Smith, were pensioned 27 Mar. 1845 at the rate of $25 per month. 1848. 1851.

Smith, John B.* —. Seaman. He was pensioned 13 May 1844 at the rate of $6 per month. 1844. 1845. 1846. 1847. 1848. 1850. 1851.

Smith, Joseph. Md. Seaman. He was pensioned as a privateer at the rate of $72 per annum from 10 Mar. 1815. 1820.

Smith, Joseph. Penn. Marine. He was pensioned 10 Apr. 1815 at the rate of $48 per annum. 1816. 1818. 1819. 1820. 1821. 1823. 1824. 1825. 1826. 1827. 1828. 1829. 1830. He was disabled at Bladensburg.

Smith, Joseph. —. Boatswain. He was pensioned 31 Dec. 1837 at the rate of $5 per month. 1837. 1839. 1840. 1841. 1842. 1842b. 1843. 1844. 1845. 1846. 1847. 1848. 1850. 1851.

Smith, Joseph. —. Lieutenant. He was pensioned at the rate of $18.75 per month. 1837. 1838. 1839. 1840. 1841. 1842b. 1843.

Smith, Julius.* —. Seaman. He was pensioned 16 May 1851 at the rate of $6 per month. 1851.

Smith, Loman.* —. Carpenter. His widow, Delilah Smith, was pensioned 31 May 1844 at the rate of $10 per month. 1844. 1845. 1846. 1847. 1848. 1850. 1851.

Smith, M. —. —. He was pensioned as a privateer at the rate of $72 per annum. 1817. 1818. 1819. 1820. 1821. 1822. 1823. 1824. 1825. 1826. 1827 for $36.

Smith, Michael. Penn. Corporal Marines. He was pensioned at the rate of $60 per annum. 1816. 1818.

Smith, Purnell, Md. Seaman. He was pensioned 16 Feb. 1815 at the rate of $48 per month. 1816. 1818. 1819. 1820. 1821. 1822. 1823. 1824. 1825. 1826. 1827. 1828. 1829. 1830 in N.Y. He served aboard the schooner *Saratoga*.

Smith, Robert. N.Y. —. He perished aboard the *Grampus*. His mother was Eliza Smith of New York, N.Y. on 6 Jan. 1844. Her eldest son, Stephen J. Smith, served aboard the *Dolphin*

Naval Pensioners of the United States, 1800-1851

under Capt. Charles H. Bell and died off the coast of Africa of fever.

Smith, Russell.* —. Carpenter's Mate. He was pensioned 2 Aug. 1842 at the rate of $7.12 ½ per month. 1842b. 1843. 1844. 1845. 1846. 1847. 1848. 1850. 1851.

Smith, Thomas. Md. Boatswain. He was pensioned 6 Apr. 1815 at the rate of $120 per month. 1818. 1819. 1820. 1821. 1822. 1823. 1824. 1825. 1826. 1827. 1828. 1829. 1830. 1835. 1836. 1837. 1839. 1840. 1841. 1842b. 1843. 1844. 1845. 1846. 1847. 1848. 1850. 1851. He was disabled at Dartmoor Prison.

Smith, Thomas.* —. Seaman. He was pensioned 5 Apr. 1839 at the rate of $5 per month. 1839. 1840. 1841. 1842b. 1843. 1844. 1845. 1846. 1847. 1848. 1850. 1851.

Smith, Thomas.* —. Ordinary Seaman. He was pensioned 23 Jan. 1843 at the rate of $3.33 1/3 per month. 1843. 1844. 1845. 1846. 1847. 1848. 1850. 1851.

Smith, Thomas.* —. Marine. He was pensioned 13 Nov. 1848 at the rate of $3.50 per month. 1850. 1851.

Smith, Thomas. —. Seaman. He was pensioned 2 Nov. 1848 at the rate of 4.50 per month. 1850. 1851.

Smith, Waters.* —. Surgeon. His widow, Hannah C. Smith, was pensioned 19 Sep. 1850 at the rate of $35 per month. 1851.

Smith, William. N.Y. Boatswain's Mate. He served aboard the *Essex*, was wounded, and died 16 Apr. 1814 at Valparaiso. His widow, Sarah Smith, was pensioned at the rate of $114 per annum. 1816. 1818. 1821. 1822. 1823. 1824. 1825. 1827. 1828. 1829. 1830.

Smith, William, 6th.* Conn. Seaman. He was pensioned 1 July 1820 at the rate of $96 per month. 1820. 1821. 1822. 1823. 1824 in Penn. 1825. 1826. 1827. 1828. 1829. 1830. He served aboard the *Franklin*.

Smith, William. —. Ordinary Seaman. He was pensioned from 1 June 1827 at the rate of $5 per month. 1835. 1836. 1837. 1839. 1840. 1841. 1842b. 1843. 1844. 1845. 1846. 1847. 1848. 1850. 1851.

Smith, William. —. Sergeant of Marines. He was pensioned 7 Jan. 1841 at the rate of $6.50 per month. 1841. 1842b. 1843. 1844. 1845. 1846. 1847. 1848. 1850. 1851.

Snell, —. —. —. Rebecca Snell was pensioned on his service as a privateer at the rate of $60 per annum. 1815. 1816. 1817. 1818. 1819 increase to $120. 1820. 1821. 1822. 1823. 1824. 1825. 1826 for $64.80.

Sniffen, John. N.Y. Carpenter's Mate. He was pensioned 8 Jan. 1815 at the rate of $72 per annum. 1816. 1818. 1819. 1820. 1821. 1822. 1823. 1824. 1825. 1826. 1827. 1828. 1829. 1830. He served aboard the *Argus*.

Snow, —. D.C. Seaman. His widow, Eleanor J. Snow, received $72 per annum. 1820. 1821. 1822. 1824. 1825. 1827. 1828.

Snow, —. Mass. Lieutenant. Sarah Snow was pensioned on his service as a privateer at the rate of $72 per annum. 1815. 1816. 1817. 1818. 1819. 1820 increased to $144. 1821. 1822. 1823. 1824. 1825. 1826. 1827. 1828. 1829. 1830. 1831. 1832. 1833. 1834. 1835. 1836 for $12.

Snowman, Samuel.* —. Seaman. His widow, Julia Snowman, was pensioned from 5 Oct. 1841 at the rate of $6 per month. 1842b. 1843. 1844. 1845. His daughter, Ellen Snowman, was pensioned 1 Nov. 1844 at the rate of $6 per month. 1851.

Naval Pensioners of the United States, 1800-1851

Somerset, Levi. —. Seaman. —. His application was rejected prior to 12 Dec. 1842. He claimed to have been wounded after the battle of Lake Erie in the last war.

Souks, Duroc. Md. Seaman. He was pensioned as a privateer from 10 Mar. 1813 at the rate of $48 per annum and paid $13.47 for 1814 and died the same year. He also appeared as Duroc Souty.

Soule, —.Mass. Seaman. Mehitable Soule was pensioned on his service as a privateer at the rate of $36 per annum. 1815. 1816. 1817. 1818. 1819. 1820 increased to $72. 1821. 1822. 1823. 1824. 1825. 1826. 1827. 1828.

Southcomb, —. Md. Commander. Margaret Southcomb was pensioned on his service as a privateer at the rate of $120 per annum. 1813. 1814. 1815. 1816. 1817. 1818 increased to $240. 1819. 1820. 1821. 1822. 1823. 1824. 1825. 1826. 1827. 1828. 1829. 1830. 1831. 1832. 1833 for $40.

Southerstate, Frederick. Md. Seaman. He was pensioned at the rate of $48 per annum as a privateer from 28 Nov. 1812. 1820.

Spalding, William M. Maine. Ordinary Seaman. He was pensioned from 1 Jan. 1825 at the rate of $72 per annum. 1827. 1828. 1829. 1830. 1836. He also appeared as William M. Spaulding. He served aboard the *General Greene*.

Sparhawk, Benjamin D. Mass. Boatswain's Mate. He was pensioned 2 Apr. 1829 at the rate of $108 per annum. 1829. 1830. 1836. He served aboard the *President* under Commander Rogers.

Sparks, —. —. —. Frances Sparks was pensioned on his service as a privateer at the rate of $36 per annum. 1813. 1814. 1815. 1816. 1817. 1818 increase to $72. 1819. 1820. 1821. 1822. 1823. 1824. 1825. 1826. 1827. 1828 for $48.

Spedden, Robert. La. Lieutenant. He was pensioned 5 Dec. 1823 at the rate of $240 per annum. 1824. 1825. 1826. 1827. 1828. 1829. 1830. 1835. 1836. 1837. 1839. 1840. 1841. 1842. 1842b. 1843. 1844. 1845. 1846. 1847. 1848. 1850. 1851. He was disabled on Gunboat No. 163. He also appeared as Robert Spedken and Robert Speddin. His disability was permanent.

Spence, Robert T.* —. Captain. His widow, Mary C. Spence, was pensioned from 26 Sep. 1826 at the rate of $50 per month. 1835. 1836. 1837. 1839. 1840. 1841. 1842. 1842b. 1845. 1846. 1848. 1850.

Spencer, Samuel B. —. Gunner's Mate. He was pensioned as a privateer from 1 Sep. 1821 at the rate of $6 per month. 1821. 1822. 1823. 1824. 1825. 1826. 1827. 1828. 1829. 1830. 1831. 1832. 1833. 1834. 1835. 1836. 1837 for $36.

Spicer, Walter. —. Ordinary Seaman. He was pensioned 19 Oct. 1845 at the rate of $5 per month. 1847. 1848. 1850. 1851.

Spiers, James.* —. Ordinary Seaman. He was pensioned 5 May 1837 at the rate of $3.75 per month. 1839. 1840. 1841. 1842b. 1843. 1844. 1845. 1846. 1847. 1848. 1850. 1851. He also appeared as James Spires.

Spinney, John A.* —. Ordinary Seaman. He was pensioned 6 Dec. 1846 at the rate of $3.75 per month. 1850. 1851. He also appeared as John A. Spimrey.

Spinney, Joseph A.* —. Orderly Sergeant. His widow, Pamela Spinney, was pensioned 1 Aug.

Naval Pensioners of the United States, 1800-1851

1848 at the rate of $8 per month. 1850. 1851.

Spooner, Samuel.* —. Ordinary Seaman. He was pensioned 15 Oct. 1838 at the rate of $1.66 2/3 per month. 1839. 1840. 1841. 1842b. 1843. 1844. 1845. 1846. 1847. 1848. 1850. 1851.

Spratt, William. N.Y. Ordinary Seaman. He was pensioned 15 Feb. 1815 at the rate of $48 per annum. 1816. 1818. 1819. 1820. 1821. 1822. 1823. 1824. 1825. 1826. 1827. 1828. 1829. 1830. He served aboard the schooner *Saratoga*.

Springer, Charles L.* N.Y. Lieutenant. He served aboard the *Enterprise* and died 24 May 1820. His widow was Eliza Scott, and she was guardian of the two children. His heirs were pensioned 7 May 1824. 1824. 1825. 1827. 1829. 1830. Mary Ann Springer was his daughter, and she was pensioned at the rate of $25 per month. 1839. 1840. 1841. 1842b. He also appeared as Charles Spinger.

Springer, Charles.* —. Gunner's Mate. His widow, Charlotte Springer, was pensioned 4 Feb. 1845 at the rate of $9.50 per month. 1851. His daughter, Eugenia Springer, was pensioned 25 Oct. 1850 at the rate of $9.50 per month. 1851.

Sproston, George S.* —. Surgeon. His widow, Jane Sproston, was pensioned from 21 Jan. 1842 at the rate of $35 per month. 1842b. 1843. 1844. 1845. 1846. 1848. 1850. 1851.

Stallings, —. —. —. Jane Stallings was pensioned on his service. 1842.

Stallings, Joseph.* —. Lieutenant. His widow, Elizabeth L. Stallings, was pensioned from 26 Apr. 1841 at the rate of $25 per month. 1841. 1842b. She was pensioned again 1 Sep. 1847 at the rate of $25 per month. 1848. 1850. 1851.

Stallings, Thomas.* —. Ordinary Seaman. He was pensioned 7 Nov. 1826 at the rate of $2.50 per month. 1839. 1840. 1841. 1842b. 1843. 1844. 1845. 1846. 1847. 1848. 1850. 1851.

Standish, —.N.Y. Seaman. Sally Standish was pensioned on his service as a privateer at the rate of $72 per annum. 1819. 1820. 1821. 1822.

Stanfield, George. —. Seaman. He was pensioned from 7 June 1837 at the rate of $6 per month. 1837.

Stanford, —. Mass. Seaman. Sarah Stanford was pensioned on his service as a privateer at the rate of $36 per annum. 1815. 1816. 1817. 1818. 1819. 1820 increased to $72. 1821. 1822. 1823. 1824. 1825. 1826. 1827. 1828. 1829. 1830. 1831. 1832. 1833. 1834. 1835 for $6.

Stanley, George. N.Y. Purser's Steward. He was pensioned 20 May 1814 at the rate of $72 per annum. 1816. 1818. 1819. 1820. 1821. 1822. 1823. 1824. 1825. 1826. 1827. 1828. 1829. 1830. He was disabled on Lake Erie. He also appeared as George Standley.

Stanwood, William. —. Seaman. His sons, Joseph Stanwood and William Stanwood, were pensioned at the rate of $4 per month from 31 Aug. 1800. Joseph Stanwood was paid to 22 Feb. 1820; William Stanwood was paid to 22 May 1821. 1843.

Staples, Nathaniel. —. Seaman. He was pensioned 1 May 1833 at the rate of $3 per month. 1835. 1836. 1837. 1839. 1840. 1841. 1842b. 1843. 1844. 1845. 1846. 1847. 1848. 1850. 1851. He also appeared as Nathan Staples.

Stark, —.* —. Corporal Marines. His widow, Elizabeth A. Stark, was pensioned from 10 Dec. 1839 at the rate of $4.50 per month. 1841. 1842. 1842b. She also appeared as Elizabeth A. Starke. [He was listed as Thomas Starke in the Old Wars pension index.]

Starr, James P. Conn. Ordinary Seaman. He perished aboard the *Epervier* 1 Sep. 1815. His father,

Naval Pensioners of the United States, 1800-1851

William Starr of Middletown, Conn., was paid $60 on 14 Apr. 1817.
Staunton, Charles.* —. Boatswain's Mate. He was pensioned 19 Feb. 1838 at the rate of $9.50 per month. 1842b. 1843. 1844. 1845. 1846. 1847. 1848. 1850. 1851.
Staunton, Peter J. R. S.C. Carpenter's Yeoman. He was pensioned at the rate of $72 per annum in 1818. 1823. 1824. 1825. 1826. 1827. 1828. 1829. He served board the brig *Spark.*
Staunton, William. Md. Quarter Gunner. He was pensioned at the rate of $72 per annum. 1818. 1819. 1820. 1821 in D.C. 1822. 1823. 1824. 1825. 1826. 1827. 1828. 1829. 1830. 1836. He served aboard the Schooner *Ontario.* He also appeared as William Stanton.
Stearns, Isaac. R.I. Private Marine. He was pensioned from 30 Sep. 1802 at the rate of $36 per annum. 1810. 1811. 1816. 1818. 1824. 1825. 1826. 1827. 1828. 1829. 1830. He served aboard the frigate *New York.*
Steel, James. Mass. Seaman. He was pensioned at the rate of $72 per annum in 1808. 1809. 1810. 1811. 1816.
Steele, Peter.* —. Sergeant Marines. His widow, Rachel Steele, was pensioned at the rate of $8.00 per month from 28 Nov. 1832. 1837. 1839. 1840. 1841. 1842. 1842b. She was pensioned again 1 Sep. 1847 at the rate of $8 month. 1848. 1850. 1851.
Steinbogh, —.* —. Boatswain. His widow, Elizabeth Steinbogh, was pensioned from 20 Nov. 1840 at the rate of $10 per month. 1841. 1842. His daughter, Wilhelmina Steinbogh, was pensioned from 13 July 1841 at the rate of $10 per month. 1841. 1842b. [He was listed as Nicholas Steinbogh in the Old Wars pension index.]
Stephenson, —.* —. Seaman. His widow, Mary Stephenson, was pensioned from Oct. 1828 at the rate of $6 per month. 1835. 1836. 1837. 1839. 1840. 1841. 1842b. She also appeared as Mary Stevenson. [He was listed as Thomas Stephenson in the Old Wars pension index.]
Stephenson, Alexander. —. Gunner. His widow, Maria T. Stephenson, was pensioned 1 Sep. 1847 at the rate of $10 per month. 1847. 1848. 1851. His children, Alonzo W. Stephenson and Ralph C. Stephenson, were pensioned 12 Feb. 1850 at the rate of $10 per month. 1850. 1851.
Stephenson, William. —. Master. His widow, Ann Stephenson, was pensioned from 27 Aug. 1813 at the rate of $20 per month. 1835. 1836. 1837. 1839. 1840. 1841. 1842. 1842b. 1845. 1846. She was pensioned again 1 Sep. 1847 at the rate of $20 per month. 1848. 1850. 1851.
Sterrett, James. D.C. Prize Master. He was pensioned as a privateer at the rate of $84 per annum from 22 Mar. 1813. 1813. 1814. 1815. 1816. 1817. 1818. 1819. 1820. 1821. 1822. 1823. 1824. 1825. 1826.
Sterrett, William C.* —. Boy. His application was rejected prior to 17 Jan. 1845. He claimed to have been injured in June 1819. The law required that a disability of more than twenty-five years' standing be proved by record evidence. There was not any.
Stevens, Benjamin. Mass. Master's Mate. He was pensioned 27 June 1814 at the rate of $120 per annum. 1818. 1819. 1820. 1821. 1822. 1823. 1824. 1825. 1826. 1827. 1828. 1829. 1830. 1835. 1836. 1837. 1839. 1840. 1841. 1842b. 1843. 1844. 1845. 1846. 1847. 1848. 1850. 1851. He was disabled on Gunboat No. 109.

Naval Pensioners of the United States, 1800-1851

Stevens, John.* —. Quartermaster. He was pensioned 21 May 1831 at the rate of $4.50 per month. 1839. 1840. 1841. 1842b. 1843. 1844. 1845. 1846. 1847. 1848. 1850. 1851.

Stevens, Joseph. —. Sailing Master. His widow, Mary Stevens, was pensioned at the rate of $20 per month from 18 Apr. 1816. 1837. 1839. 1840. 1841. 1842. 1842b. She was pensioned again 1 Sep.1842 at the rate of $20 per month. 1851.

Stevens, Leonard.* —. Sergeant of Marines. He was pensioned 27 Jan. 1837 at the rate of $3.25 per month. 1838. 1839. 1840. 1841. 1842b. 1843. 1844. 1845. 1846. 1847. 1848. 1850. 1851.

Stevens, Samuel.* —. Seaman. He was pensioned 15 Aug. 1843 at the rate of $1.50 per month. 1843. 1844. 1846. 1846. 1847. 1848. 1850. 1851.

Stevens, Thomas Holdup.* —. Captain. He was pensioned at the rate of $7.12 ½ per month. 1837. 1838. 1839. 1840. 1841. His widow, Eliza Stevens, was pensioned at the rate of $50 per month 21 Jan. 1842. 1842. 1842b. 1843. 1845. His child Eben W. Sage, was pensioned at the rate of $30 per month. 1843. 1844. 1845. 1846. 1847. 1848. 1850. 1851. The difference in the surnames of the father and son was not given. He also appeared as Thomas H. Stephens.

Steward, —. —. —. J. Steward was pensioned as a privateer at the rate of $36 per annum. 1815. 1816. 1817. 1818. 1819. 1820 increased to $72. 1821. 1822. 1823. 1824. 1825. 1826. 1827. 1828.

Stewart, —. —. Captain. His daughter, Catharine Stewart, was pensioned at the rate of $50 per month. 1837. 1842.

Stewart, Charles.* —. Gunner's Mate. He was pensioned 30 Apr. 1844 at the rate of $9.50 per month. 1847. 1848. 1850. 1851.

Stewart, Charles. Mass. Seaman. He was pensioned as a privateer at the rate of $72 per annum from 31 Jan. 1815. 1820.

Stewart, E. —. —. He was pensioned as a privateer in 1814 at the rate of $72 per annum. 1814. 1815. 1816. 1817. 1818. 1819 in the amount of $36.

Stewart, Eli. Penn. Sailing Master's Mate. He was pensioned 20 May 1814 at the rate of $84 per annum. 1816. 1818. 1819. 1820. 1821. 1822. 1823. 1824. 1825. 1826. 1827. 1828. 1829. 1830. 1835. 1836. 1837. 1839. 1840. 1841. 1842b. 1843. 1844. 1845. 1846. 1847. 1848. 1850. 1851. He also appeared as Eli Steward and Eli Stenard. He was disabled on Lake Erie. His rank was also given as sail maker's mate.

Stewart, James.* Md. Seaman. He was pensioned 14 Feb. 1820 at the rate of $72 per annum. 1821. 1822. 1823. 1824. 1825. 1826. 1827. 1828. 1829. 1830. He served aboard the *Guerriere*.

Stewart, William. Mass. Seaman. He was pensioned 10 Sep. 1812 at the rate of $48 per annum. 1816. 1818. 1819. 1820. 1821. 1822. 1823. 1824. 1825. 1826. 1827. 1828. 1829. 1830. He served aboard the *Chesapeake*. He also appeared as William Steward and William Steuart.

Still, Thomas J.* —. Marine. He was pensioned 1 Jan. 1832 at the rate of $3 per month. 1835. 1836. 1837. 1839. 1840. 1841. 1842b. 1843. 1844. 1845. 1846. 1847. 1848. 1850. 1851.

Still, William. Mass. Sailing Master. He was pensioned as a privateer at the rate of $144 per

Naval Pensioners of the United States, 1800-1851

annum from 12 July 1814. 1820.

Stillwagon, Daniel S. —. Master. His widow, Mary Stillwagon, was pensioned from 16 Nov. 1828 at the rate of $20 per month. 1835. 1836. 1837. 1839. 1840. 1841. 1842. 1842b. 1845. 1846. She was pensioned again 1 Sep. 1847 at the rate of $20 per month. 1848. 1850. 1851. She also appeared as Mary Stellwagen.

Stinger, John.* —. Landsman. His widow, Rebecca S. Stinger, was pensioned from 15 July 1839 at the rate of $4 per month. 1840. 1841. 1842. 1842b. 1843. 1845. 1846. She was pensioned again 15 July 1849 at the rate of $4 per month. 1848. 1850. 1851.

Stivers, Stephen D.* —. Landsman. His widow, Ann Maria Stivers, was pensioned from 22 Apr. 1839 at the rate of $4 per month. 1840. 1841. 1842b. 1843. 1845. 1846. She was pensioned again 1 Sep. 1847 at the rate of $4 per month. 1848. 1850. 1851.

Stockdale, William. Md. Marine. He was pensioned 26 July 1816 at the rate of $72 per annum. 1818. 1819. 1820. 1821. 1822. 1823. 1824. 1825. 1826. 1827. 1828. 1829. 1830. 1835. 1836. 1837. 1839. 1840. 1841. 1842b. 1843. 1844. 1845. 1846. 1847. 1848. 1850. 1851. He served aboard the frigate *Congress*.

Stockton, Samuel W.* —. Lieutenant. His widow, Mary H. Stockton, was pensioned at the rate of $25 per month from 20 Nov. 1836. 1837. 1839. 1840. 1841. 1842. 1842b. She was pensioned again 1 Sep. 1847 at the rate of $25 per month. 1848. 1850. 1851.

Stockwell, James.* —. Ordinary Seaman. He was pensioned 28 Feb. 1829 at the rate of $4.50 per month. 1842b. 1843. 1844. 1845. 1846. 1847. 1848. 1850. 1851.

Stoker, John.* Va. Gunner's Mate. He was pensioned 22 Feb. 1830 at the rate of $54 per month. 1830. 1835. 1836. 1837. He served aboard the *Delaware*. He also appeared as John Stoke.

Stone, John.* Me. Seaman. He was late of Kennebunk, Maine and was aboard the privateer schooner *Harlequin* of Portsmouth when he was taken by one of His Britannic Majesty's ships-of-war and taken to Halifax and thence to England. He was confined in Dartmoor Prison where he died in consequence of the bad treatment and sufferings to which he was subjected. His widow, Hannah Stone, was pensioned at the rate of $3 per month from 1 July 1815 until 1820 and $6 per month from 30 June 1834. 1835. 1836. 1837. 1839. 1840. 1841. 1842. 1842b.

Stone, John. N.Y. Seaman. He was pensioned from 13 July 1814 at the rate of $72 per annum. 1818. 1819. 1820. 1821. 1822. 1823. 1824. 1825. 1826. 1827. 1828. 1829. 1830. He served aboard the *Essex*.

Stone, Jonas A. D.C. Carpenter. He was pensioned 4 Apr. 1829 at the rate of $60 per annum. 1829. 1830. 1835. 1836. 1837. 1839. 1840. 1841. 1842b. 1843. 1844. 1845. 1846. 1847. 1848. 1850. 1851. He served aboard the *Lawrence*.

Stone, William.* Mass. Seaman. He served aboard the *Wasp* and was lost 20 Apr. 1815. His widow, Mary Stone, was pensioned 1 Jan. 1817 at the rate of $6 per month. 1818. 1819. 1821. 1822. 1823. 1824. 1825. 1827. 1830. 1835. 1836. 1839. 1840. 1841. 1842b. 1845. 1846. 1848. 1850.

Stoodley, —.* —. Sailing Master. His children, Ann Olivia Stoodley and Adelaide E. McD. Stoodley, were pensioned at the rate of $20 per month. 1837. 1842. [He was listed as

Naval Pensioners of the United States, 1800-1851

Nathaniel Stoodley in the Old Wars pension index.]
Stover, Caleb. —. Seaman. He was pensioned 6 July 1848 at the rate of $6 per month. 1848. 1850. 1851. He also appeared as Caleb Storer.
Strain, John.* —. Seaman. He was pensioned 28 Feb. 1837 at the rate of $4.50 per month. 1839. 1840. 1841. 1842. 1843. 1844. 1845. 1846. 1847. 1848. 1850. 1851.
Street, —. Mass. Seaman. Elizabeth Street was pensioned on his service as a privateer at the rate of $72 per annum. 1817. 1818. 1819. 1820. 1821. 1822. 1823. 1824. 1825. 1826. 1827 for $55.
Stricker, —.* —. Sergeant Marines. His widow, Hannah Stricker, was pensioned from 1 Oct. 1820 at the rate of $6.50 per month. 1837. 1839. 1841. 1842. 1842b. She also appeared as Hannah Striker. [He was listed as Peter Strider in the Old Wars pension index.]
Stubbs, —.D.C. Commander. His widow, Rachel Stubbs, was pensioned at the rate of $120 per annum. 1814. 1815. 1816. 1817. 1818. 1819 increased to $240. 1820. 1821. 1822. 1823. 1824. 1825. 1826. 1827. 1828 . 1829 for $127.33.
Sullivan, —. N.H. Quarter Gunner. Eunice Sullivan was pensioned on his service as a privateer at the rate of $48 per annum. 1815. 1816. 1817. 1818. 1819. 1820 increase to $96. 1821. 1822. 1823. 1824. 1825. 1826. 1827. 1828. 1829 for $64.
Sullivan, —. —. Seaman. His widow, Honora Sullivan, was pensioned from 30 June 1837 at the rate of $6 per month. 1837. 1839. 1840. 1842. She also appeared as Hannorah Sullivan.
Sullivan, —. —. Seaman. His daughters, Deborah Sullivan and Florence Sullivan, were pensioned from 7 July 1840 at the rate of $6 per month. 1841. 1842. 1842b.
Sullivan, Jeremiah.* —. Seaman. He was pensioned 30 June 1837 at the rate of $6 per month. 1839. 1840. 1841. 1842b. 1843. 1844. 1845. 1846. 1847. 1848. 1850. 1851.
Sullivan, John.* —. Fireman. He was pensioned 23 Sep. 1850 at the rate of $6 per month. 1851.
Suter, Richard S. D.C. Midshipman. He was pensioned 16 Dec. 1814 at the rate of $114 per annum. 1819. 1820. 1821. 1822. 1823. 1824. 1825. 1826. 1827. 1828. 1829. 1830. 1835. 1836. 1837. 1839. 1840. 1841. 1842b. 1843. 1844. 1845. 1846. 1847. 1848. 1850. 1851. He was disabled on the Chesapeake flotilla. He also appeared as Richard S. Sater.
Sutherland, —. —. Master's Mate. His son, George Sutherland, was pensioned at the rate of $10 per month. 1837. 1842.
Sutton, Harmon.* Penn. Seaman. He was pensioned 1 July 1829 at the rate of $3 per month. 1829. 1830. 1835. 1836. 1837. 1839. 1840. 1841. 1842b. 1843. 1844. 1845. 1846. 1847. 1848. 1850. 1851. He was disabled at the Marine Barracks in Pennsylvania.
Sutton, John. S.C. Purser's Steward. He was pensioned as a privateer at the rate of $60 per annum from 22 Mar. 1813. 1813. 1814. 1815. 1816. 1817. 1818. 1819. 1820 for $48.67.
Swann, Isaac.* —. Ordinary Seaman. He was pensioned 12 Aug. 1843 at the rate of $2.50 per month. 1843. 1844. 1845. 1846. 1847. 1848. 1850. 1851.
Swann, William S.* Va. Lieutenant. He perished aboard the *Grampus*. His lady and two children Julia C. Swann, Macon Swann of less than five years of age, and Julia Ann Taylor Swann of less than one year of age lived in Norfolk, Va. 27 Jan. 1844. His widow, Julia C. Swann, was pensioned from 20 Mar. 1843 at the rate of $25 per month. 1844. 1845. 1846. His children, William Macon Swann and Julia Ann T. Swann, were pensioned 22

Naval Pensioners of the United States, 1800-1851

June 1847 at the rate of $25 per month. 1850. 1851.
Swartwout, Augustus. N.Y. Midshipman. He was pensioned at the rate of $144 per annum in 1823. 1824. 1825. 1826. 1827. 1828.
Swasey, —. —. —. Lydia K. Swasey was pensioned on his service. 1842.

Taft, Silas. Mass. Marine. He was pensioned 1 Jan. 1806 at the rate of $36 per annum. 1807. 1808. 1809. 1810. 1811. 1816. 1818. 1819. 1820. 1821. 1824. 1825. 1826. 1827. 1828. 1829. 1830. He served aboard the *President*. He also appeared as Silas Sufts.
Taggert, —.* —. Gunner. His widow, Ann Taggert, was pensioned from 13 Dec. 1836 at the rate of $10 per month. 1839. 1840. 1841. 1842. 1842b. [He was listed as David Taggart in the Old Wars pension index.]
Talbot, Murray. Md. Seaman. He was pensioned as a privateer from 3 Aug. 1812 at the rate of $5 per month. 1812. 1813. 1814. 1815. 1816. 1817. 1818. 1819. 1820. 1821. 1822. 1823. 1824. 1825. 1826. 1827. 1828. 1829. 1830. 1831. 1832. 1833. 1834. 1835. 1836. 1837 for $30.
Tallman, John. Mass. Seaman. He was pensioned at the rate of $72 per annum. 1816. 1818. 1819. 1820. 1821. 1822.
Tanner, —.* —. Quarter Gunner. His widow, Mary Tanner, was pensioned from 22 Feb. 1834 at the rate of $7.50 per month. 1835. 1836. 1837. 1839. 1840. 1842. [He was listed as John Tanner in the Old Wars pension index.]
Tarbell, J. Va. Captain. He served aboard the *Norfolk*. He died 24 Nov. 1815 of a natural death. His widow, Elizabeth Tarbell, was pensioned at the rate of $600 per annum. 1818. 1819. 1821. 1822. 1823. 1824 in D.C. 1825. 1827. 1828. 1829.
Tarlton, —. N.H. Pilot. Abigail Tarlton was pensioned on his service as a privateer at the rate of $48 per annum. 1815. 1816. 1817. 1818. 1819. 1820 increase to $96. 1821. 1822. 1823. 1824. 1825. 1826. 1827. 1828. 1829. 1830. 1831. 1832. 1833. 1834.
Tarlton, John.* —. Ordinary Seaman. He was pensioned 8 May 1833 at the rate of $4 per month. 1835. 1836. 1837. 1839. 1840. 1841. 1842b. 1843. 1844. 1845. 1846. 1847. 1848. 1850. 1851.
Tarr, —. —. Sailing Master. His children, Abigail B. Tarr and Mary G. Tarr, were pensioned at the rate of $20 per month. 1837. 1842.
Tash, John S.* —. Ordinary Seaman. He was pensioned 6 Feb. 1849 at the rate of $2.50 per month. 1850. 1851.
Tatem, Robert S.* —. Master. His widow, Mary Ann Tatem, was pensioned 3 Jan. 1844 at the rate of $20 per month. 1844. 1845. 1846. 1847. 1848. 1850. 1851.
Tatman, —. Mass. Seaman. Mary Tatman was pensioned on his service as privateer at the rate of $36 per annum. 1815. 1816. 1817. 1818. 1819. 1820 increased to $72. 1821. 1822. 1823. 1824. 1825. 1826. 1827. 1828. 1829. 1830. 1831. 1832 for $60.
Taylor, —. N.H. Gunner. Eliza Maria Taylor was pensioned on his service as a privateer at the rate

Naval Pensioners of the United States, 1800-1851

of $60 per annum. 1815. 1816. 1817. 1818. 1819. 1820 increase to $120. 1821. 1822. 1823. 1824. 1825. 1826. 1827. 1828. 1829. She also appeared as Ella Maria Taylor.

Taylor, —. —. Captain. His daughter, Charlotte J. Taylor, was pensioned at the rate of $50 per month. 1837. 1842.

Taylor, —. Penn. Commander. His widow, Sarah S. Taylor, was pensioned at the rate of $120 per annum. 1820.

Taylor, —. —. Sailing Master. His widow, Grizel A. Taylor, was pensioned at the rate of $20 per month from 2 Jan. 1820. 1837. 1839. 1840.

Taylor, George.* —. 1st Class Boy. He was pensioned 22 Jan. 1844 at the rate of $3.50 per month. 1844. 1845. 1846. 1847. 1848. 1850. 1851.

Taylor, John.* —. Quartermaster. He was pensioned 31 May 1839 at the rate of $8 per month. 1839. 1840. 1841. 1842b. 1843. 1844. 1845. 1846. 1847. 1848. 1850. 1851.

Taylor, Owen. Mass. Seaman. He was pensioned 19 Aug. 1812 at the rate of $72 per annum. 1822. 1823. 1824. 1825. 1826. 1827. 1828. 1829. 1830. 1835. 1836. 1837. 1838. 1839. 1840. 1841. 1842. 1842b. 1843. 1844. 1845. 1846. 1847. 1848. 1850. 1851. He served aboard the *Constitution*.

Taylor, Samuel.* —. Ordinary Seaman. He was pensioned 30 Nov. 1839 at the rate of $5 per month. 1841. 1842b. 1843. 1844. 1845. 1846. 1847. 1848. 1850. 1851.

Taylor, Thomas. Mass. Gunner's Mate. He was pensioned as a privateer from 4 Nov. 1812 at the rate of $72 per month. 1812. 1813. 1814. 1815. 1816. 1817. 1818. 1819. 1820. 1821. 1822. 1823. 1824. 1825. 1826. 1827. 1828. 1829. 1830. 1831. 1832. 1833. 1834. 1835. 1836. 1837 for half a year. He was pensioned from 1 July 1837 at the rate of $6 per month. 1837. 1838. 1844. 1845. 1846. 1847. 1850.

Taylor, William. Mass. Seaman. He was pensioned at the rate of $48 per annum in 1807. 1808. 1809. 1810. 1811.

Taylor, William.* —. Ordinary Seaman. He was pensioned 27 Feb. 1845 at the rate of $3.75 per month. 1845. 1846. 1847. 1848. 1850. 1851.

Taylor, William.* —. Seaman. He was pensioned 8 Apr. 1846 at the rate of $6 per month. 1846. 1847. 1848. 1850. 1851.

Tebbets, —. N.H. Seaman. Mary Tebbets was pensioned on his service as a privateer at the rate of $36 per annum. 1815. 1816. 1817. 1818. 1819. 1820 increase to $72. 1821. 1822. 1823. 1824. 1825. 1826. 1827. 1828. 1829.

Temple, William T.* —. Lieutenant. His widow, Lucy R. Temple, was pensioned from 23 June 1830 at the rate of $25 per month. 1835. 1836. 1837. 1839. 1840. 1841. 1842. 1842b. 1845. 1846. She was pensioned again 1 Sep. 1847 at the rate of $25 per month. 1850. 1851.

Terrell, Ebenezer. —. Boatswain's Mate. His widow, Ann Terrell, was pensioned at the rate of $9.50 per annum from 8 Dec. 1846. 1847.

Terry, Julius. —. Ordinary Seaman. He was pensioned from 31 Aug. 1812 at the rate of $5 per month. 1839. 1840. 1841. 1842b. 1843. 1844. 1845. 1846. 1847. 1848. 1850. 1851.

Tewksbury, —. Mass. Boatswain. Nancy Tewksbury was pensioned on his service as a privateer at the rate of $120 per annum. 1817. 1818. 1819. 1820. 1821. 1822. 1823. 1824. 1825. 1826.

Naval Pensioners of the United States, 1800-1851

1827. 1828. 1829. 1830. 1831. 1832 for $60.

Tewksbury, James. —. Master. His widow, Elizabeth Tewksbury, was pensioned 31 Aug. 1848 at the rate of $20 per month. 1847. 1848. 1850. 1851.

Thatcher, James Swan. Mass. Purser. He perished aboard the *Grampus*. His mother was Lucy Knox Thatcher of Thomaston, Lincoln Co., Me. His brothers and sisters relinquished their claim to her. His father was the late Ebenezer Thatcher of Maine.

Theall, Halstead.* —. Sergeant Marines. His widow, Caroline E. Theall, was pensioned 11 Feb. 1847 at the rate of $8 per month. 1846. 1848. 1850. 1851.

Theobald, George.* —. Orderly Sergeant Marines. His widow, Jane Theobald, was pensioned 18 June 1849 at the rate of $8 per month. 1850. 1851.

Thomas, —, N.Y. Boatswain. Elizabeth Thomas was pensioned on his service as a privateer at the rate of $120 per annum. 1816. 1817. 1818. 1819. 1820. 1821. 1822. 1823. 1824. 1825. 1826. 1827. 1828. 1829 for $20.

Thomas, —. —. Boatswain's Mate. Martha Thomas was pensioned on his service as a privateer at the rate of $96 per annum. 1818. 1819. 1820. 1821. 1822. 1823. 1824. 1825. 1826. 1827. 1828 for $42.40.

Thomas, —. —. —. Sally Thomas was pensioned on his service as a privateer at the rate of $36 per annum. 1815. 1816. 1817. 1818. 1819. 1820 increase to $72. 1821. 1822. 1823. 1824. 1825. 1826. 1827. 1828. 1829.

Thomas, —.* —. Marine. His daughter, Mary Ann Thomas, was pensioned at the rate of $3.50 per month from 11 May 1826. 1837. 1842. [He was listed as Orreal I. Thomas in the Old Wars pension index.]

Thomas, David. Penn. Private Marine. He was pensioned 1 Jan. 1806 at the rate of $36 per annum. 1807. 1808. 1809. 1810. 1816. 1818. 1819. 1820. 1821. 1822. 1823. 1824. 1825. 1826. 1827. 1828. 1829. 1835. 1836. 1837. 1839. 1840. 1841. 1842. 1842b. 1843. 1844. 1845. 1846. 1847. 1848. 1850. 1851. He was disabled in action at Derne.

Thomas, George.* N.Y. Seaman. He was pensioned 3 Aug. 1818 at the rate of $72 per annum. 1819. 1820. 1821. 1822. 1823. 1824. 1825. 1826. 1827. 1828. 1829. 1830. He was black. He served aboard the *Washington*.

Thomas, Henry.* —. Captain of Forecastle. He was pensioned from 6 Jan. 1848 at the rate of $7.50 per month. 1850. 1851.

Thomas, Isaac.* Penn. Marine. He was pensioned 30 Oct. 1829 at the rate of $6 per month. 1830. 1835. 1836. 1837. 1839. 1840. 1841. 1842b. 1843. 1844. 1845. 1846. 1847. 1848. 1850. 1851. He served aboard the *Delaware*. He was permanently disabled.

Thomas, James.* —. Quartermaster. He was pensioned 12 Dec. 1844 at the rate of $6 per month. 1845. 1847. 1848. 1850. 1851.

Thomas, John L.* —. Lieutenant. His widow, Frances A. Thomas, was pensioned from 10 Sep. 1829 at the rate of $25 per month. 1835. 1836. 1837. 1839. 1840. 1841. 1842. 1842b. 1845. 1846.

Thomas, Lewis.* —. Private Marines. He was pensioned 11 May 1839 at the rate of $2.66 2/3 per month. 1840. 1841. 1842. 1842b. 1843. 1844. 1845. 1846. 1847. 1848. 1850. 1851.

Thomas, Richard.* —. Carpenter. His widow, Margaret M. Thomas, was pensioned 20 Dec.

Naval Pensioners of the United States, 1800-1851

1842 at the rate of $10 per month. 1842. 1843. 1845. 1846. 1847. 1848. 1850. 1851.

Thomas, William, 2d. R.I. Seaman. He was pensioned at the rate of $60 per annum. 1816. 1818. 1819. 1820. 1821. 1822.

Thompson, —. N.Y. Seaman. Rebecca Thompson was pensioned on his service as a privateer at the rate of $36 per annum. 1815. 1816. 1817. 1818. 1819. 1820 increase to $72. 1821. 1822. 1823. 1824. 1825 for $50.40.

Thompson, Charles. —. Seaman. His widow, Anna Thompson, was pensioned from 1 July 1813 at the rate of $6 per month. 1851.

Thompson, Charles C. B.* —. Captain. His widow, Emma C. B. Thompson, was pensioned from 2 Sep. 1832 at the rate of $50 per month. 1835. 1836. 1837. 1839. 1840. 1841. 1842. 1842b. 1845. 1846. She was pensioned again 1 Sep. 1847 at the rate of $50 per month. 1848. 1850. 1851.

Thompson, Giles.* La. Second Lieutenant of Marines. His application was rejected prior to 23 Dec. 1848. His claim was more than twenty-five years' standing. He also appeared as Gillis Thompson.

Thompson, James.* —. Seaman. He was pensioned 30 June 1836 at the rate of $6 per month. 1837. 1838. 1839. 1840. 1841. 1842. 1842b. 1843. 1844. 1845. 1846. 1847. 1848. 1850. 1851.

Thompson, John. —. Quartermaster. He was pensioned 23 May 1844 at the rate of $2 per month. 1844. 1845. 1846. 1847. 1848. 1850. 1851.

Thompson, John. N.Y. Quarter Gunner. He was pensioned at the rate of $108 per annum. 1820. 1822. 1823. 1825. 1826.

Thompson, John.* N.C. Seaman. He was pensioned at the rate of $72 per annum. 1822. 1824. 1825. 1826. 1827. 1829. He served aboard the schooner *Columbus*.

Thompson, John.* —. Seaman. He was pensioned 18 Mar. 1848 at the rate of $4.50 per month. 1848. 1850. 1851.

Thompson, John. Penn. Quarter Gunner. He was pensioned at the rate of $108 per annum. 1816. 1818. 1819. 1820. 1821. 1824. 1826.

Thompson, John.* —. Seaman. His widow, Hannah Thompson, was pensioned at the rate of $6 per month from 9 Apr. 1835. 1837. 1839. 1840. 1841. 1842. 1842b. She was pensioned again 1 Sep. 1847. 1848. 1850.

Thompson, Peter. Md. Seaman. He was pensioned 15 July 1825 at the rate of $72 per annum. 1827. 1828. 1829. 1830. He served aboard the *Peacock*.

Thompson, William. Mass. Boatswain's Mate. He was pensioned 1 Jan. 1816 at the rate of $114 per annum. 1818. 1819. 1820. 1822. 1824. 1825. 1826. 1827. 1828. 1829. 1830. He served aboard the schooner *Wasp*.

Thompson, William. N.Y. Seaman. He was pensioned at the rate of $72 per annum. 1818.

Thompson, William.* S.C. Ordinary Seaman. He was pensioned 20 May 1826 at the rate of $6 per month. 1827. 1828. 1829. 1830. 1835. 1836. 1837. 1839. 1840. 1842b. 1843. 1844. 1845. 1846. 1847. 1848. 1850. 1851. He served aboard the revenue cutter *Louisiana*.

Thompson, William.* —. Quartermaster. He was pensioned 21 Apr. 1849 at the rate of $8 per month. 1850. 1851.

Naval Pensioners of the United States, 1800-1851

Thompson, William G. —. Seaman. His widow, Lydia Thompson, was pensioned from 21 Nov. 1813 at the rate of $6 per month. 1851.

Thompson, William James.* —. Marine. His widow, Mary Thompson, was pensioned from 11 Oct. 1847 at the rate of $3.50 per month. 1850.

Thorn, —.* —. Surgeon. His widow, Charlotte M. R. Thorn, was pensioned from 18 Aug. 1827 at the rate of $25 per month. 1835. 1836. 1837. 1839. 1842. His children were pensioned at the rate of $30 per month from 12 Oct. 1838. 1841. 1842. 1842b. [He was listed as Robert S. Thorn in the Old Wars pension index.]

Thurston, —. —. Sergeant Marines. His widow, Catherine Thurston, was pensioned from 21 May 1839 at the rate of $6.50 per month. 1840. She and her children were pensioned on his service. His son, John L. Thurston, was pensioned at the rate of $6.50 per month from 11 Sep. 1840. 1841. 1842. 1842b.

Thurston, John C. N.Y. Seaman. He was pensioned at the rate of $72 per annum. 1816.

Tight, —.* —. Seaman. His widow, Ann Tight, was pensioned at the rate of $6 per month from 24 Mar. 1834. 1837. 1839. 1840. 1841. 1842. 1842b. [He was listed as Frederick Tight in the Old Wars pension index.]

Tilden, John. —. Seaman. His widow, Ann Tilden, was pensioned from 20 Apr. 1815 at the rate of $6 per month. 1841. 1842. 1842b. 1846. She was pensioned again 1 Sep. 1847 at the rate of $6 per month. 1848. 1850. 1851.

Timberlake, —. —. —. He died a natural death. His widow, Margaret Timberlake, applied in Aug. 1828 at the rate of $240 per annum.

Timberlake, —.* —. Purser. His daughters, Mary V. Timberlake and Margaret R. Timberlake, were pensioned at the rate of $20 per month from 2 Apr. 1828. 1837. 1839. 1840. 1841. 1842. 1842b. [He was listed as John Timberlake in the Old Wars pension index.]

Tindley, Thomas. —. Seaman. He was pensioned from 6 Apr. 1815 at the rate of $3 per month. 1838. 1839. 1840. 1841. 1842b. 1843. 1844. 1845. 1846. 1847. 1848. 1850. 1851. He also appeared as Thomas Findley. He was disabled by a gun shot wound in the hip in the Dartmoor Prison.

Tingey, Thomas.* —. Captain. His widow, Ann E. Tingey, was pensioned from 22 Feb. 1829 at the rate of $50 per month. 1835. 1836. 1837. 1839. 1840. 1841. 1842. 1842b. 1845. 1846. She was pensioned again 1 Sep. 1847 at the rate of $50 per month. 1848. 1850. 1851.

Tinkum, Peter.* N.Y. Seaman. He was pensioned at the rate of $48 per annum. 1816. 1818. 1819. 1820. 1821. 1822. 1823. 1824. 1825. 1826. 1827. 1828. 1829. 1830. He also appeared as Peter Thinkum. He served aboard the brig *Argus*. His son, Edward Thinkum, was pensioned from 31 Oct. 1836 at the rate of $6 per month. 1840. 1841. 1842.

Tinslar, B. R. —. Surgeon. He was pensioned from 31 Jan. 1832 at the rate of $6.50 per month. 1839. 1840. 1841. 1842. 1842b. 1843. He also appeared as R. R. Tinslar.

Titcomb, —. —. —. Martha Titcomb was pensioned on his service. 1842.

Tobey, —. —. Ordinary Seaman. His widow, Elizabeth Tobey, was pensioned at the rate of $5 per month from 30 Apr. 1813. 1837. 1839. 1842.

Tobey, —. —. —. His daughter, Caroline Tobey, was pensioned. 1837. 1842.

Toland, William. N.Y. —. He perished aboard the *Grampus*. His brother was John Toland of New

Naval Pensioners of the United States, 1800-1851

York, N.Y. who was out of work and destitute with a large family on 29 Jan. 1843.
Tollon, John.* —. Seaman. He was pensioned 14 May 1845 at the rate of $3 per month. 1845. 1846. 1847. 1848. 1850. 1851. He also appeared as John Tollom.
Tomerlier, John S. L. —. —. His name with no other details was on the roll for 1829.
Tompson, John. —. Seaman. His widow, Hannah Tompson, was pensioned 1 Sep. 1847 at the rate of $6 per month. 1851.
Tonkins, Jacob.* —. Marine. He was pensioned 31 May 1840 at the rate of $3.50 per month. 1840. 1841. 1842b. 1843. 1844. 1845. 1846. 1847. 1848. 1850. 1851. He also appeared as Jacob Tonkin and Jacob Tinkins.
Toohey, Edward.* —. Sergeant Marines. His widow, Eliza Toohey, was pensioned from 13 Nov. 1837 at the rate of $6.50 per month. 1839. 1840. 1841. 1842. 1842b. She was pensioned again 1 Sep. 1847 at the rate of $6.50 per month. 1851. He also appeared as Edward Tookey.
Toole, John. Ga. Midshipman. He perished aboard the *Epervier* 1 Sep. 1815. His father, James Toole, of Augusta, Ga., was paid $114 on 16 June 1817.
Tooley, Peter. —. Marine. He was pensioned 27 Jan. 1837 at the rate of $3.50 per month. 1839. 1840. 1841. 1842b. 1843. 1844. 1845. 1846. 1847. 1848. 1850. 1851. He was also known as Peter Forley.
Tourpson, William J. —. Marine. His widow, Mary Tourpson, was pensioned 11 Oct. 1847 at the rate of $3.50 per month. 1851.
Town, David. N.Y. Marine. He served aboard the schooner *Hornet* and was killed 23 Mar. 1815. His widow, Sarah Town, received $36 per annum in 1821. 1822. 1823. 1824. 1825. 1827. 1828. 1829. William Alden was guardian of the minor heirs.
Towner, —. —. —. Nancy S. Towner was pensioned on his service. 1842.
Towner, —.* —. Gunner. His children, Virginia Ann Towner and Robert Towner, were pensioned at the rate of $10 per month from 2 Sep. 1834. 1837. 1839. 1840. 1841. 1842. 1842b. [He was listed as Benjamin Towner in the Old Wars pension index.]
Townsend, Henry. N.Y. Ordinary Seaman. He was pensioned 18 Dec. 1814 at the rate of $60 per annum. 1816. 1818. 1819. 1820. 1821. 1822. 1823. 1824. 1825. 1826. 1827. 1828. 1829. 1830. 1835. 1836. 1837. 1839. 1840. 1841. 1842. 1843. 1844. 1845. 1846. 1847. 1848. 1850. 1851. He was disabled on Lake Champlain.
Townsend, Seth.* Mass. Seaman. He was pensioned 17 Apr. 1817 at the rate of $72 per annum. 1818. 1819. 1820. 1821. 1822. 1823. 1824. 1825. 1826. 1827. 1828. 1829. 1830. He also appeared as Seth Townshend. He served aboard the *Washington*.
Trainer, James. Mass. Marine. He was killed 1 June 1813 on the *Chesapeake*. His widow, Mary Trainer, was pensioned 29 Feb. 1816 at the rate of $36 per annum. 1818. 1820. 1821. 1822. 1823. 1824. 1825. 1827. 1829. 1830.
Trant, —.* —. Lieutenant. His widow, Charlotte Trant, was pensioned at the rate of $25 per annum from 11 Sep. 1820. 1837. 1839. 1840. 1842. [He was listed as James Trant in the Old Wars pension index.]
Trapnell, Joshua.* Md. Marine. He was killed 10 Sep. 1813 at Niagara on Lake Erie. His widow, Elizabeth Trapnell, was pensioned 30 May 1814 at the rate of $3 per month. 1816. 1818.

Naval Pensioners of the United States, 1800-1851

1821. 1822. 1823. 1824. 1825. 1828. 1830. 1835. 1836. 1837. 1839. 1840. 1841. 1842. 1842b. 1845. 1846. She also appeared as Elizabeth Traprell, Elizabeth Trapnall, Elizabeth Trampnell, and Elizabeth Trupnell.

Traya, Lewis. Md. Seaman. He was pensioned at the rate of $12 per annum in 1805. 1807. 1808. 1809. 1810. 1811.

Tredick, —. N.H. Seaman. Ruth Tredick was pensioned on his service as a privateer at the rate of $36 per annum. 1815. 1816. 1817. 1818. 1819. 1820 increase to $72. 1821. 1822. 1823. 1824. 1825. 1826. 1827. 1828. 1829. 1830. 1831. 1832. 1833. 1834.

Trenchard, Edward.* —. Captain. His widow, Elizabeth Trenchard, was pensioned from 3 Nov. 1824 at the rate of $50 per month. 1835. 1836. 1837. 1839. 1840. 1841. 1842. 1842b. 1845. 1846. She was pensioned again 1 Sep. 1847 at the rate of $50 per month. 1848. 1851.

Trepenny, Francis. Md. Seaman. He was pensioned at the rate of $72 per annum. 1819. 1820. 1821. 1822. 1823. 1824. 1825. 1826. 1827. 1828. He also appeared as Francis Trepanny, Francis Tripanny, and Francis Trepanney.

Trevett, —.* —. Surgeon. His son, Russell Trevett, was pensioned at the rate of $30 per month from 4 Nov. 1822. 1837. 1842. [He was listed as Samuel Trevett in the Old Wars pension index.]

Trimble, —.* —. Sailmaker. His children, John Trimble, Joshua W. Trimble, and Eliza Jane Trimble, were pensioned at the rate of $10 per month from 1 July 1837. 1837. 1839. 1840. 1841. 1842. 1842b. [He was listed as John Trimble in the Old Wars pension index.]

Tromp, —. Penn. Marine. He was lost in the *Epervier* 1 Sep. 1815. His widow, Elizabeth Tromp, received $36 in 1822. 1823. 1824. 1825. 1827. 1828. She also appeared as Elizabeth Trony and Elizabeth Trump.

Truman, John B. Penn. Ordinary Seaman. He was pensioned 5 Feb. 1816 at the rate of $60 per annum. 1819. 1820. 1821. 1822. 1823. 1824. 1825. 1826. 1827. 1828. 1829. 1830. He also appeared as John B. Trueman. He served aboard the *Guerriere*.

Trumbull, James. Mass. Ordinary Seaman. He was pensioned 6 Apr. 1815 at the rate of $60 per annum. 1818. 1819. 1820. 1821. 1822. 1823. 1824. 1825. 1826. 1827. 1828. 1829. 1830. 1835. 1836. 1837. 1839. 1840. 1841. 1842b. 1843. 1844. 1845. 1846. 1847. 1848. 1850. 1851. He was disabled in the Dartmoor Massacre. He also appeared as James Turnbull.

Trump, Philip. Penn. Marine. He perished aboard the *Epervier* 1 Sep. 1815. His widow, Elizabeth Trump, of Lebanon Twp., Lebanon Co., Penn. was paid $36 on 18 Feb. 1820.

Trusty, Samuel.* —. Ship's Cook. His widow, Jane Trusty, was pensioned from 24 July 1839 at the rate of $9 per month. 1840. 1841. 1842. 1842b. 1845. 1846. She was pensioned again 1 Sep. 1847 at the rate of $9 per month. 1848. 1850. 1851.

Tucker, —. —. Master's Mate. His daughter, Rebecca M. Tucker, was pensioned at the rate of $10 per month. 1837. 1842.

Tucker, Samuel. Maine. Captain. He was pensioned by act of Congress 3 Mar. 1821 at the rate of $240 per annum. He was in Mass. in 1824. 1825. 1826. 1827. 1828. 1830. He served in the American Revolutionary War.

Tuille, David. —. Quartermaster. He was pensioned. 1838.

Naval Pensioners of the United States, 1800-1851

Tull, James. Del. Sergeant of Marines. He was pensioned at the rate of $60 per annum. 1818. 1819. 1820. 1822. 1823. 1824. 1825. 1826. 1829. 1830. 1835. 1836. 1837. 1839. 1840. 1841. 1842b. 1843. 1844. 1845. 1846. 1847. 1848. 1850. 1851. He served aboard the schooner *Lawrence* on Lake Erie.

Tully, Philip. Penn. Seaman. He was pensioned 10 Jan. 1816 at the rate of $60 per annum. 1818. 1819. 1820. 1821. 1822. 1823. 1824. 1825. 1826. 1827. 1828. 1829. 1830. 1835. 1836. 1837. 1839. 1840. 1841. 1842b. 1843. 1844. 1845. 1846. 1847. 1848. 1850. 1851. He also appeared as Philip Tulley and Phillips Tulley. He was disabled on Lake Ontario.

Tunstall, George.* —. Seaman. He was pensioned 14 Apr. 1836 at the rate of $3 per month. 1836. 1837. 1839. 1840. 1841. 1842b. 1843. 1844. 1845. 1846. 1847. 1848. 1850. 1851.

Tupper, Charles C.* —. Captain Marines. His widow, Emily C. Tupper, was pensioned from 18 Jan. 1838 at the rate of $20 per month. 1839. 1840. 1841. 1842. 1842b. 1845. 1846. She was pensioned again 1 Sep. 1847 at the rate of $20 per month. 1848. 1850. 1851.

Turner, —. N.Y. Gunner's Mate. Mary Turner was pensioned on his service as a privateer at the rate of $48 per annum. 1815. 1816. 1817. 1818. 1819. 1820 increase to $96. 1821. 1822. 1823.

Turner, Daniel.* —. Captain. His widow, Catharine B. Turner, was pensioned 4 Feb. 1850 at the rate of $50 per month. 1850. 1851.

Turry, George.* —. Boatswain. He was pensioned 9 Aug. 1839 at the rate of $3.33 1/3 per month. 1840. 1841. 1842b. 1843. 1844. 1845. 1846. 1847. 1848. 1850. 1851. He also appeared as George Turrey.

Tuttle, Stephen. N.Y. Seaman. He was pensioned at the rate of $60 per annum. 1818.

Twiggs, Levi.* —. Major Marines. His daughter, Priscilla D. Twiggs, was pensioned. 1837. 1842. His widow, Priscilla Twiggs, was pensioned 18 Sep. 1847 at the rate of $25 per month. 1848. 1850. 1851.

Tyler, Samuel E.* Mass. Seaman. He was pensioned 1 Mar. 1824 at the rate of $48 per annum. 1824. 1825. 1829. 1830. He served on the frigate *United States*.

Tyrrell, William.* Va. Seaman. He was pensioned at the rate of $102 per annum in 1807. 1808. 1809. 1810. 1811.

Tyrrett, Ebenezer.* —. Boatswain's Mate. His widow, Ann Tyrrett, was pensioned 8 Dec. 1846 at the rate of $9.50 per month. 1847. 1848. 1850. 1851. He also appeared as Ebenezer Tyrrell.

Ulrich, George.* —. Sailing Master. His widow, Hannah Ulrich, was pensioned from 6 June 1822 at the rate of $20 per month. 1836. 1837. 1839. 1840. 1841. 1842. 1842b. 1845. 1846. She was pensioned again 1 Sep. 1847 at the rate of $20 per month. 1848. 1850. 1851. She also appeared as Hannah Ulrick.

Underwood, Benjamin. Md. Ordinary Seaman. He was pensioned 24 Apr. 1815 at the rate of $60 per annum. 1816. 1818. 1819. 1820. 1821. 1822. 1823. 1824. 1825. 1826. 1827. 1828. 1829. 1830. 1835. 1836. 1837. 1839. 1840. 1841. 1842b. 1843. 1844. 1845. 1846.

Naval Pensioners of the United States, 1800-1851

1847. 1848. 1850. 1851. He served aboard the frigate *United States*.
Underwood, John.* —. Carpenter's Mate. He was pensioned 16 Aug. 1844 at the rate of $9.50 per month. 1844. 1845. 1846. 1847. 1850. 1851.
Underwood, Joseph A.* —. Lieutenant. His widow, Sarah J. Underwood, was pensioned at the rate of $25 per month 24 July 1840. 1841. 1842. 1842b. 1843. 1844. 1848.
Upham, George. —. Marine. He was pensioned 12 July 1816 at the rate of $3 per month. 1836. 1837. 1838. 1839. 1840. 1841. 1842. 1842b. 1843. 1844. 1845. 1846. 1847. 1848. 1850. 1851. He also appeared as George Upshaw and George Upsham.
Upton, Benjamin. Mass. Commander. He was pensioned as a privateer from 6 Dec. 1812 at the rate of $120 per annum. 1812. 1813. 1814. 1815. 1816. 1817. 1818. 1819. 1820. 1821. 1822. 1823. 1824. 1825. 1826. 1827. 1828. 1829. 1830. 1831. 1832. 1833. 1834. 1835. 1836. 1837 for half a year. He was pensioned from 1 July 1837 at the rate of $10 per month. 1844. 1845. 1846. 1847. 1850.

Vail, N. —. —. He was pensioned as a privateer at the rate of $240 per annum. 1813. 1814. 1815. 1816. 1817. 1818. 1819. 1820 for $180.
Vallence, Isaac. N.Y. Quartermaster. He was pensioned 15 Mar. 1815 at the rate of $96 per month. 1816. 1818. 1819. 1820. 1821. 1822. 1823. 1824. 1825. 1826. 1827. 1828. 1829. 1830. 1835. 1836. 1837. He also appeared as Isaac Valence. He served aboard the *Essex*.
Vallie, William.* N.Y. Marine. He was pensioned 29 Dec. 1828 at the rate of $60 per annum. 1829. 1830. He served aboard the *Warren* under Lt. Hearney.
VanBebber, —. —. Purser. His widow, Betsey C. B. VanBebber, was pensioned at the rate of $20 per month. 1837.
VanBlake, Isaac. Md. Gunner. He was with the flotilla at Baltimore and died in the War of 1812. His widow, Mary VanBlake, was pensioned at the rate of $120 per annum. 1816. 1818. 1819. 1821. 1822. 1824. 1825. 1827. 1828. 1829. She sometimes appeared as Margaret VanBlake.
Vandachenhausen, —.* —. Marine. His daughter, Emily Vandachenhausen, was pensioned at the rate of $3.50 per month from 12 Mar. 1833. 1837. 1839. 1840. 1841. 1842. 1842b. [He was listed as William Vandachenhausen in the Old Wars pension index.]
Vanderfien, —.* —. Ordinary Seaman. His widow, Anna Vanderfien, was pensioned 30 June 1834 at the rate of $5 per month. 1835. 1836. 1837. 1839. 1840. 1841. 1842. 1842b. She also appeared as Anna Vanderfier and Anna Vanderfeen. [He was listed as Lucus Vandefien in the Old Wars pension index.]
Vanderford, Benjamin.* —. Master's Mate. His widow, Elizabeth Vanderford, was pensioned 22 Mar. 1847 at the rate of $10 per month. 1847. 1848. 1850. 1851.
Vanderveer, —. —. —. Lydia Vanderveer was pensioned on his service as a privateer at the rate of $36 per annum. 1813. 1814. 1815. 1816. 1817. 1818. 1819 increase to $72. 1820. 1821 for $3.
Vandervoort, —. —. —. Phoebe Vandervoort was pensioned on his service as a privateer at the

rate of $60 per annum. 1813. 1814. 1815. 1816. 1817. 1818. 1819 increase to $120.
1820. 1821. 1822. 1823. 1824. 1825. 1826. 1827. 1828. 1829. 1830. 1831. 1832.

Vandyke, Charles. N.Y. Ordinary Seaman. He was pensioned at the rate of $60 per month in 1819. 1820. 1821. 1822. 1823. 1824. 1825. 1826. 1827. 1828.

VanHorn, Gabriel.* —. Marine. He was pensioned 23 Dec. 1837 at the rate of $3.50 per month. 1839. 1841. 1842b. 1843. 1844. 1845. 1846. 1847. 1848. 1850. 1851.

Vanhorn, Jesse.* Mass. Marine. He was wounded on Lake Champlain and died 10 Oct. 1814. His widow, Lydia Vanhorn, was pensioned from 10 Oct. 1814 at the rate of $36 per annum. 1824. 1825. 1827. 1828. 1829. 1830. 1835. 1836. 1837. 1839. 1840. 1841. 1842. 1842b. 1845. 1846. She was pensioned again 1 Sep. 1847 at the rate of $3.50 per month. 1848. 1850. 1851.

Vankown, —. N.Y. Seaman. His widow, Rebecca Vankown, received $72 per annum. 1818. 1821. 1822. 1823. She also appeared as Rebecca Vanknown.

VanPatten, —.* —. Ordinary Seaman. His widow, Rachel VanPatten, was pensioned from 23 Apr. 1825 at the rate of $5 per month. 1839. 1840. 1841. 1842. 1842b. [He was listed as Cornelius VanPatten in the Old Wars pension index.]

VanVorst, Richard. —. Quarter Gunner. He was pensioned as a privateer at the rate of $60 per annum. 1829. 1830. 1831. 1832. 1833. 1834. 1835. 1836. He was pensioned from 1 Jan. 1837 for privateer service at the rate of $5 per month. 1837. 1838. 1844. 1845. 1846. 1847. 1850.

VanZandt, Joseph A.* —. 3rd Assistant Engineer. His widow, Gilbertina L. VanZandt, was pensioned 7 Apr. 1849 at the rate of $10 per month. 1850. 1851.

Varney, —.N.H. Master's Mate. Sarah Varney was pensioned on his service as a privateer at the rate of $60 per annum. 1815. 1816. 1817. 1818. 1819. 1820 increase to $120. 1821. 1822. 1823. 1824. 1825. 1826. 1827. 1828. 1829.

Varnum, George. N.Y. Seaman. He was pensioned at the rate of $72 per annum. 1816. 1818. 1819. 1820. 1821. 1822. 1823.

Vaughan, John. —. Surgeon. His widow, Virginia Smith, was pensioned at the rate of $30 per month from 25 Aug. 1848. 1848.

Vaughan, Joseph. N.Y. Ordinary Seaman. He was pensioned at the rate of $60 per annum. 1816. 1818. 1819. 1820. 1821. 1822. He also appeared as Joseph Voughan.

Veal, —. Mass. Gunner. Susan Veal was pensioned on his service as a privateer at the rate of $120 per annum. 1818. 1819. 1820. 1821. 1822. 1823. 1824. 1825. 1826. 1827. 1828. 1829. 1830, 1831. 1832. 1833.

Veazie, —. Mass. Lieutenanat. Sarah Veazie was pensioned on his service as a privateer at the rate of $144 per annum. 1817. 1818. 1819. 1820. 1821. 1822. 1823. 1824. 1825. 1826. 1827 for $120. She also appeared as Sarah Veasie.

Veazy, John. N.H. Quarter Gunner. He was pensioned 10 Dec. 1814 at the rate of $108 per annum. 1818. 1819. 1820. 1821. 1822. 1823. 1824. 1825. 1826. 1829. 1830. He served aboard the *Chesapeake*. His pension was reduced to $4.50 per month effective 18 Mar. 1824.

Venable, William. *—. Boatswain's Mate. He was pensioned 2 May 1834 at the rate of $4.75 per

Naval Pensioners of the United States, 1800-1851

month. 1835. 1836. 1837. 1838. 1839. 1840. 1841. 1842. 1842b. 1843. 1844. 1845. 1846. 1847. 1848. 1850. 1851.

Verry, Edward. —. Ordinary Seaman. He was pensioned 22 June 1842 at the rate of $5 per month. 1844. 1845. 1846. 1847. 1848. 1850. 1851.

Vestlery, David. —. Boatswain. His widow, Margaret S. Vestlery, was pensioned 7 Nov. 1828 at the rate of $10 per month. 1851.

Vial, Nicholas. Md. Commander. He was pensioned as a privateer at the rate of $240 per annum from 10 Mar. 1813. 1820.

Vickers, —. —. Seaman. His son, William Vickers, was pensioned at the rate of $6 per month. 1837. 1842.

Vincent, John S.* —. Captain of the Hold. He was pensioned 5 Apr. 1843 at the rate of $1.75 per month. 1843. 1844. 1845. 1846. 1847. 1848. 1850. 1851.

Vogle, John. Mass. Ordinary Seaman. His pension was $48 per annum. 1816. 1823.

Voorhees, Ralph.* —. Commander. His widow, Harriet Voorhees, was pensioned 27 July 1842 at the rate of $30 per month. 1843. 1844. 1845. 1846. 1851.

Wade, —. —. Lieutenant. His widow, Mary D. Wade, was pensioned at the rate of $25 per month from 15 Nov. 1816. 1837. 1839. 1840. 1841. 1842. 1842b.

Wade, Charles.* Fla. Gunner. His widow, Constance Wade, was pensioned from 27 Feb. 1841 at the rate of $10 per month. 1842b. She had her application rejected prior to 23 Dec. 1848. She was barred under the act of 11 Aug. 1848. She was pensioned 1 Sep. 1847 at the rate of $10 per month. 1850. 1851.

Wagner, William. La. Quarter Gunner. He was pensioned 1 Dec. 1819 at the rate of $108 per annum. 1822. 1824. 1825. 1826. 1827. 1828. 1829. 1830. 1839. 1840. 1841. 1842b. 1843. 1844. 1845. 1846. 1847. 1848. 1850. 1851. He served aboard the schooner *Lynx*.

Wainwright, Robert D. —. Lieutenant Colonel Marines. He was pensioned at the rate of $7.50 per month. 1837. 1838. 1839. 1840. 1841. His widow, Maria M. Wainwright, was pensioned from 6 Oct.1841 at the rate of $30 per month. 1842b. 1843. 1844. 1845. 1846. 1848. 1850. 1851.

Walcot, —. —. —. T. Walcot was pensioned on his service as a privateer at the rate of $36 per annum. 1815. 1816. 1817 for $24.30.

Waldo, Charles F.* Mass. Master's Mate. He was pensioned 18 Mar. 1813 at the rate of $108 per annum. 1816. 1818. 1819. 1820. 1821. 1822. 1823. 1824. 1825. 1826. 1827. 1828. 1829. 1830. 1835. 1836. 1837. He served aboard the *Constitution*. His widow, Sarah V. Waldo, was pensioned from 30 Aug. 1838 at the rate of $20 per month. 1839. 1840. 1841. 1842. 1842b. 1845. 1846. She was pensioned again 1 Sep. 1847 at the rate of $20 per month. 1848. 1850. 1851.

Waldron, James. Conn. Seaman. He was pensioned at the rate of $72 per annum. 1819. 1820. 1821.

Wales, John. —. Seaman. He was pensioned 25 Jan. 1847 at the rate of $1.50 per month. 1847.

Naval Pensioners of the United States, 1800-1851

1848. 1850. 1851.

Walgrove, —. N.Y. Marine. Ellen Walgrove was pensioned on his service as a privateer at the rate of $72 per annum. 1819. 1820. 1821. 1822. 1823. 1824. 1825. 1826. 1827. 1828. 1829 for $12.

Walkington, —. N.Y. Prize Master. Sarah Walkington was pensioned on his service as a privateer at the rate of $60 per annum. 1815. 1816. 1817. 1818. 1819. 1820 increase to $120. 1821. 1822. 1823. 1824. 1825. 1826. 1827. 1828. 1829.

Walkinshaw, Gavin. Mass. Seaman. He was pensioned at the rate of $102 in 1802. 1803. 1804. 1805. 1807. 1808. 1809. 1810. 1811.

Wallace, Alexander.* —. Marine. His widow, Sarah Wallace, was pensioned 14 Jan. 1847 at the rate of $3.50 per month. 1848. 1850. 1851.

Walling, —. —. Seaman. His widow, Catherine Walling, was pensioned from 3 Dec. 1813 at the rate of $6 per month. 1839. 1840. 1841. 1842. 1842b.

Walpole, Henry.* —. Seaman. He was pensioned 2 Oct. 1820 at the rate of $3 per month. 1839. 1840. 1842b. 1843. 1844. 1845. 1846. 1847. 1848. 1850. 1851.

Walsh, James L.* —. Seaman. He was pensioned from 30 Apr. 1837 at the rate of $5 per month. 1838. 1839. His widow, Susan Walsh, had her claim rejected before 10 Jan. 1844. Her husband was pensioned for wounds received in the service. For several years before his death he had left the service. She could not qualify because he did not die in the service or in the line of duty at the time of his death.

Walter, John. Penn. Seaman. He was pensioned 1 Dec. 1813 at the rate of $48 per annum. 1816. 1818. 1819. 1820. 1821. 1822. 1823. 1824. 1825. 1826. 1827. 1828. 1829. 1830. He served aboard the *Enterprise*. He also appeared as John Walton.

Walters, —. Pa. Boatswain. Martha Walters was pensioned on his service as a privateer at the rate of $120 per annum. 1817. 1818. 1819. 1820. 1821. 1822. 1823. 1824. 1825 for $60.

Ward, —. —. —. His widow, Eliza Ward, applied in Mar. 1826 at the rate of $240 per annum.

Ward, Henry.* —. Quarter Gunner. He was pensioned 27 May 1833 at the rate of $9 per month. 1835. 1836. 1837. 1839. 1840. 1841. 1842b. 1843. 1844. 1845. 1846. 1847. 1848. 1850. 1851.

Ward, Joseph. Mass. Seaman. He was pensioned at the rate of $72 per annum. 1816.

Ward, Joseph. Va. Seaman. He was pensioned 1 July 1818 at the rate of $72 per annum. 1818. 1819. 1820. 1821. 1822. 1823. 1824. 1825. 1826. 1827. 1828. 1829. 1830. 1835. 1836. 1837. 1839. 1840. 1841. 1842b. 1843. 1844. 1845. 1846. 1848. 1850. 1851. He served aboard the *Constitution*.

Ward, Joseph.* —. Gunner. His widow, Harriet Ward, was pensioned 1 Jan. 1846 at the rate of $9.50 per month. 1846. 1847. 1848. 1850. 1851.

Ward, Thomas.* —. Captain of Foretop. He was pensioned 14 Jan. 1835 at the rate of $7.50 per month. 1835. 1836. 1837. 1838. 1839. 1840. 1841. 1842. 1842b. 1843. 1844. 1845. 1846. 1847. 1848. 1850. 1851.

Ward, Thomas.* —. Ordinary Seaman. He was pensioned 5 Nov. 1845 at the rate of $5 per month. 1846. 1847. 1848. 1850. 1851.

Ward, William.* —. Seaman. He was pensioned 1 Aug. 1832 at the rate of $6 per month. 1836.

Naval Pensioners of the United States, 1800-1851

1837. 1838. 1839. 1840. 1841. 1842. 1842b. 1843. 1844. 1845. 1846. 1847. 1848. 1850. 1851.

Ward, William.* —. Sailmaker. His widow, Ann Maria Ward, was pensioned 24 May 1849 at the rate of $10 per month. 1850. 1851.

Ware, James.* N.Y. Ordinary Seaman. He was pensioned at the rate of $60 per annum in 1818. 1819. 1820. 1822. 1823. He also appeared as James Wave.

Wares, Samuel. N.Y. Commander in Flotilla. He was killed 28 Nov. 1812 or 4 Dec. 1815 on Lake Ontario. His widow, Charlotte Wares, was pensioned 27 Mar. 1817 at the rate of $20 per month. 1818. 1819. 1821. 1822. 1823. 1824. 1825. 1827. 1829. 1830. 1835. 1836. 1837. 1839. 1840. 1841. 1842. 1842b. 1845. 1846. She also appeared as Charlotte Waves. His rank was also given as Sailing Master. He served aboard the *New York*.

Warner, James.* N.Y. Seaman. He was pensioned 1 Nov. 1818 at the rate of $72 per annum. 1820. 1821. 1822. 1823. 1824. 1825. 1826. 1827. 1829. 1830. He served aboard Gunboat No.165.

Warner, John. Md. Sailing Master. He died at Bladensburg 24 Aug. 1814. His widow, Margaret Warner, was pensioned 1 Feb. 1815 at the rate of $20 per month. 1816. 1818. 1821. 1822. 1823. 1824. 1825. 1827. 1828. 1829. 1830. 1835. 1836. 1837.

Warren, —. —. Marine. His widow, Abigail Warren, was pensioned from 12 Sep. 1812 at the rate of $3.50 per month. 1839. 1840. 1841. 1842. 1842b.

Warren, Nahum.* —. Master. His widow, Martha Warren, was pensioned 10 June 1843 at the rate of $20 per month. 1844. 1845. 1846. 1847. 1848. 1850. 1851.

Washbourne, —. Mass. Seaman. Sarah Washbourne was pensioned on his service as a privateer at the rate of $36 per annum. 1815. 1816. 1817. 1818. 1819. 1820 increased to $72. 1821. 1822. 1823. 1824. 1825. 1826. 1827. 1828. 1829. 1830 for $3.

Waterman, —. N.Y. Commander. Eliza Waterman was pensioned on his service as a privateer at the rate of $120 per annum from 1 Feb. 1815. 1815. 1816. 1817. 1818. 1819. 1820. 1821 increase to $240. 1822. 1823. 1824. 1825. 1826. 1827.

Waters, —. —. —. Charlotte Waters was pensioned on his service as a privateer at the rate of $36 per annum. 1812. 1813. 1814. 1815. 1816. 1817 increase to $72. 1818. 1819. 1820. 1821.

Waters, John.* —. Seaman. He was pensioned 30 Sep. 1838 at the rate of $3 per month. 1839. 1840. 1841. 1842b. 1844. 1845. 1846. 1847. 1848. 1850. 1851.

Waters, John.* N.Y. Ordinary Seaman. He was pensioned 31 May 1824 at the rate of $5 per month. 1827. 1828. 1829. 1830. 1835. 1836. 1837. 1838. 1840. 1841. 1842. 1842b. 1843. 1844. 1845. 1846. 1847. 1848. 1850. 1851. He served aboard the *United States*.

Watson, —. —. —. Sarah Watson was pensioned on his service. 1842.

Watson, —.* —. Boatswain. His son, James A. Watson, was pensioned at the rate of $10 per month. 1837. 1842. [He was listed as James Watson in the Old Wars pension index.]

Watson, Daniel.* —. Carpenter's Mate. He was pensioned 10 May 1838 at the rate of $4.75 per month. 1840. 1841. 1842b. 1843. 1844. 1845. 1846. 1847. 1848. 1850. 1851.

Watson, Henry. Md. Seaman. He was pensioned as a privateer at the rate of $72 per annum from 31 Aug. 1814. 1814. 1815. 1816. 1817. 1818. 1819. 1820. 1821. 1822. 1823. 1824. 1825.

1826 for $55.40.

Watson, Samuel E.* —. Major Marines. He was pensioned at the rate of $18.75 per month. 1837. 1838. 1839. 1840. 1841. 1842b. 1843. His widow, Mary A. Watson, was pensioned 17 Nov. 1847 at the rate of $25 per month. 1848. 1850. 1851.

Watts, Edward.* —. Seaman. He was pensioned from 31 Dec. 1828 at the rate of $3 per month. 1838. 1839. 1840. 1841. 1842b.

Weaver, William A. —. Midshipman. He was pensioned 12 Sep. 1834 at the rate of $9.50 per month. 1836. 1837. 1838. 1839. 1840. 1841. 1842b. 1843. 1844. 1845. 1846. 1847. 1848. 1850. 1851. He also appeared as William W. Weaver.

Webb, —. N.H. Marine Officer. His widow, Nancy Webb, was pensioned on his service as a privateer at the rate of $60 per annum. 1815. 1816. 1817. 1818. 1819. 1820 increase to $120. 1821. 1822. 1823. 1824. 1825. 1826. 1827. 1828. 1829. 1830. 1831. 1832. 1833. 1834.

Webb, James. Md. Apprentice. He perished aboard the *Grampus*. His mother was Elizabeth Webb of Baltimore, Md. on 1 Jan. 1844.

Webb, John.* N.Y. Seaman. He was pensioned 5 Apr. 1822 at the rate of $48 per annum. 1823. 1824. 1825. 1826. 1827. 1828. He served aboard the *Spark*.

Webb, John M.* —. Carpenter. His widow, Julia Webb, was pensioned 16 June 1847 at the rate of $10 per month. 1848. 1850. 1851.

Webb, Richard. Penn. Ordinary Seaman. He was pensioned 1 July 1805 at the rate of $60 per annum. 1807. 1808. 1809. 1810. 1811. 1816. 1818. 1819. 1820. 1821. 1824. 1825. 1827. 1828. 1829. 1830. He served aboard the *Trumbull*.

Webb, Robert. Penn. Ordinary Seaman. He was pensioned at the rate of $60 per annum in 1826.

Webb, Stephen. Mass. Seaman. He served aboard the *Constitution*, was wounded, and died 1 Jan. 1813. His widow, Hannah Webb, was pensioned from 1 Jan. 1813 at the rate of $72 per annum. 1816. 1818. 1820. 1821. 1822. 1823. 1824. 1825. 1827. 1829. 1830. 1835. 1836. 1837. 1839. 1840. 1841. 1842. 1842b.

Webber, Benjamin W.* —. Purser's Steward. His widow, Elizabeth A. Webber, was pensioned 11 Aug. 1848 at the rate of $9 per month. 1850. 1851.

Webster, —. N.H. Lieutenant. Sally Webster was pensioned as a privateer at the rate of $72 per annum. 1815. 1816. 1817. 1818. 1819. 1820 at the rate of $144. 1821. 1822. 1823. 1824. 1825. 1826. 1827. 1828. 1829. 1830. 1831. 1832. 1833. 1834.

Webster, —.* —. Lieutenant. His widow, Electa Webster, was pensioned 25 Aug. 1825 at the rate of $20 per month. 1835. 1836. 1837. 1839. 1840. 1841. 1842. 1842b. [He was listed as Nelson Webster in the Old Wars pension index.]

Webster, John A. —. Sailing Master. He was pensioned 3 Sep. 1814 at the rate of $20 per month. 1835. 1836. 1837. 1839. 1838. 1840. 1841. 1842. 1842b. 1843. 1844. 1845. 1846. 1847. 1848. 1850. 1851. He was pensioned by special act.

Webster, John W.* —. Sergeant Marines. His widow, Lucinda Webster, was pensioned 21 July 1847 at the rate of $6.50 per month. 1850. 1851.

Wedge, John. Md. Quarter Gunner. He was killed at the Navy Yard at Washington by the bursting of a gun 21 Sep. 1813. His widow, Susannah Wedge, received $108 per annum

Naval Pensioners of the United States, 1800-1851

in 1821. 1822. 1823. 1824. 1825. 1827. 1828. 1829. His rank was also given as carpenter.

Wedger, —. —. Mass. Seaman. Rebecca Wedger was pensioned on his service as a privateer at the rate of $72 per annum. 1817. 1818. 1819. 1820. 1821. 1822. 1823. 1824. 1825. 1826. 1827. 1828. 1829. 1830. 1831. 1832 for $36.

Weed, Elijah J.* —. Quartermaster. His widow, Julia Weed, was pensioned from 5 Mar. 1838 at the rate of $20 per month. 1839. 1840. 1841. 1842. 1842b. Her pension was renewed on 5 Mar. 1843 at the rate of $30 per month. 1843. 1845. 1846. 1847. It was renewed again in 1848. 1848. 1850.

Weeks, —. —. —. Cloe Weeks was pensioned on his service as a privateer at the rate of $36 per annum. 1815. 1816. 1817. 1818. 1819. 1820 increased to $72. 1821. 1822. 1823. 1824. 1825. 1826. 1827. 1828. 1829. 1830 for $3.

Weeks, Charles.* —. Seaman. He was pensioned from 23 Feb. 1830 at the rate of $6 per month. 1835. 1836. 1837. 1839. 1840. 1841. 1842b. 1843. 1844. 1845. 1846. 1847. 1848. 1850. 1851. He served aboard the *Constellation*.

Weems, Nathaniel. Md. Surgeon's Mate. He was pensioned at the rate of $180 per annum in 1809. 1810. 1816.

Welch, Thomas.* N.Y. Quarter Gunner. He was pensioned 26 Feb. 1820 at the rate of $144 per annum. 1821. 1822. 1823. 1824. 1825. 1826. 1827. 1828. 1829. 1835. 1836. 1839. 1840. 1841. 1842b. 1843. 1844. 1845. 1846. 1847. 1848. 1850. He also appeared as Thomas Welsh. He served aboard the schooner *Franklin*.

Wells, James. Md. Seaman. He was pensioned 6 Apr. 1815 at the rate of $108 per annum. 1818. 1819. 1820. 1821. 1822. 1823. 1824. 1825. 1826. 1827. 1828. 1829. 1830. He was disabled in Dartmoor Prison.

Wells, John. —. Marine. His application was rejected prior to 17 Jan. 1845. He claimed a pension for long service in the navy and the army. The law made no provision for such. It did not appear that he was ever disabled by wounds, or otherwise, in the service.

Wells, William. N.Y. Seaman. He was pensioned 19 Mar. 1812 at the rate of $72 per annum. 1816. 1818. 1821. 1822. 1823. 1824. 1825. 1826. 1827. 1828. 1829. 1830. He served aboard the *Congress*.

Welsh, Michael. Mass. Ordinary Seaman. He was pensioned 1 Feb. 1824 at the rate of $60 per annum. 1824. 1826. 1828. 1829. 1830. He served aboard the *Boston*.

Welsh, Peter.* —. Seaman. He was pensioned 9 Oct. 1849 at the rate of $3 per month. 1850. 1851.

Welsh, Thomas. —. Ordinary Seaman. He was pensioned 1 Jan. 1822 at the rate of $2.50 per month. 1850.

Welsh, William. Mass. Seaman. He was pensioned 28 Aug. 1815 at the rate of $60 per annum. 1816. 1818. 1819. 1820. 1821. 1822. 1824. 1825. 1826. 1827. 1830. He served aboard the frigate *United States*. He also appeared as William Welch.

Welsh, William. Va. Seaman. He was pensioned 22 Feb. 1830 at the rate of $72 per annum. 1830. He served aboard the *Delaware*.

Welsh, William. Mass. Ordinary Seaman. He was pensioned 1 Jan. 1822 at the rate of $2.50 per month. 1827. 1828. 1837. 1839. 1840. 1841. 1842b. 1844. 1845. 1846. 1847. 1848. 1850.

Naval Pensioners of the United States, 1800-1851

1851.

Welsh, William S.* Penn. Seaman. He was pensioned 1 May 1827 at the rate of $6 per month. 1829. 1830. 1835. 1836. 1837. 1839. 1840. 1841. 1842b. 1843. 1844. 1845. 1846. 1848. 1851. He served aboard the frigate *United States*.

Wents, William S. —. Lieutenant. His children, William A. Wents and Matilda Wents, were pensioned 23 Dec. 1850 at the rate of $25 per month. 1851.

Wentworth, John.* —. Seaman. He was pensioned 16 May 1846 at the rate of $3 per month. 1847. 1848. 1850. 1851.

West, —. —. —. Elizabeth West was pensioned on his service as a privateer at the rate of $72 per annum. 1812. 1813. 1814. 1815. 1816. 1817 increase to $144. 1818. 1819. 1820 for $120.80.

West, —. —. —. Hannah West was pensioned on his service as a privateer at the rate of $72 per annum. 1812. 1813. 1814. 1815. 1816. 1817. 1818 increase to $144. 1819. 1820. 1821. 1822. 1823. 1824. 1825. 1826 for $54.50.

West, Ebenezer.* —. Seaman. He was pensioned 10 Feb. 1849 at the rate of $4.50 per month. 1850. 1851.

West, John W. —. Lieutenant. He was pensioned from 30 Nov. 1830 at the rate of $6.25 per month and on 21 Nov. 1844 at the rate of $9.37 ½ per month. 1839. 1840. 1841. 1842b. 1845. 1846. 1847. 1848. 1850. 1851.

West, Thomas.* —. Seaman. He was pensioned 6 June 1849 at the rate of $6 per month. 1850. 1851.

Westcott, —.* —. Lieutenant. His widow, Elizabeth Westcott, was pensioned at the rate of $25 per month from 25 Mar. 1837. 1837. 1839. 1840. 1842. His orphan, T. G. Wescott, was pensioned at the rate of $25 per month. 1841. 1842b. [He was listed as Hampton Wescott in the Old Wars pension index.]

Weston, —. —. —. His daughter, Sarah Weston, was pensioned. 1837.

Weston, Nathaniel. Mass. Seaman. He was pensioned as a privateer from 1812 at the rate of $36 per annum from 1 Sep. 1812. 1812. 1813. 1814. 1815. 1816. 1817. 1818. 1819. 1820. 1821. 1822. 1823. 1824. 1825. 1826. 1827. 1828. 1829. 1830. 1831. 1832. 1833. 1834. 1835. 1836. 1837 for half a year. He was pensioned from 1 July 1837. 1837. 1838. 1844. 1845. 1846. 1847. 1850.

Westover, Isaac. —. Coxswain. His application was rejected prior to 12 Dec. 1842. He claimed to have been wounded during the Tripolitan War more than twenty-five years ago.

Wetmore, William C.* —. Commander. His widow, Susan W. Wetmore, was pensioned 8 Aug. 1846 at the rate of $30 per month. 1847. 1848. 1850. 1851.

Whamsley, John.* —. Captain Maintop. His widow, Rebecca Whamsley, was pensioned 19 Feb. 1848 at the rate of $7.50 per month. 1850. 1851.

Wharton, —.* —. Colonel Marine Corps. His children, Franklin Wharton, Clifton Wharton, George W. Wharton, William Lewis Wharton, Alfred W. Wharton, and Henry W. Wharton, were pensioned at the rate of $30 per month. 1837. [He was listed as Franklin Wharton in the Old Wars pension index.]

Wheeler, Charles.* —. Seaman. He was pensioned 3 Oct. 1836 at the rate of $3 per month. 1837.

Naval Pensioners of the United States, 1800-1851

1839. 1840. 1841. 1842b. 1843. 1844. 1845. 1846. 1847. 1848. 1850. 1851.

Whelan, Peter. Penn. Marine. He was pensioned 1 Jan. 1806 at the rate of $36 per annum. 1816. 1818. 1819. 1820. 1821. 1822. 1823. 1824. 1825. 1826. 1827. 1828. 1829. 1830. He also appeared as Peter Wheland and as Peter Wheeler. He was disabled as a prisoner at Tripoli.

Wherrin, —. N.H. Carpenter's Mate. Lovey Wherrin was pensioned on his service as a privateer at the rate of $48 per annum. 1815. 1816. 1817. 1818. 1819. 1820 increase to $96. 1821. 1822. 1823. 1824. 1825. 1826. 1827. 1828. 1829.

Whetcroft, —.* —. Sergeant Marines. His widow, Drusilla Whetcroft, was pensioned from 29 Aug. 1834 at the rate of $6.50 per month. 1841. 1842. 1842b. [He was listed as William W. Whetcroft in the Old Wars pension index.]

Whilcom, John.* —. Master-at-Arms. His application was rejected between Mar. 1840 and 1 Jan. 1842. The surgeon who examined his wound declined certifying that his disability would be permanent.

Whipple, Abraham. D.C. Captain. He was pensioned at the rate of $360 per annum. 1816. 1818. 1819. He was a captain in the Revolutionary War.

Whipple, John. N.Y. Quartermaster. He was pensioned at the rate of $108 per annum in 1807. 1808. 1809. 1810. 1811. 1818.

Whipple, Joseph.* —. Marine. His widow, Ann Whipple, was pensioned 13 Oct. 1846 at the rate of $3.50 per month. 1847. 1848. 1850. 1851.

Whitaker, —. Pa. Lieutenant. Elizabeth Whitaker was pensioned on his service as a privateer at the rate of $144 per annum. 1817. 1818. 1819. 1820. 1821. 1822. 1823. 1824. 1825. 1826. 1827 for $72. She also appeared as Elizabeth Whitecot.

White, —. —. Quarter Gunner. His daughter, Deborah White, was pensioned at the rate of $7.50 per month. 1837. 1842.

White, Benjamin.* —. Master-at-Arms. His widow, Elizabeth White, was pensioned at the rate of $9 per month from 18 May 1815. 1837. 1839. 1840. 1841. 1842. 1842b. 1845. 1846. 1848.

White, Charles W.* —. Ordinary Seaman. He was pensioned 17 Feb. 1837 at the rate of $5 per month. 1837. 1838. 1839. 1840. 1841. 1842. 1842b. 1843. 1844. 1845. 1846. 1847. 1848. 1850. 1851.

White, James. Penn. Gunner's Mate. He was pensioned 10 Aug. 1811 at the rate of $108 per annum. 1816. 1818. 1819. 1820. 1821. 1822. 1823. 1826. 1827. 1828. 1829. 1830. He served aboard the *President* and the *Constitution.*

White, John.* —. Seaman. He was pensioned 30 May 1845 at the rate of $4.50 per month. 1845. 1847. 1848. 1850. 1851.

White, John.* —. Seaman. He was pensioned 3 Oct. 1845 at the rate of $6 per month. 1846. 1847. 1848. 1850. 1851.

White, Samuel.* —. Carpenter. His widow, Mary Ann White, was pensioned 20 Aug. 1843 at the rate of $10 per month. 1843. 1844. 1847. 1848. 1850. 1851. He also appeared as Lemuel White.

White, Solomon. N.Y. Seaman. He was pensioned 29 Feb. 1812 at the rate of $48 per annum.

Naval Pensioners of the United States, 1800-1851

1819. 1820. 1821. 1822. 1823. 1824. 1825. 1826. 1827. 1828. 1829. 1835. 1836. 1837. 1839. 1840. 1841. 1842b. 1843. 1844. 1845. 1846. 1847. 1848. 1850. 1851. He served aboard the schooner *President*.

White, Stephen. Md. Prize Master. He was pensioned as a privateer at the rate of $120 per annum from 20 Sep. 1812. 1819. 1820. 1822. 1823 for $46.33.

White, Thomas.* —. Captain Forecastle. He was pensioned 1 May 1835 at the rate of $7.50 per month. 1835. 1836. 1837. 1842. His last payment went to H. Scovell, administrator of his estate, in 1842.

Whitehorn, Daniel.* —. Quarter Gunner. He was pensioned 21 June 1842 at the rate of $7.50 per month. 1842b. 1843. 1844. 1845. 1846. 1847. 1848. 1850. 1851.

Whitehouse, —. —. —. Polly Whitehouse was pensioned on his service. 1842.

Whiteknact, Thomas. N.Y. Boatswain's Mate. He was pensioned at the rate of $114 per annum. 1816.

Whitney, William. La. Seaman. He was pensioned 1 Nov. 1818 at the rate of $96 per annum. 1818. 1819. 1820. 1821. 1822. 1824. 1825. 1826. 1827. 1828. 1829. 1830. 1835. 1836. 1837. 1839. 1840. 1841. 1842b. 1843. 1844. 1845. 1846. 1847. 1848. 1850. 1851. He served aboard the frigate *Essex*.

Whittle, —. —. —. His daughter, Elizabeth B. Whittle, was pensioned. 1837. 1842.

Whittle, John S.* —. Passed Assistant Surgeon. His widow, Sarah Ann Whittle, was pensioned 5 Apr. 1850 at the rate of $22.50. 1850. 1851.

Wickes, —.* —. Surgeon. His son, Silas D. Wickes, was pensioned at the rate of $25 per month from 21 Aug. 1819. 1839. [He was listed as Silas Wicks in the Old Wars pension index.]

Wicks, William. Del. Ordinary Seaman. He was pensioned 4 Aug. 1813 at the rate of $48 per annum. 1816. 1818. 1819. 1820. 1821. 1822. 1823. 1824. 1825. 1826. 1827. 1828. 1829. 1830. 1836. 1837. 1839. 1840. 1841. 1842b. 1843. 1844. 1845. 1846. 1847. 1848. 1850. 1851. He served aboard the *Vixen*.

Wigart, Charles.* —. Captain of the Hold. His widow, Jane Wigart, was pensioned 17 Mar. 1850 at the rate of $7.50 per month. 1850. 1851.

Wiggins, Caleb J. —. Ordinary Seaman. He was pensioned 23 May 1814 at the rate of $3 per month. 1835. 1836. 1837. 1839. 1840. 1841. 1842b. 1843. 1844. 1845. 1846. 1847. 1848. 1850. 1851.

Wilcox, Sylvester.* N.Y. Carpenter's Mate. He served aboard the schooner *Hamilton* and died 8 Aug. 1813 on Lake Ontario. His widow, Marvel Wilcox, was pensioned 1 Mar. 1816. 1818. She was pensioned again 1 Jan. 1821 at the rate of $9.50 per month. 1821. 1822. 1823. 1824. 1825. 1827. 1830. 1835. 1836. 1837. 1839. 1840. 1841. 1842. 1842b. 1845. 1846. She was pensioned again from 1 Sep. 1847. 1848. 1850. She also appeared as Manuel Wilcox. He also appeared as Sylvanus Wilcox. Her name was sometimes carried incorrectly on the rolls as the invalid pensioner himself.

Wiley, Elias. —. Ordinary Seaman. He was pensioned 10 Sep. 1813 at the rate of $2.50 per month. 1837. 1838. 1839. 1840. 1841. 1842. 1842b. 1843. 1844. 1845. 1846. 1847. 1848. 1850. 1851.

Wiley, George.* —. Seaman. He was pensioned 1 Mar. 1837 at the rate of $3 per month. 1839.

Naval Pensioners of the United States, 1800-1851

1840. 1841. 1842b. 1843. 1844. 1845. 1846. 1847. 1848. 1850. 1851.

Wiley, Robert L. —. Ordinary Seaman. He was pensioned 4 May 1846 at the rate of $5 per month. 1846. 1847. 1848. 1850. 1851.

Wilkinson, —. Md. Sailing Master. Mary Wilkinson was pensioned on his service as a privateer at the rate of $144 per annum. 1818. 1819. 1820. 1821. 1822. 1823. 1824. 1825. 1826. 1827. 1828. 1829. 1830. 1831. 1832 for $178.

Wilkinson, Stephen.* —. Passed Midshipman. His widow, Mary Stuart Wilkinson, was pensioned from 14 Nov. 1839 at the rate of $12.50 per month. 1840. 1841. 1842. 1842b. 1846. She was pensioned again 1 Sep. 1847 at the rate of $12.50 per month. 1848. 1850. 1851.

Willard, Ezra H.* —. Sergeant Marine Corps. His widow, Sarah H. [or A.] Willard, was pensioned at the rate of $6.50 per month from 30 May 1837. 1837. 1839. 1840. 1841. 1842. 1842b. 1846.

Williams, A. —. Seaman. He was slain 2 June 1813. He served with the flotilla at Baltimore. His daughter, Hannah Williams, was pensioned at the rate of $10 per month. 1829. 1837. 1842.

Williams, Charles. —. Quartermaster. He was pensioned at the rate of $9 per month. 1837.

Williams, Charles. N.Y. Ordinary Seaman. He was pensioned 7 Feb. 1815 at the rate of $48 per annum. 1816. 1818. 1819. 1820. 1821. 1822. 1823. 1824. 1825. 1826. 1827. 1828. 1829. 1830. He was disabled on Lake Erie.

Williams, Charles. N.Y. Seaman. He was pensioned 4 Dec. 1815 at the rate of $48 per annum. 1824. 1825. 1827. 1828. 1829. 1830. He served aboard the *Shark* or *Spark.*

Williams, Charles.* —. Ordinary Seaman. He was pensioned 4 Aug. 1840 at the rate of $3.75 per month. 1844. 1845. 1846. 1847. 1848. 1850. 1851.

Williams, Francis.* —. Landsman. He was pensioned 15 Jan. 1838 at the rate of $1 per month. 1839. 1840. 1841. 1842b. 1843. 1844. 1845. 1846. 1847. 1848. 1850. 1851.

Williams, George. D.C. Marine. He was pensioned 1 July 1829 at the rate of $72 per annum. 1828. 1830. He served aboard the *Delaware.*

Williams, George. D.C. Seaman. He was pensioned 1 July 1826 at the rate of $108 per annum. 1827. 1829 in Md. 1830. He served on the Chesapeake flotilla.

Williams, Henry.* —. Ordinary Seaman. He was pensioned at the rate of $3 Mar. 1838 at the rate of $5 per month. 1839. 1840. 1841. 1842b. 1843. 1844. 1845. 1846. 1847. 1848. 1850. 1851.

Williams, Henry Raymond.* —. Yeoman. He was pensioned 2 Aug. 1840 at the rate of $7.50 per month. 1841. 1842b. 1843. 1844. 1845. 1846. 1847. 1848. 1850. 1851.

Williams, Jack.* —. Seaman. He was pensioned from 22 Mar. 1828 at the rate of $6 per month. 1839. 1840. 1841. 1842b. 1843. 1844. 1845. 1846. 1847. 1848. 1850. 1851.

Williams, James. N.Y. Ordinary Seaman. He was pensioned at the rate of $60 per annum. 1808. 1809. 1810. 1811. 1818. 1819. 1820. 1821. 1824. 1825. 1826. 1827. 1828. 1829. 1830. He served aboard the *John Adams.*

Williams, James. —. Seaman. He was pensioned 9 Jan. 1847 at the rate of $6 per month. 1847. 1848. 1850. 1851.

Naval Pensioners of the United States, 1800-1851

Williams, James.* —. Seaman. He was pensioned 2 May 1850 at the rate of $3 per month. 1850. 1851.

Williams, Job G. —. First Lieutenant Marine Corps. He was pensioned from 30 June 1828 at the rate of $7.50 per month. 1838. 1839. 1840. 1841. 1842. 1843.

Williams, John. Md. Seaman. He was pensioned at the rate of $6 per month. 1816. 1818. 1820. 1821.

Williams, John. Conn. Seaman. He was pensioned 1 July 1818 at the rate of $72 per annum. 1819. 1820. 1821. 1822. 1823. 1824. 1825. 1826. 1827. 1829. 1830. 1835. 1836. 1837. 1839. 1840. 1841. 1842b. 1843. 1844. 1845. 1846. 1848. 1851. He served aboard the *Hornet.*

Williams, John, 6th.* Penn. Ordinary Seaman. He was pensioned at the rate of $96 per annum. 1819. 1820. 1821. 1822. 1823. 1824. 1825. 1826. 1827. 1828.

Williams, John.* —. First Captain of Foretop. He was pensioned 9 Sep. 1836 at the rate of $1.87 ½ per month. 1838. 1839. 1840. 1841. 1842b. 1843. 1844. 1845. 1846. 1847. 1848. 1850. 1851.

Williams, John.* —. Ordinary Seaman. He was pensioned 1 May 1843 at the rate of $2.50 per month . 1843. 1844. 1845. 1846. 1847. 1848. 1850. 1851.

Williams, Samuel. —. Quartermaster. He was pensioned 1 Sep. 1827 at the rate of $6 per month. 1839. 1840. 1841. 1842b. 1843. 1844. 1845. 1846. 1847. 1848. 1850. 1851.

Williams, Thomas. Mass. Ordinary Seaman. He was pensioned at the rate of $60 per annum in 1810.

Williams, William.* —. Marine. He served aboard the *Delaware.* He was pensioned 1 July 1829 at the rate of $6 per month. 1835. 1836. 1837. 1838. 1839. 1840. 1841. 1842. 1842b. 1843. 1844. 1845. 1846. 1848.

Williams, William F.* —. Seaman. His widow, Elizabeth Williams, was pensioned 17 Aug. 1842 at the rate of $6 per month. 1843. 1844. 1845. 1846. 1847. 1848. 1850. 1851.

Williamson, Charles L. —. Commander. He was pensioned 18 June 1844 at the rate of $40 per month. 1847. 1848.

Williamson, Frederick. Md. Seaman. He was pensioned at the rate of $72 per annum. 1816. 1818. 1819. 1820. 1821. 1822. 1823.

Williamson, J. D.* —. Commander. His children had their application rejected prior to 30 Dec. 1845. There was no law in existence which provided for the children of a deceased navy officer.

Williamson, James. —. Armorer. He was pensioned 29 Aug. 1832 at the rate of $6 per month. 1835. 1836. 1837. 1838. 1839. 1840. 1841. 1842. 1842b. 1843. 1844. 1845. 1846. 1847. 1848. 1850. 1851. He also appeared as James Williams.

Williamson, Samuel.* Penn. Quarter Gunner. He was pensioned 1 Sep. 1827 at the rate of $72 per annum. 1829. 1830. He served aboard the *North Carolina.*

Williamson, Thomas.* —. Surgeon. He was pensioned at the rate of $15 per month. 1837. 1838. 1839. 1840. 1841. 1842b. 1843.

Wills, —. —. Landsman. His widow, Eleanor Wills, was pensioned from 10 Aug. 1800 at the rate of $4 per month. 1837. 1839. 1840. 1841. 1842. 1842b. She also appeared as

Naval Pensioners of the United States, 1800-1851

Eleanor Wells.
Wilson, —. —. —. Ann Wilson was pensioned on his service as a privateer at the rate of $120 per annum. 1812. 1813. 1814. 1815. 1816. 1817. 1818 increase to $240. 1819. 1820. 1821. 1822. 1823. 1824. 1825. 1826 for $16.67.
Wilson, —. —. —. His daughter, Nancy F. Wilson, was pensioned. 1837. 1842.
Wilson, Alexander.* —. Seaman. He was pensioned 13 June 1844 at the rate of $4 per month. 1851.
Wilson, Charles.* —. Quartermaster. He was pensioned from 11 Apr. 1836 at the rate of $9 per month. 1836. 1837. 1838. 1839. 1842.
Wilson, David.* Md. Seaman. He was pensioned 9 July 1816 at the rate of $72 per annum. 1820. 1821. 1822. 1823. 1824. 1825. 1826. 1827. 1828. 1829. 1830. 1836. He was black. He served aboard the *Guerriere*.
Wilson, Enoch.* —. Armorer. His widow, Mary Jane Wilson, was pensioned from 27 July 1841 at the rate of $9 per month. 1842b. 1843. 1844. 1845.
Wilson, George. Va. Quartermaster. He was pensioned 15 Aug. 1829 at the rate of $108 per annum. 1830. He was disabled due to old age and infirmity.
Wilson, George.* —. Seaman. He was pensioned 23 Mar. 1838 at the rate of $6 per month. 1839. 1840. 1841. 1842. 1842b. 1843. 1844. 1845. 1846. 1847. 1848.
Wilson, James. N.Y. Seaman. He was pensioned at the rate of $120 per annum. 1816. 1818.
Wilson, James. N.Y. Quarter Gunner. He was pensioned at the rate of $120 per annum in 1826.
Wilson, James. Penn. Quarter Gunner. He was pensioned 1 Jan. 1820 at the rate of $120 per annum in 1818. 1819. 1820. 1821. 1822. 1823. 1824. 1825. 1826. 1827. 1828. 1829. 1830. He served aboard Gunboat No. 121.
[*N.B.* The three entries *supra* for James Wilson may pertain to two individuals or even one.]
Wilson, James. —. Quartermaster. He was pensioned 15 Aug. 1829 at the rate of $9 per month. 1835. 1836. 1837. 1839. 1840. 1841. 1842b. 1843. 1844. 1845. 1846. 1847. 1848. 1850. 1851. He was disabled by old age and infirmity.
Wilson, James P.* —. Commander. His daughter, Mary Jane Hollins Wilson, was pensioned at the rate of $30 per month 13 Mar. 1848. 1850.
Wilson, John. Md. Seaman. He was pensioned at the rate of $72 per annum. 1820. 1821. 1822.
Wilson, John. N.Y. Ordinary Seaman. He was pensioned at the rate of $60 per annum. 1821. 1822. He appeared as James Wilson in 1821.
Wilson, John. Penn. Seaman. He was pensioned 1 Jan. 1822 at the rate of $72 per annum. 1824. 1826. 1827. 1828. 1829. 1830. He served aboard the frigate *United States*.
Wilson, Richard. N.H. Boatswain. He was pensioned at the rate of $10 per month in 1803. 1804. 1805. 1807. 1808. 1809. 1810. 1811.
Wilson, Robert W. —. Master's Mate. He was pensioned 7 Mar. 1831 at the rate of $5 per month. 1835. 1836. 1837. 1838. 1839. 1840. 1842. He also appeared as Robert M. Wilson.
Wilson, William. —. Seaman. His widow, Catharine Wilson, was pensioned 13 June 1845 at the rate of $6 per month. 1850. 1851.
Wines, James. —. Seaman. He was pensioned 28 Mar. 1824 at the rate of $6 per month. 1835.

Naval Pensioners of the United States, 1800-1851

1836. 1837. 1839. 1840. 1841. 1842b. 1843. 1844. 1845. 1846. 1847. 1848. 1850. 1851.
Winn, James. Penn. Seaman. He was killed 28 Mar. 1814 at Valparaiso. He served aboard the *Essex*. His widow, Mary Winn, and their son, James Winn, received $72 in 1822. 1823. 1824. 1825. 1827. 1828. 1829. She also appeared as Mary Wine and Mary Wind and her son as James Wine. There was seemingly also a minor heir Mary Winn.
Winn, Timothy.* —. Purser. His widow, Rebecca Winn, was pensioned from 18 Feb. 1836 at the rate of $20 per month. 1836. 1837. 1839. 1840. 1841. 1842. 1842b. 1845. 1846. She was pensioned again 1 Sep. 1847 at the rate of $20 per month. 1848. 1850. 1851.
Wise, Andrew.* —. Seaman. He was pensioned 13 Dec. 1850 at the rate of $4.50 per month. 1851.
Wise, George C. —. Purser. His widow, Catharine Wise, was pensioned from 20 Nov. 1824 at the rate of $20 per month. 1835. 1836. 1837. 1839. 1840. 1841. 1842. 1842b. 1845. 1846. She was pensioned again 1 Sep.1847 at the rate of $20 per month. 1848. 1850. 1851.
Wish, —.* —. Lieutenant. His widow, Mary Wish, was pensioned from 30 June 1834 at the rate of $25 per month. 1836. [He was listed as John Wish in the Old Wars pension index.]
Woalfort, Thomas.* N.Y. Seaman. He was pensioned 1 Jan. 1827 at the rate of $72 per annum. 1829. 1830. 1835. 1836. 1837. He also appeared as Thomas Woolfort. He served aboard the *Erie*.
Wolfenden, John.* —. Seaman. He was pensioned 3 Mar. 1843 at the rate of $8.58 1/3 per month. 1843. 1844. 1845. 1846. 1847. 1848. 1850. 1851. He also appeared as John Wolfender.
Wolfley, Lewis.* —. Surgeon. His children, William J. Wolfley and Lewis Wolfley, were pensioned 21 July 1844 at the rate of $30 per month. 1848. 1850. 1851. He also appeared as Lewis Wolfey.
Wolfrom, John.* N.Y. Quarter Gunner. He was pensioned at the rate of $108 per annum. 1827. 1828. 1829. He served aboard the schooner *John Adams*.
Wood, Elijah. —. Quartermaster Marines. His widow, Julia Wood, was pensioned 5 Mar. 1848 at the rate of $30 per month. 1851.
Wood, Harry P. T.* —. Passed Midshipman. His widow, Edna Maria Wood, was pensioned from 9 Oct. 1836 at the rate of $12.50 per month. 1837. 1839. 1840. 1841. 1842. 1842b. 1845. 1846.
Wood, John. Md. Seaman. He was pensioned as a privateer at the rate of $60 per annum from 25 Mar. 1813. 1813. 1814. 1815. 1816. 1817. 1818. 1819. 1820 for $30.
Wood, John.* —. Seaman. He was pensioned 8 Oct. 1846 at the rate of $2.33 1/3 per month. 1847. 1848. 1850. 1851.
Wood, John.* —. Quarter Gunner. His widow, Mary Wood, was pensioned 23 Dec. 1842 at the rate of $7.50 per month. 1844. 1845. 1846. 1847. 1848. 1850. 1851.
Wood, Owen.* —. Marine. His widow, Elizabeth Wood, was pensioned 9 May 1843 at the rate of $3.50 per month. 1843. 1844. 1846. 1847. 1848. 1850. 1851.
Wood, William. Mass. Seaman. He was pensioned 29 July 1814 at the rate of $72 per annum. 1816. 1818. 1819. 1820. 1821. 1822. 1824. 1825. 1826. 1827. 1828. 1829. 1830. He served aboard the *Essex*.

Naval Pensioners of the United States, 1800-1851

Woodbury, Peter. Mass. Quartermaster. He was pensioned 18 Mar. 1813 at the rate of $108 per annum. 1816. 1818. 1819. 1820. 1821. 1822. 1823. 1824. 1825. 1826. 1827. 1828. 1829. 1830. 1835. 1836. 1837. 1839. 1840. 1841. 1842b. 1843. 1844. 1845. 1846. 1847. 1848. 1850. 1851. He served aboard the *Constitution*.

Woodhouse, James.* —. Seaman. He was pensioned 17 Mar. 1836 at the rate of $6 per month. 1836. 1837. 1839. 1840. 1841. 1842b. 1843. 1844. 1845. 1846. 1847. 1848. 1850. 1851.

Woodington, James.* Md. Quarter Gunner. He was pensioned at the rate of $108 per annum. 1821. 1822. 1823.

Woodruff, —. —. —. Sarah Woodruff was pensioned on his service. 1842.

Woods, —.* —. Boatswain. His son, John Woods, was pensioned at the rate of $10 per month from 1 Jan. 1839. 1839. 1840. 1841. 1842. 1842b. [He was listed as John Woods in the Old Wars pension index.]

Woods, —.* —. Boatswain. His widow, Margaret Woods, was pensioned from 31 Jan. 1836 at the rate of $10 per month. 1836. 1837. [He was listed as John Woods in the Old Wars pension index.]

Woods, Robert.* —. Seaman. He was pensioned 31 Dec. 1836 at the rate of $3 per month. 1838. 1839. 1840. 1841. 1842b. 1843. 1844. 1845. 1846. 1847. 1848. 1850. 1851.

Woolcot, —. —. —. Thirza Woolcot was pensioned on his service as a privateer at the rate of $6 per month from 1 Jan. 1815.

Woolford, William. Md. Seaman. He was pensioned at the rate of $72 per annum. 1816. 1818. 1819. 1820. 1821.

Woolsey, Melancthon T.* —. Captain. His widow, Susan C. Woolsey, was pensioned from 18 May 1838 at the rate of $50 per month. 1839. 1840. 1841. 1842. 1842b. 1845. 1846. She was pensioned again 1 Sep. 1847 at the rate of $50 per month. 1848. 1850. 1851.

Woolsey, William G.* —. Lieutenant. He was pensioned from 22 Oct. 1828 at the rate of $8.33 ½ per month. 1838. 1839. 1840. His widow, Ellen Woolsey, was pensioned on his service at the rate of $25 per month from 25 Oct. 1840. 1840. 1842. 1842b. 1843. 1844. 1848.

Worth, Algernon S.* —. Lieutenant. His widow, Margaret C. Worth, was pensioned from 3 Feb. 1841 at the rate of $25 per month. 1841. 1842. 1842b. 1845. 1846. She was pensioned again 1 Sep. 1847 at the rate of $25 per month. 1848. 1850. 1851.

Wright, James B.* —. Quartermaster. He was pensioned 1 May 1831 at the rate of $9 per month. 1835. 1836. 1837. 1838. 1839. 1840. 1841. 1842. 1842b. 1843. 1844. 1845. 1846. 1847. 1848. 1850. 1851.

Wright, John. N.Y. Quarter Gunner. He was pensioned 1 Jan. 1818 at the rate of $60 per annum. 1819. 1820. 1821. 1822. 1824. 1826. 1827. 1828. 1829. 1830. He served aboard the *Hornet*.

Wright, John. —. Quarter Gunner. He was pensioned from 6 Sep. 1835 at the rate of $6 per month. 1839. 1840. 1841.

Wright, John. —. Quarter Gunner. He was pensioned 7 Nov. 1836 at the rate of $5.62 ½ per month. 1835. 1836. 1837. 1838. 1839. 1840. 1841. 1842. 1842b. 1843. 1844. 1845. 1846. 1847. 1848. 1850. 1851.

Wright, John.* N.Y. Ordinary Seaman. He was pensioned 1 May 1822 at the rate of $60 per

Naval Pensioners of the United States, 1800-1851

annum. 1823. 1824. 1825. 1826. 1827. 1828. 1829. 1830. 1835. 1836. 1842. 1842b. 1843. 1844. 1845. 1846. 1847. 1848. 1850. 1851. He served aboard the *Franklin*.

Wright, Reuben. R.I. Carpenter's Mate. He was disabled on Lake Erie. He was pensioned 30 Aug. 1814 at the rate of $96 per annum. 1818. 1819. 1820. 1821. 1822. 1823. 1824. 1825. 1826. 1827. 1828. 1829. 1830. 1835. 1836. 1837. 1839. 1840. 1841. 1842. 1842b. 1843. 1844. 1845. 1846. 1847. 1848. 1850. 1851.

Wright, William.* —. Seaman. He was pensioned 31 Aug. 1832 at the rate of $3 per month. 1837. 1838. 1839. 1840. 1841. 1842. 1842b. 1843. 1844. 1845. 1846. 1847. 1848. 1850. 1851.

Wurts, William A.* —. Lieutenant. His widow, Matilda Wurts, was pensioned 6 Feb. 1847 at the rate of $25 per month. 1847. 1848. 1850. He also appeared as William Wurtz.

Wyer, William. Mass. Sailmaker. He served aboard the schooner *Saratoga* and was killed 11 Sep. 1814. His widow, Margaret Wyer, was pensioned at the rate of $120 per annum. 1816. 1818. 1819. 1820. 1821. 1822. 1823. 1824. 1825. 1827. 1829.

Wyman, Joshua.* —. Seaman. He was pensioned 29 Nov. 1842 at the rate of $6 per month. 1843. 1844. 1845. 1846. 1847. 1848. 1850. 1851.

Yarnall, Abner H.* —. Carpenter's Mate. His widow, Ann T. Yarnall, was pensioned from 30 Apr. 1837 at the rate of $9.50 per month. 1841. 1842. 1842b. She was pensioned again 1 Sep. 1847 at the rate of $9.50 per month. 1850. 1851.

Yarnall, John J. Penn. Lieutenant. He perished aboard the *Epervier* 1 Sep. 1815. He was the son of Mordecai and Phebe Yarnall. His sister and brother-in-law were Elizabeth Bolton and Aquila M. Bolton. His widowed mother was paid $140 on 28 May 1817.

York, —. —. —. Sarah York was pensioned on his service as a privateer at the rate of $37 per annum. 1812. 1813. 1814. 1815. 1816. 1817 increase to $72. 1818. 1819. 1820. 1821. 1822. 1823. 1824. 1825. 1826. 1827 for $54.

York, Richard G.* —. Seaman. He was pensioned 13 Jan. 1839 at the rate of $3 per month. 1842b. 1843. 1844. 1845. 1846. 1847. 1848. 1850. 1851.

Yorkley, T. —. —. He was pensioned at the rate of $36 per annum. 1814. 1815. 1816. 1817. 1818. 1819. 1820. 1821. 1822. 1823. 1824. 1825. 1826. 1827. 1828 for $7.10.

Yost, John.* —. Marine. He was pensioned 13 July 1847 at the rate of $2.33 1/3 per month. 1848. 1850. 1851.

Young, —. —. Sergeant Marines. His son, Thomas A. Young, was pensioned at the rate of $12.50 from 7 July 1835. 1837. 1839. 1840. 1841. 1842. 1842b.

Young, Charles.* Md. Private Marine. He was pensioned 1 Apr. 1805 at the rate of $36 per annum. 1805. 1807. 1808. 1809. 1810. 1811. 1816 in D.C. 1818. 1819. 1820. 1821. 1822. 1823. 1824. 1825. 1826. 1827. 1828. 1829. 1830. He served aboard the *Constitution*.

Young, Charles. Mass. Seaman. He was killed 28 Nov. 1812 on Lake Ontario. His widow, Abigail Young, was pensioned 4 Oct. 1814 at the rate of $72 per annum. 1816. 1820.

1821. 1822. 1824. 1825. 1827. 1830.

Young, John. N.Y. Quartermaster. He was pensioned again 20 Dec. 1824 at the rate of $108 per annum. 1816. 1818. 1819 in Penn. 1825. 1826. 1827. 1829. 1830. He served aboard the *Argus*.

Young, John J. —. Lieutenant. He was pensioned 8 Dec. 1834 at the rate of $25 per month. 1835. 1836. 1837. 1838. 1839. 1840. 1841. 1842b. 1843.

Young, Peter. Md. Quartermaster. He was pensioned 10 May 1811 at the rate of $72 per annum. 1816. 1818. 1819. 1820. 1821. 1822. 1824. 1825. 1826. 1827. 1828. 1829. 1830. He served aboard the *Vixen*.

Zellweger, —. —. Surgeon. His widow, Eliza Zellweger, was pensioned at the rate of $35 per month. 1837. 1842. She also appeared as Eliza Zelweger.

Naval Pensioners of the United States, 1800-1851

Index

Abbett
    Samuel 1
Abbott
    R. 19
    Robert 19
Achmuty
    Louisa 1
Ackerman
    Mary 2
Ackins
    Hannah 1
Adams
    Elizabeth 2
    Hannah 2
    Sally 1
    Sarah 1
    Thomas W. 1
Adden
    Alice B. 3
    Charles H. 3
Adee
    Amelia K. 2
Agar
    Mary E. 2
Aggens
    Frederick 2
Aikins
    Andrew J. 1,7
Akerman
    Mary 2
Albron
    George 3
Alcorn
    James 3
Alcutt
    Mary 3
Alden
    Alice B. 3
Alexander
    Eliza Jane 3
Allcom
    James 3
Allen
    -----, Lt. 55
    Lydia 4
    Mary 4
Allester
    Isaac 4

Alleston
    Isaac 4
Allinson
    Mary 4
Allison
    Mary 4
Alliston
    Mary 4
Ames
    Eliza J. 72
Amies
    Sally 6
Anderson
    Ann 5
    Ann E. 5
    Benjamin F. 5
    Catharine 5
    Emma 5
    James W. 5
    Joseph P. 5
    Laura V. 5
    Sarah Ann 5
    Sophia 5
    Virginia N. 5
    William 5
Andrews
    Cornelia 5
    Nancy L. 6
    Pamela 5
Andrus
    Robert 6
Angus
    -----, Lt. 81
    Ann W. 6
Annis
    Sarah 6
Anthony
    Anna 6
Appleton
    Abigail 6
Arbunkle
    William 6
Archbold
    Hannah 6
    J. A. B. 6
    Mary 7
Arche
    John 7

Archer
    E. M. 7
    Eliza M. 7
    Mary P. 7
    Richard 7
Ardis
    Ann 7
    Elizabeth 7
    Emma 7
    John 7
Arkins
    Andrew J. 1
    Hannah 7
Arlett
    Mary E 7
Armistead
    Catherine L 7
Armitage
    Elizabeth 7
    Samuel 7
Armstrong
    Ann E. 7
    Betsey 7
    Franklin 7
    George W. 7
    John 7
    Lawrence 7
    Thomas 7
    Thomas P. 7
    Venerado 7
    Virginia 7
    William 7
Arundel
    Margaret 7
Arundell
    Robert 7
Ashton
    Lawrence 8
Aspelin
    Robert 8
Asperlin
    Mary 8

Naval Pensioners of the United States, 1800-1851

Atkins
- James 8
- Joseph 8
- Sarah 8

Atwood
- Martha Ann 8
- Mathias C. 8

Auchmuty
- Louisa 1

Audricour
- Peter 126
- Richard Green ... 126

Audricourd
- Mary 126

Avery
- Caroline 8

Baab
- Christine 8

Babbit
- Julianna S. 8
- Maria 8
- Mary J. 8

Bache
- Eliza C. 9

Bacon
- Frederick A. 9
- Sarah A. 9

Badger
- -----, Rev. 59
- Catherin 33
- Catherine 9
- Peter 33

Bailey
- Abigail 9
- Ellen 9
- Sarah 9

Bainbridge
- -----, Capt. 6
- Susannah 9

Baker
- Jane 10

Baldwin
- Elizabeth H. 10
- George 10
- Isaac 10
- Lydia 10
- Margaretta 10
- Martha 10

- William 10

Ball
- Nancy 10

Ballagh
- Mary 10

Bank
- Grace 11

Banks
- Elizabeth 11
- Grace 11
- Joseph Potter 11

Barber
- Susan 11

Bardeen
- John 29

Barnard
- Hannah 12
- John 12
- Sarah 12

Barndollar
- Harriet D. 12

Barnes
- Dominick 29
- Elizabeth 12

Barnewall
- George 12
- Mary 12
- Peter 12

Barney
- ----, Commodore . 107
- Harriet 12

Barns
- Dominick 29

Barnwell
- Mary 12

Barrett
- Adelaide A. 13
- Hannah S. 13
- Samuel S. W. 12

Barron
- Ida 13
- Joseph 13
- Samuel 13

Barry
- Mary 13
- Polly 13
- Richard F. 13
- Robert T. 13

- Susannah E. 13

Bartholomew
- Julia Ann 13

Bartlett
- Abijah 14
- Elizabeth 14
- Mary P. 14
- William G. 14

Barton
- George 30

Bassett
- George 14
- Henry W. 14

Basson
- William 145

Bateman
- James 143

Bates
- Sally 14
- Sarah 14

Bay
- Gratia 15

Bayne
- William 9

Beadle
- Emily 15

Beale
- Emily 15

Beaty
- John 15

Bebee
- Patty 15

Beckford
- Eleanor 18
- Elizabeth 15
- William 15

Beeler
- Elizabeth 15

Beers
- Augustin P. 15
- Catherine M. 15

Beeves
- Ellen 16
- Jane 16

Beevis
- Jane 16

Beggs

197

Naval Pensioners of the United States, 1800-1851

Bell
- Sarah 16
- Charles H. 163
- Gilbert 16
- James 16
- John 16
- Marcellus 16
- Margaret 16
- Margaret E. 16
- Maria 16
- Mary Jane 16
- Phillis 16
- Sophia 16

Bellingham
- Elizabeth 16

Belmore
- Lucy 16

Bennet
- Anna 16

Bennett
- Huldah 16

Bentley
- Ann E. 17
- Michael 17

Beondi
- Antonio 18

Berchmore
- Juliana 18

Bergamer
- Jane 17
- Joseph 17

Bergen
- James 17
- William E. 17

Berger
- Peter 17

Bernard
- Peter 12

Berry
- Caroline M. 17
- Elizabeth E. A. ... 17
- John 17
- Mahala 17
- Sarah 18
- William 17

Beverly
- Henrietta B. 18

Bickford
- Eleanor 18

Biddle
- J. 142

Birchmore
- Juliana 18

Bishop
- Elizabeth 18
- Harriet 18

Bispham
- Alleta 19

Black
- Winney B. 19

Blade
- James 19
- James K. 19

Blake
- Letitia 19

Blakely
- Edna M. 20
- Jane Ann 19
- Udna M. 19

Blakslee
- John 19
- Julia Ann 19

Blaskley
- Abraham 19

Blethen
- Nathaniel 20

Bliss
- Frederick 20
- Marianna F. 20
- Martha 20
- Nathaniel 20
- Thomas J. P. 20

Bliven
- Ann 20

Bliver
- Ann 20

Blossom
- Betsey 20

Blunt
- Mary 20

Boerum
- Emily 20

Boggs
- Margaret M. 20
- William 9

Bolton
- Aquila M. 194
- Mary H. 20

Boomer
- D. 24

Booth
- Thomas A. 21
- Waller M. 21
- Waller S. 21
- Walter M. 21
- William L. 21

Boower
- David 20

Bostwick
- Lucy 21
- William W. 21

Boughan
- Eliza H. 21
- Elizabeth K. 21

Bowie
- Belinda 21
- Cecile 21

Bowne
- Sarah 22

Boyd
- Mary 22
- Mary Ann 22
- Peter 21
- Rosanna 22

Bradlee
- Eliza 22

Bradley
- Frances L. 22

Brannan
- John 22, 23

Brazier
- Hannah 23

Breckenridge
- Sarah 23

Breese
- Lucy 23

Brett
- Ellen 23

Brice
- Nancy 23

Briggs
- Nancy 23, 150

Bright
- Eliza 23

Naval Pensioners of the United States, 1800-1851

Brimblecom
    Hannah 23
Brimblecomb
    David 23
    Sarah 23
Brimblecome
    Hannah 23
Brinnisholtz
    Priscilla 24
Brooke
    Elizabeth 24
Brooks
    Betsey 24
Broom
    Mary E. 24
Broomer
    David 20
    David 20
Broughton
    Elizabeth 24
    John 24
Brown
    ----- 137
    Alexander 24
    Ann 24, 26
    Ann Eliza 24
    Benjamin 25
    Bethiah D. 126
    Collen 25
    Colton 25
    Eliza L. 24
    Emma 24
    Isaac C. 24
    Isabella 24
    James 24
    John 106
    John 24
    Lydia 25
    Margaret 24
    Maria E. 24
    Mary 24
    Mary E. 25
    Mary O. 25
    Morris 24
    Richard 24
    William 24
Browne
    Elizabeth 26, 27
Browning
    Leuright 27

    Lewright 27
Brum
    Susannah 27
Bryant
    Samuel 27
Buck
    Elizabeth 28
    Sophia H. 28
Buckley
    David Z. 28
    Eleanor 28
    James S. 28
    Thomas 28
Budd
    Charles H. 28
    Thomas 28
Bun
    Thomas 30
Bunch
    Daniel 28
Bundick
    Catherine 28
Burchmore
    Juliana 18
Burchstead
    Nabby 28
Burdett
    Mary 29
Burk
    Edward 29
Burke
    P. 67
Burnee
    Dominick 29
Burnes
    Dominick 29
Burns
    Daniel 29
    Elizabeth 29
    Mary 29
Burrell
    Lemuel 30
    Martha 30
Burvell
    Martha 30
Bury
    Mahala 17
Bush
    Sarah 30
Busvine

    Elizabeth A. 30
Butler
    Phebe 30
Butman
    T. 23
Butterfield
    Eliza 31
Byrne
    Ann 31
Cahill
    Bartholomew 31
    Mary J. 31
Cain
    Anna 31
Calalano
    Salvadore 35
Caldwell
    Elizabeth J. 31
    Hannah 31
    Hester 31
    William M. 31
Cale
    S. 32
Callamore
    Hannah 32
    Maria J. 32
Campbell
    Ann D. 32
    Isabella 32
    William 32
Cantrell
    William 32
Cape
    Isabella 32
Cardevan
    Edward 45
Cardeven
    Edward 45
Carey
    Dennis 35
Carleton
    Benjamin F. 33
Carlisle
    Nancy 33
Carlton
    Benjamin L. 33
Carman
    Frances 33
Carmick

Naval Pensioners of the United States, 1800-1851

Catharine 33	William 36	Maria 38
Margaret 33	Cavilier	Chritchet
Carmuck	Maria J. 49	Susannah 48
Catherine 33	Cerner	Clapp
Carpenter	Amasa 43	Luretta C. 38
Ann 33	Cernon	Clark
Catharine 33	Elizabeth 36	Andrew 38
Carr	James 36	Ann 38
Ann 34	Chadbourne	Christian 39
Burroughs E. 33	Sarah 36	H. 69
Ellen 33	Chaddock	James 39
John 34	Mary 36	Margaret T. 38
John A. 33	Chaldwell	Mary 39
John G. 33	John 31	Phoebe A. P. 38
Julia 34	Chalmers	Thomas J. 39
Sarah 34	Andrew 36	Clarke
Carreia	Chamberlain	John 39
Eleanor 49	Charles R. 36	Claxton
Cars	Margaret T. 36	Redelphine 39
Ellen 33	Chambers	Rodolphine 39
Carson	Elizabeth 36	Clementson
George 35	Chandler	John 40
George 36	Elizabeth E. 37	Sarah 40
Carswell	Chaplin	Clifton
Eliza Ann 34	John C. 36	Alfred Wharton ... 40
Samuel 34	Chapman	Clinton
Carter	Margaret 37	Charlotte 40
Fanny 34	Chardelle	Cloud
Jane 34	James 37	Eliza M. 40
Leah 34	Mary 37	Clough
Carter	Chase	Sarah A. 40
Harriet 34	Margaret 37	Clunet
Cary	Chauncey	Anna Maria 40
Dennis 33	Catherine 37	Clunett
Cash	Cheever	Ann M. 40
Elizabeth 35	Mary 37	Cluret
Cassin	Chew	Ann M. 40
Eliza 35	Benjamin 37	Coates
Fanny 35	Catherine 37	Russel 40
George 36	Childs	Cobert
John 35	Enos R. 37	Sarah 40
Mary A. 35	Christie	Cocke
Casted	Daniel 38	Ann V. 40
Lucinda 35	Christopher	Eliza 41
Caswell	Mercy G. 38	Eliza H. 41
Mary M. 35	Christophers	Eliza W. 41
Polly 35	George 38	Samuel B. 41
Catalano	Christy	Thomas 40
Martha 35	Caroline 38	Colby
Cathell	John W. 38	Louisa 41

Naval Pensioners of the United States, 1800-1851

Cole
    Elizabeth 41
    Elizabeth J. 42
    John David 41
Coleman
    Elizabeth 42
    Margaret 42
    Nancy 42
Collins
    Ann D. 42
Collinson
    Francis 43
Collison
    Catharine 42
Colluic
    John 42
Colston
    Samuel 43
Colter
    William 42
Colter
    James 43
Colton
    Cornelia P. 43
    Rebecca A. 43
    Samuel 46
Combs
    Essey 156
    George 44
Comyn
    James 45
Conchlin
    Zachariah 43
Concklin
    Mary 43
    Zachariah 43
Connor
    David 43
Conrad
    Ann 44
Conway
    -----, Dr. 34
    Charles 44
    Charles W. 44
    Fanny S. 44
Cook
    Andrew B. 44
    Clarissa 44
    Frances F. 44
    Frances T. 44

Cooke
    Frances F. 44
    Sarah Ann 44
Coomes
    George 44
Coon
    Eleanor 44
Cooper
    Dorothea 45
    Dorothy 45
    Eliza 44
    Elizabeth 45
    Jane A. 45
    Rebecca G. 44
    Sophia 81
    William M. 44
Cope
    William 33
Copp
    Margaret 45
Corbett
    S. 45
Corbitt
    Eunice 45
Corey
    -----, Dr. 33
Corlette
    Susan 45
Cornell
    Mary 45
    Mary W. 45
Corner
    Amasa 43
Corning
    James 45
Correia
    Eleanor 45
Coruger
    James 45
Corwer
    Amasa 43
Cotter
    William 42
Cotton
    Rebecca A. 46
Coulter
    Alexander M. 46
    Joseph H. 46
    Mary Ann 46
    Sarah 46

Cousins
    Delia 46
    Emeline 46
    John 46
Covell
    Ethalindal 46
Covenhaven
    James 46
    William 46
Covenhoven
    Francis 46
Covenhover
    Francis 46
Covington
    Caroline L. 46
Cowan
    Margaret 47
Cowell
    Abigail 47
Cowen
    Margaret 47
    William S. 47
Cox
    Eleanor 47
    Ellen 47
    Emma M. 47
Coxe
    Ellen 47
Crain
    Ann 47
    Anna 31
Crane
    Susan M. 47
Crauford
    Thomas 47
Crawford
    Mary 47
Creighton
    Harriet 47
Crickett
    Susannah 48
Cristopher
    Mercy C. 38
Cristophers
    George 38
Critchet
    John 48
    Susanna 48
Critchett
    Susannah 48

Naval Pensioners of the United States, 1800-1851

Cropper
    Isaac 143
Cross
    Celia 48
Crow
    Margaret Ann 48
Crowninshield
    Harriet 48
Crutchet
    John 48
    Susanna 48
Cummings
    Jane 48
    Jenny 48
    Margaret 48
    Marian 48
    William 48
Cummins
    Margaret 48
Cumpston
    Lucy 48
Cunningham
    Bridget 49
    Edward T. [or F.] . 48
    Elizabeth 49
    John R. 48
    Wesley 49
    William B. 48
Curillier
    Maria J. 49
Currace
    Eleanor 49
Curraeil
    Antonia 49
    Antonio 49
Currell
    Margaret 49
Currier
    Edward 49
    Elizabeth 49
    Fanny 49
    Mercy 49
    Solomon 34
Cushley
    Mary 49
Cuthbert
    Jesse 159
Cutler
    Jesse 159
Cuvillier
    Maria J. 49
Daggett
    Laura P. 50
Dale
    John P. 50
    William H. 50
Daley
    Elizabeth 50
Dallas
    Mary 50
Danagh
    Margaret 50
Danford
    Jacob 50
    Sally 50
Darragh
    Alexander P. 50
Darrah
    Margaret P. 50
Davey
    Thomas 55
    Waitstill C. 51
Davidson
    Catherine 51
    William 51
Davis
    Abijah 52
    Ann 52
    Charlotte 51
    Eliza 139
    Elizabeth C. 52
    Francis A. 52
    Martha 51
    Mary 51
    Mary Elizabeth ... 52
    Mary Frances 51
    Reliance 51
    Samuel 51
    Sarah 51, 52
    Susan 53
    Teresa 51
    William L. 52
Day
    Hannah 53
    Rebecca 53
Dean
    Hannah 53
    Samuel 53
Dearborn
    Abigail 53
Decatur
    Susan 53
Deignan
    Elizabeth 54
Deigrian
    Peter 54
Dellsil
    Mary 144
Demarest
    Emma 54
    John 54
Denham
    John E. 54
    Mary Ann 54
    Prudence 54
    Thomas S. 54
Denham
    John 54
Denison
    Eliza A. K. [or R.]
    54
    Henry 54
Dennis
    Sarah 54
Dennison
    Eliza A. R. 54
    Elmina Virginia ... 55
    Mary Ellen 55
    Susan 55
Denny
    John 54
    Penelope 55
Dent
    Elizabeth Ann 55
    John H. 55
Denton
    Margaret F. 55
Denvers
    Daniel 50
    David 50
Dern
    Jacob 57
Desha
    Franklin Wharton
    55
    Margaret Frances .. 55
Dever
    Ellen 55
    John 55

Naval Pensioners of the United States, 1800-1851

Dewey
    Waitstill C. 55
Dexter
    Ellen E. 55
Dickason
    Joanna P. 55
Dickens
    Hannah 93
Dill
    Lamartie 56
    Lamatre 56
    Lamotie 56
Dillehunt
    Henrietta 56
Diragan
    George 56
Diragen
    John 56
Ditchell
    J. 160
Dix
    Ellen 56
Dixagen
    John 56
Dobson
    Euphemia 56
    William 56
Dodge
    Hillman 56
    Shillman 56
Donegan
    Timothy 57
Donly
    Jemima 57
Donnelly
    John 57
Donovan
    Eliza 57
Dooire
    Sally 57
Dorgan
    Andrew 57
    Timothy 57
Dorne
    Jacob 57
Dornes
    Jacob 57
Dorney
    Peggy 57
Dorons

Martha L. 57
Dougherty
    Rebecca 57
Douglas
    -----, Lt. 137
    Elizabeth 58
    Matthias 58
Douley
    Gemima 58
Douly
    John 57
Dove
    Margaret 58
Dovire
    Sally 57
Downes
    Caroline Lithgow .. 58
    Deborah 58
    Maria Gertrude ... 58
    Martha E. 58
    Martha L. 58
    Nathaniel 58
    Shubal 58
Downey
    Mary A. 58
    Mary R. 58
Downs
    Albert E. 58
Doxey
    Eliza 58
Doxy
    Eliza 58
Drake
    ----- 52
    Mary Ann 58
    Sarah 52
Drew
    Sarah 58
Drinker
    Joana 125
Droun
    J. 14
Drury
    Austin 59
    John, Dr. 59
Dubois
    Arabella 59
Duendorf
    Andrew 55
Dugan

Henry 57
Duglas
    Mathias 58
Duncan
    James F. 59
    Virginia 59
Dunham
    Virginia 60
Dunlery
    Peter 60
Dunley
    Peter 60
Durham
    Silas 60
Durnell
    Joseph 59
Dusendorf
    Andrew 55
Dwight
    Harriet M. 60
Dyer
    Betsey 60
    Grace A. S. 60
    Henrietta 60
Eakin
    Susan W. 61
Earl
    John 61
Earle
    Elizabeth 61
Eaton
    Susan 61
    Susannah 61
Edgar
    Lavinia M. 61
Edwards
    Ann 62
    Ann R. 62
    Eliza 62
    Elizabeth 62
    Gardner 62
Egbert
    John 63
    Maria 62
Eichel
    Catherine 33
Elbert
    Harriet Ann 63
Elden
    Patience 63

Naval Pensioners of the United States, 1800-1851

Eldridge
- Silas 63
- Abigail 63
- Daniel 63
- Phebe 63

Elliott
- Frances C. 64
- Mary 63

Englis
- Thomas 64

English
- Susannah 64

Enoch
- Elizabeth C. 52

Erskine
- Huldah 64

Eshum
- Sarah 64

Evans
- Albert F. 64
- Dorothy M. 65
- Elisha E. 64
- Jane 64
- Samuel 64
- Susan 65

Everett
- Hannah 65

Fallabee
- John 65

Fallakee
- John 65

Falvay
- John 66

Farrell
- Nicholas T. 66

Fears
- Betsey 66
- Robert 66

Feers
- Betsey 66

Felt
- John 68
- Rachel 66

Fenimore
- Samuel 66

Fenn
- Augustus 67

Fennimore
- Elizabeth M. 67

Fenny
- Michael. 103

Ferguson
- Elizabeth 67

Fernald
- Abigail C. 67

Fernall
- Abigail C. 67

Ferrin
- Ann 67
- Thomas 67

Ferry
- Catherine 67
- Evert [?] 67
- Mary 67
- Michael 67
- Samuel 67

Finch
- William B. 130

Findley
- Thomas 175

Finney
- Robert 67

Fish
- Mary 67

Fishbourne
- John 68

Fishburn
- John 88
- Maria 88
- Maria 68

Fisher
- Christina 68
- Mary Ann 68
- Mary Jane 68

Fitt
- Rachel 68

Fitzgibbon
- Edward 68

Flagg
- Lucy 68

Flaherty
- Michael 157

Flanders
- Martha 69

Flann
- Michael 69
- Susannah 69

Flatio
- L. C. F. 66

Fletcher
- Ann 69
- Sarah 69

Flinn
- Johanna 69
- Mary C. 69
- Patrick 69

Flock
- William 69

Flood
- Jack 69

Florence
- Lydia 69

Floyd
- Elizabeth 70

Foote
- Mary 70

Ford
- Mary 70
- Theodosia 70

Forley
- Peter 176

Forrest
- Alexander 70
- Ann H. 70
- Mary 70
- Mary P. 70
- Mary T. 71

Forsaith
- Robert 71

Forsyth
- Robert 71

Fortin
- Eliza M. 71

Fossett
- Susan 71

Foster
- Catharine 71
- Delia H. 71
- Elenor Francis 71
- Mary 71

Fowler
- Elizabeth 71

Francis
- Lewis 71

Franklin
- E. 72

Franks
- Elizabeth Ann 72
- Emily 72

204

Naval Pensioners of the United States, 1800-1851

Frazier
    Henry N. 72
    Daniel 72
Frederick
    Ruth 72
Freelon
    Thomas 72
Freelow
    Lydia P. 72
Freemody
    Catharine 72
    Elie 72
Freyer
    John 73
Frost
    Sarah 72
Fryee
    John 73
Fullen
    Daniel 73
Fuller
    Abigail 132
Furguson
    James 67
Furrel
    Nicholas T. 66
Fury
    Catherine 73
Gadsden
    Mary S. 73
Gallagher
    Catherine H. 73
    George 73
Gallon
    James 74
    Mary 74
Gamble
    Frances W. C. 74
    Hannah L. 74
Ganswoort
    John M. 74
Ganzler
    George 74
Gardiner
    Esther 74
    Jerry 75
Gardner
    Ann 74
    Deborah 74
    Esther 74
    Harriet A. 75
    Harriet W. 75
    Jerry 75
    John M. 75
    Sarah 74
    Sophia 75
Garner
    Jerry 75
Garr
    John M. 115
Garretson
    Isaac 75
    Mary 75
Garrison
    Edward 75
    John 75
Gately
    Patrick 75
Gayle
    Lucretia T. 75
    Lucy G. 75
Gebhardt
    William 75
George
    Peter 17, 21
German
    Lewis 76
    Lewis S. 76
Geyee
    John 76
Geyger
    John 76
Gibson
    Mary 76
Gilbert
    Ruth 76
Gilboy
    Richard 76
Gillbody
    Richard 76
Gillen
    William 76, 77
Gillespie
    Mary 155
Gillon
    William 77
Gillone
    William 76
Gillow
    William 76, 77
Gilmore
    Caroline E. 77
Gist
    Angeline F. 77
Glass
    Mary 77
Glentworth
    Caroline E. 77
Goar
    Pinetta 77
Goddard
    Grace H. 77
    Mary 126
Goldsmith
    Abigail 77
Goldthwaite
    John 77
Goldthwart
    Elizabeth 77
Goodrum
    Dynoisia 78
Goodshull
    William 78
Goodwin
    Joan 78
    Joshua H. 78
Gordman
    Mary 4
Gordon
    Julia A. 78
    Susan 79
Gorlet
    James F. 77
Goslin
    Jane 79
    John 79
Goss
    John 79
    John A. T. 79
    Louisa 79
    Mary 79
    Thomas 79
Goudy
    Alex 48
Graffam
    -----, Mrs. 137
Graham
    Sarah E. 79

Naval Pensioners of the United States, 1800-1851

Grandso
    John 79
Gray
    Elizabeth C. 80
    Richard 80
    Robert 158
Grayson
    Eliza 80
    Elizabeth 80
Green
    Ann T. 80
    Hannah 80
    Margaret F. 80
    Sarah 80
Greener
    Elizabeth 81
Grenell
    Catharine A. 81
    Catherine 81
    Sophia 81
Griffin
    Ellen 81
    James 81
    Mary 81
    Patrick 81
    Unity 81
Griffing
    John 81
    William 81
Griffith
    Cornelia M. 81
Grimes
    Anna B. 82
Grimke
    M. A. Secunda 82
Grinke
    M. A. S. 82
Griswold
    Laura 82
Grover
    Almira 139
    Asa 139
    Benjamin 139
    Fanny 139
    Gilbert 139
    Henry 139
    Lucius 139
    Olive 82
Grymes
    Ann B. 82

    Charles 82
    James M. 82
Gulliver
    Rebecca 82
Gunnell
    Sophia 82
Gwinn
    Caroline S. 82
Hackleton
    Mary 82
Hadding
    Mary 82
Haddon
    John 82
Hagenon
    Daniel 83
Haggeron
    Daniel 83
Haggerty
    William 83
Hall
    Ann R. 83
    Eleanor 83
    Elizabeth 83
    George 83
    George Joseph 83
    Isaac 83
    Martha 83
    Martha F. 83
Halsey
    Eliza 83
Hambledon
    Samuel 83
Hambleton
    Clayton 84
Hamersley
    Phebe 83
Hamilton
    Honor 105
    William 105
Hammerley
    Phebe 83
Hammersley
    Phebe 83
Hammond
    Hannah 84
    James 84
Hanbury
    Ella Nora 84
Hand

    Mary 84
Handy
    Henrietta D. 84
    Jane 84
Hanna
    Mary 85
Hansbury
    Matthew 84
Hanscomb
    Uriah 85
Hanscombs
    Uriah 85
Haraden
    Susan 86
Harbury
    Ella Nora 84
Hardin
    Ann 85
Harding
    John Jacob 85
Hardy
    Ch. 69
Hardy
    Diana 85
Harnell
    Mary Ann 87
Harnett
    Mary Ann 87
Harraden
    Sarah 86
    Susan 86
Harriden
    Susan 86
Harris
    Eliza 86
    Lucy Ann 75
    Marianne 86
    Sarah Ann 86
    Thompson S. 86
    William Sneed ... 86
Harrison
    Andrew 85
    John 86
    John Henry 86
    Maria 86
    Maurice J. B. 86
Hart
    Sarah A. 86
    Sarah Ann 86

Naval Pensioners of the United States, 1800-1851

Hartle
    Isaac T. 88
Hartlee
    Isaac T. 88
Hartnett
    Mary Ann 86
Hartwell
    Elizabeth 87
    Elizabeth H. 86
Harvey
    Henry 89
    Mehitable 87
    Miriam S. 87
    Sally 87
Harvie
    Francis 87
Harvis
    John 86
Haskell
    Agnes 87
Hass
    Charles B. 82
Hassler
    Anna J. 87
Hatch
    Mary Rawlain 87
    Mary Roulain 87
Hatchin
    James 87
Havie
    Francis 88
Havre
    Francis 88
Hawkins
    Jane 87
Haycock
    George 87, 88
    Joseph 88
Hayden
    John 76
Haynes
    Ann 88
Hayre
    Francis 87
Hayrock
    Joseph 87
Hayward
    John 88
Hazen
    Hannah 88

Hearney
    -----, Lt. 179
Heartlie
    Isaac 88
Heartte
    Isaac T. 88
Hebard
    Sarah 88
Hebbard
    Seth 88
Heckle
    Alfred 88
    Emily 88
Heerman
    Adolphus 88
    Charles F. 88
    Clifford 88
    Theodore 88
    Valentine M. 88
Hefferman
    Mary H. 88
Heffron
    Maria 88
Henley
    Eliza 89
    John D. 137
    Mary 89
Henricks
    Garret 89
Henry
    Hetty 89
    John 89
Hensinger
    George 103
Henson
    George 89
    Mary 89
Herring
    Emily C. 108
Herringbrook
    William 85
Hervey
    Anson 87
    Miriam S. 87
    Salley 89
Hibbert
    Samuel 89
    Stephen 89
Hicks
    Elizabeth E. 89

Higdon
    Elizabeth 89
Higgins
    Rebecca 90
    Sarah 89
Hilburn
    Martha 90
Hill
    Eliza 90
    Mary Ann 90
    Sarah 90
Hillman
    Simon 90
Hilman
    Simeon 90
Hinds
    Elizabeth 90
Hixon
    Henrietta 90
Hobbs
    Cornelia 90
Hodding
    Mary 90
Hodge
    Eliza 90
    Margaret 90
Hodgerbets
    John 91
Hodgkins
    John 91
Hodgkinson
    Ann 91
Hodgson
    Margaret Ann 91
Hoffman
    Phebe W. 91
    Theresa 91
Hofford
    Mary 91
Hohn
    Henry 92
Holbert
    Mary E. 91
    Thomas 91
Holbrook
    Sarah 74
Holcomb
    Charlotte A. 91
    P. 91

Naval Pensioners of the United States, 1800-1851

Holins
    William 92
Holland
    Margaret 91
Hollis
    Phebe 91
Holm
    Henry H. 92
Holmes
    Ann J. 92
    James L. 92
    Maria P. 92
    Mary Ann. H. 92
    Samuel 92
    Sarah 92
Holms
    Charles 92
    William 92
Holt
    Susan Jane 92
Hooe
    Elizabeth M. A. G.
    92
Hook
    Susannah 92
Hooper
    Andrew 92
    Thomas T. 92
Hoover
    Conrad 93
    Godlip 93
    Hannah 93
    Henry 93
Hopkins
    Daniel 93
    Daniel H. 93
    Nathaniel G. 93
    Sarah 130
    Susan S. 93
Horsley
    Mary Ann 93
Horton
    Emma 93
House
    Thomas 105
Hove
    George 92
Howard
    Cornelia 93
Howell
    Ann 93
    Charles 93
    Henrietta 93
    John G. 93
    Martha Ann 93
    William 93
Howland
    Reuben 93
Howse
    Thomas 93
Hoxe
    John 94
Hoxie
    John 94
Hozier
    Peter 93
Huffstedler
    George 94
Hughes
    Edward 69
Hull
    Anna M. H. 94
    E. 94
    Eliza 94
Hume
    Barbara E. 94
Hunt
    Cyrus 94
    Mary Ann 94
    Sarah Ann 94
Hunter
    Eliza 94
    Elizabeth A. M. E.
    95
    Ellen 94
    Harriet L. 95
    Martha 94
    Mary S. 94
    William 94
Huntt
    Sarah Ann 94
Huston
    Pamelia 95
Igerbreton
    Nicholas 95
Inderwick
    Andrew 95
Ingerbretson
    Nicholas 95
Ingerbrettsen
    Nicholas 95
Ingraham
    Daniel 95
    Daniel G. 95
    Hannah 95
Ingram
    Edward 96
Irons
    Phoebe 96
Irwin
    Andrew 96
Isley
    Margaret 96
Jackson
    Benjamin 96
    George 96
    James 96
Jackson
    John 97, 98
    Maria Ann 96
    Mary 97
Jackson
    Susan Jane 96
James
    William 174
Jameson
    Cornelia L. T. 97
    Mary 97
Jenkins
    Ellen 97
Jewett
    Joseph 98
Johnson
    Abigail 98
    Catherine 98
    Elizabeth 98
    Henrietta 98
    John 96
    Jos. 38
    Maria T. 99
    Mary T. 99
    Nancy 98
    Susannah 98
Johnston
    Abigail 98
    Elizabeth 99
    Elizabeth A. 99
    Richard 99
Jolly
    Catharine 99

Naval Pensioners of the United States, 1800-1851

Jones
- Hannah 99
- James 99
- Jane 99
- Lucinda 99
- -----, Lt. 137
- Abigail .. 99, 100, 101
- Caroline 99
- Daniel F. 99
- Elizabeth 99, 100
- Emeline 100
- Emily 101
- Frances 99
- George W. 89
- Hetty 99
- James 139
- John D. 99
- Joseph B. 99
- Martha 99
- Mary 100
- Parmelia Ann 99
- Richard 99
- Richard A. 101
- Ruth 100
- Sarah V. 100
- Stephen 99
- Susan 100
- Theresa 99
- Thomas Ap Catesby 137
- William 99

Jordan
- Elizabeth P. 101
- Elizabeth T. 101
- Louisa 101

Joscelyn
- Elizabeth 101

Joselyn
- Elizabeth 101

Josselyn
- Joseph 101

Kearney
- Mary M. 102

Keen
- William C. 102

Keith
- Eliza M. 102

Kelley
- Joseph 102
- Thomas 103

Kelly
- Mary 145
- Ann M. 102
- Hepzibah 102
- Mary 103

Kelsey
- Susan C. 103

Kemp
- Elizabeth 143

Kennear
- William 104

Kennedy
- Ann 103
- John 103
- Mary Anne 103
- Mary E. 103

Kennon
- Britannia W. 103

Kenny
- John 103

Kerney
- Mary M. 103

Keyer
- Zenas 103

Kidwell
- John J. 104
- Theodore 104
- William E. 104

Kiggin
- John 104

Kimball
- Lucia 104

King
- Catherine C. 104
- William 104

Kingsberry
- William 104

Kingston
- Sarah 104

Kinnead
- William 104

Kinsinger
- George 103

Kipfar
- Lawrence 105

Kissam
- Harriet J. 104

Kitchen
- Abigail 104
- Mary 104

Kitts
- Eliza 104
- John 104

Klapp
- Anna P. 105

Kleim
- Nicholas 105

Klein
- Nicholas 105

Kleiss
- Daniel 105

Kline
- Nicholas 105

Knight
- Mary 105

Knose
- Thomas 105

Kolb
- Elizabeth C. 17
- Joseph 17

Kouse
- Thomas 105

Lagonce
- Elizabeth 105

Lagonee
- Elizabeth 105

Lagoner
- Elizabeth 105

Laighton
- Louisa C. 105

Lambright
- Jane 105

Lanagan
- Elizabeth 105

Lancey
- Nancy 105

Lancy
- Nancy 105

Lane
- Sally H. 105

Langrean
- Susannah 106

Laramee
- Benjamin 106

Larramee
- Abby 106

Laskey
- Mary 106

Latham

Naval Pensioners of the United States, 1800-1851

Lathrop
   Lucy T. 106
   Maria M. 106
Laughen
   John 106
Laurie
   Ann Eliza 106
Lavis
   Catherine E. 106
Lawder
   George 111
Lawrence
   Julia M. 106
Lazanno
   John 107
Leahy
   Catherine 107
Leaky
   Catherine 107
Lecchesi
   Mary 107
Leckie
   Martha 107
Lecompte
   Rebecca 107
Lee
   Elizabeth 107
   John 107
   Matilda T. 107
   Theodore 107
Lemon
   Martha 107
Lent
   Sarah Ann 107
Leonard
   Mary 8
Letson
   Alice 108
Levely
   Henry 109, 111
Levely.
   John 111
Lewis
   Daniel B. 108
   Elizabeth P. 108
   Frances M. 108
   Georgia Ann 108
   Lucien L. 108
   Maria L. 108
   Mary 108

   Mary J. 108
   Sarah F. 108
Lightelle
   Benjamin T. 109
   John 109
   John B. O. O'. 109
   William E. 109
Lindsay
   Deborah 109
   Elizabeth 109
Lindsey
   Deborah 109
Linn
   Elizabeth 109
Linsay
   Deborah 109
Linscott
   Caroline W. 109
   Jane P. 109
   Mary F. 109
Linslie
   Hannah 109
Lippincott
   Susannah 109
Lively
   Henry 111
Livingston
   Catharine 109
   James 109
Lock
   E. 110
Lockert
   Margaret E. 110
Logue
   Jane 110
Long
   Sally 110
Longiel
   Susannah 110
Longill
   George R. 110
   Susannah 110
Lonzado
   Agnes 110
Look
   Eliza 110
Lord
   Caroline 110
   John 110
Loring

   Prudence C. 111
Loud
   Rufus W. 111
Loude
   Louisa 111
Louther
   Hannah 112
Louzade
   Agnes 110
Love
   Adeline K. 111
Loversage
   William 111
Lovett
   Priscilla 1

Naval Pensioners of the United States, 1800-1851

Low
    Betsey 111
    Elizabeth 111
    Lydia 111
Lowe
    Adeline K. 111
    William 111
Lowndes
    Jane B. 111
Lowry
    James 111
Lowther
    Hannah 112
Loyed
    John 110
Lucchesi
    Mary 112
Ludlow
    Augustus C. 112
    Elizabeth Matilda
        159
    Mary W. 112
    Robert C. 112
    William B. 112
Luegler
    Joseph 112
Lugler
    Sarah J. 112
Lumbard
    John 112
    Joshua 112
Lutts
    Mehitable 112
Lyle
    Getty........... 112
    Henry 112
Lyndall
    Mary 112
Lyndell
    Mary 112
Lyne
    Elizabeth B. 112
    Wilhelmina B. ... 112
Lynn
    Ann Eliza 112
McArthur
    Mary........... 112
McCall
    Mary........... 112
McCann
    Elizabeth 113
    Mary Ann 113
    William B. 113
McCarthy
    Mary........... 113
McCarty
    Dennis.......... 113
    Hannah......... 113
    Honora 113
    Mary........... 113
McCauley
    George 113
    James........... 113
McCawley
    James B. 113
    Mary E. 113
McCloud
    Colin 117
    John 113
    Mary A. 113
McClure
    Mary D. 113
    Theophilus 113
McCollum
    Andrew 114
McConnell
    William 48
McCormick
    Martin 129
McCoy
    Mary Ann 114
    William 114
McCrea
    Thomas 114
McCreary
    George 114
McCreery
    Matilda 114
McCulloch
    Ann G. 114
McCullock
    Ann G. 114
McCulloh
    Susan 114
McCullough
    Alexander 114
    Ann 114
    Susan 114
McDermott
    Hetty 114
    Stephen 114
McDonald
    Asenath 114
    Mary........... 114
McDonnell
    James........... 115
McEvers
    Sophia.......... 115
McGee
    Rebecca 115
McGinnis
    Thomas 115
McGowan
    Celeste 115
McKennon
    Elizabeth 115
McKensie
    Matthew 116
McKenzie
    Catherine A. S. ... 116
McKernau
    John 116
McKiernan
    T. E. 31
McKim
    Elizabeth 116
McKinzie
    Alexander 116
McKnight
    Mary........... 116
McLane
    Catalina 116
McLaughlin
    Catharine 116
    G. T. 116
    Salvadora 116
    William 116
McMahon
    Jeremiah 117
    John 117
    Peter 117
McMasters
    John 117
McMenemy
    Mary Ann 117
McMuller
    John 117

Naval Pensioners of the United States, 1800-1851

McMullin
    John 117
Murray
    Catherine C. 117
McMurtrie
    Elizabeth 117
McNelly
    John 117
    Joshua 118
    Martha 117
    Mary 118
McPherson
    Mary E. 118
Macabee
    John 118
    Lydia 118
Maccabee
    Lydia 118
Macdonough
    Augustus R. 118
    Charles S. 118
    Charlotte R. 118
    Edward T. 118
    Thomas 118
Mack
    Catherine 118
    Margaret 118
Macomber
    George 118
Madding
    Mary 118
Madison
    John H. McIntosh
    118
    Maria C. 118
Magill
    Louisa 118
    Mathias 115
Mahen
    John 119
Mahon
    Maria 119
Malanson
    Sarah 119
Malon
    Sarah 119
Malone
    Michael 119
Malono
    Mary Ann 119

Malprino
    John 119
Malson
    Sarah 119
Manley
    Elizabeth 119
Manly
    Elizabeth 119
Mantz
    John 130
Marabee
    Lydia 118
Maralions
    Susan 119
Maralious
    Susan 119
Marbury
    Mary B. 119
March
    Nancy 119
Marden
    Maria 119
Marshall
    Elizabeth 120
    Elizabeth H. 120
    James 120
    Mary Ann 120
    Rachel 120
Martin
    Ann 121
    Elizabeth 121
    John H. 121
    Martha 120
    Mary E. 120
    Patrick 120
    R. 120
    William Orleans
    120
Martins
    M. 121
Marwick
    Esther 121
Mashaway
    John 129
Matteson
    Andrew 121
Matthews
    Sarah 121
Maulton
    Jane 128

Maury
    Alexander 121
    Eliza 121
    Mary G. 121
Mayer
    William 122
Mays
    Elizabeth 122
Mears
    Charles 122
Meech
    Elizabeth 122
Meiggs
    John 122
Meley
    Enoch 124
Meloon
    Sarah 119
Melville
    John 122
Melzard
    Sarah 123
Merceran
    Sarah 123
Mercereau
    Lewis 123
    Sarah 123
Mercier
    E. 123
    M. 123
    Martha 123
Meredith
    Hester 123
    John 123
Merrell
    Elizabeth 123
Merrill
    Tamizen 123
Metz
    George 123
    Susan 123
Middleton
    William 123
Midlen
    Ann 124
Midler
    Ann 124
Milburn
    Thomas 122
Mileg

Naval Pensioners of the United States, 1800-1851

Miles	Enoch	124	Morrison	Richard	127	James	129

Miles
    Enoch 124
    Martha 124
Millard
    Mary 124
Miller
    Catherine 124
    George 124
    Sarah 124
Millett
    Joseph 124
Mills
    Elizabeth 124
Mitchel
    John 125
Mitchell
    Catharine 125
    James 125
Mix
    Ann 125
    Virginia R. 125
Moffatt
    Archibald 125
Monroe
    Eleanor 128
Monteath
    Caroline 125
Montgomery
    Lawrence 125
    Mary 125
    Phebe 125
Moody
    Isabella 125
    William 126
Moran
    Alexander 126
    James 126
    John 126
    Michael 126
More
    John 126
Morgan
    Abigail 126
Morrice
    Mary Ann 127
Morris
    -----, Capt. 119
    Caroline D. 127
    Lewis R 127
    Mary P. 127

Morrison
    Richard 127
    Thomas E 127
    Mary A. 127
Morse
    Sarah 127
Morun
    William 126
Mosart
    Martha 128
Mott
    Harriet 127
    Mary Louisa 127
Moulton
    Jane 128
Mozart
    Margaret 128
    Martha E. 128
Mull
    Mary 128
Mullen
    Elizabeth P. 128
    John 128
    Judetha 128
    Judith 128
Mulleniffe
    James 128
Mulliniff
    James 128
Mulloy
    Sally 128
Munroe
    Eleanor 128
    Margaret R. 128
    Mary Ann 129
    Richard 128
Murdoch
    Thomas 129
Murdock
    Eleanor R. 129
Murphy
    Eleanor 129
    Hester 129
    Mary 129
    Mary Ann 129
    William 129
Murray
    Charles B. 129
    Cotton 129
    Hannah 129

    James 129
Mussey
    Mary 129
Myer
    Mary 129
Myers
    Augustus 130
    Charles 122
    Elizabeth 130
    George 130
    Mary 130
Nabb
    Nelson 130
Nagle
    Elizabeth 130
Nants
    Ann 130
Nantz
    Ann 130
Nason
    Sally 131
Navarre
    Margaret 131
Navarro
    Margaret 131
Neagle
    Godfrey B. 131
    Michael 131
    William 131
Neal
    Mary 131
Neale
    ----, Lt. 108
    Mary 131
Nelson
    Ann 131
    Elizabeth A. ... 131
    William 131
Nesbit
    William 131
Netto
    John 131
Netts
    Eliza 131
Nevin
    Matthew 67
Newburg
    David 131
Newbury
    David 131

Naval Pensioners of the United States, 1800-1851

Newcomb
    Rhoda 131
Newman
    Miriam S. 132
Nicholas
    Teresa 132
Nicholls
    Sarah H. 132
Nichols
    Sarah H. 132
    Teresa 132
    Thomas 132
    William 132
Nicholson
    Ann E. 132
    Charity 132
    Elizabeth R. 132
    Frederick A. G. .. 132
    James W. A. 132
    Laura C. 132
    Maria 132
    Nathaniel 132
Nickerson
    Eliza 133
    Elizabeth S. 133
Noble
    Mary 133
    Philemon 133
Norcross
    Benjamin 133
Norris
    Maria C. 133
    Otho 133
    Shubrick 133
North
    James 72
    Mary........... 133
Noyes
    Sarah L. 133
Noys
    Ebenezer 133
    Sarah L. 133
Nugent
    Jane 134
Oellers
    Rebecca 134
Olcutt
    Mary 134
Oliver
    Eliza A 134

Olliver
    Thomas 134
Omant
    Isaac 134
Ordiorne
    Samuel 134
Osbourn
    Alexander 135
    Archibald 135
    Elizabeth 134
    Margaret 135
Osgood
    Sarah 135
    Susannah L. 135
Ottenvell
    John 135
Otterwell
    John 135
Overman
    Charles Carroll .. 135
    Elizabeth 135
    Isabella 135
    John Oliver 135
    Sarah Ann 135
Overstocks
    Lucinda 135
Owmans
    Issac 134
O'Connor
    Nicholas 134
O'Hare
    Elizabeth 134
O'Neal
    Jennett 134
O'Sullivan
    Thomas 135
Packett
    John B. 135
    Mary Ann 135
Page
    Eliza 135
    Maria 135
Palmer
    Ann 136
    Cornelia 136
    G. J. O'Neill 136
    George 136
    Jane R. 135
Parcels
    Margaret 136

Parker
    Eliza 136
    Elizabeth 136
    Frances W. 136
    Lewis 136
    Louis 136
    Mary 136
    Susan Ann 136
Parkham
    Lydia H. 136
Parrott
    Abigail 136
    Nathaniel 136
Parsell
    George 136
Parsells
    Margaret 136
Parture
    Charles 137
Passenger
    Charlotte 137
Pastine
    Charles 137
Patch
    Hannah 137
    Nancy 137
Patten
    Rachel 137
Patterson
    D. T. 154
    Eunice 138
    Georgeanne 138
    John 138
    Mary Ann 138
Patton
    Sarah 138
Paul
    Mary.......... 138
Payne
    Thomas 135
Peabody
    Phebe 138
Peaco
    Georgianna A. .. 138
Pearce
    Eliza L. 138
Pearson
    Frances E. 138
Pease

Naval Pensioners of the United States, 1800-1851

Peed
- Almira 139
- Frances M. 139
- Rachel B. 139

Peirce
- George 142

Pelt
- James 142

Penny
- Elizabeth 139
- James G. 139
- William 139

Perkins
- Caroline 139
- Elizabeth 139
- Hannah 139
- Lucy 140
- Mary 139, 140
- Nancy 139

Perreau
- Margaret 140

Perry
- Alexander 140
- Elizabeth C. 140
- James Alexander 140
- James DeWolf ... 140
- Lucretia M. 140
- Nancy B. 140
- Sarah 140

Pettingell
- Eliza E. 141

Peyton
- James 138

Phillips
- Catharine 141
- Charlotte 141
- George W. 141
- Praxedes 141
- Sarah 141
- Sarah T. 141

Phippen
- Joseph 142
- Margaret 141
- Nabby 142

Pickerson
- James 133

Pierce
- Catharine Ann ... 142
- Eliza L. 142

- Wilder W. 142

Piercy
- Henrietta 142

Pillsbury
- Margery 142

Pinee
- John 142

Pinkham
- Lydia G. 142
- Lydia H. 142

Pinkney
- Emily Maria 142

Pippen
- Nabby 142

Pitman
- Susan 142

Pittman
- William 142

Pitts
- James 142

Place
- Cornelia 143
- Gilbert J. 143
- Sarah 143

Plinter
- Harriet 143

Pons
- Marie 143

Porter
- David 137, 139
- Eliphalet 145
- Eliza C. 143
- Evelina 143
- Lois 143

Pottenger
- Frances 144

Potter
- Elizabeth 111
- Hannah 143

Pottinger
- Frances 143

Potts
- Jasper 144
- Mary 144
- Sarah 144

Powell
- Angelica T. 144

Prather
- Henrietta M. 144

Pratt
- Elizabeth 144

Preble
- ----, Com. 81
- Mary 144

Prentiss
- Eleanor H. 144

Price
- George 144
- Rachel W. 144

Primrose
- Amelia 145
- Daniel 145
- Rachel Ann 145

Proctor
- Bathsheba 145
- James 90
- Mary 145

Purcelles
- Margaret 136

Quantier
- Peter 145

Quill
- David 146

Rackliff
- Benjamin 146
- Susan 146

Radcliff
- Damaris 146

Rainey
- Rebecca 146

Ramey
- Rebecca 146

Randal
- John 146

Rankin
- George 147
- Margaret 147
- Mary 146

Rantin
- Elizabeth H. 147

Rasmussen
- Catherine 147

Rassmassen
- Catherine 147

Rattler
- John 147

Ray
- Catharine S. M. . 147

Read
- Catharine C. ... 147

215

Naval Pensioners of the United States, 1800-1851

Reak
- James C. 148
- Thomas 148
- Mary 147

Reany
- John K. 147
- Mary K. 147

Redfield
- Susan M. 148

Reed
- John 147

Reid
- Mary 148

Reilly
- Mary 148

Reineburg
- Lewis 148

Renshaw
- Charlotte E. 148

Reynolds
- Amanda H. 148
- Phoebe 148
- William 148

Rhodes
- Rachel 148
- Rosmante 148
- Rosnati 148

Rice
- Eliza M. 148

Richardet
- James B. 149
- Samuel 149

Richards
- A. P. 149

Richardson
- Harriet 149
- Robert 149
- Sarah 149

Richie
- Thomas 150

Riddels
- Thomas 149

Ridgeway
- Maria 149

Ridley
- Rachel 150

Riggs
- Nancy 150

Riley
- Esther 150

Ring
- Eliza 150
- Thomas 150

Rinker
- Catharine 150

Risley
- Lavinia 150
- Rachel A. 150

Ritchey
- John T. 150

Ritchie
- Mary R. 150

Rlakeslie
- Julia 19

Roach
- Sarah 151

Roath
- Grace 154

Robenson
- John 152

Roberds
- Nelson 151

Roberts
- Elizabeth 151
- Francis 151
- Hannah 151
- Margaret 151
- Mary 151
- William 151

Robertson
- Eliza W. B. 151
- Elizabeth B. W. .. 151
- Elizabeth R. 151
- Mary E. 151
- Samuel 151
- Susan D. 151
- William J. H. 151

Robey
- Eleanor Ann 151

Robinson
- Elizabeth 152
- Martha 151
- Sarah 151
- Susan 151
- William 152

Rodgers
- Anna M. 152
- Ellen 152
- J. 89
- James 153

- John 153
- William 152

Rogers
- ----, Commander . 165
- Augustine 152
- Minerva 153
- Theophilus 152
- William 153

Rogon
- Burnett 146

Rolf
- Nathaniel 153

Rolfe
- Nathan 153

Rolph
- Nathaniel 153

Romeyn
- Jeremiah 112

Rose
- Ann 85
- Martha 153
- Mary W. 153
- Robert M. 153

Ross
- Ann J. 153
- Sarah 154

Rossmussoin
- Catherine 147

Rosson
- William 154

Roth
- G. 154

Rouley
- Alonzo 154

Rounds
- Anna 154

Row
- James 154

Rowan
- John 154

Rowe
- Polly 154

Rowland
- Edward 154

Ruff
- Sarah 154

Rumney
- Edward 154

Naval Pensioners of the United States, 1800-1851

	Eliza	154	Schnell			Shepherd	
Ruppert				Margaret V.	157		Patience	158
	Joanna	155	Schriver			Sherblock	
Rush				John	157		Edward	159
	John	137	Schroader			Sherburne	
Rusmussen				John	157		Frances P.	159
	Catherine	147	Sclosser				Louisa B.	159
Russell				Sally	157	Shoter	
	Abigail	155	Scott				Charles	158
	Edmund	155		Billinger	157	Shroeder	
	Elizabeth J.	155		Clarissa B.	157		Rosanna	159
	Mary	155		Eliza	166	Shrouder	
	Sally	155		Henry	157		John	157
Ryall			Scovell			Shubrick	
	Mary	155		H.	188		Edmund T.	159
Ryan			Scranton				Elizabeth Matilda	159
	Mary	155		Patrick	156		Esther M.	159
Sage			Searcy				Julia S.	159
	Eben W.	168		Isabella R	157	Shuburne	
	Lois	155		Robert	157		Frances P.	159
Salter			Sevier				Louisa B.	159
	Horatio	160		Elizabeth A.	157	Shurbrick	
Sanders			Seward				Elizabeth	159
	Harriet H.	156		Jane	157	Shuter	
	James	156	Seymour				Charles	158
	Robert	156		Eliza	157	Simmonds	
Sanderson				Susan	157		Nancy	159
	Hannah T.	155	Shackerly			Simmons	
Sandwith				Harriet	158		Elizabeth	159
	William	155		Mary	158		Nancy	159
Sansford				Sarah	158	Simonds	
	James H.	106	Shaler				Nancy	159
Sardo				Ann	158	Simpson	
	Ann Eliza	156	Shapeley				Sally K.	160
Sarria				John	158	Sinclair	
	Esperanza Pons	156	Shaw				Arthur	160
	Jose	156		John R.	158		George T.	160
Sater				Margaret E.	158		Gilberta F.	160
	Richard S.	170		Mary B.	158		Mary	160
Saunders			Sheed				William H.	160
	Harriet H.	156		William	149	Sisson	
Saunderson			Sheeten				Matilda	160
	Hannah T.	155		Charles	158		Sarah	160
Scates			Sheeter			Sitcher	
	Emily L.	156		Charles	158		William	160
Schannal			Sheffield			Sivers	
	Cornelius	156		Harriet E.	158		John	160
	Joanna	156	Shehan				Nancy	160
Schlosser				B.	158			
	Lewis	157		Bethiah	158			

Naval Pensioners of the United States, 1800-1851

Sivery
   Mary 160
Slam
   William 48
Sloan
   John 160
Small
   Ann 160
Smart
   Eleanor 160
Smidt
   Catharine 161
   John 161
Smiley
   Alice 161
Smith
   Alonzo P. 161
   Catharine F. 163
   Catherine 161
   Catherine M. 161
   Delilah 163
   Elisha 161
   Eliza 163
   Emeline B. 163
   Ferdinand 161
   Frederick 161
   Hannah C. 164
   Jane 161
   Jane Elizabeth ... 163
   Jno. H. 161
   Lavinia 161
   Louisa Ann 161
   Lydia 161
   Margaret 161
   Maria 161
   Mary 161, 163
   Mehitable 162
   Patty 161
   Phoebe Ann 161
   Rachel 68
   Sarah 161, 162, 164
   Stephen J. 163
   Virginia 180
   Virginia A. 163
Snell
   Rebecca 164
Snow
   Eleanor J. 164
   Sarah 164
Snowman
   Ellen 164
   Julia 164
Soule
   Mehitable 165
Southcomb
   Margaret 165
Souty
   Duroc 164
Sparks
   Frances 165
Spaulding
   William M. 165
Speddin
   Robert 165
Spedken
   Robert 165
Spence
   Mary C. 165
Spimrey
   John A. 165
Spinger
   Charles 166
Spinney
   Pamela 165
Spires
   James 165
Springer
   Charlotte 166
   Eugenia 166
   Mary Ann 166
Sproston
   Jane 166
Stallings
   Elizabeth L. 166
   Jane 166
Standish
   Sally 166
Standley
   George 166
Stanford
   Sarah 166
Stanton
   William 167
Stanwood
   Joseph 166
   William 166
Staples
   Nathan 166
Stark
   Elizabeth A. ... 166
Starke
   Elizabeth A. 166
   Thomas 166
Starr
   William 166
Steele
   Rachel 167
Steinbogh
   Elizabeth 167
   Nicholas 167
   Wilhelmina 167
Stellwagen
   Mary 169
Stenard
   Eli 168
Stephens
   Eliza 167
   Thomas H. 168
Stephenson
   Alonzo W 167
   Ann 167
   Maria T. 167
   Mary 167
Stephenson
   Ralph C 167
   Thomas 167
Steuart
   William 168
Stevens
   Eliza 168
   Mary 167
   Thomas H. 167
Stevenson
   Mary 167
Steward
   Eli 168
   J. 168
   William 168
Stewart
   Catharine 168
Stillwagon
   Mary 168
Stinger
   Rebecca S. 169
Stitcher
   Eliza 160
Stivers

Naval Pensioners of the United States, 1800-1851

Stockton
- Ann Maria 169

Stoke
- Mary H. 169

Stone
- John 169
- Hannah 169
- Mary 169

Stoodley
- Adelaide E. McD 169
- Ann Olivia 169
- Nathaniel 169

Storer
- Caleb 169

Street
- Elizabeth 170

Stricker
- Hannah 170

Strider
- Peter 170

Striker
- Hannah 170

Sullivan
- Deborah 170
- Eunice 170
- Florence 170
- Hannorah 170
- Honora 170

Sutherland
- George 170

Swann
- Julia Ann Taylor . 170
- Julia C. 170
- Macon 170
- William Macon .. 170

Swasey
- Lydia K. 170

Taggert
- Ann 171
- David 171

Tanner
- John 171
- Mary 171

Tarbell
- Elizabeth 171

Tarlton
- Abigail 171

Tarr
- Abigail B. 171

Tatem
- Mary G. 171
- Mary Ann 171

Tatman
- Mary 171

Taylor
- Charlotte J. 171
- Eliza Maria 171
- Ella Maria 171
- Grizel A. 172
- Sarah S. 171

Tebbets
- Mary 172

Temple
- Lucy R. 172

Terrell
- Ann 172

Tewksbury
- Elizabeth 172
- Nancy 172

Thatcher
- Lucy Knox 172

Thatcher
- Ebenezer 173

Theall
- Caroline E. 173

Theobald
- Jane 173

Thinkum
- Edward 175
- Peter 175

Thomas
- Elizabeth 173
- Frances A. 173
- Margaret M. 173
- Martha 173
- Mary Ann 173
- Orreal I. 173
- Sally 173

Thompson
- Anna 174
- Cornelius 77
- Emma C. B. 174
- Gillis 174
- Hannah 174
- Lydia 174
- Lydia 77
- Mary 174
- Rebecca 173

Thorn
- Charlotte M. R. . 174
- Robert S. 175

Thurston
- Catherine 175
- John L. 175

Tight
- Ann 175
- Frederick 175

Tilden
- Ann 175

Timberlake
- John 175
- Margaret 175
- Mary V. 175

Tingey
- Ann E. 175

Tinkins
- Jacob 176

Tinslar
- R. R. 175

Titcomb
- Martha 175

Tobey
- Caroline 175
- Elizabeth 175

Toland
- John 175

Tollom
- John 175

Tompkins
- Nancy 143

Tompson
- Hannah 175

Tonclier
- John 34

Tonkin
- Jacob 176

Toohey
- Eliza 176

Tookey
- Edward 176

Toole
- James 176

Tourpson
- Mary 176

Towell
- William. 90

Town
- Sarah 176

219

Naval Pensioners of the United States, 1800-1851

Towner
    Benjamin 176
    Nancy S. 176
    Robert 176
    Virginia Ann 176
Townshend
    Seth 176
Trainer
    Mary 176
Trampnell
    Elizabeth 176
Trant
    Charlotte 176
    James 176
Trapnall
    Elizabeth 176
Trapnell
    Elizabeth 176
Traprell
    Elizabeth 176
Tredick
    Ruth 177
Trenchard
    Elizabeth 177
Trepanney
    Francis 177
Trepanny
    Francis 177
Trevett
    Russell 177
    Samuel 177
Trimble
    Eliza Jane 177
    John 177
    Joshua W. 177
Tripanny
    Francis 177
Trippe
    -----, Lt. 43
Tromp
    Elizabeth 177
Trony
    Elizabeth 177
Trueman
    John B. 177
Trump
    Elizabeth 177
Trupnell
    Elizabeth 176
Trusty
    Jane 177
Tucker
    Rebecca M. 177
Tufts
    Silas 171
Tulley
    Phillips 178
Tulley
    Philip 178
Tupper
    Emily C 178
Turnbull
    James 177
Turner
    Catharine B. 178
    D. 78
    Mary 178
Turrey
    George 178
Twiggs
    Priscilla 178
    Priscilla D 178
Tyrrell
    Ebenezer 178
Tyrrett
    Ann 178
Ulrich
    Hannah 178
Ulrick
    Hannah 178
Underwood
    Sarah J. 178
Upsham
    George 179
Upshaw
    George 179
Valance
    Isaac 179
Van Cleef
    Belinda 21
VanBebber
    Betsey C. B. 179
VanBlake
    Margaret 179
    Mary 179
Vanchef
    Cornelius 22
VanCleef
    Belinda 21
Vandachenhausen
    Emily 179
    William 179
Vandefien
    Lucus 179
Vanderfeen
    Anna 179
Vanderfien
    Anna 179
Vanderfier
    Anna 179
Vanderford
    Elizabeth 179
Vanderveer
    Lydia 179
Vandervoort
    Phoebe 179
Vandyke
    Israel 143
Vanhorn
    Lydia 180
Vanknown
    Rebecca 180
Vankown
    Rebecca 180
VanNess
    Getty 112
VanPatten
    Cornelius 180
    Rachel 180
VanZandt
    Gilbertina L. ... 180
Veasie
    Sarah 180
Veazie
    Sarah 180
Vestlery
    Margaret S. 180
Vickers
    William 181
Vogle
    John 133
Voorhees
    Harriet 181
Voughan
    Joseph 180
Wade
    Constance 181
    Mary D. 181
Wainwright

Naval Pensioners of the United States, 1800-1851

Walcot
- Maria M. 181
- T. 181

Waldo
- Sarah V. 181

Walgrove
- Ellen 181

Walkington
- Sarah 181

Wallace
- Sarah 182

Walling
- Catherine 182

Walsh
- Susan 182

Walters
- Martha 182

Walton
- John 182

Ward
- Ann Maria 182
- Eliza 182
- Harriet 182

Wares
- Charlotte 183

Warner
- Margaret 183

Warren
- Abigail 183
- Martha 183

Washbourne
- Sarah 183

Waterman
- Eliza 183

Waters
- Charlotte 183

Watson
- James 183
- James A. 183
- Mary A. 183
- Sarah 183

Wave
- James 183

Waves
- Charlotte 183

Weaver
- William W. 184

Webb
- Elizabeth 184
- Hannah 184

Webber
- Julia 184
- Nancy 184
- Elizabeth A. 184

Webster
- Electa 184
- Lucinda 184
- Nelson 184

Wedge
- Susannah 184

Wedger
- Rebecca 184

Weed
- Julia 184

Weeks
- Cloe 185

Welch
- William 185

Wells
- Eleanor 190

Welsh
- Thomas 185

Wents
- Matilda 185

Wents
- William A. 185

Wescott
- Hampton 186
- T. G. 186

West
- Elizabeth 186
- Hannah 186

Westcott
- Elizabeth 186

Western
- Mary 145

Weston
- Sarah 186

Wetmore
- Susan W. 186

Whamsley
- Rebecca 186

Wharton
- Alfred W. 186
- Clifton 186
- Franklin 40, 186
- George W. 186
- Henry W.. 186
- William Lewis ... 186

Wheeler
- Peter 186

Wheland
- Peter 186

Wherrin
- Lovey 187

Whetcroft
- Drusilla 187
- William W. 187

Whipple
- Ann 187

Whitaker
- Elizabeth 187

White
- Deborah 187
- Elizabeth 187
- Mary Ann 187

Whitecot
- Elizabeth 187

Whitehead
- Elizabeth 101

Whitehouse
- Polly 188

Whittle
- Elizabeth B. 188
- Frances Munford 108
- Mary Ann 108
- Mary L. 131
- Sarah Ann 188
- William Fortescue 108

Wickes
- Silas D. 188

Wicks
- Silas 188

Wigart
- Jane 188

Wilcox
- Louis 73
- Manuel 188
- Marvel 188
- Sylvanus 188

Wilkinson
- John 71
- Mary 188
- Mary Stuart 189
- Susan 71

Willard
- Sarah H. [or A.] . 189

Willet

Naval Pensioners of the United States, 1800-1851

Williams
- Robert 156
- Elizabeth 190
- Hannah 189
- James 190
- Margaret 48

Wills
- Eleanor 190

Wilson
- Ann 190
- Catherine 191
- James 191
- Mary Jane 191
- Mary Jane Hollins 191
- Nancy F. 190
- Robert M. 191

Wind
- Mary 191

Wine
- James 191
- Mary 191

Winn
- James 191
- Mary 191
- Rebecca 192

Wise
- Catharine 192

Wish
- John 192
- Mary 192

Wolfender
- John 192

Wolfey
- Lewis 192

Wolfley
- Lewis 192
- William J. 192

Wood
- Edna Maria 192
- Elizabeth 192
- Julia 192
- Mary 192

Woodruff
- Sarah 193

Woods
- John 193
- Margaret 193
- Martha Ann 8

Woolcot
- Thirza 193

Woolfort
- Thomas 192

Woolsey
- Ellen 193
- Susan C. 193

Worth
- Margaret C. 193

Wurts
- Matilda 194

Wurtz
- William 194

Wyer
- Margaret 194

Yarnall
- Ann T. 194
- Mordecai 194
- Phebe 194

York
- Sarah 194

Young
- Abigail 194
- Thomas A. 194

Zellweger
- Eliza 195

Zelweger
- Eliza 195

www.ingramcontent.com/pod-product-compliance
Lightning Source LLC
Chambersburg PA
CBHW061442300426
44114CB00014B/1801